THE YEAR BOOK OF WORLD AFFAIRS 1984

VOLUME 38

Editors:

GEORGE W. KEETON

AND

GEORG SCHWARZENBERGER

Managing Editor:

COLIN BURNHAM

AUSTRALIA
The Law Book Company Ltd.
Sydney : Melbourne : Brisbane

INDIA
N. M. Tripathi Private Ltd.
Bombay
and
Eastern Law House Private Ltd.
Calcutta and Delhi
M.P.P. House
Bangalore

ISRAEL
Steimatzky's Agency Ltd.
Jerusalem : Tel Aviv : Haifa

MALAYSIA : SINGAPORE : BRUNEI
Malayan Law Journal (Pte.) Ltd.
Singapore

NEW ZEALAND
Sweet & Maxwell (N.Z.) Ltd.
Auckland

PAKISTAN
Pakistan Law House
Karachi

U.S.A. AND CANADA
Westview Press, Inc.
Colorado

THE YEAR BOOK

OF

WORLD AFFAIRS
1984

Published under the auspices of
THE LONDON INSTITUTE OF WORLD AFFAIRS

WESTVIEW PRESS • BOULDER, COLORADO

All editorial communications should be addressed to the
Managing Editor, Elgin Lodge, Wymondley Road,
Hitchin, Hertfordshire, SG4 9PH

Published in 1984 by
Stevens & Sons Limited of
11 New Fetter Lane, London
Computerset by
Promenade Graphics Ltd., Cheltenham
Printed in Great Britain by
Robert Hartnoll Limited, Bodmin, Cornwall

Published in the United States of America in 1984 by
Westview Press, Inc.
5500 Central Avenue
Boulder, Colorado 80301
Frederick A. Praeger, Publisher

Library of Congress Card Catalog Number 47-29156

ISBN 0-86531-796-8

CONTENTS

v

Contents

1984 AND BEYOND

"Volentem dei ducunt, nolentem trahunt"

At recent meetings, the Council of the London Institute of World Affairs has carefully reconsidered the lessons to be drawn from the Institute's record in its first half-century and reshaped its plans of activities for the 1980s. As in an earlier "cold peace" era, the Council is united in its resolve not to be taken by surprise by any of the contingencies that, on a darkening world scene, must be anticipated in medium-range planning.

It is thus only in keeping with comparable action taken in earlier phases of the Institute's existence that the Council has decided to suspend the publication of the *Year Book* after this Volume. Among the several considerations lying behind this decision is the conviction that, in the prevailing economic climate, continued publication would not be a rational use of always scarce resources by an Institute that has always placed great importance on its independence from governments, foundations and corporations.

As will become apparent from even a cursory consultation of the two cumulative indices published in Volume 25 and this Volume, the *Year Book* series provides now a library of world affairs that, in the course of nearly 40 years, has probably covered most significant facets of a world-activity area which is sadly repetitive in its actions and reactions. It is hoped that these volumes will continue to offer fresh insights to a new generation of readers. They will also be served from time to time by the publication of a series of ad hoc papers, entitled *Focus on World Affairs*.

Members of the Institute will be contacted direct by the Secretary of the Institute regarding future subscriptions.

It remains to thank the Institute publishers and our contributors for the invaluable part they have played for so long in this co-operative effort.

Council, L.I.W.A.

1

THE LONDON INSTITUTE
OF WORLD AFFAIRS
1934—1984

By

E.D. BROWN

THE London Institute of World Affairs will be 50 years old in August 1984 and it is perhaps fitting to celebrate its golden anniversary by offering a brief historical review of its origins and development and of the contribution which it has made to the study of world affairs. For the older generation of our members, such a review will serve as a somewhat nostalgic reminder of the early years of struggle in the 1930s and 1940s, when the intellectual foundations of the Institute were laid, and of some of the eminent scholars and public figures who have been associated with its work. There is, however, a more serious object to be served by undertaking this review: to demonstrate that independent, "uncommitted" research is possible under even the most adverse circumstances. At a time when more and more academics seem to assume that research and publication are well nigh impossible without generous funding from foundations and research councils, there are lessons to be learned from the experience of the Institute, particularly in its early years.

The history of the Institute falls roughly into four periods. The first period, between August and December 1934, saw the emergence of the New Commonwealth Research Bureau as an organ of the New Commonwealth Society. It is this Bureau which constituted the real beginning of what was later to be the London Institute of World Affairs. At the end of this period the Research Bureau developed into the New Commonwealth Institute, a body rather more loosely associated with the New Commonwealth Society. The second period, between 1935 and the outbreak of war in 1939, covered the formative phase of the Institute, during which some of its most characteristic features were firmly established. The war years from 1940 to 1945 witnessed the formal transformation of the New Commonwealth Institute into the London Institute of World Affairs and a remarkably fruitful period of education and publishing in very difficult circumstances. Finally, there is the period since 1945—the period of post-war reconstruction and after.

I—THE NEW COMMONWEALTH RESEARCH BUREAU
AUGUST—DECEMBER 1934

The key figure during this period was Lord Davies of Llandinam, a
co-founder of the New Commonwealth Society and Chairman of the
Welsh League of Nations Union. Monuments to this remarkable
South Wales coal baron still exist both in London and in his homeland. They include the David Davies Memorial Institute of International Studies, formerly the New Commonwealth Society, which
only recently moved from the birthplace of the London Institute of
World Affairs in Thorney House, Smith Square, Westminster, and
the Temple of Peace and Health in Cardiff, where the Welsh Centre
for International Affairs still enjoys a close relationship with the
Davies family.[1]

Lord Davies was a man with an international mission and firm
views on the means whereby "the problem of the twentieth century"
was to be solved.[2] His ambition, reflected in his writings and
summed up in the advertised "object" of the New Commonwealth
Society, was "The promotion of International Law and Order
through the Creation of an Equity Tribunal and an International
Police Force."[3] It was characteristic of the Society that, while
associate membership did "not involve the acceptance of any particular plan," it did imply "a willingness to investigate the problems
with which the Society is concerned."[4] It soon became apparent to
his more scientific colleagues that there existed between him and
them a fundamental difference in attitudes to freedom of research.
For Lord Davies it was axiomatic that the purpose of the Society's
research should be to develop persuasive arguments in favour of *a
priori* conclusions which would further the pursuit of the Society's
reformist objective, reform of the League of Nations Covenant
through the creation of an International Equity Tribunal and an
International Police Force. For Professor Jaeckh and Dr. Schwarzenberger, who joined the staff of the Society in 1933 and 1934
respectively, such "committed' research, designed to find the most
efficient means of achieving *a priori* political ends, was quite inconsistent with a scientific attitude to social studies which involved the
open exploration of alternative approaches to given problems.

---

[1] The writer is indebted to the Director of the Welsh Centre for International Affairs, Mr.
W.R. Davies, for providing him with access to the Centre's library and to Lord Davies's
works.
[2] See, *e.g.* D. Davies, *The Problems of the Twentieth Century. A Study in International
Relationships* (1930), and Lord Davies, *Force* (1934).
[3] I *The New Commonwealth Quarterly* (hereafter "N.C.Q."), Nr. 1(1935), back cover.
[4] *Ibid.*

Professor Jaeckh, formerly the President of the *Deutsche Hochschule für Politik* in Berlin, was invited to join Lord Davies in London in 1933 and became the co-founder and first Director of the International Section of the Society. It appears that, almost from the start, Jaeckh's ultimate intention was to establish a much less committed Research Institute. In the beginning, however, when Professor Jaeckh and Dr. Schwarzenberger met for the first time in London in 1934, it was considered desirable to start with a small Research Bureau.

The new approach to the study of world affairs which was the *raison d'être* of the Research Bureau was immediately apparent in the working methods of the new Bureau. A questionnaire was issued for the purpose of receiving constructive criticisms and suggestions relating to the Bureau's research into the problems of international justice and security and of enlisting the active co-operation of universities, institutes, organisations and individuals concerned with the study of international relations. By this and other means a comprehensive scheme for research was prepared and, as a result, it could later be reported that "some forty topics are being dealt with as subjects of scientific study."[5]

Another product of the early work of the Bureau was the issue of a document entitled *Research Material Nr. 1*, with contributions from such distinguished writers as Dr. Max Habicht, Professor Schücking, Dr. Schwarzenberger and Professor Verdross. This document elicited "interesting and stimulating replies and comments from several countries."[6] Those which related to the proposals which had been made for the establishment of an International Equity Tribunal and an International Police Force are analysed in a subsequent Institute publication.[7]

Whether as a reaction to the tendency of the New Commonwealth Society to concentrate its research energies on policies selected by Lord Davies as its co-founder and treasurer or as a reflection of the personalities and training of its key officers, the Research Bureau which was ultimately to evolve into the London Institute of World Affairs acquired, during these first months in 1934, characteristics which have endured throughout its 50-year history. It was an unofficial body committed to no particular party and no particular ideology; it was—or at least its Director, Professor Jaeckh and its Secretary, Dr. Schwarzenberger, were—already aware of the pitfalls of accepting financial support for scientific research; and it was

---

[5] I N.C.Q. Nr. 2 (1935), p. 151.
[6] *Ibid.*
[7] *Ibid.* pp. 151–155.

committed to uncommitted research—the critical analysis of alternative approaches to problems of world affairs.

II—THE NEW COMMONWEALTH INSTITUTE
1935—1939

This second phase of the Institute's development was characterised by an internal struggle for greater autonomy which began—earlier than Professor Jaeckh had anticipated—with the transformation of the Research Bureau into the New Commonwealth Institute and ended with the complete reorganisation of the Institute in September 1939.

The stated "object" of the new Institute was "The study of fundamental principles of international relations and research into the particular problems of international justice and security"[8] and, in seeking to realise this object, the Institute was served by a distinguished Advisory Research Committee which included Paul de Auer, P.J. Noel Baker, Max Habicht, Manley O. Hudson, Philip C. Jessup, Hans Kelsen, Georges Scelle and Alfred Verdross and drew its membership from several disciplines and many countries. The Director, until his resignation in 1939, was Professor Jaeckh and Dr. Schwarzenberger served as Secretary. Lord Davies's role as Treasurer reflected the continuing link between the New Commonwealth Institute and the New Commonwealth Society.

Harold Temperley, then Professor of Modern History at Cambridge, was the first President of the Institute and, in an elegant foreword to the first issue of *The New Commonwealth Quarterly*, summed up admirably the aims of the Institute and its Journal. Having noted that the world was "full of journals which contain the views of propagandists, of parties, witnesses prejudiced or perjured," but "much less full of journals which are calm, scientific and unprejudiced," he went on to state the aim of the new Journal as being "to see things as they are, in the high and dry light of reason, of science, of law and of history."[9] The fundamentals of the creed were stated boldly and clearly in a passage later to be recalled in an obituary penned by Professor Keeton: "The application of scientific and objective methods to the problems of jurisprudence, of diplomacy and of history is one of the most urgent needs to-day. It is the aim of this Journal. We shall invite suggestions from all sides; we shall prefer criticism to indifference and questioning to acquiescence. We shall be tolerant of differences and patient of prejudices,

---

[8] I N.C.Q. Nr. 1 (1935), front cover.
[9] *Ibid.* p. 3.

for it is by discussion and dispute that the truth emerges from darkness."[10]

1. *Widening scope of research*
Looking back, the most remarkable feature of this pre-war period in the Institute's development was the very considerable growth in its research and publishing activities.

The New Commonwealth Institute Monographs. Even as early as the first issue of *The New Commonwealth Quarterly*, April–June 1935, no less than six monographs had already been published and a further five were in preparation. Reflecting the "object" of the Institute, they were grouped under three headings: (a) Principles of International Relations: (b) Questions of International Justice, Law and Equity; and (c) Problems of International Security.
Some of these monographs were so closely tied to the conditions of the period in which they were published that they are now of little more than historical interest. What is more notable, as a reflection of the quality of the Institute's work and the calibre of its associates, is the enduring significance of many of these pioneering studies. The first category included Kelsen's *The Legal Process and International Order*. Works in the second category which are still consulted today included Max Habicht's study of *The Power of the International Judge to Give a Decision ex aequo et bono*, Wolfgang Friedmann's *The Contribution of English Equity to the Idea of an International Equity Tribunal* and Dr. Schwarzenberger's *William Ladd: An Examination of an American Proposal for an International Equity Tribunal*. The Institute's later interest in air transport was foreshadowed by one of the monograph's in the third category, Admiral Lawson's *A Plan for the Organisation of a European Air Service*, which ran to a second edition in 1936. The initial list was gradually expanded and by the end of this period included Professor Keeton's *National Sovereignty and International Order*, Karl Strupp's *Legal Machinery for Peaceful Change* and Dr. Schwarzenberger's *The League of Nations and World Order*.

The New Commonwealth Quarterly. From the beginning, those who moulded the Institute were ever conscious of the need for it to develop as an *international* Institute and nowhere is this ideal better realised than in the principal periodical publication of the Institute during this period, *The New Commonwealth Quarterly*. Its very

---

[10] *Ibid.* For Professor Keeton's obituary of Harold Temperley, see V N.C.Q. Nr. 2 (1939), pp. 95–96.

language was international. Thus, in the Editors' Foreword in the first issue, the policy of publishing contributions in English, French and German was launched with separate editorials in these languages by Harold Temperley, Georges Scelle and Ernst Jaeckh.[11]

The width of the *Quarterly's* coverage, both in a multidisciplinary sense and geographically, was ensured by the composition of its editorial team and the distinguished Advisory Research Committee already referred to above. As a glance at the contents of the *Quarterly* shows, the members of this Committee were more than general advisers; they were active collaborators and frequent contributors to the *Quarterly*.

The New Commonwealth Information Bulletin. Issued monthly, the Bulletin sought to provide its readers with "reliable data on questions of peaceful change and collective security." It was produced with the assistance of an Information Department, largely staffed by volunteers from the Society and by research students, particularly those encouraged in this direction by the Institute's President, Harold Temperley. The Institute also maintained a Translation Bureau.

Research Committees. A further source of stimulation and of publications was provided by the network of standing "International Research Committees" which were established in different fields. The General Research Committee included members from most European countries, as well as the United States and embraced a wide range of experience from academia, politics and the armed services. It was supplemented, in the United Kingdom, by four "Special Research Committees," dealing with legal, military, political and psychological aspects and by similar committees in other countries.

Research emphasis. The work of the Institute during this period was marked by increasing emphasis on a number of related themes.

Recognising the need to counter the propaganda campaign mounted by the Nazis and supported by those who sought to appease them, the Institute endeavoured to point out the dangers of seeking revision and peaceful change in isolation and laid stress upon the necessary interrelationship between peaceful change and security in international relations. And, as the consequences of ignoring this lesson became apparent with the growing military men-

---

[11] I N.C.Q. Nr. 1 (1935), pp. 3–7.

ace of the Triangle Powers, the editors of the *New Commonwealth Quarterly* devoted the journal to analyses of the transformation which was taking place from the inter-war period to a pre-war period.[12]

The original "object" of the New Commonwealth Society, identified by Lord Davies, continued to generate research during this early phase in the Institute's development. The emphasis, however, was on careful, realistic analysis of the feasibility of the Society's objectives. An attempt was made to identify possible stages of development in the movement towards these objectives and stress was laid upon the need to satisfy the requisite preconditions at each level. An important result of such inquiries was to reveal that, at a certain point, the pursuit of these aims, if it is to hold out any hope of their realisation, becomes in substance a quest for a federal as distinct from a confederate solution. Readers will find this thinking reflected in the first edition of Dr. Schwarzenberger's *Power Politics*, published in 1941, and in the increasing amount of attention paid to federalism in *The New Commonwealth Quarterly*. The two issues of the *Quarterly* published prior to the outbreak of war in 1939 and in the first months of the war[13] still make fascinating reading for the student of history and international relations. They also illustrate, perhaps better than any other Institute publications, the dynamic, creative, critical role which the Institute then played, a role which enabled it to attract the collaboration of some of the more original thinkers of the time.

The issue published in September 1939 is devoted exclusively to "Federalism and World Order" and reflects the considerable influence of such works as Clarence Streit's *Union Now*, a somewhat idealistic proposal to reorganise international society on the basis of a federal constitution resembling that of the United States, and Edward Mousley's *Man or Leviathan?*, advocating the taming of national sovereignty and the construction of a World Commonwealth around the nucleus of the British Commonwealth.[14] Mr. Mousley joined the Editorial Board at this time (together with Dr. Schwarzenberger—"in view of the part he has played in the foundation and development of the *Quarterly*"[15]) and was one of a number of contributors to this issue of the *Quarterly*. His collaborators included Clyde Eagleton on "The League of Nations and Federal

---

[12] See, *e.g.* the issue of the *Quarterly* devoted to "The Munich Settlement and After" IV N.C.Q. Nr. 3 (1938).

[13] V N.C.Q. Nrs. 2 and 3 (1939).

[14] Mr. Mousley's book, published in 1939, was reviewed by Professor Keeton in V N.C.Q. Nr. 2 (1939), pp. 177–178.

[15] V N.C.Q. Nr. 2 (1939), p. 170.

Union," F.A. von Hayek on "Economic Conditions of Inter-State Federalism" and Barbara Wooton on "Economic Problems of Federal Union." This issue of the *Quarterly* also reports a debate on "Union Now," chaired by Professor Keeton, held in the New Commonwealth Institute in May 1939 and attended by about 80 members of the London Schools and Colleges Dining Club.[16]

2. *Educational activity*

By the end of this pre-war period a link had been forged between the Institute and the University of London which was later to develop into a two-year, full-time Diploma course organised by the Institute in association with the Department of Extra-Mural Studies of the University. In 1939 the link took the form of two series of University Extension Lectures given by Professor Keeton and Dr. Schwarzenberger. Each series consisted of 10 weekly lectures given in the Institute, recognised as an Extension Centre of the University. The first series on "Making International Law Work" led to the book of that title[17] and the second, on "Federalism and World Order" was yet another aspect of the Institute's concentration on federalism. All this was in addition to the now well-established season of evening lectures arranged for members of the Institute.

3. *Growth, change and search for autonomy*

As mentioned at the beginning of this section, the second phase of the Institute's development, between 1935 and 1939, was marked by an internal struggle for greater autonomy. As has been seen, there were within the New Commonwealth Society, practically from the beginning, two incompatible attitudes towards research which made it necessary to establish first a small Research Bureau and shortly afterwards the New Commonwealth Institute. In retrospect, it is apparent that the uneasy co-existence reflected in this development was destined to lead to rupture and, as will be seen, the breach was formally finalised when the Institute decided to change its name to the London Institute of World Affairs in 1943.[18] The essential reshaping and reorganisation of the Institute had, however, taken place much earlier in 1939.

In March 1939, Professor Jaeckh resigned as Director of the Institute and was succeeded by Professor Keeton. In the same year the Institute lost its first President, Harold Temperley, who died in July.

---

[16] *Ibid.* at pp. 157–169.
[17] 1st ed. 1939, 2nd ed. 1946.
[18] Minutes of Council Meeting held on June 12, 1943.

These changes in the senior officers of the Institute took place at a time when it was becoming clear that the Institute might well be faced with the need to prepare both for the outbreak of war and possible separation from the New Commonwealth Society. It was, then, a time of transition in many senses and, not unnaturally, change brought with it a degree of stress, human and financial, for those who had to manage the Institute's affairs. The difficulties are hinted at in Professor Keeton's obituary of Harold Temperley when he recalled how, from his sick-bed, Temperley had "steered the Institute through that crisis of growth which is rarely spared to any vital and expanding body and which led, in this instance, to a complete reorganisation of the Institute in the course of this year."[19]

The principal changes are recorded in "The Institute's Diary," a regular feature in the *Quarterly*, and in the minutes of the Council of the Institute. The most important item was the formation of a governing council, independent of any external controlling organisation. Apart from the *ex officio* membership of the various officers of the Institute, the members of the Council were to be elected from the general body of members of the Institute, who could thus in future direct its policy. The composition of the new Council, which held its first meeting in June 1939, is worth recording. It consisted of the following members: Captain Edgar Abraham, Sir Montague Burton, Lord Davies, Dr. F.R. Demuth, Dr. T.R. Derry, Mr. N.B. Foot, Miss E. Gedge, Captain Liddell Hart, Mr. R.H.C. Holland, Dr. Pryns Hopkins, Professor G.W. Keeton, Señor Don Salvador de Madariaga, Mr. Harold Macmillan, M.P., Mr. Edward Mousley, Professor Denis Saurat, Dr. G. Schwarzenberger, Major-General A.C. Temperley, Sir Arthur Willets and Dr. Temple, Archbishop of York.

Another major concern during this period of growth and reorganisation was that of providing the Institute with the minimum degree of financial security without which many of its ambitious plans could not be realised or its independence guaranteed. How extensive these ambitions were is clear from the records of the time.[20] Five national research committees dealing with the political, legal, military, psychological and economic aspects of federalism were "being established in those countries in which freedom of thought is still permitted" and there were plans to establish corresponding international committees to be co-ordinated by a general international committee. In addition, four special research com-

---

[19] V N.C.Q. Nr. 2 (1939), p. 95.
[20] See, *e.g.* "A Call to Action" published in V N.C.Q. Nr. 1 (1939), pp. 3–5 and "The Institute Diary" V N.C.Q. Nr. (1939), pp. 170–176.

mittees were established in Great Britain, dealing with Central Europe, the refugee problem, public relations (propaganda in the international sphere) and far eastern questions.The ambition of the Council to extend the library, to make it gradually available for members and eventually to place at their disposal accommodation within the institute for study was of course a more substantial undertaking which would probably require new premises and therefore substantial funding.

The problem of funding an independent research institute is always a difficult one, with the ideal of complete freedom and generous funding seldom attainable. For most institutes it is a case of securing the best possible compromise which circumstances permit. The way in which this question was tackled at this point in the Institute's fortunes is still of interest and relevance today.

At the first meeting of the new governing Council in June 1939, it was resolved to establish an Endowment Fund "in order to put the Institute on a firm and permanent financial basis." At the same time, the Institute launched a membership campaign with the distribution of 3,000 reprints of a stirring "Call to Action," published in the June 1939 issue of the *Quarterly*. Clearly, the proceeds of such appeals, augmented by the publishing and lecturing activities of the Institute, would leave the Institute free of extraneous influences on its activities and some elements in the Council felt that funds so raised should be made to suffice. Others, aware of the limitations which such minimal funding was likely to imply, were in favour of seeking more generous support from the major research foundations. Thus, it was reported to the Council in June 1939 that negotiations with the Carnegie and Rockefeller Foundations had been initiated and were to be continued during a planned visit by Professor Keeton to the United States. The Nobel Institute was also approached at this time to obtain a special grant for research work which the Institute proposed to undertake for the various peace organisations.[21]

Even by September 1939, the campaign for an Endowment Fund and for members had borne encouraging fruit, the outstanding contribution being an anonymous donation of £200 in memory of the work of the distinguished psychologist, Dr. William McDougall, F.R.S. Bearing in mind that the annual membership subscription was then 25 shillings, this was a much appreciated contribution and became even more significant when it became known during September 1939 that Lord Davies intended to discontinue his donation

---

[21] Minutes of Council Meeting held on June 15, 1939.

to the New Commonwealth Society upon which the Institute had until then been dependent for a large part of its funding.

III—THE WAR YEARS 1940—1945

1. *Continuing reorganisation*

In common with other learned institutes and societies—but to a lesser extent than in the case of those with less flexible and more top-heavy administrations—the Institute was obliged to tighten its belt and curtail its activities as a result of war-time conditions. These difficulties would have existed in any event but they were considerably aggravated by the fact that they had to be endured at a time when the Institute was still in the course of completing the fundamental changes in structure and funding referred to above.

On the outbreak of war, the Director and Secretary of the Institute moved to Aberystwyth, both being members of the teaching staff of University College London which was to be evacuated to the University College of Wales at Aberystwyth. Lord Davies preferred to move the New Commonwealth Society, on the other hand, to Sarn, in Montgomeryshire.

Having established themselves in Wales, the Institute officers initiated fresh discussions with the Society on the financial position. Prior to 1939 the whole of the resources of the Institute (other than what was earned by its activities) had been derived from money which had been given to the New Commonwealth movement as a whole, and which had remained under the control of the Society. As has been seen, one of the objects of the changes introduced in 1939 was to establish an Endowment Fund, to be supplemented by membership revenue. It was assumed, nonetheless, that the bulk of the Institute's income would continue to be provided out of the resources of the New Commonwealth movement. Unfortunately, with the withdrawal of Lord Davies's donation, these resources were now seriously diminished. Already in 1938–39 the reduction of the Institute's income from £3,750 to £1,750 had created serious difficulties for the Institute in maintaining the standard of its work. This was now reduced by more than half to £800 for the budget year October 1939—October 1940. Nor was any support forthcoming from the Rockefeller and Carnegie Trusts despite, in the case of Carnegie, a further appeal after the outbreak of war when the financial situation had become acute.

In retrospect, this development can be recognised as a fundamental watershed in the Institute's history. Services formerly performed by paid employees were henceforth to be discharged on a voluntary basis. One result was that the Information Department had to be closed altogether and it became impossible to continue publication of the *Information Bulletin*, recently renamed the *New Commonwealth Digest*. There is perhaps a note of bitterness detectable in the Director's Report on the work of the Institute (July 1939–June 1940) where he wrote that, "It is a matter for the very greatest regret that none of the public trusts which we approached at this time saw fit to assist us even to the very limited extent which would have been necessary to preserve these obviously valuable services."[22] Nonetheless, the Institute's response was a positive one; it was to produce a new Monthly Forum entitled *Union*, which first appeared in January 1940, with a substantial part of its cost guaranteed for its first year by the generosity of two Institute members, Dr. Pryns Hopkins and Dr. Ernst Cohn. In the circumstances this was a brave venture and, as it turned out, a very fortunate one, since the Government was to issue an order prohibiting the publication of any new journal.[23]

Not unnaturally, the outbreak of war also adversely affected the recently launched membership campaign. When separate membership of the Institute was initiated in June 1939, the subscription was set at 25 shillings but it was reduced to 15 shillings on the outbreak of war, it being then calculated that the essential activities of the Institute could be maintained on this basis with 1,000 members. The campaign was moreover on target and indeed, "We were always slightly in advance of schedule until the Germans invaded Holland and Belgium."[24] By June 1940 membership stood at 250 and it was then calculated that, provided the officers of the Institute were prepared to continue to work in an honorary capacity, the Institute could carry on free of financial worries if 500–650 members could be secured.[25]

The stay in Wales was short-lived. The Institute returned to the South-East in August 1940. If finances were low, spirits were remarkably high. Professor Keeton generously solved the accommodation problem by offering the Institute a wing of his house near London and "Barrows," Roydon, near Ware in Hertfordshire was to be the Institute's home for the remainder of the war. As was noted at the time, "so long as London remains the unimpaired centre of the country which it is, to be close to the metropolis confers benefits with which even the Welsh hills and the sea do not compare."[26]

---

[22] VI N.C.Q. Nr. 2 (1940), p. 145.
[23] *Ibid*. at pp. 146–147.
[24] *Ibid*.
[25] *Ibid*. at p. 147.
[26] 1 *Union*, Nr. 9 (1940), p. 287.

That all was not bliss, however, is made clear in the contemporary description of the Institute's new abode, "where, despite the local bombs, work can be carried on in as peaceful surroundings as any to be found in England."[27]

As the subsequent history of the Institute amply demonstrates, a very tight budget and the lack of both full-time salaried staff and permanent accommodation do not necessarily prejudice unduly a dynamic policy of research and education. Some would argue indeed that they positively encourage it. Nonetheless, towards the end of this period, the Institute had certainly not abandoned its earlier wish to purchase "adequate headquarters in London" and sought to raise a building fund of £15,000.[28]

2. *Personnel*

The changes in personnel among the institute's officers which occurred during this period were partly a result of the war and partly of the ordinary course of events in the life of the Institute. In June 1939, it was announced that Dr. Temple, Archbishop of York as he then was, had consented to become Vice-President of the Institute[29] and he was joined by Mr. Harold MacMillan in September.[30] Following the death of Harold Temperley, Dr. Temple succeeded him as the Institute's second President in the early months of the war.[31] He in turn was succeeded in 1940 by Dr. A.D. (later Lord) Lindsay of Balliol College, Oxford who served until 1951. Another notable personality who became a Vice-President during this period was H.G. Wells. As was noted in the Institute Diary in April 1940,[32] Mr. Wells initiated his active collaboration with the Institute by publishing his "Declaration of the Rights of Man" in the January 1940 issue of *Union*. He appeared again in the May issue with a "Memorandum on the Federal Idea."

Less happy was Dr. Schwarzenberger's fate at this time, "swept away," as he was in June 1940, "to some unknown internment camp beyond any immediate hope of recall."[33] Quite apart from the personal trauma, this was a serious blow for the Institute at perhaps the most difficult time in its history. Since its inception, Dr. Schwarzenberger had played a key role in the development of the Institute and its publications and even his temporary loss could be ill afforded.

---

[27] *Ibid.*
[28] XI *London Quarterly of World Affairs*, Nr. 1 (1945), inside back cover.
[29] V N.C.Q. Nr. 1 (1939), p. 59.
[30] V N.C.Q. Nr. 2 (1939), p. 171.
[31] V N.C.Q. Nr. 3 (1939), p. 249.
[32] V N.C.Q. Nr. 4 (1940), p. 322.
[33] 1 *Union*, Nr. 9 (1940), p. 286.

The spirit of the times, as well as the recognition of Dr. Schwarzenberger's contribution to the Institute's early years, is very well reflected in this passage from the Director's Report, published in October 1940: "At the beginning of June, the Institute's Secretary, Dr. Schwarzenberger, was interned. Although under the conditions which now exist, one may understand the necessity for internment of persons who left Germany when the present regime came into power, we can nevertheless regret a situation in which this has become a necessity. Dr. Schwarzenberger has been, throughout his six years' service as Secretary, an indefatigable and loyal worker, whose one object was to see this Institute, in which he sincerely believed, established upon a broad and firm foundation. Unfortunately, we lost him at the moment when his labours were beginning to be crowned with success, and when the status of the Institute had received very widespread recognition."[34]

Dr. Schwarzenberger was succeeded as Secretary by Charles Vereker, one of the founders of *The Federal News-Letter*, which, as from August 1940, was incorporated in *Union*. Fortunately, Dr. Schwarzenberger's internment was of relatively short duration and he was released in October 1940. By July 1941 he was editing *The New Commonwealth Quarterly* and in 1943 he became Director of Studies.

3. *Publications*

Mention has already been made of the series of monographs published by the Institute. In September 1940 members had their attention drawn to "A Programme of Winter Reading," the bulk of which consisted of these works, recommended as being "of the very first importance for the work of study groups."[35] If this diet needed to be supplemented, a wealth of material continued to be made available in the pages of the *New Commonwealth Quarterly* and *Union*. While it is impossible to do justice to the range and quality of this periodical literature in a brief survey, the contribution which the Institute was able to make even in war-time may be illustrated by reference to some of the more memorable themes and authors.

An account has already been given of the Institute's interest in federalism and work continued on the question of regional federalism in the early years of the war. The December 1939 issue of the *Quarterly* was given over to the question *Union Now*? and included Professor Keeton's article on "Anglo-French Union—a Sugges-

---

[34] VI N.C.Q. Nr. 2 (1940), p. 148.
[35] 1 *Union* Nr. 9 (1940), p. 282.

tion."[36] This suggestion was explored further in the collection of
essays published in the issue of April 1940 devoted to *Anglo-French
Union?*[37] It must have been very gratifying for the Institute to report
a few months later that, "Late on the night of June 17 [1940] it
became known that the communication made by Mr. Churchill to
M. Reynaud on the previous day contained a proposal for Anglo-
French Union."[38] The proposed permanent union would have
covered foreign policy, defence, finance and economics and a common citizenship. Despite the collapse of France, the Institute advocated that the offer should be left open and, having justly claimed
for itself "the almost unique distinction of having concentrated its
efforts during the past twelve months upon a study of the question
of Anglo-French Union," felt "doubly encouraged to continue the
task" of exploring the fundamental problems of "union."[39] Mention
should also be made here of the symposium of essays on *Federal
Union* edited by M. Chaning-Pearce, a member of *Union's* Editorial
Board, to which both Professor Keeton and Dr. Schwarzenberger
contributed.[40]

Although large themes of this nature demanded and received a
major collaborative effort by the Institute, they did not of course
exclude full coverage of other aspects of world affairs. Many of
these contributions illustrate another of the Institute's valuable
assets during this period of austerity: its capacity to attract major
public figures to contribute articles without there being any question
of paying honoraria. Thomas Mann's piece on "Germany's Guilt
and Mission," published in April 1942, and an article on "The
USSR and US" by Sir Stafford Cripps, which appeared in July 1944,
both fall into this category.

When, in 1943, the Institute was renamed the London Institute of
World Affairs, it was decided that the title of the *Quarterly* should
also be changed to *The London Quarterly of World Affairs*.

4. Research methods and techniques

Another interesting development, both as a reflection of the Institute's service to its members and as a precursor of an educational
tool to be further developed later, was the publication in *Union* of a
series of "Study Outlines" on post-war reconstruction. Their purpose was explained as being "to provide our members, individually
and in study groups, with handy material for their own research on

[36] V N.C.Q. Nr. 3 (1939), pp. 230–236.
[37] V N.C.Q. Nr. 4 (1940).
[38] VI N.C.Q. Nr. 1 (1940), p. 68.
[39] *Ibid.*
[40] Cape, 1940.

the urgent problems within the purview of the Institute." The intention was to "try to avoid equally the Scylla of an over-technical approach and the Charybdis of over-simplification."[41] Over four issues of *Union*, Dr. Schwarzenberger provided such guidance on "The International Society: Forces and Structure"; "The Failure of the League Experiment"; and "The Issues at Stake."[42] Members were encouraged to proceed further to the first edition of Dr. Schwarzenberger's *Power Politics*, published in 1941. The same technique of "Study Outlines" was greatly developed later in successive editions of Dr. Schwarzenberger's *Manual of International Law.*[43]

It was in relation to this same problem of post-war planning and reconstruction that Dr. Schwarzenberger first developed the relativist approach to the problem of international planning and the technique of transcendental and immanent criticism. Proceeding from the premise that there is always more than one solution for a social dilemma, the first task of the relativist method is to survey the available patterns and analyse the conditions on which their realisation depends. Transcendental and immanent criticism fulfils an additional function—the provision of tools for the critical analysis of proposed plans. Transcendental criticism serves to identify, elaborate and clarify the often inarticulate or half-hidden assumptions on which plans are based and to examine the prospects of realising such projects in the light of social forces likely to oppose or to support them. Such transcendental criticism has to be complemented by immanent criticism, which is concerned not with the major assumptions on which plans are based but with the identification of shortcomings of plans from all possible points of view.[44]

IV—POST-WAR RECONSTRUCTION AND AFTER 1945—1984

By the beginning of the post-war period the Institute's characteristic features had been clearly formed and the history of this final period is one of the further development of the Institute's activities in research, publication and education.

1. *Research and publication*

The fruits of the Institute's labours in promoting research and writing on world affairs during this period appeared in the Institute's

---

[41] "Preface to Study Outlines" II *Union*, Nr. 3 (1941), pp. 94–95.

[42] II *Union*, Nrs. 4, 6, 7 and 8 (1941).

[43] See latest edition: G. Schwarzenberger and E.D. Brown, *A Manual of International Law* (6th ed., Revised Second Impression, 1978), at pp. 326–533.

[44] See further G. Schwarzenberger, *Power Politics* (1st ed. 1941), Chap. 1.

Quarterly periodical (down to October 1951), in the 38 volumes of *The Year Book of World Affairs* and in 69 volumes published in *The Library of World Affairs*.

It was announced in October 1946 that, since the title *The London Quarterly of World Affairs* implied "a certain restriction of the field covered by the *Quarterly*," the "Old Series" would terminate with Volume 12 and a "New Series" would come out under the title *World Affairs*, thus indicating that it was "intended to cater for those interested in World Affairs in the widest sense."[45] Lest it be thought that this reflected a mere whim, it should be added that the first issue of *World Affairs* carried Dr. Schwarzenberger's editorial "Defining World Affairs," in which it was explained why "world" was preferred to "foreign" or "international," and "affairs" was favoured rather than "politics."[46]

In 1950 the purpose of the *Quarterly* was reconsidered in an Editorial Note which also reflects the gratifying reception accorded to the *Quarterly* by its readers.[47] The *Quarterly* had been conceived as a means of popularising for the benefit of a wider public the research published in more extended forms in the *Year Book* and the *Library of World Affairs*. Recognising, however, that its readers tended to belong to a rather uniform group of serious students of world affairs, it was decided to abandon this distinction and to bring *World Affairs* into line with the other Institute publications. Acknowledging the support received from teachers who had found the *Quarterly* useful in their university and adult educational work, the editors pledged themselves to fulfilling even more effectively in the future the functions of providing for readers material of a factual character, as well as interpretations of long-term trends on a more technical level. Alas, it was not to be; in October 1951, ever-mounting increases in printing costs and the price of paper forced the Institute to suspend—in fact, as it turned out, terminate—publication of *World Affairs*.[48] Thus ended the Institute's *Quarterly* which, under various names and in varying sizes, had appeared for 16 years and had even managed to come out on its appointed dates during the War. As the last issue sorrowfully recorded, " . . . the fate which has overtaken *World Affairs* is symptomatic of the growing difficulties which are experienced by voluntary associations bent on their independence from governmental quarters, sectional private interests, and groups with any particular axe to grind."[49] However, the

---

[45] 12 *London Quarterly of World Affairs*, Nr. 3 (1946), p. 193.
[46] 1 *World Affairs*, New Series, Nr. 1 (1947), pp. 1–3.
[47] 4 *World Affairs* Nr. 1 (1950), pp. 1–2.
[48] 5 *World Affairs* Nr. 4 (1951), p. 385.
[49] *Ibid*. p. 386.

Council philosophically took the view that what might be lost in topicality would be gained by concentrating still more on what was of permanent significance. The role of the *Year Book* was thereby enhanced for the future.

Volume 1 of the *Year Book of World Affairs* was published in 1947. The intention was to enable the Institute to deal adequately with topics which required a fuller and more thorough treatment than it was possible to give in the *Quarterly* but which did not require the space of a book.[50] The format adopted for the first volume set the pattern which was followed for the first 25 volumes down to 1971. Volume 1 contained 12 substantial articles and a series of "Reports on World Affairs," the title given to extensive surveys of current literature on the various aspects of world affairs— economic, geographical, institutional, legal, psychological, educational and sociological. Only those involved in the organisation or writing of these invaluable surveys could appreciate the work involved in supplying them over a quarter of a century and it was with great regret they were abandoned after 1972.

Two new features appeared in volume 26 (1972): "Research Programs" and "Trends and Events." Under the heading of Research Programs, the Institute announced its intention of sponsoring the following research programs in the fields of international law and organisation: (1) comparative study of the history of international law; (2) functional sovereignty; and (3) the use of blueprints of international organisation for purposes of international legislation.[51]

The introduction of the annual survey of "Trends and Events" was prompted by the realisation that, "with every additional volume of this *Year Book* . . . , it becomes more difficult for new readers to derive the fullest benefit from the material available in the previous volumes."[52] Noting the "stereotyped and, largely, repetitive character of international affairs," it was hoped that these surveys would demonstrate to readers, that, "frequently, a 'new' happening or 'modern' development [had] been dealt with and largely anticipated in one or more earlier volumes of the *Year Book*."[53] Five issues were selected for such treatment in 1972 and this had grown to 10 in the 1983 volume. While it would be invidious to try to identify the more memorable or seminal *Year Book* contributions which have appeared over the 38 years of publication, the reader will find a use-

---

[50] 1 *Year Book of World Affairs* (hereafter "Y.B.W.A.") (1947), p.v.
[51] 26 Y.B.W.A. (1972), pp. 1–2.
[52] *Ibid.* p. 3.
[53] *Ibid.*

ful analytical guide in these annual reviews, as well as in Mr. Burnham's survey of the first 29 volumes of the *Year Book* as "A Living and Expanding Library of World Affairs," published in the 1979 volume.[54] A more comprehensive guide to the *Year Book's* coverage will be found in the cumulative indices published in the 1971 volume (covering volumes 1–25)[55] and in the present volume

Little need be added about the third tier of the Institute's publishing activities. It was natural that an Institute endeavouring to offer an independent centre for the constructive study and teaching of world affairs should include among its functions the establishment of a *Library of World Affairs*. The best measure of the success of this enterprise is provided by the list of 69 books in the *Library* list of publications which will be found at the end of this volume.

No account of the Institute's publishing record would be complete without reference to the many individuals who have contributed to its success. The roles played by Professors Keeton and Schwarzenberger pre-war and during the war have been referred to above. This fruitful partnership has continued down to the present time and, as a token of the Institute's affection and gratitude, Volume 36 of the *Year Book* was dedicated to Professor Keeton on his eightieth birthday in 1982. During the post-war period, Professor Schwarzenberger in particular provided the dynamic, creative leadership needed to ensure the publication of a continuous flow of high quality research work both in the Institute's periodicals and in the monographs which appeared in the *Library of World Affairs*. He was aided by a series of able Assistant and Managing Editors, Dr. Suse Schwarzenberger, Professor L.C. Green, Dr. F. Parkinson and the present Managing Editor, Colin Burnham. No less important was the support, especially in the early years, of Stevens & Sons Ltd. Taking over from Hammond, Hammond & Co. Ltd. as the Institute's publishers in 1946, Stevens helped to launch the *Year Book of World Affairs* in 1947 and undertook publication of the *Library of World Affairs*. Particularly valuable was the encouragement offered by Hilary Stevens, a director of Stevens who became a member of the Institute's Council in 1946. Writing in the *Year Book* in 1962, following his death, the Editors recalled that, "it was one of the remarkable features of this relationship that it was hardly ever necessary for the officers of the Institute to persuade him of the value of any of the projects put before him by the Institute. If anything it was he who continuously prodded us to be more forthcom-

---

[54] 33 Y.B.W.A. (1979), pp. 9–14. See also C.G. Burnham, "Focus on World Affairs: Selected L.I.W.A. Material, 1934–1984" in the present volume.
[55] 25 Y.B.W.A. (1971), pp. 303–343.

ing with new and challenging ideas."[56] His associates and successors
have continued in the same tradition.

2. *Education*

The Institute has been concerned with education in world affairs
since its inception in 1934 and, as has been seen, promoted discussion groups among its members and organised series of lectures
and short conferences before the war and, to the limited extent
possible, during the war years. In particular, the Institute had
played its part in satisfying the increased demand for education in
international relations shortly before the outbreak of war. As was
noted earlier, the Institute's close collaboration with the Extra-
Mural Department of the University of London resulted in the first
University Extension course in international relations, given in
1938–39 by Professor Keeton and Dr. Schwarzenberger. Continuity
was preserved during the war when the Institute's officers found
themselves evacuated to Aberystwyth in 1939 and Cambridge in
1940, evening lectures on international relations being delivered in
both places.

The Diploma in International Affairs. Towards the end of the
War, at one of several Council meetings arranged in London
"enemy action permitting," it was agreed that one of the post-war
activities of the Institute should be "The promotion of University
Extension courses in international affairs, colonial problems and
allied political and economic subjects in co-operation with the
Extension Department of the University of London."[57] Already,
discussions had taken place with the University and proposals made
for additional University Extension Diplomas. The result of this
initiative was the inclusion among the University's diplomas in the
Humanities of a Diploma in International Affairs in November
1945.

In the beginning, candidates for the Diploma were drawn from a
wide cross-section of the community and were not required to possess formal education qualifications such as matriculation. They
earned their Diplomas by attending part-time courses over a period
of four years and passing examinations in one area of international
relations at the end of each year. Before long, however, a new
demand for more intensive, full-time study was recognised. As the
first Organising Tutor of the Institute has put it, "With the progress

[56] 16 Y.B.W.A. (1962), pp. 1–2.
[57] Minutes of Meeting of Council held on July 1, 1944.

of constitutional development in the Asiatic portions of the British Commonwealth and the growing awakening of national conscious- ness in the Middle East, it was found that many students from India, Pakistan, Burma, Siam, Israel and the Arab countries were anxious, while studying in this country for the Bar or similar professions, to acquire a wide knowledge of international affairs."[58] The Council and Board of Studies of the Institute realised the difficulty of orga- nising any such course within the established format for the Extra- Mural Department's diplomas in the humanities. Nonetheless, aided by the goodwill of the Department's Director, Dr. McPhee, the Institute was able to persuade the University to accept, as an alternative to the four-year scheme, a new two-year, day-time scheme covering a slightly wider range of subjects. The new scheme started in October 1948, initially on an experimental basis. Perhaps recognising the valuable purpose which this experiment served by providing crash courses for potential leaders of emerging Third World countries, the Extension Council, of which Professor Keeton was a distinguished member, soon agreed to the continuation of the new scheme on a permanent footing.

In re-designing the scheme of studies for the new Diploma courses, the Board of Studies was able to draw upon the experience gained in conducting the part-time courses. During their first year, students were required to study International Relations since 1870; International Law, and International Economics. Successful candi- dates then proceeded to the study in the second year of Inter- national Institutions and International Economic Law. When, in 1975, it was decided to terminate the Diploma courses, the scheme of study had, by and large, stood the test of time and was little altered. International Relations since 1870 had been replaced by International History since 1914 as a first-year subject and English Language had been added to assist the large proportion of overseas students attending courses. The second-year subjects had been expanded to include International Relations and candidates were also required to take the final essay paper, designed to test their capacity for the more extended treatment of one of a number of topics.

As the numbers attending the Diploma courses swelled, the duties of the Organising Tutor correspondingly became more oner- ous, as did the problem of securing adequate teaching accommo- dation and library facilities. Throughout the 30–year period during which Diploma courses were organised, the organising tutors, in

---

[58] L.C. Green, "A New Departure in the Teaching of International Relations" 3 *World Affairs*, New Series, Nr. 3 (1949), pp. 310–320.

keeping with the Institute tradition, worked on a part-time basis with nominal honoraria. The Institute similarly benefitted from the generous co-operation of Dr. S.D. Malaiperuman, Director of the Y.M.C.A. for Indian Students, which provided teaching accommodation in its premises in Gower Street and later in Fitzroy Square for a period of 12 years down to 1964. Thereafter, courses were held in the Extra-Mural Department's premises in Tavistock Square.

At its peak in 1966, the Diploma courses were being attended by 48 first-year students and 23 second-year students. With few exceptions, students were recruited from other countries, especially Third World States, with a fair proportion of young diplomats serving in the London Embassies and High Commissions. The decision to discontinue the Diploma Courses in 1975 was based mainly on the fact that, reflecting the increased provision made elsewhere for higher education in international relations, the supply of adequately qualified applicants had fallen away. However, by that time, the Institute had performed the task it had set itself: to make a significant contribution to the training at a very modest cost, of the post-war generation of Third World leaders.

The Associateship of the Institute. For the small proportion of Diploma students and other advanced students wishing to proceed to further studies and to be trained in research techniques, the Institute introduced Associateship courses in 1962. The Associateship is awarded on the basis of a dissertation prepared over, usually, one academic session under the supervision of a teacher appointed by the Director.

Education in air and space law. A further educational experiment commenced in 1954, when it was decided to establish a Diploma in International and Comparative Air Law. Reflecting technological advances and corresponding changes in the law, the title of the Diploma was subsequently changed to Diploma in Air and Space Law. Candidates for the Diploma examinations are largely drawn from the evening course given under Professor Bin Cheng's direction at University College London. Though it has now been in existence for 30 years, the Diploma remains one of the very few professional qualifications in Air and Space Law available throughout the world. Like the Diploma in International Affairs, this Diploma caters for students from all parts of the world and, during the past decade, the Diploma has been awarded to an average of about nine candidates per annum.

3. *Institute organisation and finance*

Organisation. The Institute's form of government remained remarkably stable throughout this period. The Council, on which Institute officers are joined by distinguished colleagues from many areas of academic and public life, is the principal policy-making body, chaired by the President. The Board of Studies, chaired by the Director, advises the Council on matters of educational policy. Its members have included the Organising Tutor, teachers of Diploma courses and officers of the Department of Extra-Mural Studies of the University of London.

There has been relatively little change too in the division of responsibilities among the key Institute officers. In 1943, when the Institute adopted its present name, the opportunity was taken to introduce a number of constitutional changes, partly to provide safeguards against takeover bids from other organisations and partly to amend the designations and functions of the principal officers. Professor Keeton was appointed Principal and Dr. Schwarzenberger Director of Studies. In 1952 Professor Keeton succeeded Lord Lindsay of Birker as President and the office of Principal was dispensed with. Dr. Schwarzenberger was appointed Director of the Institute in 1962.

The other key administrative posts have been those of the Secretary, the Organising Tutor and the Treasurer. In 1949 Mr. L.C. Green added the burdens of Secretaryship to those of the Organising Tutor which he had assumed in 1946. He served in both capacities until he was appointed to the Chair in International Law in Singapore in 1960. His considerable contribution to the development of the Institute as teacher, editor and administrator was recognised by his election to Life Membership in 1960. Since 1960 a number of colleagues have served in these positions, Dr. F. Parkinson, Dr. Hilde Jacobi, Mrs. Olive Curry, Mr. R.H.F. Austin, Mr. A.M. Sutton and Mrs. J.A. Brown. The present writer has been privileged to serve the Institute since 1962, first as Organising Tutor and Secretary and subsequently as Deputy Director.

Reference has already been made to the constructive, supportive role played by officers of the Department of Extra-Mural Studies in launching the full-time Diploma course. The Institute is especially indebted to a number of those officers who took a particular interest in education in world affairs. Dr. McPhee helped to establish the strong links between the two bodies in the early post-war years and Werner Burmeister, who had been associated with the Institute and served on the Council since the War, re-enforced and developed these links when he succeeded Dr. McPhee in 1961. The Institute also enjoyed the helpful collaboration of his Deputy, Mr. Cyril Tho-

mas and of Mr. Douglas Maylor, both in his capacity as a senior officer in the Department and as a teacher of History on Diploma
courses.

Finance. Throughout its 50-year history, the Institute has had to
reconcile itself to one of the financial facts of life: a centre for
research and education in world affairs which insists on independence from governments, companies or foundations has to learn to
deploy its minimal resources with maximum efficiency and to rely
heavily upon the goodwill and loyalty of its staff and members. In
such an Institute the role of Treasurer is a vital one and the London
Institute of World Affairs has been well served for the greater part
of the post-war period by Professor Keeton, who includes among his
many other virtues a shrewd financial acumen. This role is now
played by Professor Bin Cheng.

In retrospect, it is possible to identify several characteristic features of the Institute's financial affairs. The negative consequence of
independence is constant wariness of accepting financial support
from governments, companies and foundations. The positive consequence is that it encourages self-reliance and economy. It has
meant, for example, that the Institute has always tried to ensure that
each of its activities should be at least self-supporting. It has in part
been responsible for the Institute's practice of offering only a symbolic honorarium by way of a contribution to expenses to contributors to the *Year Book of World Affairs*. It says something for the
reputation acquired by the *Year Book*, as well as for the enthusiasm
of its contributors, that there has never been any difficulty in per-
suading leading specialists to write for the *Year Book*.

It cannot be denied that adequate accommodation, including a
library, and full-time staff would have enabled the Institute to develop its works more fully than has been possible in recent years.
Nonetheless, given the non-monetary assistance provided by a
number of institutions, particularly the Department of Extra-Mural
Studies and University College London, and the part-time labour of
its officers, the Institute has survived and developed during peace
and war and in times of prosperity and recession alike. Indeed, it is
not perhaps immodest to suggest that the record of the Institute in
research, publication and education over a period of 50 years com-
pares not unfavourably with that of other educational centres which
enjoy the luxury of ample external funding.

V—THE INSTITUTE'S FIRST 50 YEARS: LESSONS IN RETROSPECT

In the introductory section of this brief history, it was suggested that there were lessons to be learned from the experience of the Institute, particularly in its earlier years. Looking back over the record of Institute activities presented above, a number of conclusions suggest themselves.

The most striking feature of the Institute's history is that, where enthusiasm and drive exist, an independent centre for research and education can do very valuable work on a very small budget. One is tempted at times to think that some variant of Parkinson's Law may well be operating in some centres at the present time. Too often, generous funding for a succession of dubious research projects leads to the recruitment of short-term research workers and the production of reports which impress more by their quantity than their quality. The unfashionable discipline of relative poverty may have its advantages.

A second lesson which can be drawn from the Institute's history is that there is perhaps an optimal size and range of activities which can be undertaken by an independent research centre of limited means. The Institute has learned over the years the desirability of never attempting to do more than can be handled by its officers working largely in an honorary capacity. Provided this restriction is accompanied by a determination never merely to duplicate work being done elsewhere, it still leaves room for a valuable and distinctive contribution to research and education. It is hoped that this necessarily brief survey has shown that this has indeed been the achievement of the Institute's first 50 years.

FOCUS ON WORLD AFFAIRS
SELECTED L.I.W.A. MATERIAL:
1934–1984

By

COLIN BURNHAM

ABBREVIATIONS

A. *Institute Monographs*
  (i) New Commonwealth Institute Monographs:
      See list at the end of G. Schwarzenberger, *The League of Nations and World Order* (1936).
  (ii) London Institute of World Affairs Monographs:
      See list in the Institute leaflet at the end of this volume.

B. *Institute Quarterly*
  (i) 1935–43: New Commonwealth Quarterly (N.C.Q.)
  (ii) 1943–46: London Quarterly of World Affairs (L.Q.W.A.)
  (iii) 1947–51: World Affairs (W.A.)

C. *Institute Year Book*
  1947–84: *Year Book of World Affairs* (Y.B.W.A.)
  See also Cumulative Indexes in Vol. 25 (1971) and in this volume.

D. *Institute Monthly*
  1940–41: *Union — Digest, Forum* and *Review* of the New Commonwealth Institute (*Union*).

(The sequence of papers included in the following survey is in chronological order under each heading.)

1 — INTERDISCIPLINARY ASPECTS

1. *World Society*
Schwarzenberger, Suse, *Trends of Thought in Germany* (2 W.A. 1948).
Strange, Susan, *In Praise of Inconsistency* (5 *ibid*. 1951).

Parkinson, F., *Social Dynamics of Underdeveloped Countries* (14 Y.B.W.A. 1960).
Vincent, R.J., *The Factor of Culture in the Global International Order* (34 *ibid.* 1980).
Zuckerman, Lord: *The Risks of a No-Risk Society* (34 *ibid.* 1980).

2. *Study of International Relations*
Green, L.C., *A New Departure in the Teaching of International Relations: The University of London Diploma in International Affairs* (3 W.A. 1949).
Alexandrowicz, Ch., *The Study of International Economics* (4 Y.B.W.A. 1950).
Lasswell, H.D., *The Scientific Study of International Relations* (12 *ibid.* 1958).
Burton, J.W., *Recent Developments in the Theory of International Relations* (18 *ibid.* 1964).
Banks, M.H., *Two Meanings of Theory in the Study of International Relations* (20 *ibid.* 1966).
Kaplan, M.A., *New Approaches to International Relations: Progress on Retrogression* (22 *ibid.* 1968).
Goodwin, C., *International Relations and International Studies* (27 *ibid.* 1973).
Kimminich, O., *International Relations and International Law* (27 *ibid.,* 1973).
Rosenau, J.N., *International Studies in the United States* (27 *ibid.* 1973).
Curle, A., *Peace Studies* (30 *ibid.* 1976).
Joynt, C.B., *Behavioural Science in International Relations* (33 *ibid.* 1979).

3. *International Law and Society*
Schwarzenberger, G., *International Law and Society* (1 Y.B.W.A. 1947).
Corbett, P.E., *Law and Society in the Relations of States* (4 *ibid.* 1950).
Schwarzenberger, G., *Neo-Barbarism and International Law* (22 *ibid.* 1968); *Détente and International Law* (35 *ibid.* 1981).

4. *World Order*
Lytton, Lord, *Conditions of International Order* (4 N.C.Q. 1938).
Falk, R.A., *The Logic of State Sovereignty Versus the Requirements of World Order* (27 Y.B.W.A. 1973).
Schwarzenberger, G., *Civitas Maxima?* (29 *ibid.* 1975).

Falk, R.A., *The Decline of International Order* (36 *ibid.* 1982).

5. *Federalism*
Eagleton, C., *The League of Nations and Federal Union* (5 N.C.Q. 1939).
Hayek, F.A. von (*et al.*), *Federalism and World Order* (5 *ibid.* 1939); *The Economic Conditions of Inter-State Federalism* (5 *ibid.* 1939).
Keeton, G.W., *Federalism and World Order* (six parts *Union* 1939–40).
Wootton, N., *The Economic Problems of Federal Union* (5 N.C.Q. 1939).
Wells, H.G., *Memorandum on the Federal Idea* (*Union* 1940).
Young, Sir George, *Federating and Federalising* (*ibid.* 1940).
Oppenheimer, F., *Federalism, Democracy and Capitalism* (6 N.C.Q. 1941).
Keeton, G.W., *Federation?* (9 *ibid.* 1943).
Beloff, Lord, *Federalism as a Model of International Integration* (13 Y.B.W.A. 1959).

II — HISTORICAL ASPECTS

1. *The League of Nations and the Quest for Security*
Capper-Johnson, K.M., *The Proposed Anglo-French Air Pact and the Problem of Collective Security* (1 N.C.Q. 1935).
Korovine, E., *Les Pactes de Non-Aggression Economique et la Preservation de la Paix* (1 *ibid.* 1935).
Kraus, H.N., *The Revision of the Peace Treaties ex aequo et bono* (1 *ibid.* 1935).
Potter, P.B., *Lessons from the Wal-Wal Arbitration between Ethiopia and Italy* (1 *ibid.* 1935).
Auer, P. de (*et al.*), *Proposals for the Reform of the* [*League of Nations*] *Covenant* (2 *ibid.* 1936).
Davies, Lord, *Lessons in the Italo-Abyssinian Dispute* (2 *ibid.* 1936).
Jenks, C.W., *The Montreux Conference and the Law of Peaceful Change* (2 *ibid.* 1936).
Rappard, W.E., *Switzerland and Collective Security* (2 *ibid.* 1936).
Lytton, Lord, *The Lessons of the League of Nations Commission of Enquiry in Manchuria* (3 *ibid.* 1937).
Mowat, R.B., *The Limits of Peaceful Revision* (3 *ibid.* 1937).
Keeton, G.W., *The Breakdown of the Washington Treaties and the Present Sino-Japanese Conflict* (4 *ibid.* 1938).
Keith, A.B., *The Policy of Appeasement and the League of Nations* (4 *ibid.* 1938).

Schwarzenberger, G., *A New Method of Revision: Limited Rights in Foreign Territory* (5 ibid. 1939).
Bettany, A.G., *The German and Hungarian Minorities in Czechoslovakia* (11 L.Q.W.A. 1946).

2. *The Inter-War Years*
Shotwell, J.T., *The American Problem* (two parts 1 N.C.Q. 1935).
Jäckh, E., *Welt-Zeit* (1 ibid. 1935).
Bustamante, A. de, *The Results of the Pan-American Peace Conference* (2 ibid. 1937).
Eagleton, C., *The USA and the Far Eastern War* (3 ibid. 1937).
Mitrany, D., *The USA Neutrality Act of May 1, 1937* (3 ibid. 1937).
Undén, Ö., *Le Différend d'Alexandrette entre la France et la Turquée* (3 ibid. 1937).
Schmid, Carlo, *Gedanken zum Problem einer allgemeinen internationalen Gerichtsbarkeit* (3 ibid. 1938).
Nicholas, H.G., *American Secession and European Anarchy: A Comparison* (5 ibid. 1940).
Noel-Baker, F., *Spain: A Fascist Pocket in Western Europe* (2 W.A. 1948).
See also below II(6) Crises: Munich and After.

3. *The Second World War, Conferences and Tribunals*
Keeton, G.W., *Anglo-French Union: A Suggestion* (5 N.C.Q. 1939).
Eastwood, W.M., *England as a Future Continental Power* (*Union* 1940).
Friedmann, W., *Aims and Problems of Anglo-French Union* (5 N.C.Q. 1940).
Gollancz, O., *Practical Steps Towards Anglo-French Union* (5 ibid. 1940).
Gooch, G.P., *Germany After the War* (*Union* 1940).
Johnson, D., *Geopolitics of the War* (ibid. 1940).
Keith, A.B. (*et al.*), *Anglo-French Union?* (5 N.C.Q. 1940); *Constitutional Aspects of Anglo-French Union* (5 N.C.Q. 1940).
Temperley, A.C., *Is There a War?* (*Union* 1940).
Tyler, J.E., *Military Aspects of Anglo-French Union* (6 N.C.Q. 1940).
Mann, Thomas, *Germany's Guilt and Mission* (7 ibid. 1942).
Thomson, D., *The Future of France* (8 ibid. 1942).
Cripps, Sir Stafford, *Shall the Spell Be Broken?* (9 ibid. 1943).
Thomson, D., *The Undertones of Dumbarton Oaks* (9 L.Q.W.A. 1945).

Schwarzenberger, G., *Power Politics, the Rule of Law and the Crimea Declaration* (11 *ibid.* 1945).
Ma, Y.C., *Problems of Post-War Economic Reconstruction in China* (12 *ibid.* 1946).
Honig, F., *Nuremburg — Justice of Vengeance?* (1 W.A. 1947).
Schwarzenberger, G., *The Judgment of Nuremberg* (2 *ibid.* 1948).
Honig, F., *Powers Behind the Nazi Throne* (4 *ibid.* 1950).

4. *After 1945*
MacDanald, M., *The British Commonwealth and Empire Today* (9 L.Q.W.A. 1946).
Rose, W.J., *Poland in Perspective* (11 *ibid.* 1946).
Edelman, M., *Russia — War or Peace?* (1 W.A. 1947).
Thomson, D., *The Anglo-French Alliance* (1 Y.B.W.A. 1947).
Bindoff, S.T., *Peacemaking at Paris* (1 W.A. 1947).
Schmid, Carlo, *The Work of Bonn* (3 *ibid.* 1949).
Thomson, D., *The Middle Way in France* (3 *ibid.* 1949).
Strange, Susan, *Strasbourg in Retrospect* (4 W.A. 1950).
Cheng, B., *The Anglo-Iranian Dispute* (5 *ibid.* 1951).
Fifield, R.H., *American Foreign Policy in the Far East, 1945–50* (5 *ibid.* 1951).
Frankel, J., *The Background in French Indo-China* (5 *ibid.* 1951).
Thomson, D., *A New Phase in France* (9 Y.B.W.A. 1955).
Parkinson, F., *European Integration: Obstacles and Prospects* (13 *ibid.* 1959).
Younger, the Rt. Hon. K.G., *Britain's Point of No Return* (22 *ibid.* 1968).
Strange, Susan, *The Commonwealth and the Sterling Area* (13 *ibid.* 1969).
Penrose, E.F. and E., *The Third World and International Politics* (33 *ibid.* 1979).
Shearman, H., *Conflict in Northern Ireland* (36 *ibid.* 1982).

5. *The Middle East*
Brodetsky, S., *The Jewish Problem* (8 N.C.Q. 1943).
Parkes, J., *The Future of the Jews* (10 *ibid.* 1944).
Bentwich, N., *The Palestine Mandate and the League of Arab States* (11 L.Q.W.A. 1945).
Eban, A.S., *The UN and the Palestine Question* (2 *ibid.* 1948).
Moyal, M., *Post-Mortem on the Arab League* (3 *ibid.* 1949).
Strange, Susan, *Palestine and the United Nations* (3 *ibid.* 1949).
Wright, W., *Egypt: Nationalism in Adolescence* (4 *ibid.* 1950).
Moyal, M., *The Middle East and the Western World* (4 *ibid.* 1950).

6. *Crises: Munich and After*
Macartney, C.A., *The Principle Underlying the Munich Settlement*
    (4 N.C.Q. 1938).
Schwarzenberger, G. (ed.), *The Munich Settlement and After* (4
    ibid. 1938).
Willert, Sir Arthur, *Munich and the Issues for Democracy* (4 *ibid.*
    1938).
Strange, Susan, *Suez and After* (11 Y.B.W.A. 1957); *Cuba and
    After* (17 *ibid.* 1963).
Hilton, R., *Castrophobia in the United States* (18 *ibid.* 1964).
Parkinson, F., *Santo Domingo and After* (20 *ibid.* 1966).
Burnham, C.G., *Czechoslovakia: Thirty Years After Munich* (23
    ibid. 1969).
Joynt, C.B., *The Anatomy of Crises* (28 *ibid.* 1974).
Nicholson, M., *Catastrophe Theory and International Relations* (35
    ibid. 1981).
Bell, Coral, *Crises and Survival* (36 *ibid.* 1982).

III — GEOPOLITICAL ASPECTS

1. *The Shape of World Politics*
Moodie, A.E., *The Straits and the World* (12 L.Q.W.A. 1946).
Kaplan, M.A., *Theoretical Enquiry and the Balance of Power* (14
    Y.B.W.A. 1960).
Schwarzenberger, G., *From Bipolarity to Multipolarity?* (21 *ibid.*
    1967).
Seara Vazquez, M., *Zones of Influence* (27 *ibid.* 1973).
Buchan, A., *An Expedition to the Poles* (29 *ibid.* 1975).
See also under IV — Political Aspects, (1) The Realities of Power.

2. *America, Russia and Europe*
Cripps, Sir Stafford, *The USSR and the US* (10 N.C.Q. 1944).
Milward, M., *Argentina: The Key to South America* (11 L.Q.W.A.
    1945).
Bettany, A.G., *Czechoslovakia Between East and West* (1
    Y.B.W.A. 1947).
Burmeister, W., *Western Germany and Western Europe* (3 W.A.
    1949).
Daniel, J., *Conflict of Sovereignties in the Antarctic* (3 Y.B.W.A.
    1949).
Schwarzenberger, G., *The North Atlantic Pact* (3 W.A. 1949).
Seton-Waltson, H., *Eastern Europe* (3 Y.B.W.A. 1949).
Sorokin, P.A., *The Real Causes of the Russo-American Conflict* (3
    W.A. 1949).

Seton Waltson, H., *Eastern Europe Since Stalin* (11 Y.B.W.A. 1957).

Gladwyn, Lord, *Britain and Western Europe* (15 *ibid.* 1961).

Burmeister, W., *Brandt's Eastern Policy* (27 *ibid.* 1973).

Northedge, F.S., *America, Russia and Britain* (28 *ibid.* 1974).

Schmidt, Helmut, *New Tasks for the Atlantic Alliance* (29 *ibid.* 1975).

Friedlander, R.A., *The Problem of the Mediterranean: A Geopolitical Perspective* (32 *ibid.* 1978).

Berner, M.F.C., *The Panama Canal and the Future United States Hemisphere Policy* (34 *ibid.* 1980).

Rubin, A.P., *The Panama Canal Treaties: Locks on the Barn Door* (35 *ibid.* 1981).

Mendl, W., *Western Europe and Japan* (37 *ibid.* 1983).

3. *India and the Far East*

Keeton, G.W., *The USSR and the Far East* — two parts (9 N.C.Q. 1944); *The French Problem in Indo-China* (W.A. 1947).

Fisher, C.A., *China and her South-Western Neighbours* (4 *ibid.* 1950).

Purcell, V., *Indo-China and the Prospect in South-East Asia* (9 Y.B.W.A. 1955).

Alexandrowicz, C.H., *India's Himalayan Dependencies* (10 *ibid.* 1956).

Burton, J.W., *Western Intervention in South-East Asia* (20 *ibid.* 1966).

Bell, Coral, *The Containment of China* (22 *ibid.* 1968).

Loescher, G.D., *Power Politics in Indo-China* (37 *ibid.* 1983).

IV — POLITICAL ASPECTS

1. *The Realities of Power*

Greenleaf, W.H., *Imperialism and Geopolitics* (1 W.A. 1947).

Morgenthau, H.J., *Neutrality and Neutralism* (11 Y.B.W.A. 1957).

Schwarzenberger, G., *A Grammar of Power Politics in Disguise* (5 W.A. 1951); *Hegemonial Intervention* (13 Y.B.W.A. 1959); *The Scope for Neutralism* (15 *ibid.* 1961); *Beyond Power Politics* (19 *ibid.* 1965).

Andreski, S., *Imperialism, Past and Present* (29 *ibid.* 1975).

Rostow, E.V., *The Politics of Force: Analysis and Prognosis* (36 *ibid.* 1982).

See also under III — Geopolitical Aspects, (1) The Shape of World Politics.

2. *Nationalism*

Ker, E., *The Nemesis of Nationalism* (*Union* 1940).
Fawcett, C.B., *Nationalism and World Order* (7 N.C.Q. 1941).
Keeton, G.W., *Nationalism in Eastern Asia* (1 Y.B.W.A. 1947).
Frankel, J., *Nationalism on Trial* (11 *ibid.* 1957).

3. *Foreign Policy*

Chaput, R.A., *The Traditions of British Foreign Policy* (4 N.C.Q. 1938).
Gurian, W., *Permanent Features of Soviet Foreign Policy* (1 Y.B.W.A. 1947).
Keeton, G.W., *The Future of British Foreign Policy* (2 *ibid.* 1948).
Gascoigne, Sir Alvary, *Soviet Foreign Policy* (9 *ibid.* 1955).
Katona, K.P., *Soviet Propaganda to the Colonial World* (9 *ibid.* 1955).
Morgenthau, H.J., *United States Foreign Policy* (9 *ibid.* 1955).
Nicholas, H.G., *The New Administration and United States Foreign Policy* (11 *ibid.* 1957).
Northedge, F.S., *Parties and Foreign Policy in Britain* (14 *ibid.* 1960).
Houghton, N.D., *Social Structures and Foreign Policy in the United States* (15 *ibid.* 1961).
Hanek, H., *Soviet Foreign Policy since Khruschev* (20 *ibid.* 1966).
Morgan, R.P., *The Scope of German Foreign Policy* (20 *ibid.* 1966).
Ginsburgs, G., *Soviet Internationalism and State Sovereignty* (25 *ibid.* 1971).
Johnson, J.T., *The Indo-China War and American Values* (25 *ibid.* 1971).
Vincent, R., *Kissinger's System of Foreign Policy* (31 *ibid.* 1977).
Smith, M.J. and Carey, R., *The Nixon Legacy and American Foreign Policy* (32 *ibid.* 1978).
Rosenau, J.H. and Holsti, O.R., *The United States in (and out of) Vietnam* (34 *ibid.* 1980).

4. *The Super-Powers*

Schlesinger, R., *The Soviet Commonwealth* (9 N.C.Q. 1944).
Ovey, Sir Esmond, *The Soviet Challenge* (3 W.A. 1949).
Moodie, A.E., *The Cast Iron Curtain* (4 *ibid.* 1950).
Thompson, K.W., *American Approaches to International Politics* (13 Y.B.W.A., 1959).
Schwarzenberger, G., *From Bipolarity to Multipolarity?* (21 *ibid.* 1967).
Ginsburgs, G., *The Constitutional Foundations of the "Socialist Commonwealth"* (27 *ibid.* 1973).

Geusau, A. von, *Détente After Helsinki* (32 *ibid.* 1978).
Home, Lord, *The Scope and Limits of Détente* (34 *ibid.* 1980).
Friedlander, R.A., *United States Foreign Policy Towards Armed Rebellion* (37 *ibid.* 1983).

5. *The Third World*
Parkinson, F., *Bandung and the Underdeveloped Countries* (10 Y.B.W.A. 1956).
Harrod, J., *Non-Governmental Organisations and the Third World* (24 *ibid.* 1970).
Bull, H., *The Third World and International Countries* (33 *ibid.* 1979).
Mugomba, A.T., *Small Developing States and the External Operational Environment* (33 *ibid.* 1979).
Heeger, G., *Turmoil and the Politics of the Third World* (35 *ibid.* 1981).
See also under VII — Economic Aspects, (3) The Third World.

6. *Southern Africa*
Haarhoff, T.J., *South Africa and the Crisis of Modern Civilisation* (6 N.C.Q. 1941).
Stent, G.D., *Colour Problems of South Africa* (2 Y.B.W.A. 1948).
Longmore, T., *The South African Dilemma* (8 *ibid.* 1954).
Doxey, G.C. and Margaret P., *The Prospects for Change in South Africa* (19 *ibid.* 1965).
Legum, C., *South Africa: The Politics for Détente* (30 *ibid.* 1976).
Butterworth, R., *The Future of South Africa* (31 *ibid.* 1977).
Bissell, R.E., *The Ostracism of Southern Africa* (32 *ibid.* 1978).
Shaw, T.M., *Southern Africa: From Détente to Deluge* (32 *ibid.* 1978).
Legum, C., *Foreign Intervention in Africa* (34 *ibid.* 1980).
Doxey, M.P., *The Making of Zimbabwe: From Illegal to Legal Independence* (36 *ibid.* 1982).
Legum, C., *South Africa's Search for a New Political System* (36 *ibid.* 1982).
Woods, D., *Escalation in South Africa* (36 *ibid.* 1982).

V — DIPLOMATIC ASPECTS

Mowat, R.B., *Diplomacy and the [Munich] Crisis* (4 N.C.Q. 1938).
Strange, Susan, *Secrecy Acheson's Total Diplomacy* (4 W.A. 1950).
Morgenthau, H.J., *Neutrality and Neutralism* (11 Y.B.W.A. 1957).
Frankel, J., *Rational Decision-Making in Foreign Policy* (14 *ibid.* 1960).
James, A., *U Thant and His Critics* (26 *ibid.* 1973).

Doxey, Margaret P., *Sanctions Against the Soviet Union — the Afghan Experiment* (37 *ibid.* 1983).
James, A., *Kurt Waldheim: Diplomat's Diplomat* (37 *ibid.* 1983).

VI — Strategic Aspects

1. *Pre-Nuclear Strategy*
Lyddell-Hart, B.H., *Military and Strategic Advantages of Collective Security in Europe* (4 N.C.Q. 1938); *The Defence of Western Civilisation* (5 *ibid.* 1939).
Werner, M., *La Puissance Militaires Dictateurs* (5 *ibid.* 1939).
Lyddell-Hart, B.H., *The German Invasions of the West — The Basic Factors* (*Union* 1940).
Keeton, G.W., *The British Army and the War* (7 N.C.Q. 1941).
Ker, E., *World Security* (9 *ibid.* 1944).

2. *The Nuclear Age*
Mott, F.C., *The Atomic Bomb and World Affairs* (11 L.Q.W.A. 1945).
Strange, Susan, *Strategic Embargoes* (2 Y.B.W.A. 1948).
Tunstall, B., *The Military Power of Western Union* (3 W.A. 1949).
Boyle, Sir Dermott, *Thoughts on the Nuclear Deterrent* (16 Y.B.W.A. 1962).
Bull, H., *Two Kinds of Arms Control* (17 *ibid.* 1963).
Groom, A.J.R., *The United States and the British Deterrent* (18 *ibid.* 1964).
Joynt, C.B., *Arms Races and the Problem of Equilibrium* (18 *ibid.* 1964).
Douglas-Home, C., *The Arms Sales Race* (23 *ibid.* 1969).
Erickson, J., *The World Strategic Balance* (23 *ibid.* 1969).
Lee, R., *Safeguards Against Nuclear Proliferation* (23 *ibid.* 1969).
Coffey, J.I., *The Limitation of Strategic Armaments* (26 *ibid.* 1972).
Owen, the Rt. Hon. David, *Western Naval Strategy in the Eighties* (28 *ibid.* 1974).
Ranger, R., *Arms Control in Theory and in Practice* (31 *ibid.* 1977).
Keohane, D., *Hegemony and Nuclear Non-Proliferation* (35 *ibid.* 1981).
Young, W. and E., *Disarmament Now: Catching Up with Crucé* (36 *ibid.* 1982).
Downey, J., *The Ageing of Deterrence* (37 *ibid.* 1983).

VII — Economic Aspects

1. *The World Economy*
Neurath, O., *Planning or Managerial Revolution* (7 N.C.Q. 1943).

Strange, Susan, *Changing Trends in World Trade* (16 Y.B.W.A. 1968).
Modelski, G., *The Corporation in World Society* (22 *ibid.* 1968).
Rose, L.W., *Flexible Exchange Rates* (30 *ibid.* 1976).
Vaizey, J., *International Inflation* (30 *ibid.* 1976).
Cohen, P.M., *The Future of Gold* (31 *ibid.* 1977).

2. *Eastern Europe and the West*
Alexandrowicz, C., *COMECON: The Soviet Retort to the Marshall Plan* (4 W.A. 1950).
Paenson, I., *The Problems of East-West Trade* (10 Y.B.W.A. 1956).
Nussbaumer, A., *The Economic Systems of Socialist Eastern Europe: Principles, Development and Operation* (29 *ibid.* 1975); *Industrial Co-operation and East-West Trade* (32 *ibid.* 1978).

3. *The Third World*
Parkinson, F., *Soviet Aid to Underdeveloped Countries* (11 Y.B.W.A. 1957).
Strange, Susan, *The Commonwealth and the Sterling Area* (13 *ibid.* 1959).
Parkinson, F., *The Alliance for Progress* (18 *ibid.* 1964).
Mahajani, U., *Foreign Aid at the Operational Level in South-East Asia* (19 *ibid.* 1965).
Levi, W., *Are Developing States More Equal than Others?* (32 *ibid.* 1978).
Wionczek, M.S., *External Indebtedness of Less Developed Countries* (35 *ibid.* 1981).
See also under IV — Political Aspects, (5) The Third World

4. *Oil and the Middle East*
Birdwood, C.B., *Oil in the Middle East* (4 W.A. 1950); *The Economic Development of the Middle East* (4 *ibid.* 1950).
Penrose, E., *Monopoly and Competition in the International Petroleum Industry* (18 *ibid.* 1964).
Odell, P., *The International Oil Companies in the New World Oil Market* (32 *ibid.* 1978).
Shaw, C.A., *Energy and a New Economic Order* (36 *ibid.* 1982).

VIII — ETHICAL ASPECTS

1. *Human Rights and World Politics*
Wells, H.G., *The Rights of Man* (*Union*, 1940).
Thomson, D., *The Four Freedoms* (7 N.C.Q. 1941).
Wells, H.G., *Homo Sapiens* (7 *ibid.* 1942).

Grace, H.M., *Conflict and Race Discrimination* (12 L.Q.W.A. 1946).
Martin, A., *The Universal Declaration of Human Rights* (3 W.A. 1949).
Green, L.C., *The European Convention on Human Rights* (5 ibid. 1951).
Vickers, Dame Joan, *Missing Persons* (28 Y.B.W.A. 1974).
Franck, T., *"Congressional Imperialism" and Human Rights Policies* (35 ibid. 1981).
Glazov, Y., *Dissent in Post-Stalinist Russia* (35 ibid. 1981).
Reoch, A.P., *"Disappearances" and International Protection of Human Rights* (36 ibid. 1982).
Vincent, R.J., *The Reagan Administration and America's Purpose in the World* (37 ibid. 1983).

2. *Moral Issues and Values*
Griffin, Cardinal, *A Christian New Order* (2 W.A. 1948).
Smith, H.A., *The Problem of the Just War* (2 ibid. 1948).
Morgenthau, H.J., *The Moral Dilemma in Foreign Policy* (5 Y.B.W.A. 1951).
Tunstall, B., *The Papacy and World Peace* (5 ibid. 1951).
Aaronson, M., *Political Aspects of International Drug Control* (9 ibid. 1955).
Dimbleby, G.W., *Restoring the Ecological Balance* (23 ibid. 1969).
Roberts, A., *Civil Resistance as a Technique in Foreign Policy* (24 ibid. 1970).
Szamuely, T., *Student Revolt in East and West* (24 ibid. 1970).
Kalmus, H., *Living Together Without Man* (25 ibid. 1971).
Hambro, E., *The Human Environment: Stockholm and After* (28 ibid. 1974).
Shaw, C.A., *Dilemmas of Super-Growth* (30 ibid. 1976).

IX — LEGAL ASPECTS

1. *International Jurisprudence*
Schwarzenberger, G., *The Frontiers of International Law* (6 Y.B.W.A. 1952); *Equity in International Law* (26 ibid. 1972).
Connelly, A.M., *The History of International Law in a Comparative Approach* (32 ibid. 1978).
Kittrie, N.N., *Reconciling the Irreconcilable: The Quest for Agreement on International Crime and Terrorism* (32 ibid. 1978).
Johnson, D.H.N., *International Arbitration Back in Favour* (34 ibid. 1980).

Watson, J.S., *A Realistic Jurisprudence of International Law* (34 *ibid.* 1980).

Schwarzenberger, G., *The Credibility of International Law* (37 *ibid.* 1983).

2. *Inner and Outer Space*

Johnson, D.H.N., *The Geneva Conference on the Law of the Sea* (13 Y.B.W.A. 1959).

Brown, E.D., *Deep-Sea Mining: The Legal Régime of "Inner Space"* (22 *ibid.* 1968).

Dickstein, H.L., *International Law and the Environment* (26 *ibid.* 1968).

Cheng, B., *The 1968 Astronauts Agreement* (23 *ibid.* 1969).

Brown, E.D., *The Anglo-French Continental Shelf Case* (33 *ibid.* 1979).

Schwarzenberger, G., *Trends in the Law of the Sea* (33 *ibid.* 1979).

3. *Social Law*

Brown, E.D., *International Social Law in Europe* (19 *ibid.* 1965).

4. *State-Capitalist Approaches*

Schapiro, L., *The Soviet Concept of International Law* (2 Y.B.W.A. 1948).

Ginsburgs, G., *Specialist International Law and State Sovereignty* (25 *ibid.* 1951).

Butler, W.E., *Eastern European Approaches to International Law* (26 *ibid.* 1972).

Lapenna, I., *The Soviet Concept of Socialist International Law* (29 *ibid.* 1975).

5. *Armed Conflict*

Radojkovic, M., *Les Armes Nucleaires et le Droit International* (16 Y.B.W.A. 1962).

Dinstein, Y., *Another Step in Codifying the Laws of War* (28 *ibid.* 1974).

Schwarzenberger, G., *The Law of Armed Conflict: A Civilised Interlude?* (28 *ibid.* 1974).

Dinstein, Y., *The New Geneva Protocols* (33 *ibid.* 1979).

Schwarzenberger, G., *Present-Day Relevance of the Hague Peace System 1899–1979* (34 *ibid.* 1980).

X — ORGANISATIONAL ASPECTS

Scelle, G., *Théorie du Gouvernment International* (1 N.C.Q. 1935).

Politis, N., *La Souveraineté et la Police Internationale* (2 *ibid.* 1936).

Green, L.C., *The Security Council in Action* (2 Y.B.W.A. 1948); *The "Little Assembly"* (3 *ibid.* 1949).

Hambro, E., *The International Court of Justice* (3 *ibid.* 1949).

Schapiro, C.B., *Soviet Participation in International Institutions* (3 *ibid.* 1949).

Parry, C., *The Secretariat of the United Nations* (4 W.A. 1950).

Cadogan, Sir Alexander, *The United Nations: A Balance Sheet* (5 Y.B.W.A. 1951).

Johnson, D.H.N., *Trusteeship: Theory and Practice* (5 *ibid.* 1951).

Belof, Lord, *Problems of International Government* (8 *ibid.* 1954).

Cheng, B., *International Law in the United Nations* (8 *ibid.* 1954).

Green, L.C., *The Security Council in Retreat* (8 *ibid.* 1954).

Strange, Susan, *The Economic Work of the United Nations* (8 *ibid.* 1954).

Friedmann, W., *Limits of Functionalism in International Organisation* (10 *ibid.* 1956).

Toussaint, Charmian Edwards, *The Colonial Controversy in the United Nations* (10 *ibid.* 1956).

Cheng, B., *The First Twenty Years of the International Court of Justice* (20 *ibid.* 1966).

Mitchell, C.R., *Peace-Keeping: The Police Function* (30 *ibid.* 1976).

Prott, L.V., *The Future of the International Court of Justice* (33 *ibid.* 1979).

See also under II — Historical Aspects, (1) The League of Nations and the Quest for Security.

POWER POLITICS
AND INTERNATIONAL ORDER

Pre-Charter Origins and Post-Charter Views

By

ROBERT A. FRIEDLANDER

ON January 22, 1917, at a time of bloody stalemate during the First World War, President Woodrow Wilson went before the United States Senate to advocate a negotiated settlement based upon "peace without victory." Three months later America itself had taken up arms, according to Wilsonian rhetoric, for the purpose of fighting "for democracy, for the rights and liberties of small nations, (and) for a universal dominion of right . . . ." Wilson's peace programme received the enthusiastic support of war-weary peoples everywhere, but not the endorsement of their national leaders.

Public opinion on both sides of the trenches believed that the forthcoming peace settlement would represent the establishment of a new world order based upon Wilson's proposed "free association of peoples" adhering to a revolutionary doctrine of "open covenants openly arrived at." Wilsonian idealism, at least in the eyes of its proponents, thus stood for a repudiation of the pre-war and wartime imperial politics of expediency which had characterised the behaviour of every European government and that of the United States in the first two decades of the twentieth century. Wilsonianism ultimately came to imply the righteous pursuit of idealistic principle in place of tainted national self-interest,[1] while the failed diplomacy of the interwar period seemed to bear out Wilson's many warnings against the perpetuation of traditional power politics in the international arena.[2]

I—THE INTERWAR BACKGROUND

The most effective official critique of interwar diplomatic dissembling and of the near fatal consequences of fascist aggression was to

---

[1] *cf.* R.E. Osgood, *Ideals and Self-Interest in America's Foreign Relations: The Great Transformation of the Twentieth Century* (1953), pp. 112–113, 172–194, and 223–263; M. Pomerance, "The United States and Self-Determination: Perspectives on the Wilsonian Conception" 70 *American Journal of International Law*, Nr. 1 (1976) pp. 1–27.

[2] E.H. Carr, *The Twenty Years' Crisis, 1919–1939: An Introduction to the Study of International Relations* (1942), pp. 186–215, remains an insightful and instructive analysis.

be found in the Atlantic Charter of August 1941. Prime Minister Winston Churchill, the British Cassandra of the Appeasement Decade, and President Franklin D. Roosevelt, the faithful disciple of Wilsonian principles, joined forces to strengthen the faith of freedom-loving peoples throughout the Western world. The eight principles, proclaimed by that historic document promised the resurrection of the rule of law and, by implication, the final interment of Global Darwinism. Others, equally concerned with the meaning of past events, were not so sure.

In their negative reaction to the diplomatic consequences of American participation in the Great War, many United States historians, analysts, and political commentators shared a common belief that self-interest, national interest, and power politics were essentially the same. The only beneficiaries of United States involvement in the First World War, from this point of view, were the war profiteers, the munitions makers, and the discredited European Allies. Charles A. Beard, the influential American historian, summed up the feelings of his fellow contemporaries in a study entitled *The Idea of the National Interest*, written during the early 1930s. Beard, echoing conclusions by other economic determinists, defined the national interest as representing material gain and commercial enterprise. He argued that the United States government interpreted its "national interest primarily in terms of domestic economy . . . ."[3] Unrestrained capitalism thus became the prime motivating factor, and diplomacy merely provided the means by which national self-interest could be achieved.

Several years later, almost coincidentally with the outbreak of the Second World War, the distinguished British historian and political scientist, Edward Hallett Carr, published his landmark analysis of the international system between the wars. A Marxist in personal philosophy, Professor Carr lashed out at Western idealism and utopianism as causative factors in the collapse of world order. "The doctrine of the survival of the fittest," he somberly intoned, "proves that the survivor was, in fact, the fittest to survive." The State, of necessity, becomes a "repository of political power," and one entity cannot impose moral conduct on another.[4] Power is equated with success, and this determines the nature of political order.[5] If Carr's reasoning is valid, then ideology serves only as a superficial symbol,

---

[3] C.A. Beard, *The Idea of the National Interest: An Analytical Study in American Foreign Policy* (A. Vagts and W. Beard Eds., 1966), p. 436.

[4] Carr, *op. cit.* in note 2 above, pp. 86 and 204.

[5] *Ibid.* p. 297. Carr also observes "that power is always an essential element of politics," which means "power is an indispensable instrument of government." *Ibid.* pp. 131 and 137.

rather than providing a motivation through itself. And nowhere in Carr's analysis does he make reference to the rôle of law.

Although he clearly foresaw the implication of Europe's gradual political breakdown, President Franklin D. Roosevelt demonstrated the popular American attitude of moral aloofness in his public pronouncements dealing with European events. He likewise refrained from reviewing Latin American problems in terms of legal issues, as his predecessors had done for more than a half-century. With the German invasion of Poland in September 1939, and Hitler's *Blitzkrieg* in the West during the spring and summer of 1940, any lingering illusions held by the White House over the short run benefits of objective neutrality were quickly shattered. Within less than two years after the Polish collapse, the American President was preparing to go to war,[6] but Pearl Harbour saved Roosevelt from having to relive the trauma of Woodrow Wilson's war declaration. Aggression had now become synonymous with power on the international scene, and military strength was deemed to be the only means of assuring national survival.

II—THE WAR-TIME LESSONS

There can be no doubt that the great majority of the Anglo-American citizenry looked upon the Second World War not only as a struggle for survival, but also—to use General Dwight D. Eisenhower's felicitous phrase—a crusade for freedom. The Second World War then and now was considered to be a just war according to the classic legal definition.[7] The Allied commitment was widely viewed as a necessary response to naked aggression and a warning to power-hungry national leaders. But there were also those analysts and commentators who realised that the attempt at the international exercise of political power represented more than mere Axis strongarm tactics.

In 1941, when the shadows of war looked darkest for the British people, Georg Schwarzenberger published the first edition of his celebrated *Power Politics*. Already a prominent legal scholar, the author defined power politics "as a system of international relations in which groups consider themselves as ultimate ends . . . ."[8] Tak-

---

[6] R. Dallek, *Franklin D. Roosevelt and American Foreign Policy 1932–1945* (1979), p. 285.

[7] M. Walzer, "World War II: Why Was this War Different?" in M. Chohen, T. Nagel, and T. Scanlon (Eds.), *War and Moral Responsibility* (1974) p. 93, asks: "Does the existence of a Nazi regime in Germany justify the war?" And then answers: "I am inclined to think that it does . . . ."*cf.* T. Taylor, *Nuremberg and Vietnam: An American Tragedy* (1970), pp. 74–76.

[8] G. Schwarzenberger, *Power Politics: A Study of World Society* (First published in 1941; 3rd ed., 1964), p. 14.

ing power to represent the mean between influence and force, Schwarzenberger argued that international law was subservient to power politics, and that morality at best plays only a minor role on the world political stage. The mistakes of the interwar period (repeated again after the Second World War) could be attributed to the refusal of national leaders to recognise that the world community, despite the creation of international organisations such as the League of Nations (and the United Nations), was merely "a system of power politics in disguise."[9] Adolf Hitler held no democratic illusions, and his use of power, when others refused to recognise or to deal with the results, led to a second international conflagration within a generation.[10] Schwarzenberger's study, in revised and expanded form, was to have its greatest impact in the new postwar era.

A second opinion shaper on the other side of the Atlantic, also influential in formulating postwar thought, was the American journalist and political philosopher, Walter Lippman. Although a former Wilsonian who helped to prepare the American peace programme during the period of United States participation in the First World War and the Paris Peace Conference, Lippman had shed most of his youthful idealism by the time of America's second wartime crusade. In a thoughtful and thought-provoking study published in the midst of the Second World War, Lippman conceded the existence of a régime of power politics, but he also insisted that it could be organised and regulated by careful calculation. Statesmen have been unable to pass from one order of power to another without major and prolonged conflict.[11] Thus, Great-Power politics have become a twentieth-century fact of life.

Lippman was one of the first commentators to claim that the United States went to war in 1917 "in order to preserve American security,"[12] and since American security was directly threatened by the Axis military machine in the Second World War, it was only natural to conceive of a postwar settlement which had to be built upon the structure of Great-Power co-operation. Lippman, therefore, specifically proposed the formation of a "nuclear alliance," meaning a close co-operation of what then appeared to be America's "natural and permanent allies" Great Britain and the Soviet Union.[13] Ironically, this vision of a peace maintained by the Great

---

[9] *Ibid.* pp. 14 and 29.
[10] *Ibid.* p. xix. One should not overlook his further analysis entitled *International Law and Totalitarian Lawlessness* (1943).
[11] W. Lippman, *U.S. Foreign Policy: Shield of the Republic* (1943), pp. 101 and 108.
[12] *Ibid.* p. 37.
[13] *Ibid.* pp. 164–166.

Powers was similar to ideas put forward a generation before by the arch enemy of Woodrow Wilson, Senator Henry Cabot Lodge of Massachusetts.

Despite the growth of a new realism on the part of such analysts as Schwarzenberger and Lippman, the flame of Wilsonian idealism was rekindled during the Second World War when the planning for a new world organisation got underway. The leading scholar of Roosevelt's foreign policy asserts that the American President was far less concerned with Wilsonian idealism than with a process "for permanently involving the United States in world affairs."[14] Undersecretary of State Sumner Welles had been the keeper of the Wilsonian flame in the Roosevelt war-time Administration,[15] and political necessity took precedence over legal principle, but there can be no doubt that Roosevelt truly wished for some kind of international peacekeeping mechanism.

When his successor, President Harry S. Truman, appeared before the final plenary session of the United Nations San Francisco Conference on June 26, 1945, the hopes and expectations of the victorious allies were reflected in Truman's eloquent address. "You have created a great instrument for peace and security and human progress in the world," Truman congratulated the assembled delegates. But then he cautioned, in a somewhat prophetic tone, that the powerful nations have a duty "to assume the responsibility for leadership toward a world of peace . . . . By their own example the strong nations of the world should lead the way to international justice."

The nature of that justice was intended to be seen in the Nuremberg and Tokyo Tribunals. Both the Nuremburg and Tokyo judgments were supposed, dramatically, to demonstrate the importance of the international rule of law, and that power politics, when the end result is aggressive war, "is essentially an evil thing."[16] In the long run Nuremberg failed as a symbol and as legal precedent to criminalise power politics when based upon military force.[17] The issue of aggression continued as a source of debate and disagreement for more than a generation. Finally in December 1974, a United Nations definition was adopted by consensus, but it has remained simply that—a definition without clarification or implementation.

---

[14] Dallek, *op. cit.* (in note 6 above), p. 536.

[15] *Ibid.* p. 421.

[16] Nuremberg Judgment, quoted in G. Schwarzenberger, *International Law: As Applied by International Courts and Tribunals*, Vol. 2 (1968), p. 485.

[17] *cf. ibid.* pp. 524–546; E. Davidson, *The Trial of the Germans: An Account of the Twenty-Two Defendants before the International Military Tribunal at Nuremberg* (1966), pp. 580–594; B. Smith, *Reaching Judgment at Nuremberg* (1977), pp. 299–306.

III—THE POST-WAR REALISTS

The harsh realities of the Cold War, and the strategy of containment developed by the United States Department of State, combined to foster a new realism among American scholars and analysts. Hans J. Morgenthau, professor of political science at the University of Chicago, literally launched a generation of controversy with the publication of his *Politics Among Nations* in 1947. Morgenthau had already gone on record one year earlier with his suspicion of international law and his dislike of international lawyers.[18] He preferred instead, as he came to call it in his second edition, a realist theory of international politics,[19] which emphasised political power and downgraded both moralism and legalism. "International politics," he declared, "like all politics is a struggle for power . . . . [P]ower is always the immediate aim."[20]

One year later, in the October 1948 issue of *World Politics*, Morgenthau pointedly criticised Edward Hallett Carr for setting out to explore a new morality which the latter asserted had become part of the political world without first having a clear notion of what constituted morality *per se*. Rejecting any attempt to balance the equities, Professor Morgenthau warned against the notion that superior power could also become the repository of superior morality. The political moralist will inevitably become snared in the trap of corrupting power lacking the strength provided by "a transcendant standard of ethics." But Morgenthau likewise rejected the role of law as an alternative to power politics. Writing shortly after the formal establishment of the United Nations, he indicated strong misgivings about an international law governing sovereign States by way of an international organisation. Those who viewed the creation of the United Nations as a victory of law over traditional power politics were actually engaging in self-deception. And this was particularly true of President Truman and Secretary-of-State Byrnes in their misplaced reliance upon the new world organisation as a prime instrument of United States foreign policy.[21]

Nearly a decade later, Morgenthau was still decrying the legalistic approach to international law. The precarious consensus which

---

[18] H. Morgenthau, *Scientific Man vs. Power Politics* (1946), pp. 108–121. His conclusion is particularly sharp: "questions which the law and the lawyer can answer are largely irrelevant to the fundamental issues upon which the peace and welfare of nations depend . . . ." *Ibid*. p. 121.

[19] H. Morgenthau, *Politics among Nations: The Struggle for Power and Peace* (2nd ed. rev. 1956), pp. 5–13.

[20] *Ibid*. p. 25.

[21] H. Morgenthau, "Traditional and United States Diplomacy" 55 *Yale Law Journal*, Nr. 5 (1946), pp. 1067–1080.

exists among interested States parties is not the same as a functional legal system, he argued, and the United Nations structure was merely old wine in a new bottle.[22] Self-interest should be the primary force motivating any nation's foreign policy, and to lose sight of that reality is to court danger and even disaster. "It goes without saying," Morgenthau cautioned the American Political Science Association in 1965, that "the image of what the United States thinks it ought to be, requires a predominant power not available to the United States."[23] This led Morgenthau in that same decade to become one of the foremost academic critics of American involvement in the Vietnam conflict. But as American historian, Gordon A. Craig, has noted, an emphasis upon power at the expense of the spirit also corrupts values and stunts political growth. Unrestricted self-interest, in the long run, may be self-defeating, if principle and power are not interrelated.

Morgenthau was not alone in opposing the international idealism manifested by American political leaders and opinion makers at the conclusion of the Second World War. The new realist who appeared to have had the most dramatic impact among the widest audience was former Ambassador George Kennan. Author of two extraordinarily influential articles in *Foreign Affairs* at the beginning of the post-war era, when he headed the Policy Planning Staff of the United States Department of State, Kennan is generally credited with having been the first to formulate the defensive Cold War strategy of containment. Kennan's most famous study, *American Diplomacy: 1900–1950*, was derived from a series of lectures delivered at the University of Chicago in 1950 and published by the University of Chicago Press the next year. It has gone through several editions and a large number of printings, in no small part due to the fact that it has been required reading for many years in American undergraduate history and political science courses.

Kennan, like Morgenthau, abjured the notion that the United States had to make itself a slave "of the concepts of international law and morality" in the pursuit of foreign policy. He bluntly condemned past reliance on legal norms and moral principles, and claimed that by substituting these false notions for the more realistic motivation of national interest, America had created many of its own difficulties and uncertainties in foreign relations. "I see the

---

[22] H. Morgenthau, *The Impasse of American Foreign Policy* (1962), pp. 112–113, 120–121. See also, pp. 33–35.

[23] H. Morgenthau, "Emergent Problems of United States Foreign Policy" in K. Deutsch and S. Hoffman (Eds.), *The Relevance of International Law* (1971), p. 78. Morgenthau viewed power as "a psychological relationship." See H. Morgenthau, *The Restoration of American Politics* (1962), pp. 7–14.

most serious fault of our past policy formulation," he admonished, "to lie in . . . the legalistic-moralistic approach to international problems. This approach runs like a red skein through our foreign policy of the last fifty years."

Legal rules and restraints, according to Kennan's analysis, are best suited to domestic rather than international systems. It is foolish and self-defeating to create rules for a game in which the only one abiding by the rules is the nation which created them. This implies an emotional commitment to self-appointed goals, rather than a rational exercise of international power. The only means to a successful end is diplomacy "in the most old-fashioned sense of the term." There can be no effective alternative, for "law is too abstract, too inflexible, too hard to adjust to the demands of the unpredictable and the unexpected."[24] And in a prophetic warning for the second half of the twentieth century, Kennan noted that "the legalistic approach to international affairs ignores in general the international significance of political problems and the deeper sources of international stability. It assumes that civil wars will remain civil and not grow into international wars."[25]

Kennan's pragmatic realism, plus his controversial years as United States Ambassador in Moscow subsequent to the Chicago lectures, created the appearance of an intellectual cold warrior who recognised the utility of power politics, and who sought to combat the Soviet Union on its own terms. This was a misconception. What most of Kennan's early admirers failed to recognise was the unanticipated change in his career from professional diplomat to distinguished academic likewise brought about a transformation in his geopolitical worldview. Kennan, the historian, carefully modified his earlier judgments with a firmer grasp of the uncertain historical process, and, thus, contrasted with Kennan, the diplomat, who drew upon personal experience obtained in such crisis posts as Beneš's Prague, Hitler's Berlin, and Stalin's Moscow.

In another series of lectures delivered four years after his Chicago presentation, Kennan continued to disparage rigid legal norms and to approve the virtues of diplomatic expediency. But he also now recognised "the importance of traditional international law," as long as it did not interfere with vital issues of national interest and military security. His distaste for morality providing a criteria for State action, however, remained undiminished. Moral concepts, he maintained, are simply not relevant to the behaviour of govern-

---

[24] G.F. Kennan, *American Diplomacy: 1900–1950* (1951), pp. 54, 84, 95–100.
[25] *Ibid.* p. 99.

ments which are themselves agents and not principals.[26] In fact, there is almost no mention of human rights in any of his writing with the exception of a few pages relating to the Helsinki Accords and the difficulties of Soviet-American relations contained in a study published a decade and a half later.[27] And his suspicion of the United Nations as an instrument of international conflict resolution has continued unabated.

Despite his increasing fears of a nuclear holocaust, and his new role as the self-appointed apostle of nuclear arms control, Kennan would bar the United Nations from being an arena for meaningful international agreement. It is instead, he maintains, a modality of "irresponsibility and emotional instability," and by its words and deeds "has constituted a destructive abuse of the value of universal organization per se."[28] Although still unable to bring himself, despite current dangers of nuclear annihilation, to advocate an international régime of the rule of law, the distinguished diplomat-scholar has finally conceded the merits of "a system of international law on a regional basis . . . ."[29] Perhaps he has at last come to recognise that a diplomacy of sheer expediency may also provide the road to self-destruction.

Although it is rarely acknowledged, the foremost advocate of the new realism among postwar practitioners of the diplomatic art was the American Secretary of State, Dean Acheson. Admonishing an audience at the annual meeting of the American Society of International Law a decade after he left cabinet office, Acheson bluntly declared that "[t]he survival of states is not a matter of law." Although a legalist by training and a lawyer by profession, Acheson saw himself rather as an international strategist who placed pragmatic realism above moral idealism.[30] Sharply critical of many of his successors, particularly John Foster Dulles, Secretary Acheson cited with approval the aciduous observation of the Seventeenth-century French philosopher, Blaise Pascal: "Justice without power is impotent; power without justice is tyranny."[31]

Unlike Morgenthau and Kennan, who held international law to be inherently suspect and potentially harmful to the national inter-

---

[26] G.F. Kennan, *Realities of American Foreign Policy* (1954), pp. 36–39, 48–50.
[27] G.F. Kennan, *The Cloud of Danger: Current Realities of American Foreign Policy* (1977), pp. 212–218.
[28] *Ibid.* p. 30.
[29] G.F. Kennan, "On Nuclear War" 28 *The New York Review of Books*, Nrs. 21 and 22 (January 21, 1982), p. 8.
[30] D. Acheson, *This Vast External Realm* (1973), pp. 136–137.
[31] Acheson, "Foreign Policy and Presidential Moralism" *The Reporter* (May 2, 1957), p. 12.

est, Acheson did not disdain the value of legal principles. But he did view post-Charter developments in international law with scepticism, and cautioned the attendees of the 1963 American Society of International Law conference that "[m]uch of what is called international law is a body of ethical distillation, and one must take care not to confuse this distillation with law." Punishing one's allies in the name of a higher cause made bad politics and worse sense. Diplomacy had to guard against "a combination of phoney law and fuzzy morals," and embarking upon diplomatic crusades or civilising missions had led, not infrequently, to the undercutting of vital interests.[32]

What was needed most of all, he insisted, was a "strategic approach to practical objectives, concretely and realistically conceived, ahead of generalizations, even those wearing the garb of idealism."[33] Acheson claimed that under his steward-ship the diplomatic position of the United States grew in strength and in stature, though his critics have argued otherwise. The balance between principle and pragmatism which he continued to advocate throughout the remainder of his life depended upon clarity of vision and resoluteness of purpose, a precarious combination for the instruments of modern diplomatic practice.

It is, by now, generally accepted that the most influential advocate of the new realism among legal commentators, following the Second World War, was Professor Georg Schwarzenberger of the University of London Faculty of Law, who has remained down to the present day the most prominent and effective critic of the Post-Charter global order. (He prefers his own term, quasi-order). As co-founder and co-editor of this *Year Book*, Schwarzenberger created a particularly effective forum where his myriad ideas and propositions reached an academic and governmental readership far greater than otherwise would have been the case for a mere specialised journal of international law. In fact, a large number of his more controversial and challenging essays have made their initial appearance in the *Year Book of World Affairs*.

Being the first scholar of serious reputation to call attention to the role of a power politics which both undermined and diminished the existing international legal system prior to the Second World War,[34] Schwarzenberger also has been consistently harsh in his post-war

---

[32] *Ibid.* p. 14.

[33] D. Acheson, *Present at the Creation: My Years in the State Department* (1969), p. 727.

[34] See Schwarzenberger, *Power Politics, op. cit.* (in note 8 above); *International Law and Totalitarian Lawlessness, op. cit.* (in note 10 above).

judgments on a reorganised world community.[35] He has never deviated from the view that "the law and order of societies are laws and orders of power. If possible, they rely on self-co-ordination but, if necessary, on a rising scale of pressures and in the last resort, force."[36] Like his American counterpart, Hans Morgenthau, Georg Schwarzenberger believes that force historically has served as both the ends and means of national foreign policy. Thus, contemporary international law in the Post-Charter era continues to operate as a "quasi-order . . . of power politics in disguise."

From this perspective, the principles and precepts of public international law past and present, whether invoked by either custom or treaty, have only had a limited effect upon the world political arena. Throughout the centuries, dating from the time of Hugo Grotius and the Peace of Westphalia, the lack of enforcement sanctions has seriously impeded the growth and actually aided the promotion of violence in the world societal structure. According to Schwarzenberger, international law is not only a system susceptible to ideology and power, it is also at times a co-operative enterprise based upon reciprocity. The operative catalyst is order which almost invariably controls the legal superstructure. In practice, therefore, international law is only able to offer an alternative set of behavioural standards applicable to sovereign States on a slightly higher plane than that of power politics.

Perhaps the key to the Schwarzenberger construct is to be found in his analysis of the nature of sovereignty. Political sovereignty in effect supervenes the principles of the United Nations Charter, undermines general international obligations, and minimises the requirements of good faith. Since the end of the Second World War, the super-Powers, or new Leviathans, have not infrequently placed themselves above the law, or at least outside of prevailing international norms. As a result, post-1945 world society has developed out of an "oligarchic nucleus . . . formed by hegemonial super-Powers, surrounded by junior partners and satellites."[37] Competition for global influence and a cosmic-like arms race have caused the current international legal régime to maintain a very precarious balance, and the prognosis for the future in an uncontrolled community of nuclear sovereignties is at best uncertain.

---

[35] The following analysis is based, unless otherwise noted, upon material presented in R. Friedlander, "Power Politics and the Rule of Law: Professor Schwarzenberger Reconsidered" 24 *De Paul Law Review*, Nr. 4 (1975), pp. 836–852.

[36] G. Schwarzenberger, "International Law and the Problem of Political World Order: Inter-Disciplinary Working Hypotheses and Perspectives" in Bin Cheng (Ed.), *International Law: Teaching and Practice* (1982), p. 57.

[37] *Ibid.* p. 58.

The real fear, to use the words of British military historian John Keegan, is "that some states, being richer or stronger than others, will place a higher value on their own sovereignty and what is due to it than they do on that of their weaker neighbours." Both Schwarzenberger and Keegan see a potential for endemic disorder in the post-1945 Charter régime of absolute equality of nations and through the sovereignty explosion which began in the 1960s. The inevitable consequence in the ensuing decade of the 1970s and that of the early 1980s has been "a world-wide system of local pecking orders, understood in a visceral way by all . . . ."[38] Since a meaningful substantive reform of the legal and political character of the United Nations is probably unattainable, the likelihood of achieving "an essentially hegemonial world confederation" in this century is virtually non-existent.[39] But the price for ongoing international instability due to the worldwide politics of power becomes even more costly, despite obvious dangers to the survival of humankind as we know it.

IV—HENRY KISSINGER
AND THE DECLINE OF WORLD ORDER

If George Kennan's influence as one of the first Cold-War apostles of the new realism (before his ultimate conversion to détente and nuclear freeze) was due in good measure to his distinguished foreign service record in the Department of State, as well as "to the fact that he writes in a language which is always intelligible and at times powerful,"[40] then Henry Kissinger's impact upon modern international political theory gained its strength as much from his later diplomatic status as from his early scholarly writings. One academic colleague and commentator has recently claimed that not until the appearance of Henry A. Kissinger, did the new realism, which developed after the Second World War, finally reach its apotheosis.[41] It is indeed ironic that in the years since Dr. Kissinger left public office, he has been more remembered, and occasionally honoured, for what he has said, than for what he actually accomplished, or claimed to have accomplished.

Speaking in Pretoria, South Africa, on September 6, 1982, Kiss-

---

[38] J. Keegan "Pecking Orders" 29 *The New York Review of Books*, Nr. 14 (September 23, 1982), p. 29.

[39] G. Schwarzenberger, "Civitas Maxima?" 29 Y.B.W.A. (1975), pp. 361–363.

[40] W. Laqueur, "What We Know about the Soviet Union" 75 Commentary, Nr. 2 (February 1. 1983), p. 14. See, also, P. Seabury, "George Kennan Vs. Mr. 'X' " *The New Republic* (December 16, 1981), pp. 17 and 20.

[41] S. Huntington, "Human Rights and American Power" 72 *Commentary* Nr. 3 (September, 1981), p. 37.

inger warned his audience that "[h]istory is kind to political leaders, who use a margin of choice while it is still available. Those who wait on events are usually overwhelmed by them." This was not only meant as pointed though friendly advice to the beleaguered South African Government, but it also reflected an overriding concern of Kissinger's personal worldview, first developed as a Havard graduate student at the beginning of the 1950s. His doctoral dissertation, completed in 1954 but not published (as his second book) until three years later, centred on the Congress of Vienna and the formation of the European Concert system from 1812 to 1822. His prime concern was the maintenance of minimum world order, and an examination of the techniques of statesmanship required for the preservation of that precarious condition. The true test of a statesman, he steadfastly maintained, is found in "his ability to recognise the real relationship of forces and to make this knowledge serve his ends."[42] Adamant in rejecting the claims of social determinists, Kissinger has never wavered in his conviction that political leadership, and the role of choice, provide the basic keys to political survival in the world community.

From the time he entered the Nixon White House, Henry Kissinger found himself often assailed by a wide variety of critics for an inexorable infatuation with power politics and for being overly obsessed with the techniques of power. American political analyst Ronald Steel, for example, writing in *The New Republic* of December 13, 1979, accuses the former Secretary of State of seeking "a Hobbesian world where power is the only arbiter and the only morality," and where "the weak are meant to be victims and that the strong can avoid that fate only by being merciless." Steel concludes that Kissinger envisions a world "where power is exercised for its own sake," devoid of any moral restraint, and at times even lacking a rational objective. From his very first book, the still-relevant *Nuclear Weapons and Foreign Policy* (1957), Kissinger has been fascinated by the relationship between force and diplomacy, and by "the task of strategic doctrine to translate power into policy."

With the publication, one year after receiving his doctorate, of a controversial essay on "American Policy and Preventive War" in the *Yale Review* (Spring 1955), Kissinger manifested a non-interest and disregard for the role of international law which has continued to the present day. Rejecting the "never-never land of formal agreement," and its concomitant "lawyer-like evasions," the newly-

---

[42] H. Kissinger, *A World Restored: Metternich, Castlereagh and the Problems of Peace, 1812–1822* (1957), p. 325.

minted scholar exalted diplomacy as the best means of restraining the exercise of power. According to this reasoning, power politics did not derive from ineluctable forces and movements, but was rather the direct result of an interplay of the human personality as it encountered the contingent and unforeseen. Individual choice, he argues, becomes the true catalyst for the political process,[43] and Kissinger in theory and practice has never failed to emphasise the importance of choice for dealing with pressing issues of statecraft.

From the Kissingerian perspective, diplomacy and personality are so inextricably intertwined that one perspicacious individual can affect the course of world events to a considerable degree. It may very well be that this idealisation of nineteenth-century diplomatic history left an indelible mark upon his own twentieth-century approach to diplomatic practice. How else does one explain the curious romanticised notion of an aloof, detached national leader, venturing out into the unknown, as a sort of Western-style cowboy folk hero, responsible for the maintenance of international order?[44] Scholars are not exempted from dreams of glory, though few are so fortunate as to ultimately partake of their own fantasies.

"Error has never approached my spirit," the nineteenth-century Austrian Imperial Chancellor, Prince Clemens von Metternich, once observed. Henry Kissinger's numerous detractors have caustically attributed to him a similar ideology and rhetoric, but their Metternich analogy is both misleading and misapplied. Prussia's Otto von Bismarck, not Metternich, is the historical figure that Kissinger has most admired, and for good reason. International relations consists of Great-Power politics, and the history of the modern State system, dating from the advent of the French Revolution, presents an inexorable struggle between the forces of disruption and the conservators of world order. Bismarck's legendary effectiveness, in the words of Henry Kissinger, reflected "the realities of power rather than the canons of legitimacy."[45] The wily Prussian statesman was an opportunism above all else, though it was an opportunist employed, since German unification, for the ends of stability and order.

Kissinger's prime concern throughout his entire career has not been with power politics so much as it has been with *balance-of-*

---

[43] S. Graubard, *Kissinger: Portrait of a Mind* (1974), p. 11. This sympathetic study by an academic colleague and friend gives a detailed analysis of Kissinger's scholarly writing and political thought.

[44] *cf.* H. Kissinger, "American Policy and Preventive War" 44 *Yale Review*, Nr. 3 (March 1955), p. 336; O. Fallaci, *Interview with History* (1977) p. 41.

[45] H. Kissinger, "The White Revolutionary: Reflections on Bismarck" 97 *Daedelus*, Nr. 3 (Summer 1968), p. 913.

power politics. His major contribution to the theory and practice of the new realism is thus misunderstood and even neglected by critics and admirers alike. What they often overlook is the fact that Kissinger's major focus centred on the limits of power and on the long-range debilitating consequences attached to the erosion of traditional political authority structures. This led him in turn to a deeply inbred pessimism—indeed an almost crushing fatalism—as to the future of Western liberal pluralistic society. "Our margin of survival has narrowed dangerously," he warned nearly a generation ago. "We are not omnipotent. We are no longer invulnerable."[46]

Ironically, Kissinger himself presided over the retreat of American power in South-East Asia, Latin America, and the Middle East. The lessons of Cambodia, Chile, OPEC, and Helsinki, disillusioned his supporters and fired up his critics. The end result, during the 1970s was that "the new realism came to be challenged by the 'new moralism' and the pendulum that had swung in one direction after World War II now swung far over the other side."[47]

CONCLUSIONS

Present-day Western democracies have largely condemned the practice of power politics as international illegality, and some even infer that it constitutes quasi-criminality. Certainly, there can be no question that the majority of international legalists denounce both its practice and its precepts. Israel, the most consistent State-party adherent to that now suspect doctrine, is barely tolerated in the international community, and probably would not be that, except for the indispensible support of its ally and protector, the United States. The United Kingdom, asserting its claim of right by force of arms in the Falkland Islands strife, nonetheless fell victim to serious economic dislocation and political dispute on the home front. Liberal pluralistic societies have yet to resolve satisfactorily the irrepressible tension between national security interests and the rule of law.

Following the Second World War, the United States, which had assumed by default the leadership of the free world, found itself immediately involved in foreign political quarrels. Traditional United States historians and commentators have viewed America's decision to intervene in the Korean conflict as a challenge to unpro-

---

[46] H. Kissinger, *The Necessity for Choice: Prospects of American Foreign Policy* (1961), p. 2.

[47] Huntington, *op. cit.* (in note 41 above), p. 42. This explains the growing importance attached to the international protection of human rights by the intellectual adversaries of power politics.

voked aggression and a commitment to the international peacekeeping function. Revisionist historians and analysts, on the other hand, have treated the American role in the Korean War as an exercise of power politics, pure and simple, and have denounced President Harry Truman and his Secretary of State, Dean Acheson, as Cold-Warriers *par excellence*. It is by now an historical common-place to say that the Vietnam experience encouraged the decline of American power in both theory and practice.

The rise of the new realism in the conduct of American foreign relations by a generation of scholar-activists after the Second World War, and the enormous influence of its proponents on strategic planning, resulted in a conscious repudiation of the Wilsonian tradition. Despite the laudable idealism associated with the establishment of the United Nations and the ensuing attempt to create a viable international order, the twentieth century neither abjured competing ideologies nor foreswore the politics of power. If might no longer made right, it still formed the basis for national survival.

Although their influence has waned considerably, advocates of the new realism never lost the ability to recognise precarious positions for what they were. The world today is once again delicately balanced upon a dangerous political tightrope, but now there is less room for effective manoeuvre than ever before. The next collapse of minimum world order may well be the last.

THE FLEET, THE FALKLANDS
AND THE FUTURE

By

DAVID GREENWOOD

IN the first half of 1981 the then Secretary of State for Defence, Mr. (now Sir) John Nott, conducted a far-reaching review of the United Kingdom's defence programme and budget. The exercise yielded a comprehensive blueprint for Britain's future defences whose essential features were set out in a White Paper entitled *The United Kingdom Defence Programme: The Way Forward*.[1] Among other things this document foreshadowed a significant rundown in the manpower strength of the Royal Navy and a reduction in the size of its surface fleet, together with the closure of one major dockyard and contraction at others.

The appearance of *The Way Forward* was followed by nine months of animated discussion and keen criticism of the Secretary of State's prescription for the Fleet. Although the cuts proposed were not without a sound strategic and economic rationale, a strong naval lobby pressed vigorously for modification—if not abandonment—of the planned diminution. A few friends were won and a few people influenced by the arguments. But the Government remained unmoved.

Then General Galtieri took it into his head to invade the Falkland Islands. With remarkable despatch, an impressive naval task force was assembled and put to sea. It sailed south and took station in the Roaring Forties, providing that visible expression of preparedness to oust the invader which—it was hoped—might lead to a peaceful withdrawal. And when diplomacy failed it put ashore troops which duly besieged Argentina's occupying forces and succeeded in securing their surrender. The Royal Navy had a little bit of help from its friends—the Army and the Royal Air Force—not to mention massive support from the mercantile marine. But it was the Commander-in-Chief Fleet who actually commanded Operation Corporate (from his Northwood Headquarters). It was the Chief of the Naval Staff or First Sea Lord and the Chief of the Defence Staff—as it happened, an Admiral too—who were the most visible figures in the higher direction of the undertaking (in Whitehall). It was the Rear Admiral in charge

---

[1] *The United Kingdom Defence Programme: The Way forward*, Cmnd. 8288 (1981) (London, H.M.S.O.

59

of the ships at sea with whom, in the popular eye, the key front-line responsibility lay (at least until ground forces had established themselves ashore). The business of "restoring British administration" to the Falkland Islands thus had all the appearance of a "Navy show." Small wonder therefore that, during and after the undertaking, the Government was urged from many quarters to reconsider the proposed naval rundown, to re-examine the apparent down-grading of the maritime element in British defence priorities, and even to reappraise the balance struck in *The Way Forward* between security provision for Europe, European waters and the North Atlantic on the one hand, and farther-flung national responsibilities on the other.

Ministers did revise their ideas. However, the policy statement *The Falklands Campaign: The Lessons*—published in December 1982— did no more than outline necessary changes in plans for the future Fleet arising from battle losses and the new obligation to patrol the South Atlantic. It did not offer the Lords of the Admiralty *carte blanche* for expansion. Nor did it foreshadow a fundamental re-ordering of strategic priorities. Indeed it was stressed that the major threat to the security of the United Kingdom continued to be the might of the Soviet Union and its Warsaw Pact allies in and around Europe.[2] To be sure, seeing references to more money and new construction, naval lobbyists claimed a triumph, a vindication of their critique of the preceding 18 months; or, rather, the not-so-perceptive among them did. Wiser men saw that not a lot had altered.

Yet after an episode like the liberation of the Falklands things could never be quite the same again. If the changes were less than the critics claimed they also amounted to more than the Government admitted. In fact, by 1983 it could be argued—and it will be argued in what follows—that the maritime and global perspectives in British defence policy-making and planning had definitely gained at the expense of the continental and Eurocentric. The effects of this transformation might not be immediately discernible. But its potential impact, in the event of either further internal budgetary pressure on the defence effort or a burgeoning of interest in Alliance-wide specialisation in the fulfilment of roles and responsibilities, is none the less significant for that.

I—NOTT'S BLUEPRINT

The background to the defence review of January-June 1981 has been explained elsewhere.[3] Essentially, what Secretary of State

---

[2] *The Falklands Campaign: The Lessons*, Cmnd. 8758 (1982) (London, H.M.S.O.).

[3] See, *e.g.* D. Greenwood, *Reshaping Britain's Defences*, Aberdeen Studies in Defence Economics (ASIDES), Nr. 19 (Summer 1981).

John Nott found on taking over at the Ministry of Defence was a programme-in-being characterised by (a) an overall force structure too extensive and planned force levels too high in relation to the resources likely to be available to sustain the defence effort; and (b) a capital stock too much of which was in the form of large and costly weapons platforms—*e.g.* ships and aircraft—masking inadequate provision of actual weapons, ammunition stocks and suchlike. Accordingly he set about a rationalisation of the business, to curtail the scope of the nation's defence dispositions so that the funds actually available should not be spread too thinly and to restore balance to the stock of capital equipment.

The outcome of the exercise was *The Way Forward*. The main features of this "blueprint for Britain's future defences " were (i) confirmation of the previous year's decision to acquire a next-generation strategic nuclear force based on the American Trident missile, the C4 variant being the candidate for purchase at this juncture; (ii) reaffirmation of the high priority to be accorded to protection of the United Kingdom itself, with special attention to modernising the nation's air defences; (iii) endorsement of the commitment to provide a major contribution to NATO's order of battle for land-air warfare on the Alliance's Central Front—the British Army of the Rhine (BAOR) and RAF Germany (RAFG) in the Federal Republic plus other formations at home—but with a remodelled Rhine Army and a scaled-down air force structure; (iv) endorsement of the commitment to provide naval and maritime-air forces for the Eastern Atlantic, but with a shift of emphasis in that provision involving fewer surface ships than had been envisaged hitherto.

As for safeguarding Western security interests beyond NATO's formally-defined boundaries, the White Paper stressed that existing garrisons outside Europe would be maintained and plans in train to improve the Services' abilities to operate worldwide would be continued.[4]

What was foreshadowed for the Fleet evoked a storm of protest from former naval peers and politicians. Yet Mr. Nott had really done no more than spotlight the questionable judgments and assumptions implicit in the naval plans he saw and some of the striking disproportionalities embodied in them.

To elaborate on the first of these points: the Minister discovered that the Royal Navy was planning to invest in a remarkably expensive three-way bet. It wanted ships to enable it (i) to carry the battle to the Soviet opponent in far northern waters (*i.e.* conduct a forward defence at sea); (ii) to perform anti-submarine barrier oper-

---

[4] Cmnd. 8288, paras. 32–36 (p. 11).

ations in the Greenland-Iceland-U.K. gap; and (iii) to provide local protection for reinforcement and resupply shipping on transatlantic passage—all this primarily to safeguard the sea line of communication across the North Atlantic so that land-air warfare might be prosecuted on the European mainland for weeks rather than days, yet all at the expense of funds for ready forces on the Central Front which were actually so undernourished that they might be hard pressed to survive for hours against a determined onslaught (which is the only sort the Warsaw Pact would ever be likely to embark upon). That did not make sense. Needless to say, the Minister was told of the dangers of robbing the Fleet to pay the Army's re-equipment bills. For even though keeping the first line of deterrence in good repair mattered most, a hedge against protracted hostilities had to be preserved. What he saw most vividly, though, was the futility of mustering the means to win tomorrow's battles by starving the forces needed to fight today's.

As for "disproportionalities" in some of the Navy's ways of doing things, Mr. Nott noted that there were warships which cost tens of millions to build, and hundreds of thousands to run each year, whose principal lethal punch was one missile launcher or ageing torpedoes. He observed too an intention to retain older hulls whose long refits and mid-life modernisations would entail indordinate expenditure and time out of commission, not least because of the huge overheads and archaic work habits of Her Majesty's Dockyards. He questioned the wisdom of spending scarce money on such vessels while more modern ships lay alongside for want of fuel and stores; and, no less significant, while private warship designers were claiming that for similar outlays equally effective new types could be constructed.

It was, of course, irreverent thus to question cherished priorities and practices. But it was not ridiculous. Indeed, the Secretary of State came up with a prescription for the future Fleet which was more rational than his critics gave him credit for. At the heart of his design was the decision to run a smaller surface fleet. To this end, he intimated that only two of the *Invincible*-class carriers should be commissioned, while in due time other "ships of high quality" should be paid off together with a dozen or so older destroyers and frigates. He envisaged, in fact, that the number of escorts in service should be brought down to 42, or three-quarters of the then existing tally, by the mid-1980s. The number of nuclear-powered Fleet submarines was not to be cut, however. Nor was the conventionally-powered submarine force, the intention being that a new class should be built to enter service well before the last of the *Oberons* had become obsolescent.

But the key thing is that reduction in the nominal size of the Fleet was not seen as an end in itself but as a means to an end. With fewer hulls, more money could be devoted to those that remained: to give them up-to-date weapons systems, to buy the fuel and stores to enable them to provide a presence-at-sea (rather than the presence-in-port which is all that many warships had provided through much of 1980–81). At the same time, the process of contraction would enable long refit and refurbishing costs to be avoided, freeing funds for new construction, perhaps of more novel and more economical designs built to commercial scantlings and with modular modernisation in mind (and thus unlikely to need extensive and frequent dockyard maintenance).

All but the most ardent naval lobbyists recognised that a "new look" Navy fashioned in this way would cut no less impressive a figure than the old in the eyes of the potential adversary (or those of Allies for that matter). For no marked degradation was implied in the two parts of the "three-way bet" most directly relevant to Soviet calculations. The United Kingdom would still muster a "mix" of naval capacity and maritime-air effort—the latter improving all the time—sufficient to give, with Allies' help, good cover of the "choke points" which the Russians must negotiate to reach the shipping lanes of the North Atlantic. The Fleet would still have, on top of that, the wherewithal to run interference in the far north-east from time to time, sufficient to deny the Soviet Navy effective sanctuary there. If fewer hulls meant a reduced capability for convoy protection, across the ocean and en route to Norway, did that matter? After all the NATO Alliance was paying more attention to pre-positioning and bringing increasing numbers of wide-bodied jets into service, so that the relative importance of seaborne reinforcement and resupply was diminishing steadily. If a smaller Fleet meant less scope for detaching task groups to sail distant seas, was that important? After all the United Kingdom no longer claimed global aspirations, and it would be feasible to despatch a few warships, occasionally, to show the flag in the Indian Ocean and the South Atlantic.

In sum, there was a lot less wrong with Mr. Nott's way forward for the Royal Navy than his critics alleged. There was even less cause for opposition after the autumn of 1981 when, following further reflection on the blueprint, the Secretary of State opted to retain the assault ships *Fearless* and *Intrepid* which he had first thought could be dispensed with. The trouble was no-one saw fit to use the opportunity of the southern hemispheric summer of 1981–82 to despatch one of those occasional task groups mentioned in the White Paper to the South Atlantic. And so a nervous General in Buenos Aires inferred that the time might soon be ripe for a decisive move to evict the British from the *Islas Malvinas* to which his country had long laid claim.[5]

<h2 style="text-align:center">II—THE FALKLANDS CAMPAIGN AND AFTER</h2>

Just over nine months after the appearance of *The Way Forward* that move was made. It evoked an immediate and impressive response, and one in which the Senior Service played a leading role. The question is: did the Royal Navy's performance of that role constitute a vindication of the critics of "Nott's blueprint"; or was the entire—and eventually successful—contingency operation essentially a sideshow, affording no justification for a fundamental reappraisal of the preceding year's decisions?

To form a judgment on this calls for attention to three themes. First, is it true—as was asserted at the time—that, had the naval reshaping foreshadowed in *The Way Forward* run its course, it simply would not have been possible to assemble a balanced task force to sail south, isolate the occupying garrison (and, while doing so, exact a toll from the adversary's naval and air forces), and then land troops to besiege and ultimately oust the invader? Secondly, did the actual conduct of operations shed any light on the "disproportionalities" argument, and specifically on the proposition that the Fleet-in-being contained too many ships with inadequate armament? Thirdly, should one regard the experience as a whole as evidence that the United Kingdom cannot, and should not, tailor its force structure to European and North Atlantic requirements?

(a) *The task force*

The capital ships around which the naval task force was composed were the venerable *Hermes* and the relatively recently commissioned *Invincible*. Neither figured in Secretary of State Nott's plans for the mid-1980s Fleet. The older vessel was slated for the scrapyard, failing the appearance of a potential purchaser. The newer was marked down for sale to the Australians (as a replacement for the ageing HMAS *Melbourne*), the Government having decided to retain only the second and third of this class, *Illustrious* and *Ark Royal* (both of which were still at the shipyard in April 1982). Commentators made great play with the irony here; heads were shaken and shoulders shrugged as people observed that "if Galtieri had only waited a few months, we would not have been able to mount

---

[5] See *Falkland Islands Review*, Report of a Committee of Privy Counsellors (Chairman: Lord Franks), Cmnd. 8787, *passim*.

the operation." But this was a careless—or, in some cases, a wilful—misreading of the official plan. It was never intended that the disposals should take place before the brand new ships entered service. And there was similar misrepresentation regarding the assault ships which, as noted, the Government had opted to keep long before the Falklands crisis loomed.

Nor was there any substance to the allegations that the proposed rundown in the escort force (destroyers and frigates) would have so depleted the Royal Navy's front line as to have precluded the formation of a flotilla such as was sent to the South Atlantic. For the essence of the Nott design was a reduction in the *nominal* size of the surface fleet to permit an increase in the proportion of the total strength in commission at any one time.

Lastly, it ought to be remembered that a majority of the vessels which actually went to the 8000-mile-distant area of operations were "ships taken up from trade" (including the liner *Canberra* which sailed to the heart of the battle zone at the time of the May landings). The 1981 review had not incorporated proposals for a slimmed-down merchant marine!

To the first of the posers just put there is, therefore, a straightforward answer. It is *not* true that one, two or even five years later it would have proved impracticable to conduct the Falklands campaign as it was in fact conducted for lack of suitable ships.[6]

(b) *Operations*

Furthermore, focusing attention on what transpired when the Fleet found itself engaged in combat, the "Falklands experience" confirmed rather than contradicted the reasoning in *The Way Forward*. Specifically, the desirability of laying greater stress on "weapons" rather than "platforms" was emphatically underscored. The vulnerability of front-line warships without a close-in defence system capable of dealing with low flying aircraft and sea-skimming missiles was particularly evident, and tragically demonstrated, *e.g.* in the early loss of the destroyer *Sheffield*. Nor is the tally of ships sunk or crippled the only relevant index in this connection. After the initial successes of the Argentinian air force, the naval commander judged it prudent to station his main force out of harm's way—well to the north-east of the Falkland Islands—at least during daylight hours, and was thereby prevented from sustaining round-the-clock pressure on the adversary. When there was no alternative but to commit ships close inshore to effect the landing of ground

---

[6] For details of the composition of the Task Force see Cmnd. 8758.

troops (and much equipment), high risks were run and the task force enjoyed greater good fortune than it was entitled to expect.[7]

In the realm of air operations there was another striking demonstration of the "disproportionality" thesis. Vulcan bombers and carrier-based Harrier aircraft flew many sorties with the aim of putting the Port Stanley airfield out of action. Yet these costly "platforms" had only limited success, essentially because the "weapons" or munitions which they delivered were not up to the job.[8]

All in all, the conclusion to be drawn on the second of the themes identified earlier is that the fighting generally bore eloquent testimony to the good sense of Mr. Nott's basic disposition in favour of combat effectiveness rather than nominal strength.

(c) *Strategic priorities*

On the third theme—the proposition that the contretemps with Argentina lent weight to the argument of those unhappy about the growing Eurocentricity of the British defence effort—there are several points to be made. That the Falkland Islands were invaded in the first place was, indisputably, a failure of deterrence. It is hardly admissible, however, to proceed from that acknowledgment to the assertion that, wherever in the world the nation's interests might be challenged, sufficient forces must be maintained "in place" to dissuade any would-be adversary. Not even in the Imperial heyday did London's writ run, or Britannia rule the waves, to that extent. Then as now, calculations about stationing involved a complex reconciliation of formal commitments in relation to available resources, made against a background of equally complex evaluations of the capabilities and intentions of potential challengers in relation to the United Kingdom's own capacities; and into the last of these elements were to be counted, and still are to be counted, not only military might but also a range of political, economic and cul-

---

[7] There is a large literature on the operations. For useful general discussions see L. Freedman, "The War of the Falklands 1982" 61 *Foreign Affairs* (Fall 1982), pp. 196–210, and N. Kerr, "The Falklands Campaign," XXXV *Naval War College Review (US)*, Nr. vi. (November-December 1982), pp. 14–21. For generally well-informed evaluations of the performance of particular types of equipment see the several issues of *International Defense Review* for the second half of 1982. Other useful essays include the five pieces in the journal *Defence* of November 1982; Ezio Bonsignore's article "Hard Lessons from the South Atlantic" *Military Technology* (August 1982), pp. 31–36; E.F. Gueritz, "The Falklands: Joint Warfare Justified," 128 *Journal of the Royal United Services Institute (RUSI)*, Nr. 1 (March 1983), pp. 33–38 and the front-line commanders' account, J. Moore and J. Woodward, "The Falklands Experience" in the same issue of this journal.

[8] For a semi-official account of air operations generally, see J. Curtiss, "Reflection on the Falklands Crisis" *The Hawk* (Journal of the Royal Air Force Staff College) (February 1983), pp. 257–263.

tural denominations in the mysterious currencies of power and influence.

It could be claimed, though, that for British sovereign territory at least it would be reasonable to expect definition and communication of a clear-cut military obligation. All very well in principle: but would one follow the logic of that through to, say, maintaining in Hong Kong forces actually sufficient to deter Chinese annexation of the Crown Colony, or keeping in Gibraltar a garrison (and guard-ships) adequate to defend the Rock against a Spanish *coup de main*? Obviously not. In fact the idea of the token presence, buttressed by special intelligence effort plus regularly-tested contingency plans for rapid reinforcement, is what would commend itself more often than not. On that basis, the crucial "lesson" of the Falklands experience may be that it is inviting trouble to provide one of these compo-nents—the token presence—without the others; and, where this is the most the nation is able or willing to do, there is really nothing for it but acknowledgment of that fact and (i) attention to creating and maintaining a stable and durable *modus vivendi* with local powers or (ii) frank admission of an untenable position.[9]

Having said that, there is a loose formulation of that protest against Eurocentricity which was prompted by the Falklands Cam-paign. It runs roughly as follows. The episode demonstrated that there can be challenges to British interests outside the NATO area, and in forms which make it imperative that steps be taken—with or without allies' help—to restore the *status quo ante*. In such circum-stances naval forces have a particular utility. It is ill-advised, there-fore, (i) generally to make security policy calculations on the basis of the dominant threat (which admittedly is in and around Europe) and (ii) specifically to deplete that naval capacity which confers par-ticular flexibility and versatility (and in which numbers count).

The imprecision of this formulation notwithstanding, those whose critique of strategic (and defence programme) priorities rested on such reasoning had, and have, a case that must be answered.

In its December 1982 White Paper *The Falklands Campaign: The Lessons* the Government did not give a clear-cut answer. Formally the official line was that the concentration of the defence effort on Europe and the North Atlantic should continue; and that the naval rundown must proceed, subject only to some "rescheduling" made necessary by the need to replace battle losses and sustain a naval

---

[9] See J. Cable, "Gunboat Diplomacy and the Conventional Wisdom" 70, *Naval Review*, Nr. 3 (July 1982), pp. 174–179.

patrol in the South Atlantic. However, the specific amendments to "Nott's blueprint" outlined in the document went a bit further than this. They did not amount to that fundamental re-ordering of priorities and reprieve for the Fleet for which many had clamoured in the second half of 1982.[10] But they were significant enough to indicate that a somewhat different view might be taken in future of the "proper" balance between NATO and non-NATO commitments in defence planning, and of the "proper" place of naval power in the national force structure.[11]

III—THE FUTURE

In fact, reading *The Lessons* carefully, one detects a paradox. Although acclaimed in many quarters as amounting to rejection of the 1981 prospectus, the major hardware decisions—orders for new warships and naval aircraft plus amendments to the timetable for paying-off older ships—emphatically did not signal a fresh approach to the Royal Navy's place in the national order of battle and to priorities generally. Yet the assertions that there would be no such change did not really square with several minor programme decisions, while the enhancement of extra-European capabilities as a by-product of provision for protecting the Falklands was bound to be a factor in future planning, even though coming about for reasons other than strategic reappraisal.

Regarding hardware, the White Paper highlighted three consequences of the campaign. The government said, in effect, (i) we find ourselves short of four major warships, some Harrier aircraft and several helicopters; (ii) we have the job now of mounting, for a few years at least, a South Atlantic patrol (a commitment not bargained for, or budgeted for, hitherto); and (iii) we realise that it is unwise to sail ships into danger without proper air defence, including organic airborne early warning (AEW). And the document spelt out three responses, which may be summarised as follows. (1) It will be necessary to buy some replacement frigates; and, because they are required urgently, they will be of the Type 22 variety which is in production. Fixed- and rotary-wing aircraft losses must be made good promptly also. (2) The Fleet must be kept up to strength while new ships are being built, because of the new commitment. So a number of older hulls will be kept going instead of being retired. Moreover, *Invincible* will not be sold (and, in fact, extra planes—needed to

---

[10] One of the most consistent voices was that of *The Times*.

[11] That was not the view which the present writer took in an initial comment on the December 1982 White Paper, published in the *Sunday Times*, December 19, 1982). It is the result of further reflection!

equip two carriers in commission—will be procured). Exactly when the total escort strength can be allowed to drop to 50—and whether there will be only 42 "running" ships or a few more than that—depends on the duration of the need for a continuous presence in Falklands waters. (3) The lesson of the losses has been learnt and "high value" warships will get some AEW and decent close-in anti-air weapons.

All this, though, added up to adjustment of the programme sketched in *The Way Forward*—for the short-to-medium term—and not a "reprieve for the Royal Navy." As for the announced plans for purchase of wide-bodied tanker/transport planes, additional air defence fighters and surface-to-air missile units, extra medium-lift helicopters—these decisions, too, were related to the need to carry on defending the Falklands without a major diversion of effort from other tasks. They could not be construed as reflecting a reordering of priorities, viz. a positive preference for bolstering "out of area" capabilities.

However, when the wide-bodied tanker/transports, the extra helicopters and suchlike are acquired, the United Kingdom will have got itself a better capability for tasks outside the NATO area. And the December 1982 White Paper had things to say about making the Army's 5th Infantry Brigade into a properly-constituted force capable of rapid deployment for contingency operations more or less worldwide (reminiscent of the Strategic Reserve of the 1960s), a transformation which would probably not have been set in hand if the Falklands fracas had not demonstrated the weakness of relying on a token capability for extra-European missions. In other words, the low priority "out of area" element in the national defence effort now features more prominently than it did, notwithstanding official protestations that nothing has really changed.

Perspectives have altered. With what effect on decision-making for defence in the future, it is too soon to tell. Suffice it to note that, because of this, the national reaction to particular pressures for change which are likely to impinge on policy calculations in the next few years could well be very different than it would have been before "the Falklands experience."[12]

For instance, it is probable that the overall size and shape of the United Kingdom's defence effort will come under scrutiny yet again in 1984/85 (as it did in 1964/65 and 1974/75). This is because, successful though Mr. John Nott's review of 1981 was in striking a balance between resources and commitments for the time being,

---

[12] The detailed information in the foregoing paragraphs is based on Cmnd. 8758, especially its third part (on "The Future").

several significant things have happened since his "way forward" was outlined—quite apart from the Falklands affair. Defence's appetite for resources shows no sign of abating, despite official steps to check the rising real cost of equipment. Yet finding extra resources for defence is something that the second Thatcher administration may not be *able* to do (because a well-sustained economic recovery is not assured), and may not be *willing* to do (because of its conviction that total government spending must fall, at least as a proportion of Gross Domestic Product). What is more, the expense of some items to which the Conservatives are strongly wedded—like the Trident missile system—is going to be greater than was envisaged in 1981.

In this eventuality, which options for adjustment of the national force structure (and force levels) are most likely to find favour? Almost certainly not measures which involve diminution of the extra-European capabilities for which a programme of enhancement is in train. Almost certainly not measures which involve modification of the revised naval construction plans so recently drawn up.[13]

A second potential source of "pressures for change" in the mid-1980s is NATO-wide attention to the possibilities of an Alliance division of labour, based on specialisation in the fulfilment of military tasks. This is a notion which has been around a long time. But as all nations wrestle with the problem of rising real costs and tight budgets the impulse to try this and other means of making more effective use of resources grows stronger year by year. Indeed with a powerful current running in NATO circles in favour of improving the Alliance's conventional capabilities, so as to reduce what is generally perceived as an excessive reliance on nuclear weapons, this impulse is gaining particular strength just now.[14]

If the Western allies do begin to take this idea seriously, in which aspects of defence provision are they likely to look to the United Kingdom for particular contributions? Almost certainly in capacities for operations outside the NATO area, for as long as apprehension

---

[13] By the middle of 1983 the likelihood of further budgetary pressure on the defence programme had grown to near certainty, following the remarks of the Chancellor of the Exchequer (Mr. Nigel Lawson) in the first debates of the new Session of Parliament following the General Election of June 9, 1983.

[14] See D. Greenwood, "Allocating Resources for Western Europe's Defence" in 27 *NATO's Fifteen Nations*, Nr. 5 (October–November 1982); and for evidence of official interest in the "division of labour" concept *Defense Daily* (U.S.) (February 24, 1983). On the pressures for improvement of NATO's conventional capabilities, see General Bernard Rogers, "Enhancing Deterrence—Raising the Nuclear Threshold" 30 *NATO Review*, Nr. 6 (1983) and "Strike Deep: a new concept for NATO," 5 *Military Technology*, (1983), plus the Report of the European Security Study, R.R. Bowie *et al. Strengthening Conventional Deterrence in Europe: Proposals for the 1980s.* (1983).

about potential challenges there persists and for as long as the number of States capable of furnishing relevant forces for contingencies outside Europe is so few. Almost certainly in the domain of maritime, especially naval, power: if only because this is where, certainly among the North European members of the Alliance, the British have a clear comparative advantage.

LATIN AMERICA
AND THE FALKLANDS CONFLICT

By

GORDON CONNELL-SMITH

DURING the Falklands crisis, much was spoken and written about the reaction of "Latin America" to the hostilities and the dispute which led to them. In Britain, critics of the Government declared that good relations with Latin America were being sacrificed by its policy of using military force to regain the islands, which presumably the critics would have been prepared to leave in Argentina's possession. "Latin Americanists" in the United States likewise argued that the Reagan Administration was putting inter-American relations at risk by its support of the United Kingdom. The main object of this paper is to examine how far the 20 republics which comprise Latin America were united on the Falklands issue, and the extent to which their relations with the United States and the United Kingdom appear to have been damaged by the war. This examination will be made against the background of the broader, related question: how far has "Latin America" played a distinctive role in world affairs?

I—THE BACKGROUND

The Falklands conflict, and Latin American reaction to it, both have their roots deep in the international history of the region; but they also reflect a number of significant contemporary developments. The major historical factors are linked to Latin America's colonial heritage, and the region's traditional relationship with the United States. The contemporary developments are related to the Cold War, the emergence of the Third World and Latin American self-identification with it, and recent efforts to fashion a distinctive Latin American role—a regional identity—in world affairs.

1. *The colonial heritage*

Eighteen of the Latin American republics were formerly ruled by Spain. Sixteen[1] of these became national sovereign States as a result of the wars of independence fought between the years 1810 and

---

[1] Cuba and Panama did not become national sovereign States (and then closely tied to the U.S.A.) until the beginning of the 20th century.

73

1824. Territorial disputes among them were an ominous part of their colonial heritage. For, while they agreed in principle that the boundaries of the new States should normally coincide with the administrative divisions of the former Spanish empire, these seldom were clearly demarcated, and offered considerable scope for argument. Not a few of the many ensuing disputes led to hostilities, and some have remained unsolved. Among the latter is one between Argentina and Chile over possession of a number of islands in the Beagle Channel, which links the Atlantic and Pacific oceans south of Tierra del Fuego. This dispute almost brought the two countries to war in 1978. There were hostilities between Ecuador and Peru over their boundary dispute in 1981. Bolivia and Peru have not forgotten the territories they lost to Chile in the early 1880s following their defeat in the War of the Pacific.

In addition to boundary disputes between Spanish American States, there were others between some of them and Brazil, the former Portuguese American empire[2]: again, part of the region's colonial heritage. The most important of these disputes concerned the Banda Oriental, or eastern shore of the River Uruguay, occupying a strategic position at the mouth of the River Plate, which had been fought over by Spain and Portugal during the colonial period, and became an object of rivalry between Argentina and Brazil. These two countries went to war for possession of the territory in 1826. Significantly, it was diplomatic pressure from Great Britain which led to the creation of Uruguay as an independent buffer State between the rivals in 1828. For Britain at this time was the most influential external power in Latin American affairs.

Great Britain herself had dependencies in Central and South America, which were claimed by neighbouring countries as heirs of Spain. Guatemala asserted her right to British Honduras, and Venezuela to more than three-fifths of British Guiana. These claims are still vigorously asserted, even though the territories are now the independent States of Belize and Guyana. The Falkland Islands, or Islas Malvinas, were a subject of dispute between Great Britain and Spain during the colonial period. Following independence, the new government in Buenos Aires regarded itself as inheriting Spain's claim to the islands, and attempted to assert it. But in 1833 a British expedition expelled the small partyy of Argentinian soldiers sent there, and since then the Falklands—together with the South Georgia and South Sandwich groups—have remained under continuous occupation and administration by Britain.

---

[2] In the settlement of almost all of these disputes Brazil gained territory at the expense of her Spanish American neighbours.

2. *The traditional relationship with the United States*

The British occupation of the Falkland Islands took place 10 years after President James Monroe of the United States made his famous pronouncement in which he said, among other things, that "the American continents . . . are henceforth not to be considered as subjects for future colonisation by any European powers."[3] The United States was, by her own origins, "anti-colonial." But the Monroe Doctrine was directed against the extension of *European* power and influence in Latin America. Indeed, United States leaders coveted portions of Spanish America, notably Cuba, and had already acquired Florida from Spain. Later the United States was to secure, by conquest, half of the national territory of Mexico. But she lacked the power to end the British occupation of the Falkland Islands in 1833, even had she wanted to do so.

The Monroe Doctrine was concerned, naturally enough, with the interests of the United States, whose leaders declared, in Monroe's words, "that we should consider any attempt on their (that is, the European Powers') part to extend their system to any portion of this hemisphere as dangerous to our peace and safety." Monroe claimed that "America" (in the hemispheric sense) had a "system" essentially different from that of Europe, and it was upon this claim that the inter-American (or Pan American) system, embracing the United States and Latin America, was established. The inter-American system postulated a community of interests, shared by the two Americas, which would be threatened by "extra-continental intervention." It took the form of a series of international conferences, held from 1889 onwards, and a growing number of institutions created to promote inter-American co-operation in many fields.[4] But inter-American harmony has been very difficult to achieve, because of the immense imbalance of power between the United States and the Latin American countries. For the United States, the inter-American system has been essentially an instrument for maintaining her hegemony over Latin America by limiting the influence of non-American Powers in the region. She herself has intervened frequently in Latin America, sometimes with military forces, in order, her leaders have claimed, to forestall extra-continental intervention. Franklin Roosevelt's "Good Neighbour policy" in the 1930s, which involved repudiating *armed* intervention, improved inter-American relations only temporarily.

---

[3] The text of what has been called "The Original Monroe Doctrine," from which the above quotations are drawn, is contained in D. Perkins, *A History of the Monroe Doctrine* (1955), pp. 394–396.

[4] For a history of the inter-American system and the Organisation of American States, see G. Connell-Smith, *The Inter-American System* (1966).

Nevertheless, the inter-American system was formalised in 1948 with the adoption of the Charter of the Organisation of American States (OAS). Moreover, it now included a mutual security pact: the Inter-American Treaty of Reciprocal Assistance, signed at Rio de Janeiro on September 2, 1947. The Rio treaty was to operate against an armed attack occurring within a defined region.[5] This region embraces North and South America, together with Greenland, the Arctic and Antarctic regions adjacent to the North and South American continents, and all of the area lying between.[6] Within it are the Falkland, South Georgia and South Sandwich Islands. In a statement included in the Final Act of the Rio conference (at which the treaty was signed), Argentina reaffirmed her claim to these islands. Whereupon the United States recorded her position that "the Treaty of Rio de Janeiro has no effect upon the sovereignty, national or international status of any of the territories included in the region."[7]

Argentina was not the only Latin American country to make such a statement: Guatemala reiterated her claim to British Honduras (Belize). Venezuela did not make a comparable statement on this occasion, but she still maintained her claim to a substantial portion of British Guiana. The claimants in these cases declared the territories in question to be "occupied" by the United Kingdom and vestiges of British colonialism. A resolution adopted at the Ninth International Conference of American States (at which the OAS Charter was signed) declared that the historical process of the emancipation of America would not be complete as long as such territories were occupied by non-American countries.[8] Moreover, a resolution of the Tenth Inter-American Conference (1954), supporting self-determination for the peoples of European colonies in the western hemisphere, expressly excluded its application to "territories that are the subject of litigation or claim between extracontinental countries and some American republics."[9] In other words, the claims of the Latin American countries concerned involve denying the right of self-determination to the peoples of these territories. Yet Argentina has presented her case in terms of "anti-colonialism," and in 1965 the United Nations General Assembly called

---

[5] The Rio treaty also provides for defence against aggression other than by armed attack. Consequently, it has been invoked against "communist subversion."

[6] The region is defined in Article 4. The text of the treaty is contained in Pan American Union, Washington, D.C., *The International Conferences of American States, Second Supplement, 1942–1954* (1958), pp. 142–150.

[7] *Ibid.* pp. 157–158.

[8] *Ibid.* p. 271.

[9] *Ibid.* p. 438.

upon her and the United Kingdom to discuss the issue bilaterally, though bearing in mind its own Resolution 1514 on decolonisation, which asserted the right of dependent peoples to self-determination.

3. *The Cold War*

In spite of the establishment of the OAS in 1948, the concept of a special relationship between the United States and Latin America proved increasingly difficult to sustain. In the years immediately following the end of the Second World War, as the Cold War developed in other parts of the world, Latin America was regarded by United States leaders as a low priority area. The Latin Americans were not allies in the sense that the West Europeans were: no military organisation on the lines of NATO was built upon the Rio treaty. Much the greatest share of United States economic aid went to other regions of the world, and Latin Americans complained that their interests were being neglected.[10] When the Cold War eventually came to Latin America, inter-American relations grew even more strained as the United States pressed for support of policies directed against Latin American governments which she accused of being communist. These policies were criticised as leading to intervention in the affairs of the countries concerned, as indeed they did. In 1954 the United States Central Intelligence Agency (CIA) engineered the overthrow of President Arbenz of Guatemala; and in 1961 endeavoured, but without success, to do the same to Fidel Castro, the Cuban leader. The question of revolutionary Cuba dominated relations between the United States and the other countries of Latin America during the 1960s, and has remained of fundamental importance ever since. The United States is far from reconciled to the permanence of Cuba's alignment with the Soviet Union, and has been determined to prevent the spread of left-wing revolution in Latin America. Under strong pressure from Washington, the Cuban Government was excluded from the OAS in 1962 and further sanctions were subsequently imposed upon it. The United States encouraged the Brazilian military to overthrow President Goulart in 1964; in the following year her forces intervened in the Dominican Republic to prevent a possible "second Cuba"; and in 1973 she played a significant role in the downfall of President Allende of Chile. In 1979 the United States faced a new challenge when the Nicaraguan

---

[10] They were particularly disappointed that there was no "Marshall Plan" for Latin America.

dictator, Somoza, was overthrown by the Sandinistas.[11] In addition, a left-wing coup occurred in Grenada in the same year. The United States accused the new Nicaraguan Government—in collaboration with Cuba and the Soviet Union—of aiding left-wing guerrillas in El Salvador, which has become the focal point of the Cold War in Latin America. There is ample evidence of CIA involvement in efforts to "destabilise" the Sandinista Government. Interestingly, Argentina has actively supported the United States in Central America.

4. *Latin America and the Third World*

Their concern over United States anti-communist policies in the region, and continuing dissatisfaction with her response to their perennial requests for more economic aid and better terms of trade,[12] encouraged Latin American countries to broaden their international relationships outside the OAS. It is noteworthy that such strongly anti-communist governments as those of Argentina and Brazil greatly increased their trade with the Soviet bloc as well as with western Europe and Japan. Argentina became a very important trading partner of the Soviet Union, taking advantage of the United States boycott following Russia's intervention in Afghanistan greatly to increase her sales of grain to Moscow.

Of wider significance was the growing self-identification of the Latin American countries with the Third World, whose members (mainly African and Asian nations) rejected the Cold War concept of confrontation between "free" and "communist" countries (the East-West struggle), and regarded as crucial a division between "developed" and "developing" (the North-South dialogue). Within the context of the Cold War, Latin America (excepting Cuba since her revolution) formally was part of the "free world" through its membership of the OAS and adherence to the Inter-American Treaty of Reciprocal Assistance. But in a division between developed and developing countries, Latin Americans felt themselves to be among the latter: in other words, members of the Third World. This was evident when the First United Nations Conference on Trade and Development (UNCTAD) was held at Geneva in 1964. The conference highlighted the conflict of interests between the developed and developing countries, with the United States as the

---

[11] The Sandinistas took their name from Augusto César Sandino, the patriot who opposed the United States intervention in Nicaragua during the late 1920s and early 1930s. Sandino was murdered in 1934 on the orders (it is generally accepted) of Anastasio Somoza, founder of the Somoza "dynasty" and father of the dictator overthrown in 1979.

[12] In 1961 President Kennedy launched the "Alliance for Progress": an ambitious programme of economic and social development. Its failure served to heighten Latin American dissatisfaction, and to stimulate the search for broader international relationships and new efforts to form an effective regional grouping among themselves.

leading member of the first group and the Latin American countries among the second. The latter formed the "Group of 77"[13]: the "South" in the North-South dialogue.

Latin American participation in the non-aligned movement, which was established in Belgrade in 1961, was more limited. Only a minority of the republics became full members, though others sent observers to its conferences.[14] But among the full members was Argentina, whose former president, Juan Perón, actually pioneered the idea of a "Third Position" in world affairs. The most prominent Latin American member of the non-aligned movement, however, has been Cuba, whose leader was its president during the early 1980s. Cuba's role, in spite of her close ties with the Soviet Union, reflects the movement's propensity to be more critical of the West than of the Soviet Union and its hostility towards (western) "imperialism." This is the case with the Third World as a whole, which explains why Argentina's essentially colonialist claim has been widely supported in the United Nations General Assembly, as well as at conferences of the non-aligned movement.

5. *Towards a regional identity?*

A broadening of Latin American international relationships outside the western hemisphere was linked with new efforts to establish a regional identity in world affairs. This link was logical, since the traditional association with the United States effectively limited Latin America's international relations and inhibited the development of Latin American, as distinct from inter-American, organisations. As relations between the United States and the Latin American republics became more strained, owing to both Cold War and economic issues, the latter were increasingly inclined to have recourse to the United Nations rather than to the OAS. Within the world body, they co-operated more closely with each other, as well as with the growing number of Third World countries, on major issues. Prior to the first UNCTAD the Latin/American governments endeavoured to formulate a common position to be taken at Geneva, and subsequently they set up a Special Commission for Latin American Co-ordination (CECLA), which operated within the "Group of '77."

The most important efforts to establish a regional identity have been in the economic sphere. Two agreements to promote economic integration in the region were signed in 1960: the Treaty of Montevideo, instituting the Latin American Free Trade Association

---

[13] It now has 125 members.
[14] See note 23 below.

(LAFTA), to which eventually all ten South American republics and Mexico adhered, and the General Treaty of Central American Integration. But neither proved successful. Economic nationalism, the disparity of economic strength between the larger countries and the smaller, and the small proportion of Latin America's foreign trade which takes place between the republics, were among the most important reasons for the lack of success. War between El Salvador and Honduras in 1969 dealt a severe blow to the Central American Common Market. In 1975 the Latin American Economic System (SELA) was set up, with Cuba a member. SELA is essentially a Latin American forum for economic co-operation and consultation. It has so far made only modest progress towards attaining such objectives as the formulation of common policies on international economic and social issues, and the establishment of multinational enterprises to promote development in the region.

In both the economic and political spheres the Bolivarian vision of a unified Latin America playing a significant role in world affairs[15] has made little progress towards becoming a reality. Would the Falklands conflict provide an occasion for Latin America to play a distinctive and influential role in a major international crisis, and thus strengthen prospects for unity? Or would it confirm the differences which have undermined Latin American solidarity in the past, and perhaps make it even more difficult to achieve in the foreseeable future?

II—The Conflict

The crisis began when, after years of intermittent discussions, during which it proved impossible to reconcile Argentina's insistence that her sovereignty over the Falklands was not negotiable, and the United Kingdom's refusal to transfer sovereignty without the consent of the islanders, the military junta in Buenos Aires led by General Galtieri sent armed forces to "reoccupy" the islands on April 2, 1982. On the following day, the United Nations Security Council adopted a Resolution (502) demanding the cessation of hostilities and an immediate withdrawal of all Argentinian forces from the Falkland Islands; and calling upon the governments of Argentina and the United Kingdom to seek a diplomatic solution to their differences and to respect fully the purposes and principles of the United Nations Charter. But Argentina refused to withdraw her

---

[15] Simón Bolívar, the greatest hero of the wars of independence, is also regarded as the apostle of Latin American unity. In 1813 he wrote: "Divided we will be weaker, less respected by enemies and neutrals. Union under a single supreme government will provide our strength and will make us formidable before all."

forces from what her leaders described as Argentinian territory, which she would defend if attacked.

At first sight, the Falklands conflict appeared an auspicious occasion upon which to demonstrate Latin American solidarity, for support of Argentina's case against Britain was virtually unanimous. The Falkland Islands and dependencies—as we have seen—were considered "occupied territories" and, both geographically and historically, part of Latin America. The only acceptable solution was their return to Argentina, the rightful owner. The United Kingdom's commitment to the self-determination of their inhabitants was viewed as either irrelevant or merely an excuse for holding on to the territories. The other Latin American countries had already supported Argentina's case in international forums, criticising Britain for the long delay in reaching a satisfactory settlement. But they did so with varying degrees of warmth, even before serious misgivings were widely aroused over Argentina's resort to force to assert her claim: a clear breach of international law, and a dangerous precedent in the light of other oustanding territorial disputes in the region (and, of course, elsewhere in the world).

Not surprisingly, Venezuela and Guatemala were among Argentina's warmest supporters—and the most interested in the outcome of the conflict—because of their own comparable claims to "occupied territories." Peru and Panama also supported Argentina strongly. By contrast, Chile was very concerned over the use of force to make good a territorial claim, and feared the possible effects of the Falklands conflict upon her own dispute with Argentina over the islands in the Beagle Channel. Brazil also adopted a cautious position. Her desire to pay lip service to the idea of Latin American solidarity was reinforced by her military government's fears of a political upheaval in Argentina should the junta in Buenos Aires be defeated. But friendly ties with Britain, and the important role played by the City of London in the management of her huge foreign debt—added to her long-standing rivalry with Argentina—determined that Brazil would not be very helpful to her sister republic. Mexico had for a long time worked to increase the authority of the United Nations (notably in relation to the OAS), and was greatly concerned by Argentina's resort to armed force and refusal to comply with the Security Council's Resolution 502. Both Mexico and Brazil favoured a diplomatic solution through the United Nations. Colombia, like Chile, was very reluctant to support Argentina.[16] But Buenos Aires received warm backing from Cuba, especially after the

---

[16] Colombia's policy on the Falklands conflict was affected by the recently revived claim of the Nicaraguan government to certain islands in the Pacific.

European Community and the United States came down on the side of Britain, when the Falklands conflict could be depicted as a North-South struggle. This situation presented Castro with a good opportunity further to break down Cuba's isolation from the rest of Latin America which had followed her exclusion from the OAS. For comparable reasons, the Sandinista Government of Nicaragua voiced its warm support for Buenos Aires, in spite of Argentina's co-operation with the United States in Central America.[17]

Among the Latin American countries, only Panama was a member of the Security Council at this time, though Latin America as a geographical region traditionally has occupied two of the non-permanent seats on that body. The second such seat was held by Guyana. Panama was the only member of the Council to vote against Resolution 502.[18] Guyana voted for it: understandably, in view of Venezuela's claim to so much of her territory. The United States also voted for it. The Soviet Union and China abstained: both supported Argentina's claim. With Argentina refusing to respond to the Security Council's call to remove her forces from the islands, strenuous efforts were made to reach a diplomatic solution while a British task force was sailing towards the South Atlantic.

The United States was particularly anxious to find a peaceful solution to the conflict, which had placed her in a very difficult position. Argentina was her ally as a co-signatory of the Rio Treaty; and the special relationship with Latin America was also involved. Moreover, the Reagan Administration wanted to retain Argentina's support in Central America, and to avoid action which might drive the junta in Buenos Aires to form closer ties with Russia. But Great Britain was a much closer and more important ally. Moreover, her international position made it impossible for the United States to do other than condemn Argentina's use of armed force, whatever the merits of the case. Thus, in spite of warnings from the "Latin Americanists" among the members of the Administration,[19] there could be no doubt that, given the necessity of choosing between the two allies, the United States would have to side with Britain. And this she eventually did: though not firmly until after her Secretary of State, Alexander Haig, had made considerable efforts to resolve the dispute before British forces were in a position to open their campaign to retake the Falkland Islands.

---

[17] But see note 16 above.

[18] Other Latin American delegates, speaking in the debate (but having no vote), supported Argentina's claim and appealed for a diplomatic solution to the conflict.

[19] Prominent among these was Mrs. Jeane Kirkpatrick, United States chief representative at the United Nations, who was particularly concerned to retain Argentina's support of Washington's policy in Central America, of which she was a very strong advocate.

III—THE ROLE OF THE OAS

Mr. Haig was still engaged in his peace efforts when the dispute was considered for the first time by the Permanent Council of the OAS, a body upon which all members of the organisation are represented at ambassadorial level. The situation was potentially very embarrassing for the United States. The historic thrust of her Latin American policy had been to prevent "extra-continental intervention" in the region. It had even been claimed that the purpose of the Monroe Doctrine was to protect Latin America from such intervention, though few outside the United States took that claim seriously. For the last three decades the United States had been anxious to utilise the OAS to combat the threat (as she saw it) of "international communism" in Latin America. And now, when the issue before the OAS again was likely to be one of extra-continental intervention, the extra-continental power in question was her closest ally! But at this point, in the light of Mr. Haig's peace mission, the Council adopted, on April 13, 1982, an innocuous resolution offering its friendly co-operation to both Argentina and the United Kingdom in reaching a peaceful settlement of their dispute. No reference was made to Security Council Resolution 502, though a number of British Commonwealth countries, which had joined the OAS after gaining independence,[20] endeavoured to have it cited.

On April 20, with the British task force poised for action in the South Atlantic, Argentina invoked the Rio treaty and called for a meeting of OAS Foreign Ministers: a "Meeting of Consultation" under the treaty. Eighteen countries voted to call the meeting, with the United States, Colombia and Trinidad and Tobago abstaining. Since the last named was the only new member of the OAS to have signed and ratified the Rio treaty, she alone among them was represented. The Twentieth Meeting of Consultation of American Foreign Ministers opened at the headquarters of the OAS in Washington on April 26, the day after British troops had retaken South Georgia. Its first session lasted until April 28. It was clear from the beginning that, whatever degree of diplomatic support might be forthcoming for Argentina, very little by way of military assistance could be expected from the other Latin American countries. The

---

[20] From 1967 there has been a notable increase in the membership of the OAS. All the new members were until recently dependencies of European Powers: in all but one case, Suriname (formerly Dutch Guiana), that Power was the United Kingdom. The British Commonwealth members are Antigua and Barbuda, Barbados, the Commonwealth of Dominica, Grenada, Jamaica, Saint Lucia, Saint Vincent and the Grenadines and Trinidad and Tobago. The admission of these new members has weakened the OAS as embodying the special relationship between the United States and Latin America.

Argentinian government was well aware of this. Its Foreign Minister declared that, at this stage, it did not intend formally to request either economic sanctions or military assistance against the United Kingdom. He received qualified diplomatic support. Argentina's right to sovereignty over the Falkland Islands was recognised, and the United Kingdom was urged "to cease immediately the hostilities it is carrying on within the security region established by Article 4 of the Inter-American Treaty of Reciprocal Assistance and to refrain from any act that could affect inter-American peace and security."[21] But the OAS Foreign Ministers did not demand the withdrawal of the British fleet from the South Atlantic as Argentina wanted. The Argentinian Government itself was urged to take no action that might exacerbate the situation. Both countries were urged to call an immediate truce and resume negotiations for a peaceful settlement of their dispute. Sanctions which had been imposed upon Argentina by members of the European Community and other States were deplored, and the governments concerned were asked to lift them. The final resolution of the meeting was carried by 17 votes, with four abstentions: the United States, Chile, Colombia and Trinidad and Tobago. During the debate, Mexico and Colombia had joined with the United States in arguing that the proper forum for action on the dispute was the United Nations within the framework of Resolution 502, reference to which was made in the preamble to the OAS resolution. But there was a great deal of criticism of the United States during the meeting.

Before the OAS Foreign Ministers resumed their consideration of the Falklands crisis, a number of significant developments took place. Mr. Haig finally gave up his peace mission, blaming Argentina for his failure and announcing that the United States was now aligning herself with the United Kingdom. There followed two further, and likewise unsuccessful, peace initiatives, one by the President of Peru, the other by the Secretary-General of the United Nations. Meanwhile, hostilities intensified as the British task force began the operation of landing troops on the Falklands. On May 27, the OAS Foreign Ministers met again to consider Argentina's case against "British aggression." They did so in the knowledge that the most powerful member of their organisation was opposed to any resolution calling for economic or military measures against the United Kingdom and, indeed, was giving sizeable assistance to that country. Mr. Haig reiterated the United States view that, since Argentina had been the first to use force by invading the Falkland

---

[21] Quoted in *The Times*, (April 29, 1982).

Islands, there were no grounds for taking collective action under the terms of the Rio treaty: there had not been extra-continental aggression. Nevertheless, the fact remained that an extra-continental Power was engaged in hostilities against a Latin American country—and with the support of the United States. It is hardly surprising that feelings ran high, and Argentina and her warmest supporters were bitterly critical of Washington.

But there was no serious prospect of the OAS Foreign Ministers agreeing to collective measures against the United Kingdom. Brazil and Mexico reportedly advised the meeting to avoid linking support for Argentina to the Rio treaty, and continued to maintain that the United Nations was the appropriate forum in which to pursue a peaceful solution to the dispute. A resolution was finally adopted (on May 29) which "condemned most vigorously the unjustified and disproportionate attack perpetrated by the United Kingdom"[22]; urged the United States to end sanctions against Argentina, to cease giving military assistance to Britain, and to respect the principle of inter-American continental solidarity under the Rio treaty; and called upon members of the OAS to offer Argentina whatever aid they found appropriate. It was carried by seventeen votes, with four abstentions: as previously, the United States, Chile, Colombia and Trinidad and Tobago.

Although hard information has been difficult to come by, it is clear that what the members of the OAS considered "appropriate" support for Argentina did not, in the event, amount to much. Venezuela had earlier suspended negotiations for the purchase of British aircraft, and Brazil was reported to have lent Argentina some reconnaissance planes as a gesture of support. But Peru denied reports that she had sent Buenos Aires six of her Mirage aircraft, though she apparently gave some limited military assistance. No fellow Latin American government severed commercial links or broke off diplomatic relations with the United Kingdom on Argentina's account. There was evidence that Chile importantly assisted British intelligence during the hostilities, although both countries denied that this was so.

Just over two weeks after the OAS Foreign Ministers adopted their resolution, the Argentinian troops on the Falkland Islands surrendered, and British sovereignty was restored. This came as a shock to Argentina's strongest supporters, but for most of the other Latin American countries, especially the largest ones, it must have brought a welcome end to a most embarrassing affair. Bitter denun-

---

[22] *Ibid.* (May 31, 1982).

ciation of the role of the United States could not hide the poor performance of the Latin American members of the OAS, underlined
by the contrast between the lack of tangible support given to Argentina and the often extravagent rhetoric in which so many of their
delegations indulged at the Meeting of Consultation.

IV—THE AFTERMATH

Following upon the OAS Meeting of Consultation, the Argentinian
Foreign Minister went to a conference of the non-aligned movement
being held in Havana. There he received an effusive welcome from
Fidel Castro. The conference condemned the United Kingdom for
her action over the Falklands (though not as strongly as Argentina
might have hoped); urged an immediate end to hostilities; and
called upon the United States to cease her military support of
Britain. Moreover, it declared the South Georgia and South Sandwich Islands, as well as the Falklands, to be an integral part of Latin
America. This was likewise the position taken at the Seventh Conference of the Heads of State or Government of the Non-aligned
Countries held in Delhi in March 1983, when the presidency of the
movement passed from Dr. Castro to Mrs. Gandhi of India. Significantly, there had been a notable increase in the Latin American
membership of the movement during the Cuban leader's term of
office.[23] The Cubans collaborated closely with the Argentinians at
the Delhi summit conference, where President Bignone[24] of Argentina was fulsome in his praise of Dr. Castro.

Meanwhile, Cuba had been actively involved when Argentina
took her case to the General Assembly of the United Nations in the
previous autumn. She joined the other 19 Latin American countries
in tabling a resolution calling for direct negotiations between the
United Kingdom and Argentina over the Falkland Islands. It was
supported by the Soviet Union, China, and other members of the
Soviet bloc, as well as by a large number of Third World countries.
To Britain's disappointment, the United States also voted for the
Latin American resolution. Britain felt that such a vote, in the face
of Argentina's refusal to declare a formal cessation of hostilities in
the South Atlantic, amounted to condoning the use of force by the
Buenos Aires government. Obviously, the United States wanted to
repair the damage caused to her relations with Latin America by her

---

[23] Argentina, Bolivia, Colombia, Cuba, Ecuador, Nicaragua, Panama and Peru were full
members of the Delhi conference. Brazil, Mexico and Venezuela were represented by official
observers. Chile, though not invited, apparently sent an unofficial observer: *Latin America
Weekly Report* (March 25, 1983), p. 3.
[24] Bignone became president in July 1982 after Galtieri had resigned.

support of the United Kingdom, particularly in the light of the situation in Central America. When the OAS General Assembly met in Washington for its annual conference later in November, it passed a resolution on the Falklands similar to the one adopted by the United Nations body. At the end of the month President Reagan began a visit to four Latin American countries: Brazil, Colombia, Costa Rica and Honduras. Arrangements were made for him to see the Presidents of El Salvador and Guatemala during his trip. Apparently, Mr. Reagan would have liked to meet President Bignone at some convenient place on the Brazilian border. But United States support of Argentina in the recent United Nations vote proved insufficient to make such a meeting acceptable at that stage.[25]

V—SOME FINAL COMMENTS

Thus the Falklands conflict did not evoke a truly "Latin American" response. Rather did reaction to it confirm the heterogeneous character of the region. But, more than that, the crisis revived interest in the many conflicting territorial claims which Latin American States have against each other. We noted how the positions on the issue taken by various governments were strongly influenced by their own claims or fears of those of others against themselves. Divisions were sharpened, and the Falklands conflict has given further impetus to the current arms build-up in the region.

The search for a regional identity has been importantly linked to relations with the United States: a united Latin America would be in a much stronger position to deal with the over-powerful northern neighbour. But within the inter-American system the United States seldom has been confronted by "Latin America."[26] Only on some general issues, such as United States intervention and the demand for better terms of aid and trade, have the Latin American countries adopted something close to a common position. On particular issues, such as the Cuban problem and the (related) situation in Central America today, they have usually been divided over United States policies. The Falklands conflict was another such issue, in spite of the rhetoric suggesting otherwise.

But if the rhetoric of Latin American solidarity was mocked by reality, so was that of inter-American solidarity. For while the other

---

[25] *The Times*, (November 19, 1982).

[26] One very important factor has been the role of Brazil. Historically, she has been more friendly towards the U.S.A. than have the large Spanish American countries. This has aroused the suspicions of the latter, especially those of Argentina, Brazil's traditional rival for leadership in Latin America. Moreover, Brazil's ambition to be a world power clearly limits her commitment to establishing a regional identity.

Latin American countries were divided on the degree of support to be given to Argentina, the United States actually took Britain's side. In the OAS, where the divisions were so evident, another chapter was written in the story of its decline. But talk of replacing it with a new regional grouping excluding the United States was no more than that, though further encouragement was given by the Falklands affair to the development of closer relations between Latin American countries and wider international organisations.

The Falklands conflict underlined Latin America's weakness, as well as divisions among the republics; so that even Argentina and her warmest supporters, who felt the greatest bitterness towards the United States, could not afford to allow their relations with her to suffer lasting damage. Moreover, the Falklands issue would become less significant as the crisis in Central America deepened, causing increasing concern and bringing further divisions within Latin America.

Nor do relations between Great Britain and the countries of Latin America appear to have suffered as much as had been feared. It may be difficult to envisage one of Argentina's neighbours granting Britain in the near future the facilities she needs to lessen the formidable task of maintaining her position in the Falkland Islands; but factors other than fear of prejudicing good relations with "Latin America" are likely to persuade her eventually to seek an accommodation with Argentina over the issue.

THE FALKLANDS,
THE LAW AND THE WAR

By

LESLIE. C. GREEN

WHENEVER there is any question as to sovereign rights in the southern hemisphere, whether the area in issue relates to Antarctica or to the Falklands, to some intra-continental boundary dispute, or even if there is discussion as to the rights of aboriginal peoples in the New World as against the claims of existing sovereign Powers, there is reference to a variety of Papal Bulls issued during the fifteenth century. Of these, the most important appears to be that known as the Bull *Inter Caetera*[1] issued by Alexander VI after Columbus returned from his first voyage. By this, the Pope purported to divide the undiscovered and unclaimed or unsettled parts of the world between Spain and Portugal. Alexander granted Ferdinand and Isabella all lands lying west of the Azores, including regions discovered and unknown, so long as they had not already been seized by any other Christian Prince. The subjects of other States were not allowed to enter this domain without the consent of the Spanish King. Lands east of the line were awarded to Portugal. It is clear from the wording of this Bull that the Pope, and it might have been presumed all Christian kings and princes owing him allegiance, believed that the world belonged to God and that the administration and disposition thereof were within the jurisdiction of the Pope as His representative. Moreover, the language makes it clear that the Pope regarded his award as a legal grant giving the Spanish and Portuguese monarchs full power of sovereignty and jurisdiction over the territories concerned, with the primary objective of spreading Christianity: " . . . on one of the chief of these aforesaid islands [discovered by Columbus] the said Christopher has caused to be put together and built a fortress fairly equipped, whereon he has stationed as garrison certain Christians . . . who are to make search for other remote and unknown islands and mainlands, ... Wherefore, . . . you [Ferdinand and Isabella] have purposed . . . to bring under your sway the said mainlands and islands with their residents and inhabitants and to bring them to the Catholic faith . . . . And in order that you may

---

[1] Davenport, *European Treaties Bearing on the History of the United States and its Dependencies* (1917) p. 17 (Latin text p. 75; the Latin text is also reproduced in Perl, *The Falkland Islands Dispute in International Law and Relations* (1983) p. 89.

enter upon so great an undertaking with greater readiness and heartiness endowed with the benefit of our apostolic favour, we, of our own accord, not at your instance nor the request of anyone else in your regard, but of our own sole largesse and certain knowledge and out of the fullness of our apostolic power, by the authority of Almighty God conferred upon us in blessed Peter and of the vicarship of Jesus Christ, which we hold on earth, do by tenor of these presents, should any of said islands be found by your envoys and captains, give, grant, and assign to you and your heirs and successors, . . . forever, together with all their dominions, cities, camps, places and villages, and all rights, jurisdictions, and appurtenances, all islands and mainlands found and to be found, discovered and to be discovered towards the west and south, by drawing and establishing a line from the Arctic pole . . . to the Antarctic pole . . . , no matter whether the said mainlands and islands are found in the direction of India or towards any other quarter, the said line to the distant one hundred leagues from any of the islands commonly known as the Azores and Cape Verde. With this proviso however that none of the islands and mainlands, found and to be found, discovered and to be discovered, beyond the said line, towards the west and south, be in the actual possession of any Christian king or prince up to the birthday of our Lord Jesus Christ just past from which the present year one thousand four hundred and ninety-three begins. And we make, appoint and depute you and your said heirs and successors lords of them with full and free power, authority, and jurisdiction of every kind; with this proviso however, that by this our gift, grant, and assignment no right acquired by any Christian prince, who may be in actual possession of said islands and mainlands prior to the said birthday of our Lord Jesus Christ, is hereby to be understood to be withdrawn or taken away. . . . Furthermore, under penalty of excommunication *late sententie* to be incurred *ipso facto*, should anyone thus contravene, we strictly forbid all persons of whatsoever rank, even imperial or royal or of whatsoever estate, decree, order, or condition, to dare, without your special permit or that of your aforesaid heirs and successors, to go for the purpose of trade or any other reason to islands or mainlands, found and to be found, discovered and to be discovered . . . apostolic constitutions and ordinances and other decrees whatsoever to the contrary notwithstanding . . . . Let no one, therefore, infringe, or with rash boldness contravene, this our recommendation, exhortation, requisition, gift, grant, assignment, constitution, deputation, degree, mandate, prohibition, and will. Should anyone presume to attempt this, be it known to him that he will incur the wrath of Almighty God and of the blessed apostles Peter and Paul . . . ."

That the rulers of Spain and Portugal considered the Pope's grant as being completely effective is evidenced by the Treaty of Tordesillas (1494),[2] whereby they shifted the 100 league line demarcating their spheres of ownership to 370 leagues west of the Cape Verde Islands. While dividing the seas between them, they recognised the right of each to cross into the territory of the other to the extent that this should be necessary, but affirmed the exclusive ownership of each within his area. This amendment to the Bull *Inter Caetera* was sanctified by Julius II in his Bull *Ea Quae* of 1506.[3] While the monarchs of Spain and Portugal accepted the Pope's decree as holy writ, not all European sovereigns were so disposed. Thus Francis I of France, the "Most Christian King," asked to be shown the will of Adam whereby he had been deprived of the right to acquire territory in the New World.[4] Protestant monarchs were even more sarcastic as may be seen from Elizabeth's rejoinder to the Spanish Ambassador Mendoza who had protested at Drake's activities in that part of the world[5]: "she would not persuade herself that [the Indies] are the rightful property of Spanish donation of the pope of Rome in whom she acknowledged no prerogative in matters of this kind, much less authority to bind Princes who owe him no obedience, or to make the New World as it were a fief for the Spaniard and clothe him with possession: and that only on the ground that the Spaniards have touched here and there, have erected shelters, have given names to a river or promontory: acts which cannot confer property. So that this donation of *res alienae* which by law (*ex jure*) is void, and this imaginary proprietorship, ought not to hinder other princes from carrying on commerce in these regions and from establishing colonies where Spaniards are not residing, without the least violation of the law of nations, since without possession prescription is of no avail (*haud valeat*), nor yet from freely navigating that vast ocean since the use of the sea and air is common to all men; further that no right of the ocean can insure to any people or individual since neither nature nor any reason of public use permits occupation of the ocean."

Even the opponents of this Papal largesse, when issuing commissions to their own explorers/land-grabbers, instructed them not to seize land already claimed in the name of another Christian

---

[2] Davenport, *op. cit.* (in note 1 above), p. 93 (Perl. p. 103), confirmed by Treaty of Madrid (1495), *ibid.* p. 104.

[3] *Ibid.* p. 110.

[4] Fauchille, *Traité de Droit International Public*, Vol. I, Pt. II, (1925), p. 687: "Le roi de France, François Ier demanda à voir le testament d'Adam qui le dépouillait d'acquérir des territoires dans le Nouveau Monde."

[5] Camden, *Annales Rerum Anglicae*, Vol. 2 (1717) pp. 359–360.

prince, although in practice the Papal disposition seems not to have been regarded as sufficient warrant of title. Consequently there was much debate as to who had first discovered any particular part of the New World[6] and as to the evidence that would indicate a true title consequent upon such discovery. In fact, it soon became clear that mere discovery without the establishment of some sort of permanent settlement was inadequate to establish title to sovereignty and to exclude others from claiming the territory as *terra nullius* and thus open to occupation by the newcomer.

Regardless of any claim based on prior discovery, it seems to be agreed that earliest settlement of the Falklands dates from the eighteenth century. The first serious landfalls in the area occurred in 1706 and 1707 by vessels from St. Malo, although as early as 1690 an English privateer named Strong had made a casual landing and named the islands the Falklands.[7] This period saw the beginnings of a dynastic struggle between France and Spain, as well as conflicts, in which England too was involved, concerning commerce, and particularly relating to the *assiento*, the right to participate in the slave trade. In 1764 an expedition under Bougainville, which had set out like the French predecessors from St. Malo, established a settlement, took possession of the territory in the name of Louis XV and called it Les Malouines, which became, for the Spaniards, Los Malvinas. Two years later a British garrison was set up at Port Egmont.

"In the meantime, Spain formally protested to the French Government and her rights of dominion were recognised. King Louis XV ordered Bougainville to hand over Port Louis [where his settlement had been established] on the compensatory payment of all expenses incurred in. The transfer was solemnly held in a ceremony held on 1 April 1767 in Port Louis itself, thus recognizing the legal right of the Spanish Crown to these Islands [—this is true, however, only in so far as France was concerned]. Previously, the Government had issued a Royal Bill, dated 4 October 1766 which declared the Islands to be dependencies of the Captaincy General of Buenos Aires, and Don Felipe Ruiz Puente was designated Governor. The Spanish were thus left in possession of the Port, whose name was changed to Port Soledad with Spanish settlers about [*sic*] and a military establishment located.

"On Saunders Isle [off West Falkland], however, there was still the small British garrison of Port Egmont, which had been set up in

---

[6] A detailed account of the various voyages leading to claims of discovery of the Falklands is to be found in Goebel, *The Struggle for the Falkland Islands* (1927; 1982 ed.), Chaps. I–III.
[7] *Ibid*. pp. 140–146, 136–137, respectively.

1766.[8] At the time of the transfer of Port Louis by France to Spain, the British had been silent and made no reservations regarding their presumed sovereignty. [It should here be mentioned that there could be no obligation upon England to assert any claim in her own name at a time when that claim was not been challenged and it was only a question of French rights as against Spain which were in issue.[9]] Once her difficulties with France were solved, Spain turned her attention to Port Egmont, and the British garrison was evicted from Saunders Isle by the Spanish forces of the Rio de la Plata Fleet under the command of the Governor of Buenos Aires, Buccarelli, on 10 June 1770. Spain had thus reacted clearly and categorically in the face of both intruders and ensured respect for her sovereign rights, since the French had withdrawn after diplomatic pressure and the British after force had been exercised."[10]

Great Britain, however, unlike France was not prepared to accept this expulsion quietly. After all, the British had landed a bare two years after the French and 14 months before the Spanish took possession, and as early as 1765 Egmont had written[11]: " . . . as to Spain, it is impossible even their pretended title from the Pope's Grant or any Treaty . . . can give them the least claim to an Island lying 80 or 100 leagues in the Atlantick Ocean eastward of the Continent of South America, to which it cannot be deem'd appurtenant. And the attempt of France to settle there seems to confirm this argument against all that be urg'd hereafter by either of these powers to that effect." Moreover, when, in 1769, the local Spanish authorities had threatened to use force to expel the English, Captain Hunt replied[12]: " . . . the said Islands belong to his Britannic Majesty, my master, by right of discovery as well as settlement, and . . . the subject of no other power whatever can have any right to be settled in the said Islands without leave from his Britannic Majesty, taking the oath of allegiance and submitting themselves to his government, as subjects to the crown of Great Britain. I do, therefore, in his Majesty's name and by his orders warn you to leave the said

---

[8] Cdre. Byron, commander of the expedition, states "of this harbour and all the neighboring Islands, I took possession for his Majesty, King George, the Third, of Great Britain, by the name of Falkland's Islands," *An Account of a Voyage Round the World, Hawkesworth Voyages*, Vol. 1 (3rd ed., 1785), p. 58; *cf.* Goebel, *op. cit.* (in note 6 above), p. 232.

[9] See, *e.g.* Award of Judge Huber in *Palmas Case* (1928) 2 R.I.A.A. 829, 843.

[10] Statement by Ruda, Argentine Representative at Subcommittee III of the UN Special Committee on the Situation with respect to the Implementation of the Declaration on the Granting of Independence to Colonial Countries and Peoples, September 9, 1964, Perl, *op. cit.* (in note 1 above), pp. 351, 355–356.

[11] Goebel, *op. cit.* (in note 6 above), p. 236.

[12] *Ibid.* p. 274.

island . . . ." However, as we have seen, these brave words came to nothing in the end and it was the English who withdrew.

England immediately demanded reparation for an act described by George III as one whereby "the honour of my Crown and the security of my people's rights were become deeply affected."[13] Ultimately the issue was settled peaceably on the basis of the *status quo ante*. The Spanish declaration read[14]: "His Britannick Majesty having complained of the violence which was committed on the 10th of June, 1770, at the island commonly called the Great Malouine, and by the English Falkland's Island, in obliging, by force, the commander of the subjects of his Britannick Majesty to evacuate the port by them called Egmont; a step offensive to the honour of his crown;—the Prince de Maserano, Ambassador Extraordinary of his Catholick Majesty, has received orders to declare, and declares, that his Catholick majesty, considering the desire with which he is animated for peace, and for the maintenance of good harmony with his Britannick Majesty, and reflecting that this event might interrupt it, has seen with displeasure this expedition tending to disturb it; and in the persuasion in which he is of the reciprocity of sentiments of his Britannick Majesty, and of its being far from his intention to authorise anything that might disturb the good understanding between the two Courts, his Catholick Majesty does dosavow the said violent enterprise,—and, in consequence, the Prince de Maserano declares, that his Catholick Majesty engages to give immediate orders, that things shall be restored in the Great Malouine at the port called Egmont, precisely to the state in which they were before the 10th of June, 1770: For which purpose his Catholick Majesty will give orders to one of his Officers, to deliver up to the Officer authorised by His Britannick Majesty the port and fort called Egmont, with all the artillery, stores, and effects of his Britannick Majesty and his subjects which were at that place the day above named, agreeable to the inventory which has been made of them.

"The Prince de Maserano declares, at the same time, in the name of the King, his master, that the engagement of his said Catholick Majesty, to restore to his Britannick Majesty the possession of the port and fort called Egmont, cannot nor ought in any wise to affect the question of the prior right of sovereignty of the Malouine islands, otherwise called Falkland's Islands . . . ."

Despite this reservation of sovereignty on behalf of Spain, the declaration remains ambiguous. In the first place the act of displacement of the English settlers was expressly disowned making the Spa-

---

[13] Address from the throne at prorogation of Parliament (1770), *ibid.* p. 303.
[14] 22 B.F.S.P. 1387 (*ibid.* pp. 358–359).

nish action one of private depradation, but in respect of which the Spanish crown offered an apology. Moreover, the reference to the desire not to disturb the good understanding between the two countries is itself an acknowledgment of the existence of British claims, which acknowledgment is reiterated by the agreement to restore matters to the pre-existing situation, when it was known that at that time the British claimed sovereignty, and an injury could have occurred only if a right had in fact been interfered with. The British acceptance[15] of the Spanish declaration makes no reservation of sovereignty, but, for the reasons just explained, together with the resumption of possession and re-establishment of the settlement, it would appear that no such reservation was needed: "His Catholick Majesty having authorized the Prince de Maserano, his Ambassador Extraordinary, to offer, in his Majesty's name, to the King of Great Britain, a satisfaction for the injury done to his Britannick Majesty by dispossessing him of the port and fort of Port Egmont; and the said Ambassador having this day signed a declaration . . . expressing therein, that his Catholick Majesty, being desirous to restore the good harmony and friendship which before subsisted between the two Crowns, does disavow the expedition against Port Egmont, in which force has been used against his Britannick Majesty's possessions, commander, and subjects; and does also engage, that all things shall immediately be restored to the precise situation in which they stood before the 10th of June, 1770; and that his Catholick Majesty shall give orders, in consequence to one of his Officers to deliver up to the Officer authorized by his Britannick Majesty, the port and fort of Port Egmont, as also all his Britannick Majesty's artillery, stores, and effects, as well as those of his subjects, according to the inventory which has been made of them. And the said Ambassador having moreover engaged, in his Catholick Majesty's name, that what is contained in the said declaration shall be carried into effect by his said Catholick Majesty . . . ; his said Britannick Majesty, in order to shew the same friendly disposition on his part, has authorised me to declare, that he will look upon the said declaration of the Prince de Maserano, together with the full performance of the said engagement on the part of his Catholick Majesty, as a satisfaction for the injury done to the Crown of Great Britain . . . ."

The Spanish representatives had sought throughout the negotiations to secure a commitment from Great Britain that, after satisfaction had been given for the 1770 incident, the settlement would in fact be withdrawn. However, the English consistently pointed out

---

[15] 22 B.F.S.P. 1387–1388 (Goebel, pp. 359–360).

that the question of abandonment could not be discussed prior to the return of possession and when in 1774 the English did withdraw this was done as a matter of economy. The Earl of Rochford, Secretary of State for the Northern Department, explained the reason to Lord Grantham, British Ambassador in Madrid[16]: " . . . Lord North, in a Speech some days ago in the House of Commons, on the subject of the Naval Establishment for this year, mentioned the intention of reducing the Naval Forces in the East Indies, as a material object of diminishing the number of Seamen; and at the same time hinted, as a matter of small consequence, that, in order to avoid the expense of keeping any Seamen or Marines at Falkland Islands, they would be brought away, after leaving there the proper marks or signals of possession, and of its belonging to the Crown of Great Britain. As this measure was publicly declared in Parliament, it will naturally be reported to the Court of Spain . . . ; . . . it is neither more nor less than a small part of an economical Naval regulation." In accordance with this intention, the garrison was withdrawn and an inscription engraved on lead was affixed to the blockhouse[17]: "Be it known to all nations that the Falkland Islands, with this fort, the storehouses, wharfs, harbors, bays, and creeks thereunto belonging are the sole right and property of His Most Sacred Majesty George the Third, King of Great Britain, France and Ireland, Defender of the Faith, etc. In witness thereof this plate is set, and his Britannic Majesty's colors left flying as a mark of possession by S.W. Clayton, commanding officer at Falkland Islands, A.D. 1774."

There is no question that as the law had developed by the twentieth century[18] a mere assertion of title, even by way of an inscribed plate installed *in situ*, does not confer sovereignty in the absence of some exercise of jurisdiction or other evidence of occupation. However, it was a common practice during the era of discoveries during the sixteenth and seventeenth centuries to assert sovereignty by way of a plaque bearing the royal arms,[19] although English practice required some token possession of the soil.[20] Equally, abandonment

---

[16] (February 11, 1774), 22 B.F.S.P. 1393, reprinted Smith, *Great Britain and the Law of Nations*, Vol. 2 (1932), pp. 55–56.

[17] Goebel, *op. cit.* (in note 6 above) p. 410.

[18] See *Clipperton Island Case* (1931) 2 R.I.A.A. 1108.

[19] *E.g. The Voyages of Jacques Cartier*, (translated by Biggar) Publication of Public Archives of Canada, Nr. 11 (1924), pp. 64–66, 85, 225; Williams, *The Voyages of the Cabots* (1929), p. 30; Coxe, *Account of the Russian Discoveries between Asia and America* (1804), pp. 1–2, 33.

[20] *E.g.* Drake's circumnavigation of the globe, Purchas, *Hakluytus post humus*, Vol. 2 (1905), p. 129; C.Keller *et al.*, *Creation of Rights of Sovereignty through Symbolic Acts* (1967), p. 57; Gosch (Ed.), *Danish Arctic Exploration 1605–1620* (1894), p. 10.

of possession only amounted to an abandonment of sovereignty if there was a clear *animus reliquendi*, and it would seem that the installation of a plaque maintaining title was tantamount to evidence that no such *animus* existed, "and the fact that authority has not been exercised in a positive manner does not imply the abandonment of an acquisition already definitively acquired."[21] Moreover, Spain was informed of the reasons for the withdrawal. By a treaty of 1790,[22] Great Britain and Spain signed a treaty relative to America. By article III they "agreed that their respective Subjects shall not be disturbed or molested either in navigating or carrying on their Fisheries in the Pacific Ocean, or in the South Seas, or in landing on the Coasts of those Seas, in places not already occupied, for the purpose of carrying on their commerce with the Natives of the Country, or of making Settlements there." However, by article VI "it is further agreed, with respect to the Eastern and Western Coasts of South America, and to the Islands adjacent, that no Settlement shall be formed hereafter, by the respective Subjects, in such parts of those Coasts as are situated to the South of those parts of the same Coasts, and of the Islands adjacent, which are already occupied by Spain; provided that the said respective Subjects shall retain the liberty of landing on the Coasts and Islands so situated, for the purposes of their Fishery, and of erecting thereon huts, and other temporary buildings, serving only for those purposes."

At the time of the signing of this treaty, Spain was still in possession of its settlement at Solidad, but her colonists were withdrawn following the decision of 1811 to discontinue the colony,[23] that is to say some five years before the United Provinces of Rio de la Plata, with its seat of government at Buenos Aires, declared its independence from Spain. This hiatus in sovereign administration is important since it raises doubts as to the validity of the doctrine of *uti possidetis*[24] whereby the independent countries of South America claim to be the direct successors in title to the territories formerly owned by Spain. Four years after the establishment of the Republic of the United Provinces a ship was sent by the Republic and formal possession of the Islands was proclaimed; in 1823 a Governor was appointed and the right to exploit and fish was granted to Vernet, who was named Political and Military Commandant of the Islands in

---

[21] *Clipperton Island, loc. cit.* (in note 18 above), p. 1111.
[22] Perl. *op. cit.* (in note 1 above), p. 145.
[23] Goebel, *op. cit.* (in note 6 above), p. 433.
[24] See *e.g. Guatemala-Honduras Boundary* arbitration (1933) 2 R.I.A.A. 1307, 1323–1325; Waldock, "Disputed Sovereignty in the Falkland Islands Dependencies" 25 B.Y.I.L. (1948), pp. 311, 325–326.

1829.[25] This appointment acquires major significance in view of events that occurred shortly thereafter. Before examining Vernet's actions, which led to the expulsion of the Argentinian settlers, it is worth reproducing the comments of H.A. Smith on this "appointment." He states that the new government at Buenos Ayres "was wholly unable to exercise any effective control over a group of islands more than a thousand miles from its own capital,"[26] but does not explain why the Government of Spain or of Great Britain was able to exercise effective control of any of its possessions in the New World thousands of miles from home. He goes on to state[27]: "A 'governor' of the Falklands was appointed in 1823, but this was clearly an appointment *in partibus infidelium*, for he never visited his province. In 1826 an American adventurer named Louis Vernet [—according to Goebel[28] 'Vernet was of French origin, but as he had resided for a long time in Hamburg he was generally spoken of as a German. He was a man of character and by no means the uncultivated barbarian that he was pictured in the American diplomatic correspondence'—] established a colony on the islands. This action was nominally legalised by a concession from Buenos Ayres, and the concession was followed in 1829 by a decree appointing Vernet as governor, but these documents were transparent fictions and Vernet was never at any time subject to any real governmental control. The text of the decree, which is dated 10th June, 1829, in effect admits that 'circumstances' had hitherto prevented any real exercise of sovereignty—'When by the glorious Revolution of 25th of May, 1810, these Provinces separated themselves from the Dominion of the Mother Country, Spain held the important Possession of the Islands of the Malvinas, (Falkland Islands), and of all the others which approximate to Cape Horn, including that under the denomination of Tierra del Fuego[29]: this Possession was justified by the right of the first occupant, by the consent of the principal Maritime Powers of Europe, and by the proximity of the Islands to the Continent which formed the Viceroyalty of Buenos Ayres, unto which Government they depended. For this reason, the Government of the Republic, having succeeded to every right which the Mother Country previously exercised over these Provinces, and which its Viceroys possessed, continued to exercise acts of Dominion in the

---

[25] Ruda statement, *loc. cit.* (in note 10 above), pp. 360–361.

[26] *Op. cit.* (in note 16 above), p. 57.

[27] *Ibid*. pp. 57–59 (italics added). This proclamation is reproduced in Perl. *op. cit.* (in note 1 above), pp. 156–157.

[28] *Op. cit.* (in note 6 above), p. 435.

[29] Title to Tierra del Fuego was disputed by Chile, which received the greater part of the island by its treaty with Argentina of 1881, Smith, *op. cit.* (in note 16 above), pp. 58n., 262.

said Islands, its Ports, and Coasts, notwithstanding *circumstances have hitherto prevented* this Republic from paying the attention to that part of the Territory which, from its importance, it demands. Nevertheless the necessity of no longer delaying *such precautionary measures as shall be necessary to secure the rights of the Republic*; and at the same time to possess the advantages which the productions of the said Islands may yield, and to afford to the Inhabitants that protection of which they stand in need, and to which they are entitled; the Government has ordered and decreed, as follows:

Art. I. The Islands of the Malvinas and those adjacent to Cape Horn, shall be under the command of a Political and Military Governor, to be named immediately by the Government of the Republic.

Art. II. The Political and Military Governor shall reside in the Island de la Soledad, on which a Battery shall be erected under the Flag of the Republic.

Art. III. The Political and Military Governor shall cause the Laws of the Republic to be observed by the Inhabitants of the said Island, and provide for the due performance of the Regulations respecting Seal Fishery on the Coasts . . . .'

"The reader will note that this decree claims title by succession from Spain, and dates Argentine independence from 1810. In actual fact Ferdinand VII was nominally acknowledged as sovereign until the 9th July, 1816, and all official acts were promulgated in his name.[30] But it would have raised fresh difficulties for the Buenos Ayres government to have admitted that the Spanish title survived until 1816. Not only had the islands been completely evacuated in 1811, but the government of Buenos Ayres only controlled part of the vast territory included in the Spanish viceroyalty of Rio de la Plata. The territory included the republics of Bolivia, Paraguay, and Uruguay, as well as Argentina, and any one of these might have had as good a claim as the government of Buenos Ayres to succeed to the Spanish title in the Falklands. In actual fact no control over the islands was exercised by the genuine authority of any government until the British re-occupation in 1832. In a report to Buenos Ayres Vernet himself admitted that the foundation of the colony was entirely his own work, that he received no assistance at any time from the government, that he was paid no salary as 'governor,' and

---

[30] Note from American Chargé d'Affaires to Buenos Ayres Minister (July 10, 1832) 20 B.F.S.P. 338, Perl. *op. cit.* (in note 1 above), pp. 180, 191.

that the islands were exempt from taxation.[31] It seems clear that the 1829 decree was merely an attempt to cover with a show of legality the actions of an individual adventurer whom the Argentine government was in fact wholly unable to control." While it may be true that the Argentine Government's statements are somewhat *parti pris* it would appear that, in the light of the official documents and proclamations, this is no less true of Smith's assessment.

It is interesting to note that in its Proclamation the Republic makes no reference to Papal Bulls nor to first discovery. Even the assertion as to occupation only has validity so long as the area in question is effectively administered and the title of the administrator is acknowledged by third parties. In view of the British attitude— and of the United States as shown shortly after its promulgation— this is hardly the case, and in 1829 Britain in fact protested the proclamation on the ground that Port Egmont had never been abandoned.[32] As to the doctrine of proximity, while this may have certain apparent attractions, it is generally accepted that the position in international law is as stated by Judge Huber in the *Palmas* case[33]: " . . . Although States have in certain circumstances maintained that islands relatively close to their shores belonged to them in virtue of their geographical situation, it is impossible to show the existence of a rule of positive international law to the effect that islands situated outside territorial waters should belong to a State from the mere fact that its territory forms the *terra firma* (nearest continent or island of considerable size). Not only would it seem that there are no precedents sufficiently frequent and sufficiently precise in their bearing to establish such a rule of international law, but the alleged principle itself is by its very nature so uncertain and contested that even Governments of the same State have on different occasions maintained contradictory opinion as to its soundness. The principle of contiguity [—proximity—], in regard to islands, may not be out of place when it is a question of allotting them to one State rather than to another, either by agreement between the Parties, or by a decision not necessarily based on law; but as a rule establishing *ipso jure* the presumption of sovereignty in favour of a

---

[31] In fact, the Decree of January 5, 1828, "ceded," with certain exceptions, "the Island of Statenland, and all the lands of the Island of Soledad . . . with the object, and under the express condition, that, within 3 years of the date hereof, a Colony shall be established . . . ," Perl. *op. cit.* (in note 1 above) p. 262. As regards the absence of governmental financial assistance, Vernet states that payment in respect of disbursements was made "with the product of the Fishery," Report of the Political and Military Commandant—Vernet (May 10, 1832) *ibid.* pp. 211, 164.

[32] British Chargé d'Affaires to Buenos Ayres Minister (November 19, 1829), *ibid.* pp. 188–189.

[33] *Loc. cit.* (in note 9 above), pp. 854–855, 869.

particular State, this principle would be in conflict with what has been said as to territorial sovereignty and as to the necessary relation between the right to exclude other States from a region and the duty to display therein the activities of a State. Nor is this principle of contiguity admissible as a legal method of deciding questions of territorial sovereignty; for it is wholly lacking in precision and would in its application lead to arbitrary results . . . . The title of contiguity, understood as a basis of territorial sovereignty, has no foundation in international law." Insofar as the argument based on succession to Spain is concerned, the comments by Smith and the arguments put forward above with regard to the hiatus in Spanish occupation suffice to negate that claim.

Acting as Governor and seeking to protect the fishery, Vernet forbade foreign fishing in the region on penalty of seizure and despatch to Buenos Ayres for trial. In 1831 three American vessels, the *Harriet, Superior* and *Breakwater* were seized and Vernet accompanied the *Harriet* to Buenos Ayres. The Americans protested the seizure, maintaining that their fishermen were entitled to operate in the area and the *U.S.S. Lexington* was sent to Port Soledad. Its captain, Commander Duncan, destroyed the settlement and sailed off with one of Vernet's lieutenants, whom he had invited on board, and five of the settlers in irons.[34] The United States condemned Vernet's seizure of the vessels as "lawless and piratical [which] could not permit the President to believe that they were authorised by a friendly power" and Vernet was described as a private individual and the decree forbidding fishing and threatening seizure as a mere pretence for piratical acts.[35] The seizures were condemned as the "lawless, and indeed piratical acts of Vernet and his band . . . . [H]is settlement is composed of deserters from our ships, and renegades from all nations,[36] governed by no laws but the will of Vernet, [which] show clearly that it is an establishment dangerous to our commerce, [and] which it is necessary that we should break up, *whether the Government of Buenos Ayres have the title to the jurisdiction of the islands, or have not.* If they have the jurisdiction, they have no right so to use it in any way to interfere with our right of fishery, established by long usage; but above all to use in the irregu-

---

[34] Goebel, *op. cit.* (in note 6 above), pp. 438–447; most of the documents relevant to these incidents are reproduced in Perl, *op. cit.* (in note 1 above), pp. 153–298.

[35] Secretary of State Livingston to Baylies, U.S. Chargé d'Affaires, Buenos Ayres, (January 26, 1832) 1 Moore, *Digest of International Law*, pp. 876–883.

[36] A table prepared by Captain Onslow, *H.M.S. Clio* (January 16, 1833), lists 18 settlers at Soledad (Port Louis)—a French merchant in charge of the flag, an Irishman, an English labourer, a German agriculturist and a carpenter, a Jamaican carpenter and 12 Argentinians, Public Record Office, F.O. 6/500. None had been there longer than 5 years.

lar manner stated . . . , which they do not repress; and whether the omission proceeds from the want of means, or of inclination, the obligation of our Government to protect its own citizens, in either alternative, is equally imperative."[37]

It would appear that, despite the fulminations against Vernet, the United States was not certain that he was not a representative of the government of the Republic. This was the view of the Circuit Court of Connecticut when faced with a suit by Americans claiming to own seal-skins seized by Vernet, and which they described as having been seized piratically. Circuit Justice Thompson stated[38] "[I]f these islands were held in the possession and under the jurisdiction of the Buenos Ayrean government, and *Vernet's establishment then was under the authority and protection of that government, as it clearly was*, and even admitting that Vernet had abused his power, Captain Duncan [of the *Lexington*] could have no right, without express directions from his government, to enter into the territorial jurisdiction of a country at peace with the United States and forcibly seize upon property found there and claimed by citizens of the United States. Such a principle would be too hazardous to the peace of nations to be admitted in practice . . . .Our government must have been fully apprized of the course pursued by the government of Buenos Ayres; for the decree [of June 1829] was undoubtedly the decree under which Vernet was acting. And that decree, . . . in terms declares, that the Falkland Islands shall be governed by a military and civil governor, to be appointed by the government of the republic, and whose residence should be on the island of Solidad, and that he should see to the regulations of the fisheries on that coast. . . . [O]ur government four years after the seizure of the Superior, and, as must be presumed, with full knowledge of the fact, treated this right [to fish] as a subject for negotiation between the two governments, and does not undertake to affirm such seizure to be a piratical act." However, in *Williams* v. *Suffolk Insurance Co.*[39] the Supreme Court refused to go behind a government statement, holding that "inasmuch as *the American government has insisted and still does insist* through its regular executive authority, *that the Falkland Islands do not constitute any part of the dominions within the sovereignty of the government of Buenos Ayres*, the action of the American government of this subject is binding . . . as to whom the sovereignty of these islands belongs . . . ."

---

[37] Livingston to Baylies (February 14, 1832) 1 Moore, *op. cit.* (in note 35 above), pp. 884–885 (italics added).

[38] *Davison* v. *Seal-skins* (1835) 2 Paine 324 (Perl, *op. cit.* (in note 1 above), pp. 343, 347–348. italics added).

[39] (1839) 13 Peters 415 (Perl, *op. cit.* (in note 1 above), pp. 335, 342—italics added).

The United States maintained its attitude that Vernet was a pirate and his acts unlawful and those of the *Lexington* fully justified throughout the nineteenth century. Thus, in his annual message of December 1885, President Cleveland stated[40]: "The Argentine Government has revived the long dormant question of the Falkland Islands by claiming from the United States indemnity for their loss attributed to the action of the commander of the sloop of war *Lexington* in breaking up a piratical colony on those islands in 1831 and their subsequent occupation by Great Britain. In view of the ample justification for the act of the *Lexington* and the derelict condition of the islands before and after their alleged occupation by Argentine colonials this Government considers the claim as wholly groundless."

Consequent upon the destruction of the Argentine settlement by the *Lexington*, in December 1832 *H.M.S. Clio* arrived at Port Egmont, and formally resumed possession in the name of the King. In reply to the Argentine protest, Palmerston asserted the British claim on the basis that there had been no *animus reliquendi* at the time of the earlier withdrawal, denied that there had been any secret undertaking not to exercise sovereignty and pointed out that "the Government of the United Provinces could not reasonably have anticipated that the British Government would permit any other state to exercise a right as derived from Spain which Great Britain had denied to Spain itself.[41] In reply to an American enquiry as to the British attitude towards foreign fishing and taking cattle on the Falklands, "Lord Palmerston was of opinion that when there was a force at the Falkland Islands adequate to prevent these depradations the Americans should be requested to desist, and if they persevered in such practices they should be prevented; but he thought it would not be proper or expedient to interfere with them so long as they only resorted to the islands for shelter or refreshment."[42] These facts were brought to the notice of the United States government which "published a Notice warning their citizens of the penalties they would incur if they committed spoliations in the Falkland Islands, which they believed would put a stop to the depradations complained of."[43] In fact, with the establishment of effective policing power two Americans were convicted in 1854. The United States government protested, and in their protest maintained that even if the Falklands were in fact British the penalties were excessive.[44]

---

[40] Goebel, *op. cit.* (in note 6 above), p. 463.
[41] (January 8, 1834) 22 B.F.S.P. 1384, *ibid.* p. 457.
[42] *British Digest of International Law*, Vol. 2b, p. 615.
[43] *Ibid.* p. 616.
[44] *Ibid.* pp. 616–617.

While the United States might have acquiesced in the British occupation tacitly, other European States appear to have afforded a more open acknowledgement, making no protest when their whaling companies were required to seek licences from the Falkland authorities. Moreover, in so far as South Georgia is concerned "in 1905 a two-year lease of grazing and mining rights was granted to a Chilean company. In 1906 a twenty-one-year lease of 500 acres was granted to an Argentine company at a rent of £250 which has been paid to the Falkland Islands Government ever since . . . [and] in 1903 the Scottish National Antarctic Expedition used Laurie Island in the South Orkneys as their base, establishing a meteorological station ashore. W.S. Bruce, the leader, failing to get the necessary funds from Great Britain, offered to the Argentine Meteorological Department through the British Minister to convey four Argentine scientists to the island in his own ship, the *Scotia*, to take charge of the observatory. In 1904, an Argentine team, financed by their Meteorological Department, duly took over the observatory. There was no ceremony of taking possession but the Argentine flag was hoisted over the station[45] and the party came armed with stamps[46] and a special post-mark, 'Orcadas del Ind. Distrito 24.' The latter appears to have been primarily a philatelic speculation and the letters were taken away for posting at Cape Town."[47] These activities are consistent with an effective British presence and administration, continuous since the restoration of the colony and legitimised in English law by the Act of 1843 "to enable Her Majesty to provide for the Government of Her Settlements on the Coast of Africa and in the Falkland Islands,"[48] on the authority of which the various Orders in Council imposing the necessity to secure licenses were issued.

---

[45] The raising of a flag without some related exercise of jurisdiction, has no more value than the symbolic planting of a cross or leaving of a replica of the national coat of arms or portrait of a monarch. When done with the consent of the local authority, which continues to exercise jurisdiction, it lacks even this symbolic value.

[46] The mere printing of a postage stamp has no political or legal significance, as may be seen in the case of the Provisional Government of Free India (Green "The Indian National Army Trials," 11 *Modern Law Review* (1948), pp. 47, 48) or of the Republic of South Moluccas. Even if stamps are accepted for international postal purposes, this is not evidence that the issuing authority exercises sovereignty. By the Constitution of the Universal Postal Union (2 Peaslee, *International Governmental Organisations* (1961), p. 1821), the postal administrations of members of the Union are listed to include "the whole of the British overseas Territories, including the Colonies, the Protectorates, and the territories under trusteeship . . . ," Art. 4. There is no reference to any overseas or colonial territory of Argentina.

[47] Waldock, *loc. cit.* (in note 24 above), pp. 327–331.

[48] 6 Vict. c. 13 (31 B.F.S.P. 1211).

Regardless of the British attitude or that of the United States[49] or other countries, Argentina has never acquiesced in the British claim to sovereignty, even though long periods of quiescence have elapsed between its public manifestations of protest. In 1841 there was a formal diplomatic protest against the British "spoliation" of Argentinian sovereignty and territory,[50] and in the first edition of his *Derecho Internacional* published in 1868 Calvo condemned the British take-over of the islands as a graver breach of international law than the British occupation of Copenhagen in 1807.[51] New opportunities for protest and in a much more public manner, and in a more sympathetic arena, arrived with the creation of the United Nations and adoption by the General Assembly of its Declaration on the Granting of Independence to Colonial Countries and Peoples.[52] While Resolutions of the General Assembly do not for the main part carry any legal obligation,[53] there is a tendency to treat Declarations as if they were something more,[54] and Declarations frequently form the basis of majority policy in the Assembly with the principles of the Declaration being treated as if they constituted a modern "Sermon on the Mount."[55] In fact, "From the inception of the [United Nations], Argentina was well aware of the importance of Art. 73e of the Charter.[56] As soon as ever Great Britain began to supply information on the Malvinas, the Argentine Republic informed the United Nations—as it had done so often in the past—of its rights of sovereignty over the territory. And thus, through the General Assembly, Argentina yearly reminded the organization of its rights, and stated that the information supplied by the United Kingdom on the Malvinas Islands, the Georgias and

---

[49] In 1982 Enders, Assistant Secretary of State for Inter-American Affairs, stated that "the United States takes no position on the merits of the competing claims to sovereignty, nor on the legal theories on which the parties rely," Perl, *op. cit.* (in note 1 above), p. 18. Perl states this to be "in line with the conclusions reached in an internal Dept. of State research project conducted in 1947: (a) the U.S. accepts and works with the de facto situation; (b) It accepts tacitly but by unmistakable implication the de jure sovereignty of the U.K. over the Islands, although there has been a tendency even in intra-departmental statements to avoid clear cut, categorical recognition of British sovereignty; (c) It seeks to avoid exacerbating Argentine susceptibilities by refraining so far as possible from public explicit commitment on the dispute," *ibid.* p. 19.

[50] (December 18, 1841) 31 B.F.S.P. 1003.

[51] Vol. 1, s.129, pp. 227–230.

[52] Res. 1514 (XV) (1960).

[53] See, *e.g.* Separate Opinion by Judge Lauterpacht in *South-West Africa—Voting Procedure* [1948] I.C.J. 90, 115.

[54] See, *e.g.* Statement by Legal Dept., U.N. Secretariat, (April 2, 1962), Schermers, *International Institutional Law*, Vol. 2 (1972), p. 500.

[55] See *e.g. Namibia (South-West Africa) Opinion* [1971] I.C.J. 16, 46 *et seq.; Western Sahara* [1975] I.C.J. 4, 31 *et seq.*

[56] "to transmit to the Secretary-General for information purposes . . . information . . . [on] the territories for which they are respectively responsible . . . ."

the South Sandwich [parts of the Dependency] in no way affected
Argentine sovereignty over these territories, that the occupation by
Britain was due to an act of force, never accepted by the Argentine
Government and that it reaffirms its imprescriptable and inalienable
rights. At the same time, in the Organization of American States,
[Argentina] has advocated an end to colonial situations in Amer-
ica . . . .

"The Malvinas Islands are in a different situation from that of the
classical colonial case. *De facto* and *de jure*, they belonged to the
Argentine Republic in 1833 and were governed by Argentine authorities and occupied by Argentine settlers. These authorities and
these settlers were evicted by violence[57] and not allowed to remain
in the territory. On the contrary, they were replaced, during those
131 years of usurpation, by a colonial administration and a population of British origin. Today the population amounts to 2172 souls,
and it is periodically renewed to a large extent by means of a constant turn-over; thus in 1962, 411 persons left and 268 arrived; in
1960, it was 292 that left and 224 who arrived. This shows that it is
basically a temporary population that occupies the land and one that
cannot be used by the colonial power in order to claim the right to
apply the principle of self-determination.

"Our Government holds . . . that this principle of self-determination of peoples, as set forth in Article 1, paragraph 2, of the
Charter, must in these exceptional cases, be taken in the light of the
circumstances which condition its exercise . . . . The basic principle
of self-determination should not be used in order to transform an
illegal possession into full sovereignty under the mantle of protection that would be given by the United Nations."[58]

This must be the first occasion on which it has been suggested that
for a nation or a people to enjoy the right of self-determination the
population must be static and immigration and emigration
unknown. Nor does one often come across so blatant a denial of the
rights of the only people resident in the territory, a position that
reminds one of Indonesia's actions on West Irian or Spain's attitude
to Gibraltar, both of which have received United Nations acquiescence, if not approval. Moreover, Article 1 of the Charter is merely a
declaration of principles. It contains no legal obligation. The reference to "respect for the principle of equal rights and self-determination of peoples" in 1945, when the Charter was adopted, could

---

[57] According to Leibniz he is sovereign who can defend his sovereignty, Jones, "Leibniz as
International Lawyer" 22 B.Y.I.L. (1945), pp. 1, 4.
[58] Ruda statement, *loc. cit.* (in note 10 above); Perl, *op. cit.* (in note 1 above), pp. 367–369
(italics added).

only mean, in the philosophy of the Charter, respect for the independence of States, especially as the concept of a "people" was at that time completely unknown in international law. Further, the references to "illegal possession" are so widely framed as to legitimise any recidivist movement however tenuous its historic or other claims to independence might be. It would also enable any territory the sovereignty of which had been changed by conquest, by peace treaty or even a simple cession to argue, in the absence of a plebiscite, that the actual sovereign was a usurper and that the territory should be returned to whomever claims to be the aboriginal inhabitants—hardly a claim that would go down with the members of the Organisation of African Unity or, for that matter, the countries of Latin America all of which are pledged to maintaining their existing frontiers, even though the boundaries in question are legacies from colonial days.

Interpreting the Declaration on the Granting of Independence to Colonial Countries and Peoples, the General Assembly called for an end to colonialism everywhere, including the Falkland Islands, and invited the two governments concerned to enter negotiations with a view to implementing this Declaration bearing in mind the objectives of the Charter, the provisions of the Declaration and "the interests of the population of the Falklands,"[59] and urging them "to put an end to the colonial situation."[60] In normal circumstances one might have imagined that an end to colonialism, particularly if the interests of the population of the area were to be considered, would be intended to lead to independence, in which case only the colonial administrator and the local population would be involved, with third parties becoming affected if differences between the government and the inhabitants were likely to threaten the peace. As has been noted, this was not the view of Argentina,[61] nor was it the view of the Inter-American Juridicial Committee of the Organisation of American States. This Committee deplored the fact that "territories occupied by foreign powers still remain in American lands, despite the repeated claims of Latin American states calling for their return since they constitute an integral part of their national territories . . . . Recall[ed] the just title the Republic of Argentina possesses to sovereignty over the Malvinas Islands, based on the international rules in force at the time the dispute began . . . . Declares (1) That the Republic of Argentina has an undeniable right of sovereignty over the Malvinas Islands, for which reason the basic question to be

---

[59] Res. 2065 (XX), 1965 (Perl, *op. cit.* (in note 1 above), p. 373.
[60] Res. 3160 (XXVIII), 1973 (*ibid*. p. 381).
[61] See text to note 58 above.

resolved is that of the procedure to be followed for restoring its territory to it; (2) That the 'Shackleton Mission'[62] [sent to make an
'economic and fiscal evaluation' of the archipelago and surrounding
areas], sponsored by the Government of the United Kingdom . . .
amount to making a change unilaterally, and therefore is in contradiction to resolutions . . . of the United Nations; (3) That the presence of foreign warships in waters adjacent to American states and
the intimidatory announcement by British authorities of the sending
of other ships constitute threats to the peace and security of the continent, as well as flagrant violations of the international rules on
non-intervention [—a somewhat new view of nonintervention, since
the vessels were sent to the vicinity of territory recognised by the
majority of nations in the world as constituting part of the British
Commonwealth]; (4) That all of that amounts to hostile conduct
intended to silence the claims of the Government of Argentina and
to obstruct the course of the negotiations recommended by the
General Assembly of the United Nations."[63]

It is clear that, even if the Committee might have had ground for
referring to the law at the time the conflict arose, in accordance with
the principles of international law concerning inter-temporal effects
on title,[64] it would have been impossible to have ignored the fact
that Britain had been effectively administering the territory for
more than a century, and to acknowledge this fact would have
meant recognising the presence of English settlers whose expressed
desire was to remain British.[65]

Efforts to negotiate a satisfactory future for the Islands which
would be acceptable to both Argentina and the United Kingdom
proved fruitless, partly because the United Kingdom maintained
that it was necessary to respect the "wishes" of the inhabitants,
while the Argentine maintained that it was merely necessary to

---

[62] HMSO, *Economic Survey of the Falkland Islands* (1976).

[63] January 26, 1976 (Perl, *op. cit.* (in note 1 above), p. 387).

[64] *Palmas* case (in note 9 above), pp. 845–846: "As regards the question which of different
legal systems prevailing at successive periods is to be applied in a particular case (the so-called
intertemporal law), a distinction must be made between the creation of rights and the existence of rights. The same principle which subjects the act creative of a right to the law in force
at the time the right arises, demands that the existence of the right, in other words its continued manifestation, shall follow the conditions required by the evolution of law. International law in the 19th century . . . took account of a tendency already existing and
especially developed since the middle of the 18th century, and laid down the principle that
occupation, to constitute a claim to territorial sovereignty, must be effective, that is, offer certain guarantees to other States and their nationals." Arbitrator Huber described this as a
"rule of positive law."

[65] See *e.g.* statement by elected Falkland councillors that "islanders would be prepared to
accept renewed air and trade links with Argentina *provided there was no challenge to British
sovereignty*," *The Times* (August 26, 1983) (italics added).

respect their "interests," and maintained that this could best be done by maintaining the territorial integrity of the "country," especially as, according to Argentina, "approximately 40 per cent. of the population consists of British civil servants and employees of a private company which owns nearly 50 per cent. of all property in the islands."[66] Assuming these statements to be correct, it is somewhat difficult to perceive their relevance or how they affect the situation. Nor is the situation changed, from the point of view of Argentina's argument on "interest," by the signature of an agreement concerning communication between the Islands and the Argentine mainland,[67] for such an agreement in no way affects the legal relationship and it can hardly be said that a bilateral communications agreement to facilitate the position of one party's population can be used by the other party to strengthen its alleged legal claims. In April 1980 the United Kingdom and the Argentine resumed discussions and the General Assembly deferred consideration of the dispute because of this. The British attitude had changed. While sovereignty was still maintained and the wishes of the inhabitants were held to be paramount, it became clear that, provided the latter agreed, the United Kingdom was prepared to consider the possibility of an outright transfer of sovereignty to Argentina, the institution of a condominium similar to that which had existed between herself and France for the New Hebrides, the breaking off of all negotiations, or a lease-back proposal, whereby title would be ceded to Argentina which would then grant a lease to the United Kingdom which would remain as the de facto administrator. Under such an arrangement, the settlers were promised that their "life style would not be changed, and there would be new financial benefits from fishing, tourism, and oil, which would commence as soon as possible after the change."[68] The Legislative Council of the Territory, however, requested the Government to continue negotiations to find an agreement, but with the sovereignty dispute frozen temporarily. Argentina, however, rejected a freeze during further discussions, but it was reported that "the Argentine delegation, in a direct appeal to the councillors [present as members of the British delegation], had offered to make the islands 'a most pampered region' and to maintain the democratic, legal, social and educational systems of the Territory, if the inhabitants gave up United Kingdom sovereignty in favour of Argentine sovereignty." Since, however,

---

[66] Letter from Argentine Representative to U.N. to Special Committee with regard to Implementation on Granting of Independence to Colonial Countries and Peoples (May 7, 1976), Perl, *op. cit.* (in note 1 above), pp. 399, 401.

[67] Agreement of August 5, 1971, T.S. Nr. 64 (1972), Cmnd. 5000. See, also, note 65 above.

[68] *The Times* (November 27 and 28, 1980).

new Council elections were due to be held before December 1981, the existing Council thought the matter should be left for decision by the new one when elected.[69]

There matters rested, but in March 1982 a group of Argentine scrap-merchants landed on South Georgia without a British licence or permit and refused to leave, and received Argentine support. The United Kingdom referred this matter to the Security Council which called on the two States to continue negotiations and settle their issues peacefully. On April 2, however, Argentina launched a military invasion resulting in the surrender of the small British garrison and leading the President of Argentina to proclaim that[70]: "Safeguarding our national honour and without rancour or bitterness, but with all the strength that comes from being in the right, we have recovered a part of our national heritage." Despite this emotional and lofty statement, the Security Council condemned the invasion, finding that a breach of the peace existed and demanded an immediate cessation of hostilities and the immediate withdrawal of all Argentine forces from the Islands. It again called upon the two countries to settle their differences diplomatically and in accordance with the Charter.[71]

Although she did not regard the Argentine act of aggression as a *casus belli* necessitating a declaration of war, Great Britain mounted a major military operation which, after suffering relatively heavy casualties, recaptured the Islands and restored the British administration. While it would appear that the civilian population of the United Kingdom was fully supportive of the government's actions, there was much political controversy with some Members of Parliament contending that force was not the answer, that Britain should continue negotiations and even criticising the manner in which the military operations had been conducted. These criticisms were strengthened somewhat when it became clear that Argentina would continue with its protests at the British presence, and announced its intention to re-establish its own sovereignty, threats that acquired reality in view of the proximity of the Argentina mainland which would necessitate the continued presence of a British garrison larger than the entire local population and at what the critics considered to be inordinate expense.

It is not the purpose of this paper to follow the course of the con-

---

[69] Report of the Special Committee (August 5, 1981) (Perl, *op. cit.* (in note 1 above), pp. 403, 408).
[70] Statement by Argentine representative to Security Council (April 3, 1982) (Perl, *op. cit.* (in note 1 above), pp. 403, 408).
[71] S.C. Res. 502, April 3, 1982 (*ibid.* pp. 419).

flict or the sinuosities of the political debates that followed in the United Nations or in the United Kingdom. Rather, it is intended to comment upon some of the legal issues involved. In the first place it must be remembered that the United Nations, like the Organisation of American States, the majority of whose members fully backed the Argentine claims which, in ideology at least, were so similar to their own historic attitudes, is not a court, nor are its representatives necessarily lawyers. Both organisations are political, the members are States, the decisions, however they are phrased, are political and the delegates of member States participating in debates are political appointees deciding on their votes in accordance with the political instructions they receive from their political masters. This was clearly indicated by the International Court of Justice in its advisory opinion on *Reparation for Injuries Suffered in the Service of the United Nations*[72]: "[T]he Organisation is a political body, charged with political tasks of an important character, and covering a wide field . . . and in dealing with its Members it employs political means."

It must also be remembered that over the years the nature of the United Nations has changed. With the increase in the number of members, particularly with the admission of a multitude of newly independent States many of which have a grudging attitude towards their former imperialist rulers and their allies in the developed world, many of the resolutions of the United Nations reflect this antagonism and indicate a desire to give vent to ideological belief rather than any intent to examine issues objectively or to uphold the rule of law.[73] As one commentator has expressed it[74]: "The United Nations seems to be more adept at orchestrating tensions than at calming tempers; more adroit at arousing passions and inflaming prejudice than at achieving accommodation; more artful at acting out real or simulated rage than at resolving disputes. And the world body is never more vulnerable than when called upon to deal with issues that involve moral considerations and moral actualities. Human aggression, violence and destruction are unleashed when nations seek and find sanction to act freely and punitively in the name of humanity's ideals."

The only trouble with the United Nations' attitude to the Argentine adventure in the Falklands was a willingness to indulge in verbal condemnation of the act of aggression, but no willingness "to act

---

[72] (The Bernadotte Case) [1949] I.C.J. 174, 179.
[73] See, *e.g.* Green, "The Impact of the New States on International Law," in *Law and Society* (1975), Chap. V.
[74] Moskowitz, *The Roots and Reaches of United Nations Actions and Decisions* (1980), p. 171, see, also, pp. 2, 7–8.

freely and punitively in the name of humanity's ideals," if they be understood as synonymous with the maintenance of peace and the rule of law. At no time was the United Nations willing to take any form of sanction against the Argentine, even though the United States and the members of the European Economic Community were prepared to support Britain and treat the Argentine as an aggressor.[75] Insofar as the British reaction to Argentina's military activites is concerned, the United Kingdom was fully entitled under Article 51 of the United Nations Charter to resort to such measures as were considered necessary by way of self-defence in response to an armed attack, in whatsoever part of its territory that attack occurred. The fact that military action had ceased because of the local surrender in no way inhibited the United Kingdom from taking the requisite action until the Security Council itself took such action "as it deems necessary in order to maintain or restore international peace and security." The fact that the Security Council had called for a cessation of hostilities without putting forward any alternative action of its own did not mean that the United Kingdom was under any obligation to cease its activities directed at restoring the *status quo ante*, particularly as the Council's call for Argentine withdrawal had been ignored, leaving Britain with force as the only means of restoring its own rights and, at the same time, acting as the enforcing authority to give effect to the withdrawal call of the Security Council.[76]

The activities of the Security Council in this matter gradually weakened in that, while the original resolution called for a cease-fire and immediate withdrawal of Argentine forces, later proposals omitted the latter requirement and as a result failed to be adopted in accordance with Article 27(3) of the Charter, in that both the United Kingdom and the United States possessed the right of "veto" so that their negative votes prevented adoption of any resolution. In the meantime, the United Kingdom put forward proposals which indicated a willingness to discuss the future of the Islands, including the issue of sovereignty, so long as there was no prejudgment of the question, and so long as the freedoms and rights of the islanders were preserved, and they were enabled "to continue to participate in the administration of their affairs and to ensure that they could express freely their wishes about the future of the Islands, in accordance with the principle of self-determination."[77]

---

[75] See *e.g.* HMSO, *Falkland Islands: Negotiations for a Peaceful Settlement* (May 21, 1982) (Perl, *op. cit.* (in note 1 above), p. 485).

[76] See, *e.g.* letter by Professor Rosalyn Higgins, *The Times* (April 30, 1982).

[77] Perl, *op. cit.* (in note 1 above), p. 486.

In the interim Britain was prepared to accept a temporary United Nations administration. Argentina refused to accept such arrangements arguing that Britain was not prepared to withdraw its own forces—ignoring the fact that such withdrawal would leave the Islands open to a second Argentine occupation at any time that Argentina saw fit to act in this way—and while "Argentina had been prepared not to place any preconditions on the negotiations in view of its confidence in its legitimate authority, recognised by both OAS[78] and the Non-Aligned Movement; however, the United Kingdom had sought to place conditions on the negotiating process by insisting on a United Nations administration which would retain a colonial administrative structure which could prejudge and place conditions on the substantive issues."[79] The record of the United Nations throughout the "war" is by no means impressive. With the termination of active hostilities consequent on the Argentine surrender on June 14 there was no longer any need for positive action by the Security Council. However, the issue remained on the agenda of the United Nations and was included in that of the 1982 session of the General Assembly at the request of 20 Central and Latin American countries which sought a continuance of the negotiations under United Nations auspices, and in due course the Assembly adopted a resolution calling for further negotiations with the Secretary-General of the United Nations undertaking a renewed mission of good offices.[80] The resolution was adopted by 90 votes to 12, with 52 abstentions. With the exception of the United Kingdom, New Zealand and Oman, the negative votes were cast by smaller Commonwealth countries.

Although there had been no declaration of war,[81] the two parties were bound to recognise the relevance of the law of armed conflict. Argentina and the United Kingdom are parties to the four Geneva (Red Cross) Conventions of 1949. Article 2 of each of these provides[82]: " . . . the present Convention shall apply to all cases of declared war or *of any other armed conflict* which may arise between two or more of the High Contracting Parties, *even if the state of war is not recognized by one of them.* The Convention shall also apply to all cases of *partial or total occupation of the territory* of a High Con-

---

[78] Res. April 27, 1982, *The Times* (April 28, 1982).

[79] Working Paper prepared by UN Secretariat, August 10, 1982 (Perl, *op. cit.* (in note 1 above), pp. 600–601).

[80] November 6, 1982 (*ibid.* pp. 677–681).

[81] Hague Convention III, 1907.

[82] I—Wounded and Sick; II—Wounded, Sick and Shipwrecked; III—Prisoners of War; IV—Civilians, Schindler and Toman, *The Laws of Armed Conflicts* (1981), pp. 307, 336, 361, 433, respectively (italics added).

tracting Party, *even if* the said occupation *meets with no armed resistance . . . .*" Despite this, initial errors were made by the United
Kingdom in construing its obligations during the conflict. Originally,
Prime Minister Thatcher was of the opinion, presumably in accordance with advice given her by the relevant legal officers, that personnel taken during the fighting were "not prisoners of war. A state of
war does not exist between ourselves and the Argentine."[83] Fortunately, her advisers subsequently reminded themselves of the 1949
Prisoners of War Convention and changed the advice given. Even
so, they appeared prepared to ignore the obligation that all prisoners must be treated in accordance with the Convention and were
originally prepared to make Commander Astiz, commander of the
Argentine garrison at Grytviken, South Georgia, available for questioning by both Sweden and France,[84] in relation to alleged crimes
committed by him against their nationals in Argentina before the
outbreak of the conflict, conduct in fact which had nothing to do
with the conflict or with Great Britain. To this end he was held separately on Ascension Island.[85] Had this intention been carried
through it would have been improper in the light of Article 85 of the
Convention. This provides that "Prisoners of war prosecuted *under
the laws of the Detaining Power* for acts committed prior to capture
shall retain, even if convicted, the benefits of the present Conventions."[86] There is no provision in the Convention for the extradition
of prisoners in respect of what might be regarded as ordinary criminal acts committed against a third State, nor does the Convention
allow for a prisoner to be made available for interrogation by any
authority other than that of the Detaining Power, its allies or the
International Committee of the Red Cross, although it is open to
the Detaining Power to ask him whatever questions it pleases.[87]
There is, however, no obligation for him to provide any information
beyond his name, rank, date of birth and army number.[88] Astiz
refused to answer any other questions and was repatriated.[89]

One action by the British in relation to their own repatriated prisoners raises questions as to legality. British personnel captured during the initial Argentine assault were repatriated by Argentina and
some of them were returned to the Falklands where they partici-

---

[83] Mrs. Thatcher, House of Commons (April 26, 1982), *The Times* (April 27, 1982).
[84] For the French request, see *The Times* (May 13, 1982).
[85] Mrs. Thatcher, House of Commons (May 13, 1982), *The Times* (May 14, 1982).
[86] Italics added.
[87] Letter by Professor Col. Draper, *The Times* (May 19, 1982).
[88] Convention, Art. 17.
[89] *The Times* (May 26, June 1, 1982). See, also, Int'l Comm. of Jurists, *The Review*, Nr. 28
(June 1982), p. 3.

pated in combat as members of the British expeditionary force. *Prima facie* this would appear to be contrary to Article 117 of the Convention which provides that "no repatriated person may be employed on active military service." The problem here is that the Part (IV) of the Convention which relates to the question is concerned with the repatriation of the seriously wounded and sick and of those whose imprisonment has continued over a long period of time. For the main part the arrangements for repatriation are envisaged as being with the assistance of a neutral Power, or the International Committee of the Red Cross. In fact, prior to the repatriation of Argentine military personnel and civilians examination of their condition and of their treatment by the British was undertaken by the Red Cross.[90] Insofar as able-bodied prisoners are concerned, and the majority of the British personnel were unwounded, their repatriation depends upon special agreements made by the parties to the conflict. If such agreements make no reference to the non-employment of the personnel concerned in further combat duties, it may be argued that such employment is not forbidden.[91]

On one matter the British were meticulous in their observance of the Convention. Under Article 121 of the Convention "Every death or serious injury of a prisoner of war caused or suspected to have been caused by a sentry, . . . or any other person, . . . shall be immediately followed by an official enquiry by the Detaining Power. A communication on this subject shall be sent immediately to the Protecting Power. . . . If the enquiry indicates the guilt of one or more persons, the Detaining Power shall take all measures for the prosecution of the person or persons responsible." At the end of April it was announced that an Argentine prisoner had died in a "serious incident" and as a result of the inquiry it was ascertained that he had been shot by a British soldier and buried with full military honours. The Brazilian authorities as the Protecting Power and the International Committee of the Red Cross were informed.[92] At the court of enquiry it was ascertained that the incident occurred when Argentine naval prisoners were helping to move a disabled submarine. The guards had been instructed to shoot if there was any attempt to scuttle or sabotage the vessel, and one of the guards misconstrued the action of a petty officer who moved to turn the controls in compliance with an order to blow air into the ballast tanks. The guard fired under the impression that the officer concerned was

---

[90] *The Times* (May 10, 1982).
[91] See, also, letters by Shaw and Draper, *ibid.* April 29, June 8, 1982).
[92] *Ibid.* (April 29, May 13, 1982).

attempting to sink the submarine, endangering all on board. As a result it was considered no blame could be attached to the soldier concerned.[93]

Perhaps the most serious allegation of a breach of faith, if not of law, directed against the United Kingdom concerned the sinking of the Argentine cruiser *The General Belgrano*. At the beginning of the operations Britain proclaimed an exclusion zone of 200 miles around the Islands. This was to apply to the craft of all nations[94]: " . . . the exclusion zone will apply not only to Argentine warships and naval auxiliaries but also to any other ship, whether naval or merchant vessel, which is operating in support of the illegal occupation of the Falkland Islands by Argentine forces.

"The zone will also apply to any aircraft, whether military or civil, which is operating in support of the Argentine occupation. Any ship and any aircraft, whether military or civil, which is found within this zone without authority from the Ministry of Defence in London will be regarded as operating in support of the illegal occupation and will therefore be regarded as hostile and will be liable to be attacked by British forces . . . .*These measures are without prejudice to the right of the United Kingdom to take additional measures which may be needed in exercise of its rights of self-defence* under Article 51 of the United Nations Charter."

The Belgrano was sunk with heavy loss of life outside the declared zone but not far from it. The sinking was carried out by submarine and there was some confusion as to whether this was a decision by the officer on the spot or by the Ministry of Defence. But this distinction is irrelevant. A cruiser is obviously part of the belligerent forces and could only have been in the area in which it was sunk as part of its duties as such. It was perfectly reasonable for the authorities ordering the sinking to act on the presumption that the ship was or was intended to become engaged in the operations, and was in any case, as a naval cruiser, a legitimate object of attack, especially as "the Royal Navy was convinced she was about to attack the British aircraft carriers, and feared she was part of a three-pronged naval assault on the task force."[95] Moreover, the proclamation in no way gave immunity to war vessels outside the declared zone and in any case reserved to Great Britain the right to

---

[93] *Ibid.* (July 2, 1982). See, also, *ibid.* April 12, 1983, for report of the killing by a British sergeant of an Argentine prisoner who had been badly burned in an explosion and was shot to put him out of his misery. "The facts [were] explained to Argentine officers who accepted them and did not pursue them further."

[94] *Ibid.* (April 29, 1982) (italics added).

[95] *Ibid.* (October 4, 1982).

take any additional measures considered necessary in exercise of its right of self-defence.[96]

Accusations of disregard of the law of armed conflict were also directed against Argentina. There were allegations that napalm shells and "dum-dum" bullets were found among the munitions left behind by the Argentine forces.[97] Moreover, it was alleged that when *H.M.S. Endurance* went in to take the surrender of Southern Thule her personnel were told to land "where troops were ready to surrender, but a trap had been prepared. The figure H painted on a helicopter landing strip was to lure them into a minefield."[98] It was also reported by "Jeremy Hands, an Independent Television News correspondent, . . . that at least one British soldier was killed at Goose Green when Argentine soldiers raised the white flag of surrender and then opened fire as troops came forward to take them prisoner.[99] It has even been claimed that, regardless of the official citation of his Victoria Cross, the British soldier shot in these circumstances was, in fact, Lt. Col. Herbert Jones.[1]

It has already been pointed out[2] that an occupant is obliged to comply with the law of armed conflict even if there has been no opposition to his occupation, and by Article 6 of Geneva Convention IV (Civilians) this obligation continues until the occupation terminates. It was reported that the Argentine occupying forces detained local settlers, including the medical officer, that homes and property were ransacked and looted and that "Nazi tactics" had been employed.[3] More serious than these apparent breaches of the law was the threat by the Argentine authorities to deny immunity to British hospital ships, in particular *H.M.S. Canberra*.[4] The threat to regard this and other vessels as legitimate targets was, however, never carried out.

Shortly after the Argentine surrender, and once it was clear that Argentina was not about to resume hostilities, having in fact informed the United Kingdom, through the Swiss, that a "de facto cessation of hostilities" existed[5] some four weeks after the cease fire, arrangements were made for the repatriation of surviving Argentine prisoners, the *junta* having previously ignored requests to

---

[96] *Ibid.* (May 12, 1982).
[97] *Ottawa Citizen*, June 2, *The Times* (June 15, 1982).
[98] Statement by Lieut. David O'Connell, *The Times* (August 21, 1982).
[99] *Ottowa Citizen* (June 3, 1982).
[1] *Ibid.* (June 2, 1982).
[2] Text to note 82 above.
[3] *The Times*, (May 19, June 1, 7, 1982).
[4] *Ibid.* (May 24, 31, 1982).
[5] *Ibid.* (July 13, 1982).

grant safe passage to the British vessels that would be used in repatriating such personnel.[6] Despite the end of hostilities, the British have continued to maintain a "no-go" zone round the Islands,[7] while Argentina has refused to "make peace." As a result there has been no advance towards a negotiated settlement and both sides have maintained their respective claims.

A variety of proposals have been made to solve the problem, regardless of the validity of either side's claims to sovereignty. Among such suggestions have been the transfer of the territory to Argentina, a condominium, a lease-back, United Nations and even United States administration. None, however, has proved acceptable and the situation continues to fester the relations between Great Britain and Latin America. So far the British Government has declared it is not prepared even to discuss sovereignty until there is a guarantee that the rights of the inhabitants will be protected and their wishes properly taken into consideration. In the meantime a British garrison remains. There have been reports of Argentine probing expeditions, which to date have not been followed through. There is no guarantee that if they were the British garrison would be able to deal with them. It has now been stated, in fact, that under the proposals in the 1981 Defence White Paper it would be impossible in the 1990s to maintain or mount a Falklands-type operation.[8] It is to be hoped that if Argentina mounted a further act of aggression, even its political sympathisers would agree that such acts cannot be tolerated if the rule of law is to prevail. Equally it is to be hoped that in such circumstances they would now be prepared to take the necessary steps to restore the status quo at least temporarily. It is also to be hoped, should there be a recurrence, that the leaders of the English churches would abstain from proclaiming that the response constituted a just war. Such contentions by both Cardinal Hume and the Archbishop of Canterbury[9] cast doubts upon the commitment of the English churches to peace and the rejection of war, and even raise doubts over their attitude to nuclear weapons, particularly as it is known that some British vessels participating in the Falkland campaign were so armed. In the meantime it should be noted that in December 1983, on the establishment of a democratically elected civilian government in Argentina, Britain extended its congratulations and good wishes for the

---

[6] *Ibid.* (June 7, 1982).

[7] A year after the cessation of hostilities Britain was still maintaining a ban on the import of books from Argentina, *Globe and Mail* (Toronto), (September 7, 1983).

[8] *Ibid.* (August 24, 1983).

[9] *Ibid.* (April 30, May 3, 8, 1982).

future of the new president, thus holding out promise of a relaxation in tension.

While there seems little doubt that the British claim based on prolonged occupation and administration seems to be fully in accord with generally accepted rules of international law with regard to the acquisition of sovereignty, it must not be overlooked that these rules are considered by the new countries to be somewhat out of date and representative of a colonial ideology. There may be much truth in the contention that self-determination for the Falklands means that the decision as to sovereignty should rest with the inhabitants. On the other hand we must not overlook the fact that there is no agreed definition of self-determination, and "in his study on the right of self-determination for the UN Commission on Human Rights (UN doc. E/CN.4/Sub.2/204 paras 267–79 [3 July 1978]), Mr. Aureliu Cristescu formulated the 'elements of a definition' which have emerged from discussions in the United Nations. The relevant elements are that the term 'people' denotes a social entity possessing a clear identity and its own characteristics,[10] and that it implies a relationship with a territory, even if the people in question has been wrongfully expelled from it and artificially replaced by another population.

"If these principles are accepted, it would seem that Argentina as well as Britain can make a claim based on the principle of self-determination . . . . [But be that as it may, t]heir claim does not, of course, entitle Argentina to attempt to seize the islands by force. If such a right were accepted the fragile peace of the world would be even more seriously endangered, having regard to the numbers of disputed territories and frontiers throughout the world."[11]

Not only would international peace be endangered by such methods or the adoption of the Cristescu definition of self-determination, but so would every country in which there is an aboriginal population claiming that it is the "original people" wrongly displaced from its homeland by alien invading settlers.

---

[10] See the World Court Definition of a "community," *Greco-Bulgarian Communities* (1930) P.C.I.J. Ser. B, Nr. 17, 21 (2 Hudson, *World Court Reports*, pp. 641, 653–654).
[11] Int'l. Commn. of Jurists, *loc. cit.* (in note 89 above), p. 24.

AMERICA'S DIPLOMATIC INITIATIVE IN THE MIDDLE EAST

PROSPECTS AND PERILS

By

ROBERT G. NEUMANN

CONTINUITY, consistency and predictability are the hallmarks of a successful foreign policy. But to apply these in the United States political system is extraordinarily difficult.

Each change in administration brings to office a considerable number of inexperienced people who tend to view their predecessors with suspicion and disdain. Campaign oratory has emphasised change and new directions, which the new team attempts to apply. Yet, in foreign affairs, facts do not change because of elections. Many factors are beyond the control of even the most powerful national governments. After a year or so, every new American administration discovers that it must deal with the same facts as its predecessors and its conclusions are unlikely to be very different.

Thus, even in the United States, there is continuity—but a continuity interrupted every four or eight years when new directions are sought, not found or found wanting, followed by a return to the main line of past administrations.

I—EARLY ABERRATIONS

The Reagan Administration is no exception. It focused strongly and primarily on the East-West conflict and its first priority was to restore the long neglected defence structure of the United States, believing that "a window of vulnerability" was bound to exist for several years during which the threat of Soviet aggression would be at its maximum.

It is not the purpose of this article to examine whether the Reagan Administration's thesis was correct or not but rather to look at the consequences of that thesis for United States Middle-East policy. There is little doubt that those consequences produced an initial period of misdirection and confusion. The American side, led by former Secretary of State Alexander M. Haig, believed so strongly in the priority of the Soviet danger that it felt the Palestinian problem could be consigned to a secondary place, and also that in some fashion a strategic consensus (which was never defined) could gradually emerge among the nations of the Middle East—a consensus to counter the Soviet threat. This orientation was also encouraged by those supporters of Israel who welcomed an opportunity to push the Palestinian issue away from the centre of the stage.

Only gradually did it dawn on the new Administration that nobody in the Middle Eastern region shared this assessment, neither Arabs nor Israelis. The Israelis, knowing American politics better than the Arabs, frequently played up to the American fear of the Soviet Union. But, as clearly indicated by former Israeli Defence Minister Ariel Sharon's speech of December 15, 1981, in Tel Aviv, the Israeli government regarded the Soviet threat as an indirect one, with the Soviets benefiting from regional subversion and corrosion rather than from frontal attack.

The Reagan Administration began to realise that sharp regional conflicts and in particular the unsolved Palestinian problem consigned to the realm of illusion any hope for a "strategic consensus." President Reagan became increasingly irritated by the growing stridency in the declarations of Israeli Prime Minister Menachem Begin and Defence Minister Sharon. However, further consequences of his irritation were prevented by the influence of the strongly pro-Israeli Haig who regarded Israel as a military asset in any possible conflict with the Soviet Union. The American government further felt a need for caution in view of the then approaching date (April 25, 1982) for the evacuation of the last remnant from the Sinai Peninsula under the Camp David agreement. The Administration was most eager, as were the Egyptians, to do nothing which would give Israel an excuse for thwarting or delaying the evacuation.

General relief was experienced by everyone that that event finally took place on time. But by then there was growing apprehension about increasing tension in Lebanon. It was hardly a secret that Israel was looking for a plausible cause to intervene despite the fact that Northern Galilee had been exceptionally free from PLO attack ever since the summer of 1981, when Ambassador Philip Habib was able to negotiate a cease fire agreement.

Among President Reagan's advisers there were sharp differences concerning the manner in which to counter that threat of conflict. Again Haig generally prevailed in preventing greater American pressure on Israel. To be sure, American pressure on Israel did increase as the signs of an impending Israeli invasion multiplied, but the relatively muted tone and the known position of Haig must have given the Israeli leaders the impression that the American government would accept military action albeit grudgingly. And even after hostilities began, Haig's frequent press briefings created the impression among both Arabs and Israelis that perhaps the American government was either not wholly opposed to the course of events or at least saw "opportunities" for greater stability in the Middle East in the wake of a quick Israeli surgical strike into Lebanon and the destruction of the PLO.

Increasingly Reagan's advisers realised that Haig's policies brought the entire Arab world, including the most pro-Western and moderate countries into ever sharper conflict with the United States. At the same time there can be little doubt that the President, a warmly humanitarian man, was appalled by the daily spectacle of the destruction and suffering caused by the invasion of Lebanon. Moreover, that war, like no other event before it, underlined the importance of the Palestinian problem and its central place in any scheme for peace in the Middle East.

II—AMERICAN POLICY REVERTS TO EARLIER POSITIONS

Haig's removal from office put an end to these divergencies inside the Administration and refocused American Middle-East policy on the Palestinian problem as it had existed towards the end of the Carter Administration. Eventually this found its expression in President Reagan's speech of September 1, 1982. That speech was criticised for having come one and a half years too late. Both in Europe and the Arab world there was disappointment that it remained within the Camp David framework. The government of Israel accused the President of departing from it. But late as the speech was, it benefited from a significant shift in American public opinion which began with the growing criticism of Israel's harsh occupation measures and grew steadily as the war in Lebanon appeared on America's television screens. Thus, when the President spoke, he could count on a broader support basis than any American leader before him in addressing the problems of the Middle East. Had the President gone further, in advocating for instance an independent Palestinian State or immediate direct contacts with the Palestinian Liberation Organisation (PLO), or an abandonment of the Camp David framework, that support would have rapidly diminished.

In particular, the Camp David agreement has remained popular in America. What was significant was not that President Reagan retained the Camp David framework but that he restored America's original understanding of it. That agreement, as will be remembered, was firmly based on United Nations Security Council Resolution 242, which had envisaged the withdrawal of Israeli forces from most of the occupied regions coupled with the recognition of Israel's existence and security by the Arab States. To prepare the population of the West Bank and Gaza for this eventual reversion of the

territories to Arab control, an autonomous régime was to be negotiated as a transitional arrangement.

Subsequent difficulties revealed what should have been known
earlier, namely that there never had been a true agreement at Camp
David. Former President Carter's memoirs show how strongly
Begin had resisted any mention of Resolution 242. When that
failed, he reiterated with great emphasis his previous interpretation
that the West Bank and Gaza, or "Judea and Samaria" as he preferred to call them by their biblical names, had been "liberated" not
"occupied" territories and that Resolution 242 therefore did not
apply to them.

Thus, while the American and Egyptian interpretation of the
Camp David agreement was that the autonomy period was to
lead to the return of the occupied regions to Arab control, the
Israeli interpretation detached the transitional arrangements from
their final disposition of the land and left them hanging in a
vacuum with the clear intention that the outcome would be
Israel's annexation of those lands in more or less open fashion.
What President Reagan's speech did was to reassert strongly the
American interpretation and to restore Resolution 242 to its original central place in the Camp David agreement, a process which
the President specified in the felicitious phrase "territories for
peace."

It marked a return of America's foreign policy to that of all its
predecessors since 1967, a recognition that the twin pillars of Resolution 242, return of land, and recognition and security for Israel,
had been joined by the awareness that Palestinian nationalism was
here to stay. As long as that nationalism remained unfulfilled, it
would remain a major source of destabilisation in the Middle East
and a rallying point for all dissident elements and movements. Its
fulfilment could be achieved only by giving it a territorial base, however reduced, *i.e.* the West Bank. In fact one might even say that
the Israelis, by waging a campaign to have Jordan declared "the
Palestinian State," implicitly recognised that argument even if they
do not want it applied to the West Bank. All concerned had come a
long way since 1967. In the original 1967 version of Resolution 242
Palestinians were not even mentioned; the UN Resolution merely
spoke of "refugees."

In this context Prime Minister Begin's violent reaction to the Reagan speech was fully understandable. Begin had never departed
from his insistence that the West Bank and Gaza must "forever
remain Israel." He had faced down President Carter at Camp
David. Although settlement movements on the West Bank started
under the preceding Labour Governments, it was under Begin's

régime that 75 per cent. of the present settlements took root on the West Bank.

To return a moment to Israel's invasion of Lebanon, this had been long planned. Initially its announced aim was a security zone adjacent to Northern Israel, but it quickly became clear that Israel's objectives went must farther. Its true aim was the destruction of the PLO as both a political and military movement with the expectation that the Arab population of the West Bank would then have no alternative but to emigrate or to turn to co-operation with Israel through the Israeli sponsored "village leagues." Also Israel expected to help establish in Lebanon a Christian Maronite government with strong ties to Israel. In the meantime, the Israeli government unleashed a determined campaign which proclaimed that "Jordan is Palestine," *i.e.* that a Palestinian State already existed in Jordan and Palestinians ought to settle there. This in time would invariably lead to destabilisation of that country. If that were to get out of hand the Israelis would be there to impose their version of order. It is perhaps not too far fetched to look farther, to the time when Jordan would come under Israeli pressure; the Israelis expected this in turn would cause shock waves transmitted to Saudi Arabia to frighten that country into withdrawing financial support from the PLO and other Arab movements.

All this was now endangered by the Reagan plan, which came at the time when the opposition to Israel's Lebanon adventure was growing inside Israel and was causing significant divisions within the American Jewish community. The Reagan speech threatened all of Israel's gains in Lebanon. It seemed therefore essential to Begin not only to defeat the Reagan proposal but to do so in such a manner that no future American government would feel encouraged to go in the same direction. He wanted the Reagan plan to go the way of the only dimly remembered Rogers plan of 1969.

As 1982 drew to a close, the diplomatic lines were clearly drawn. The Arab States had wanted to go farther than the Reagan plan. At the Arab summit meeting in Fez the Arabs had reaffirmed their advocacy of an independent Palestinian State and the PLO had emerged from the ashes of its military destruction to an unprecedented political status in which it not only held virtual veto power over the other Arabs but also saw the consolidation of Yasser Arafat's power with that many faceted movement. But in asserting their objectives, the Arab countries were careful not to condemn the Reagan initiative. For that they were able not only to marshal the support of the moderates but also of other Arabs including the PLO. Only Libya stayed away in a huff. Egypt, still outside the Arab fold, was not invited.

The Arabs in Fez realised clearly that the Reagan formula of "territories for peace" shifted both their own ideas and those of Reagan into a common diplomatic perimeter. Both envisaged eventual return of the occupied regions to Arab control. Moreover, King Hassan II of Morocco, speaking as conference chairman at the close of the Fez summit mentioned "non-belligerency" as the next step. And both King Hussein of Jordan and PLO Chairman Yassir Arafat tried to work out a common framework for co-operation between them, clearly designed to satisfy President Reagan's requirement of an "association" between Palestinians and Jordan.

But on the other side remained the unequivocal "no" of Israel. The American government had expected this but had been too optimistic in hoping that it might be able to overcome it in a relatively short period. In 1956 the Ben-Gurion government had grudgingly given in to President Eisenhower's firm resolve and had backed down, as had the United Kingdom and France, then in league with Israel. But to Ben-Gurion the retention of occupied regions had been a tactically desirable situation, not an article of faith as it was to Begin.

III—THE JORDANIAN OPTION

To overcome this problem American diplomacy developed the following tactical line: King Hussein of Jordan had always been considered crucial to peace in the Middle East and this was stated in the Camp David agreement. President Reagan's "territories for peace" formula was unequivocal and Reagan had not been known to waver as had his predecessor, Carter. If, based on these assurances and American resolve, King Hussein could be brought to the negotiating table, Begin, so it was argued, could not refuse to do likewise. The ensuing diplomatic climate would create irresistible pressures in the world at large and in Israel proper either to bring Begin around or to cause a change in Israel's government.

This assumption undoubtedly appeared too optimistic an expectation for the highly experienced King Hussein. He had no doubt about President Reagan's intentions and his personal relationship with the President was infinitely better than the bitter one which characterised his dealings with Carter. But although Reagan's mounting irritation with Begin was evident, the President still hesitated to approve concrete sanctions against Israel's immobility. There was always the danger that to do too much too fast might unify divided Israel and deprive President Reagan of the above-mentioned broad support for his policy.

To Hussein, sympathetic as he was to the President's design, going to the negotiating table could easily become a trap. What counted for him was not whether the Israelis would come to the table but what they would do there. And if they were simply to come in order to reiterate, endlessly, their determination to keep the West Bank in their grip, Hussein would merely be made to look foolish and his rule over a country which already has a Palestinian majority might be endangered. He could come to the table only if he were reasonably assured that the subject for discussion would not only be the "transitional" autonomy provision, but also at least in broad outlines the eventual disposition of the territory. Or at the very least it would have to be made certain that eventual disposition remained open and had not been definitively foreclosed by Israel. That, however, Hussein could not provide. Only the Americans could if anyone could. As minimal evidence that this was indeed possible there had to be an absolute freeze on further Jewish settlements on the West Bank and on the enlargement of those already existing. In addition, the King demanded the reiteration, by all parties, of the principles of UN Resolution 242 as everybody in the world except Begin understands it, as well as preconditions which would make it certain that any discussion of "transitional" provisions would be limited in time and that the eventual negotiations would speedily come to the main point—the future of the West Bank. In addition, King Hussein was determined to remain strictly within the confines of the Rabat summit negotiations of 1974 which had recognised the PLO as "sole representative of the Palestinian people." He expected to move forward therefore only if he could reach an agreement with the PLO; contrary to many public press assertions, King Hussein never aspired to a mandate to negotiate alone for the Palestinians, nor were the PLO leaders likely to give him such a mandate. To do otherwise would be unrealistic within the Arab world and would also endanger the King's position in his own country where a large number of Palestinians reside.

Prime Minister Begin and other Israeli government leaders had repeatedly reiterated that "King Hussein should come to the negotiating table without preconditions." However, that conveniently overlooked the fact that preconditions already existed, namely those of Israel, whose government has never tired of claiming that the West Bank belonged to Israel "forever." Hence the above-mentioned preconditions which King Hussein and the PLO leaders had in mind if the Jordanians and the Palestinians were not to be backed into the kind of process which had been encountered by Anwar Sadat and the Americans. Sadat at least obtained the return of the Sinai Peninsula but Hussein, in a weaker position, could not afford such a situation. There had to be reasonable expectations that an acceptable outcome was at least realistically possible. However, it was equally clear that Prime Minister Begin had no intention whatsoever of relinquishing his control over the West Bank which had been a central aspiration for him and for his movement throughout his entire life. Hussein's preconditions were therefore bound to be rejected out of hand by Begin.

Even a successful outcome of the Hussein-Arafat negotiations for a joint negotiating team and formula could have produced only Israeli objection. The value of such a declaration would nevertheless have been politically very high. It would have made it possible for the Reagan Administration to put increasing pressure on Israel and it would have created a lively discussion both in Israel and among America's Jewish population as half of Israel and most American Jews have never been too sympathetic to Begin's annexationist aspirations.

IV—Confusion Over Preconditions

But somehow the Reagan Administration remained optimistic that some formula could ensue which would result in actual negotiations. Therefore the PLO leadership and Hussein thought it necessary to evolve a realistic framework for their co-operation and negotiation, and not merely one which would produce a political document without immediate negotiating effect. This lack of realism contributed vastly to the failure of the Hussein-Arafat talks. Arafat would have greatly preferred an independent Palestinian State and regarded a Jordanian association only as a transitional and not as a final step. Hussein realised that such a provision would place insurmountable obstacles in the way of any negotiations and was more than President Reagan could politically support. Moreover the PLO wanted to be recognised and represented as such on the team, as co-equal to King Hussein and his Jordanian advisers, but in particular they insisted that negotiations should deal with the "Palestinian issue" as a whole and not merely with those Palestinians who lived on the West Bank.

Syria was opposed to such close relations between the PLO and Jordan and mobilised more radical PLO groups and leaders against such an agreement. A further and decisive detriment was also that America's diplomacy had been extremely slow in moving after the President's speech of September 1 and had given no evidence that it was willing or capable to put the kind of pressure on Israel which in the views of virtually all Arabs would be necessary to reopen the question of the future of the West Bank. President Reagan gave strong expressions of support to King Hussein, but his statement that he would "do his best" was considered insufficient evidence that "his best" would include such pressures. As the credibility of America once again declined, the PLO leadership once again turned toward the assertion of its unity rather than its willingness to take risks for a venture which appeared increasingly dubious.

Thus the negotiations failed. Nobody benefited except Israel and although everybody blamed everybody else there was plenty of blame to go about. The United States was blamed for its relative inactivity after President Reagan's September speech and its failure to gain credibility among the Arabs by its permissive attitude towards Israel. America in turn blamed the Palestinians for not seizing the chance to make progress and creating political conditions favourable to their cause and especially to the Palestinians on the West Bank. Yasser Arafat in particular was blamed for not having had courage to risk a split in his ranks in order to move toward a more responsible position. Hussein was blamed for not striking out on his own and the Saudis for not putting sufficient pressure on the PLO. Everybody thought everybody else should take these difficult and dangerous steps. As much hope had been aroused—well beyond reason—there was now disappointment and bitterness. Both President Reagan and Secretary Shultz placed principal responsibility on the PLO and wondered aloud whether the PLO was truly the representative of the Palestinians or whether, having let this opportunity slip through its fingers, it deserved to exercise such a responsibility.

These remarks can be excused as understandable human emotions but they have little basis in reality. The PLO is representative of the Palestinians because it was the banner carrier and there is no one else to take its place. During the Carter Administration Brzezinski made a famous comment, in a comparable situation, "bye-bye PLO," but it was not long before it was realised there was no way around the PLO if Palestinian issues were to be discussed. Moreover, it is a historical fact that exile movements find it very difficult to achieve unity and preserve it; when the movements tend to fragment before action can be taken. There are always revolutionaries who live in a permanent world of violence and revolution and know no other world.

The best that can be said is, that the end of this endeavour did not reflect well on the tactical skill and understanding of the Arabs' concern, especially the PLO leadership. However, in the Middle East nothing ever returns to square one. The attempt by Hussein and Arafat, while not successful, did not exclude a similar action from being resumed at some future period.

V—THE FUTURE OF THE REAGAN PLAN

Does this mean that President Reagan's policy is doomed? Not necessarily but it is likely that it could not be expected to succeed while Menachem Begin remained Prime Minister of Israel. Therefore the target of Reagan's speeches and of American diplomacy was the Israeli public—Israel's public opinion—rather than the Likud government. To be sure there are people in the American government who still believe, against all evidence, that somehow Israel can be prevailed upon to negotiate a genuine settlement of the West Bank issue. I do not see any evidence whatsoever in the entire record of either Begin, or Shamir or the Likud party. Israel's public opinion is already strongly and feverishly debating the issues. But is more likely to be affected by the spectre of the gradual deterioration of its American lifeline than by the sudden shock of sanctions which might become counter-productive and arouse Israel's defiance. In other words the American policy has to be based on a far more long-range strategy than the United States Administration had ever expected. Such a calm, long-range strategy is not easy in the face of both Israeli and radical Arab recalcitrance.

It has often been said that America's ability to prevail in its Middle East policy has not been a question of capability but of will. In the case of the Reagan Administration one could add that this "will" is not so likely to be broken, as to be frittered away by a lack of strategy, by partial action being undertaken without reference to an overriding concept and by bogging down in innumerable skirmishes which prevent the American government from coming to grips with the main issue, the Palestine problem.

Unfortunately the Arab camp shows some of the same weaknesses. There the absence of Egypt, formerly the "natural" leader, is sorely felt and not quickly repaired. No other Arab country is able to fill this void. Iraq tried but then bogged down in its endless war with Iran. Saudi Arabia, while rich, is too vulnerable to step far beyond the Arab consensus. Syria, ruled by a minority sect, is forever struggling to divide its opponents, external and internal by an endless series of blocking actions. Jordan tried bravely but then failed to hammer out a common negotiating formula with the PLO, as we have seen. In the Arab camp, as in the American one, there are common aspirations but no common strategy. Thus opportunities are constantly missed, while unrealistic hopes for American action to bail everybody out rise, and then fall, in growing disappointment and dismay.

The government of Israel alone has a policy, a strategy and a game plan. But it is a policy which makes peace impossible. Its principal features are clear beyond any reasonable doubt. They are: to keep permanent control on the West Bank and Gaza, to defeat the Reagan plan thoroughly so as to discourage future American administrations from trying similar schemes again, to drive a wedge between America and any Arab country with which the United States seeks closer relations, with special emphasis on Saudi Arabia, in which Israel sees the archenemy who keep Palestinian and other Arab resistance alive. Beyond that, some of the more extreme Likid leaders would like to push the Palestinians out of the West Bank and into Jordan. That this would endanger King Hussein's stability has been recognised by Sharon, who has stated that if it were up to him he "would give King Hussein twenty-four hours to get out of Amman." Since nobody in his or her right mind would argue that Israel's security would be enhanced if Yasser Arafat were to rule in Amman instead of King Hussein, the only possible Israeli objective can be the destabilisation and "Lebanonisation" of Jordan with eventual Israeli intervention, in one form or another which would bring Israel, the overwhelming military power in the Middle East, to the borders of Saudi Arabia.

Neither the Reagan Administration nor any other American administration, Republican or Democratic can or will support this extreme Israeli policy. Its logic would create a permanent Israeli hegemony over the region, and neo-colonialism in the occupied territories which no Arab nation would accept. Its support by America would totally isolate the United States in the region and would give the Arab régimes no choice but to turn to the Soviet Union or lose out to more radical forces which would do the same.

Such a turn of events is clearly unacceptable to the United States and hence the policies of the Likud government are bound to come into conflict with every American government, Republican or Democratic. In view of Israel's large dependence on America, Begin's course is tenable only if he continues to destabilise the American political process, to use his influence with Congress to thwart or intimidate the Executive Branch and to bank on the fact that since President Eisenhower left office, no president has been able to win or complete two full terms. This breaks with the previous tradition according to which electorates were unlikely to deny a second term to an elected president who sought it. As long as one term presidents are the rule, the increasingly long American nomination and election process benefits the lobbies and special interest groups whose favour a candidate may feel he has to court.

The case of President Reagan, however, is different. By all indications the American electorate is primarily focused on the state of the economy which has unquestionably improved. Hence, if Reagan were to decide to seek a second term he would very probably win, regardless of any opposition on the part of Israel or the pro-Israeli lobby in America. In that event Reagan would have six years in which to implant his Middle East policy. In that longer period Israel's opportunity of derailing Reagan's policy would be much diminished, a fact which the Israeli electorate could not help but notice.

Everything that has been written above underlines the fact that peace in the Middle East is impossible unless Israel changes its policies towards the future of the West Bank. As the Likud government, committed as it is to the retention of the West Bank "forever," is unlikely to change its ways, that means that a different government would have to come to power in Israel. Recent opinion polls in Israel have shown for the first time that such a political change has become possible as the expected fruits of Israel's invasion of Lebanon continue to elude it. However, a basic change in Israel's policy constitutes at best the opening of the door to peace. To walk through that door considerable changes will have to occur on the Arab side as well.

In an overall sense the Arab and American positions have become closer. Both envisage a return of most of the West Bank to Arab control even though there is a difference between the two regarding the desirability or undesirability of establishing a separate Palestinian State. However, there is another significant point in which the two positions are not identical. The American position is and has been all along that if there is to be peace in the Middle East all sides will have, eventually, to negotiate with one another and that means to accept and recognise one another. Privately most Arabs would concede that point but even moderate Arabs still hope that America can "deliver" Israel and thereby make it unnecessary for the Arabs to take the politically difficult steps of recognition and negotiation. That is not the intention of the American government, nor is it desirable that the Arabs be taken off that hook. Not only is this necessary if peace negotiations are eventually to take place but also as peace requires more than just agreement on paper; it requires a process of conciliation which cannot take place without direct contact.

If all this were not difficult enough, the problem of removing foreign forces from Lebanon has immeasurably complicated the entire Middle East scene. In and of itself Lebanon is not directly tied into the quest for Middle East peace. However, the Reagan Administration bound them inextricably together by proclaiming that the withdrawal of foreign forces from Lebanon was its first priority, and by placing Ambassador Philip Habib in charge of

American diplomacy for both problems. This gave the Israelis and the Syrians an opportunity to defeat the Reagan policy by stalling endlessly on withdrawal from Lebanon. Habib's progress slowed down to a crawl thereby teaching the lesson (which should have been learned from the Strauss and Linowitz experiences) that shuttle diplomacy, when too long extended, becomes devalued.

VI—THE LEBANON QUAGMIRE

Realisation that shuttle diplomacy had run its course brought Secretary of State George Shultz to the Middle East. The resulting withdrawal agreement concluded between Israel, Lebanon and the United States on May 17, 1983 was hailed as a considerable achievement. In fact it made the situation worse.

Under American initiative, the United Kingdom, France, Italy and the United States had previously sent military contingents to Lebanon to provide a safety screen behind which the PLO fighters could safely be evacuated from the Beirut area. This had been accomplished successfully. Multinational forces were, in May 1983, persuaded to return to provide an aura of security and stability in which the new Lebanese government of President Amin Gemayel could broaden its base, bring Lebanon's nearly ten-year-old civil war to an end and extend its authority throughout the country after the withdrawal of all Israeli, Syrian and PLO forces would be assured. But the incredible complexity of Lebanese realities defeated that purpose.

For centuries Lebanon had been a cruel killing ground. Various groups identified by their religious denominations had staked out various areas for themselves. In their constant struggles they had acquired foreign patrons. Favoured by Europeans, especially French, one group, the Maronite Christians had acquired political and economic predominance. In 1943, as European domination of the Levant was predictably ending, an unwritten "national compact" had been concluded which reconfirmed the Maronite predominance by reserving the presidency for a Maronite and the prime ministership for a Sunni Moslem.

As the years passed, this national compact corresponded less and less to rapidly changing demographic realities. By the 1980s the Maronites had become a minority comprising no more than about 24 per cent. of Lebanon's population. On the Moslem side the hitherto predominant Sunnis had been overtaken by the Shiites who, with an estimated 28 per cent., had become the largest single group. The Druze remained small with 8 per cent. but retained their

close cohesion. Within each group many sub-groups and local chief-
tains fought each other.

More important than numbers was that the Shiites represented
the most disadvantaged classes and bitterly resented Maronite
domination and Sunni superiority. Virtually all non-Maronites
resented Maronite attempts to remain aloof from a broad Arab consensus. During the ten-year civil war the Maronites had been saved
from defeat by the Syrians whose intervention had been requested
by the pro-Syrian Maronite President Suleiman Franjieh and sanctioned by a decision of the Arab League. Meanwhile the sizeable
Palestinian refugee population had established a virtual State within
the State and various PLO groups had generally sided with the Moslems against the Maronites. It was not long before the Syrians
changed sides as Franjieh's weak successor, Elias Sarkis, was not
able to hold even the Maronites together.

Within the latter group the authoritarian and militant "Phalange"
forces had gained predominance under a young, brutal, but charis-
matic warlord, Bashir Gemayel. His militia had long been trained
and equipped by the Israelis who dreamed that the Phalange-domi-
nated Lebanon would conclude peace and a quasi-alliance with
Israel. This had been one of the objectives of Israel's invasion of
Lebanon. But in Sharon's final assault on Beirut the Phalange stood
aside. Then, in the aftermath of that terrible destruction, Lebanon
experienced a brief moment of national hope and unity when even
the Moslems threw themselves into Bashir Gemayel's arms. His
election as President by a parliament elected 13 years earlier might
have been meaningless in other periods but did represent an authen-
tic moment of national unity.

Sensing this, Bashir Gemayel attempted to distance himself from
his hitherto close ties to Israel, very much to Menachem Begin's
fury. But Bashir was assassinated shortly thereafter, before he was
able to assume office. It will forever remain conjectural whether he
might have been able to force upon his own Phalange meaningful
moves toward genuine reconciliation which would have required
then, as now, a sizeable shrinkage of Maronite power. In his place,
his older brother Amin Gemayel was elected President. For a short
moment he inherited his late brother's role as a symbol of unity.
Alas, that moment was all too brief. Amin had neither the drive nor
the control nor the skill of Bashir. He proved unable or unwilling,
perhaps both, to push for a rapid restructuring of the government.

By autumn 1983, the American Marines who, with their British,
French and Italian colleagues had come to Lebanon as neutral peace-
keepers and providers of stability, were perceived increasingly as
allies of the Maronites. This impression deepened when the Israelis,

realising the failure of their Lebanese policy, and under mounting domestic pressure, withdrew unilaterally from the Shouf Mountains, the heart of the Druze area, into which they had previously invited Phalangist infiltration. The result was a renewed outbreak of savage warfare between Druze and Phalangist, in which the latter were defeated. But as the Druze moved closer to Beirut, the partly-reconstituted Lebanese army made a stand at Sukh al Gharb and the American forces became even more partisan by supporting them through naval artillery. The situation became further confused through massive explosions which took many casualties at the American and French positions. It became difficult to draw clear distinctions between justified retaliation and partisan intervention.

In all this, Syria had become the controlling force in Lebanon and, in the eyes of the Reagan Administration, the principal obstacle. Syria's hold on the Lebanese groups opposing the Gemayal government was further enlarged by the terms of the Israeli–Lebanon–United States withdrawal agreement which did give Israel a quasi-peace treaty and special privileges in Lebanon. These were opposed by all Arab countries, including those which had little love for Hafez al-Assad and were particularly chagrined over his attempt to wipe out Yasser Arafat's leadership of the PLO.

The Reagan Administration stuck to the May 17 agreement, judging that Syria had to be reined in by a show of force. The instrument of this "balancing force" was to be Israel and that was to be projected by the revival in a new and unspecified form of the United States–Israeli Strategic Co-operation Agreement which had been concluded earlier during the Haig régime and cancelled shortly thereafter when Israel's army crashed into West Beirut.

However, the Syrians remained unimpressed. They had taken severe losses from Israeli airstrikes during Israel's invasion of Lebanon and yet held their ground. They were aware that public opinion polls in Israel demonstrated a growing majority in favour of withdrawal from Lebanon and that even among Likud hawks there was opposition to bailing out America's failing policy.

On top of that, the diplomatic climate between the Soviet Union and the United States chilled. Moscow made it clear that it would support Syria to the hilt and give whatever military equipment was needed. That created a growing, though still controllable, danger of super-Power confrontation in the already explosive Middle-East situation.

When all these factors are taken together, when one adds growing popular and Congressional resistance in America to the continuation of the Lebanon policy as well as comparable second thoughts in France, Britain, and Italy, one has to come to the inevitable conclusion that the withdrawal of the Multinational Force can be only a question of time—and a short time at that. Of American policy in the Middle East, little was left.

At the end of 1983 the Reagan Administration attempted to revive the President's peace plan of September 1, 1982. Both King Hussein of Jordan and PLO Chairman Yasser Arafat—the latter evacuated once more from Lebanon (Tripoli)—showed some cautious interest. This was supported by a surprise meeting between Egypt's President Mubarak and Arafat in Cairo in December 1983. Yet the basic conditions which might make progress feasible in the peace process had not changed. Israel, under Prime Minister Yitzak Shamir, was as deadset against relinquishing any part of the West Bank and Gaza as it had been under Begin. "Autonomy" under Israeli rule has little appeal to even the most moderate Arabs. Moreover, Shamir's declaration, after the Mubarak-Arafat meeting, that Israel would not negotiate with the PLO directly or indirectly makes it even more difficult for King Hussein to move. Syria, in its new, powerful, position would not take kindly to any process which excludes it.

Credible steps towards peace, *i.e.* a solution of the Palestinian problem, are unlikely to occur as long as the Likud government remains in office in Israel and as long as a representative Palestinian leadership is unprepared to accept formally the existence of Israel. Both conditions might be met at some time in the future. But as the year 1983 came to a close, all prospects for peace in the Middle East, in Lebanon, in the Gulf, and especially on the central Palestinian problem, appeared bleak indeed.

PLURALISM AND FOREIGN POLICY

THE STATES AND THE MANAGEMENT
OF AUSTRALIA'S EXTERNAL RELATIONS

By

BRIAN HOCKING

OBSERVERS of Australian foreign policy during the years of the Whitlam Labour Party (ALP) Governments and the Conservative Liberal-National Party (L-NP) Coalition of the Fraser era might, on occasions, have been tempted to speculate as to precisely which level of government within the federal system, Federal or State, was responsible for the conduct of the country's external relations.[1] The idiosyncratic premier of Queensland, Mr. Bjelke-Petersen was to be found in Tokyo launching the State's Tokyo Office and inviting a bemused Japanese audience to "come to Queensland, not to Australia." During 1982, he was the recipient of a letter from the Prime Minister of South Africa thanking Queensland for the "support" that it had provided South Africa—an event hardly consistent with Malcolm Fraser's firm anti-apartheid policy and concern with North-South relations. Nor was it the case that State involvement in Australia's external relations was limited to economic and human rights issues on the international agenda. Political parties of both the left and right in West Australia appeared, during 1982, to commit themselves to creating a "defence ministry" within the State government whilst the decision of the newly-elected ALP government in Victoria to ban United States nuclear-powered or nuclear-armed ships from Melbourne cast doubt (or so the Federal government claimed) on Australia's capacity to fulfil its role as alliance partner within the framework of the ANZUS treaty.

A propensity for regional authorities to engage in international relations is not without precedent; it has, for example, become the subject of intensive study in Canada where the aspirations of the French community are reflected not only in Quebec's concern to develop an international role, but in the re-orientation of Canadian foreign policy itself.[1a] But Australia, despite the wave of post-war

---

[1] Research for this paper was carried out whilst the author was a visiting fellow in the Department of Political Science, Research School of Social Sciences, Australian National University.

[1a] For an analysis of the impact of Quebec on Canadian foreign policy see J.P. Schlegal, *The Deceptive Ash: Bilingualism and Canadian Policy in Africa, 1957–71* (1978).

immigration, is an ethnically homogeneous society; what is it, therefore, that motivates the States to involve themselves with foreign
affairs? And with what consequences for the substance of Australian foreign policy and the processes attendant on its formulation? It
is with these two questions that this paper is concerned.

I—THE STATES AND FOREIGN AFFAIRS:
RESPONSE AND INTERPRETATION

State involvement in Australia's relations with her international
environment is capable of exciting fury and condemnation in some,
concern and interest in others. The phenomenon of State Premiers
making quasi-official visits to other countries, the maintenance of
State offices overseas are, by many, regarded as aberrations, albeit
dangerous aberrations, in terms of their effect on the conduct of
Australian foreign policy. Not unexpectedly, perhaps, such a view
has been expressed by Federal politicians who resent the intrusion
of the States in an area which the Federal Constitution reserves to
the Canberra government. Both Whitlam and Fraser were moved,
in rather different contexts, to condemn the interference of certain
State governments in areas of Australia's external relations, arguing
the need for centralised control of foreign policy and the dire consequences of its absence. Support for this position is to be found in
several directions. There are those arguments (essentially exten-
sions of the propositions concerning the problems of conducting
foreign policy in a democracy) with blend political philosophy and
constitutional theory in pointing to the dangers confronting federal
polities in the conduct of their foreign policies. De Tocqueville,
Dicey and Bryce each emphasise the weakness which, they argue,
characterises federal systems and flows from the waste of resources
that conflict between different levels of government entails, combined with an inherent slowness to adapt to changing circumstances.
De Tocqueville's cautious observation that the United States' isolation from the mainstream of international affairs meant that the
country's political structure presented no immediate threat,[2] is
echoed in Wheare's proposition that the need to balance regional
interests within a federation will lead a government to pursue an iso-
lationist or neutralist foreign policy.[3] "Federalism and a spirited
foreign policy go ill together," concludes Wheare.[4]

---

[2] Alexis de Tocqueville, *Democracy in America*, (ed. Phillips Bradley 1953), Vol. 1, pp.
171–2.
[3] K.C. Wheare, *Federal Government* (1953), p. 196.
[4] *Ibid*.

Further sustenance for the belief that the involvement of regional governments in foreign affairs is akin to deviant behaviour is supplied by constitutional lawyers concerned with the formal distribution of powers within the political system, together with international lawyers for whom, "recognition of the division of competence inherent in federal states would have meant a serious encroachment on one of the most basic principles of international law, that of state sovereignty."[5] Although the politicians and the academic analysts may be arguing from different positions, they are united in their assumption that foreign and domestic policy are essentially different in their nature and that the former demands special qualities for its successful formulation and implementation.

A rather different interpretation of phenomena such as the involvement of regional authorities in the international milieu is to be found in the writings of those who argue that developments of this kind reflect the realities of foreign policy management in a period of rapid change and growing complexity. Whether these are ascribed to the growth of "interdependence" or in less ambitious and macrocosmic terms, there is an emphasis on the contextual changes which confront the policy-maker and the agencies, such as foreign ministries, traditionally vested with the responsibility for managing external policy.[6] Expansion of the foreign policy agenda itself has, it is argued, enhanced the fluidity of the boundaries between "foreign" and "domestic" policy. As a result, domestic politics frequently become "internationalised" whilst international politics become "domesticised." Which policy issues belong where becomes increasingly unpredictable. This tendency is accompanied by the diversification of actors, both within and without national societies, concerned with international politics. Increasingly, "access" to the societies of other States, whether on the part of other governments or non-State actors, becomes a significant test of the capacity to exercise influence: increasingly, domestic political actors, such as regional governments and their agents, find themselves propelled into the international environment and the (not always willing) objects of interest from other actors within that environment. In this interpretation, therefore, when attempting to explain the international concerns of the Australian States, we are confronted not by aberrant behaviour, deviating from a norm which

---

[5] I. Bernier, *International Legal Aspects of Federalism* (1973), p. 6.

[6] For a discussion of the likely impact of interdependence on the machinery of foreign policy-making see M.A. East and L.H. Solomonsen, "Adapting Foreign Policy-Making to Interdependence: a Proposal and some Evidence from Norway," 16 *Cooperation and Conflict* (September 1981), pp. 165–182.

prescribes the proper channels for the conduct of relations between societies and their governments, but with one dimension of enhanced complexity in the management of foreign policy. Politicians' appeals to the need for "coherence" in that policy appears not simply as self-serving (in the sense that appeals to the "national interest" usually are) but also as insensitive to changes in the climate in which policy evolves. It is not that coherence is irrelevant but that the attempt to use it as a totem, whereby the problems of control and co-ordination in the foreign policy arena may be reduced, is doomed to failure and discourages an appreciation of that mix of qualities (of which coherence, more precisely defined, is one) necessary to the management of foreign policy in an increasingly fragmentary international and domestic environment. It will be suggested that this second interpretation, rather than the first, offers a fruitful basis for understanding the forces impelling the Australian States and the constituencies residing within them to involvement in international politics.

II—THE AUSTRALIAN STATES
AS INTERNATIONAL ACTORS

Without doubt the enhanced scope of international politics has been one of the major factors responsible for encouraging State interest in Australia's international environment. As issues within the jurisdiction of State governments have acquired international implications, so has the need arisen for the Federal government to develop means of responding to State interests, whether by co-operation or coercion, particularly where international agreements require the enactment of legislation by State parliaments. Whilst this, of itself, is not a new phenomenon having arisen, for example, with the need to give effect to ILO conventions, the lessening of those Cold-War preoccupations so notable in Australian domestic politics during the 1950s and 1960s, together with changes in the pattern of Australia's external economic relations and internal economic structure, have encouraged the States to develop direct contacts with the international system.

1. *External economic relations and internal economic structure*

The emergence of Japan as Australia's dominant trading partner has encouraged all the State governments to concentrate on the Japanese market. By 1982, each State except Tasmania was operating an office in Tokyo and the problem of regulating this multiplicity of interests was the subject of the Myer Committee enquiry into the management of Australia-Japan relations.[7] In its report, the Committee analysed the problem in the following terms: "As Australia's economic relations with Japan have grown in extent and importance so has rivalry between the states in seeking to attract Japanese expertise, investment, trade and tourists. . . . [this] has helped to sharpen the conflict between the powers which the Constitution reserves to the Commonwealth, such as external affairs, external trade and export licensing powers and those which lie with the States such as the right of tenement and the right of each state to promote its own development."[8] However, the situation was complicated by the increasing importance of mineral resources in Australian exports to Japan and the regional location of these resources.

The centre of industrial wealth and political power within Australia has, historically, been located in the populous States of the south-eastern area. The more geographically remote States, particularly Queensland and Western Australia, have tended to regard their own special concerns as neglected by successive Federal governments, resulting in centre-periphery tensions which have, on occasions produced separatist sentiments.[9] The development of Australia's mineral wealth has simultaneously transformed the economic structure of Australia and reinforced the traditional strains in the federal political system. One consequence of minerals development has been to emphasise the distinctive qualities and concerns differentiating the remoter States from those of the historic political and economic centre, reflected in the tendency, particularly noticeable in the cases of Queensland and West Australia, to develop and maintain contacts with overseas interests. Because the exploitation of mineral resources has been heavily dependent on foreign investment and because mineral products are largely exported, the links between the resource-rich States and the international community have developed, whilst these States remain outside the "core" of States constituting the south-east region. Here, the transfer of mineral resources between New South Wales, South Australia and Victoria reinforces traditional economic links between those States whilst Western Australia and Queensland find themselves increasingly pulled towards the international community through the development of their own mineral wealth: "The mineral boom has tended to strengthen the links between the outlying states and the external markets and financial centres of Japan, the United

[7] See "Report of the Ad Hoc Working Committee on Australia-Japan Relations," Canberra, Australian Government Publishing Services (1975), especially Chap. 7.
[8] *Ibid.* pp. 156–157.
[9] G. Stevenson, "Western Alienation in Australia and Canada," in L. Pratt and G. Stevenson (eds.) *Western Separatism: the Myths, Realities and Dangers* (1981), pp. 119–133.

States and Europe, rather than tightening the links between these
states and the industrialised south-east of Australia."[10]

But as a result of these developments, the nature of the States'
overseas links themselves have become the subject of conflict
between Canberra and the State governments, due in no short
measure to the constitutional division of powers whereby the States
exercise control over mineral resources within their borders whilst
the Federal government is able through its control of trade and commerce, to exercise a degree of indirect supervision. During the
1960s, as mineral exports accounted for an ever-larger share of Australia's exports, so Canberra's desire to intervene in the minerals
industries grew, reaching their peak during the Whitlam period
(1972–75). The increasing demand for minerals from Japan,
together with a growing recognition of the potential power of
resource-producing States in the OPEC era, strengthened the determination of the Federal Labour government to control the rate of
exploitation of resources, the terms under which they were exported
and to promote their internal redistribution within Australia. In this
sense, the States' overseas relations became an increasingly controversial issue, and reflected differing interests and priorities at the
national and sub-national levels. In the Whitlam era, the question of
foreign investment, regarded by the States as essential to the development of their mineral resources came under scrutiny, as did the
overseeing of export contracts to ensure that Australian resources
were not being underpriced on world markets. The result was that
the States began to engage in their own "resources diplomacy."
When, for example, the Japanese imposed a ban on the import of
Australian beef, an action threatening the Queensland beef industry, the Queensland premier retaliated by threatening to use State
powers over on-shore mining to deny Japan access to Queensland
coking coal.[11]

2. *Foreign affairs, domestic politics and federalism*

Apart from the pressures on the States to develop overseas links
as a result of economic change within Australia, the attitudes of the
political parties towards the federal system itself have encouraged
the exploitation of domestic-international issue linkages for the
attainment of political goals. The ALP has, traditionally, exhibited
little sympathy for federalism and the Whitlam government early in
its life made it clear that it regarded the external affairs power (Art.

---

[10] G. Stevenson, *Mineral Resources and Australian Federalism*, Canberra, Centre for
Research on Federal Financial Relations, ANU (1976), p. 10.
[11] H.S. Albinski, *Australian External Policy under Labor* (1977), p. 275.

51(xxix) of the Constitution) as a means of expanding its jurisdiction at the expense of the States. When criticising previous governments for acceding to ILO conventions in the knowledge that the States would refuse to implement them, Whitlam expressed his belief that the Federal government possessed the power under section 51(xxix) to implement such conventions irrespective of State attitudes. It was, however, the attempt to employ the external affairs power to gain control of off-shore mineral resources and the continental shelf that set the scene for the bitterest contest between the two levels of government. Ultimately the States were to take the Seas and Submerged Lands Act—through which the Labour government sought to gain its objective—to the High Court which, in turn, upheld the act as a legitimate use of the external affairs power.[12]

Despite the Fraser government's commitment (under the banner of the "new federalism") to enhanced co-operation between Canberra and the States, disputes concerning the extent of the external affairs power continued. In response to a case brought against the Queensland government in the High Court, accusing it of breaching the 1975 Racial Discrimination Act by refusing to approve the acquisition of pastoral leases in northern Queensland by an Aboriginal community, the State government argued that this legislation (giving effect to Australia's ratification of a United Nations convention on the elimination of racial discrimination) was an invalid use of the external affairs power.[13] The decision of the High Court to find in favour of the Federal government in 1982 was regarded as a significant development in the interpretation of the latter's powers under section 51(xxix) but is unlikely to have lessened centre-region conflict on the jurisdictional implications of growing foreign-domestic policy linkages.[14]

In addition to constitutional disputes regarding the effects of the internationalisation of policy issues on the powers of the two levels of government, it is not unknown for politicians, whether State or Federal, to exploit the linkages between foreign and domestic policy for their own short term political advantage. A clear example arose during 1982 following the announcement by the newly-elected ALP government in Victoria that the State was henceforth a nuclear-free zone and that the port facilities of Melbourne would no longer be available to visiting nuclear powered or nuclear armed ships.[15] Whilst from the Victorian perspective, the concerns of the State

---

[12] *Ibid.* p. 276.
[13] "The Age" *Canberra Times* (Melbourne, May 13, 1982).
[14] *Ibid.*
[15] "The Age" *Canberra Times* (Melbourne, June 13, 1982).

government (confused as these may have been) were clearly domestic and related to the differences between the political parties over
the mining and export of uranium, the Fraser government presented
the issue in terms of a foreign policy crisis. According to the Federal
government, not only was the general principle of its rights to determine Australia's foreign and defence policy at stake, but also the
future of her membership of the ANZUS alliance. Implicit in that
alliance, Fraser argued, was the commitment to provide facilities for
allied naval ships of whatever kind. The motivations of the Federal
government in emphasising the international implications of Victoria's action were to be found in the domestic political situation with
which it was confronted. Embarrassing attacks on Canberra's
attitude to tax-avoidance schemes, a worsening economic climate,
dissension within the ALP on the issue of the Australian-American
relationship appeared to harden Fraser's determination to find an
external policy issue which could be exploited as the time for the
next Federal election grew nearer. Even after the Victorian government had retreated, acknowledging Canberra's authority on
defence-related issues, Fraser seemed intent on keeping the issue
before the public, calling for Federal legislation to prevent State
governments from actions which "threatened" Australia's external
relations.

A further dimension of the domestic-foreign policy linkage which
has promoted the States' international concerns is the development
of an increasingly articulate public, intent on using the whole range
of forums, sub-national, national and international, to influence the
substance of Australian policy in a variety of areas. Whereas the fact
that the Australian party system is organised on a State basis has
always provided one very important connection between the political centre and the regions and ensured that Federal-State politics
rests on an intricate pattern of relationships, the proliferation of
interest groups with a variety of concerns has added to this complexity. One of the better publicised manifestations of such a tendency has been the use by Aboriginal groups of international
agencies to project their grievances against the Western Australian
and Queensland governments on the issues of land rights and mining and prospecting on Aboriginal lands. An increasingly well-
organised campaign focusing on the UN and its sub-committees cul-
minated in attempts by Aboriginal groups to exert pressure on the
OAU and Third World member States of the Commonwealth
generally, to boycott the Commonwealth Games scheduled for Brisbane in 1982.[16] In this situation, as a result of pressure group activi-

---

[16] *Sydney Morning Herald* (September 29, 1981).

ties, the Queensland government found itself the subject of unwelcome international attention and criticism from a variety of countries and other international actors one of which was the World Council of Churches.[17] (It was in the context of these events that the South African Prime Minister despatched the letter to Bjelke-Petersen referred to above.) The strategy of the Aboriginal groups was to exploit the connections between Queensland's policy towards her Aboriginal population, the concern with human rights in the international community, and a central plank in Fraser's foreign policy, namely Australia's links with the Third World and interest in North-South relations. Clearly, the hope was that these links would encourage Canberra to cease pursuing a policy of persuasion over Queensland's Aboriginal policies and to use its powers to intervene directly and assume control in this area.

3. *The States and the foreign policy machinery*

It might be expected that the foreign policy-making machinery would have developed means of responding to this increasingly fragmented policy environment with its plurality of interests and actors. In fact, it is the very nature of the bureaucratic processes associated with the formulation of external policy that has enhanced the desire of the States to involve themselves in foreign affairs. The Department of Foreign Affairs (DFA) has very weak links with the States. This is to be explained in part by the heavy emphasis in post-war foreign policy on issues of military security and alliance relationships as the stuff of foreign policy which did not demand regular liaison between the national and sub-national levels of government.[18] As the foreign-policy agenda changed during the 1960s and 1970s, however, and the DFA's focus of concern broadened, thereby making contact with the States a more obviously desirable objective, an old problem, that of departmental jealousies, loomed into view. Within the Canberra bureaucracy, the DFA is a relatively new department, assuming its present size and form after the Second World War; primary responsibility for specific areas of Australian external policy (such as trade and immigration) was already vested in the powerful "older" departments; Trade and Resources, Immigration and Treasury, for example.[19] The growing linkage between foreign and domestic policy issues set the scene for numerous inter-

---

[17] *National Times* (May 23–29, 1982).

[18] T.B. Millar, "The Official formulation and execution of Australian foreign policy," Australian Political Studies Association Conference, Perth (August 1982), p. 8.

[19] T.B. Millar, "Managing the Australian Foreign Affairs Department" 37 *International Journal*, Nr. 3 (Summer 1982), pp. 442–443.

departmental battles concerning responsibility over areas now firmly located within the foreign-policy spectrum and the relative weakness of the DFA, together with the success of other departments in defending their external policy responsibilities, has had two effects. First there is a strong element of "diffusion" of responsibility between public service departments in the management of Australian foreign policy; secondly, the DFA has been discouraged from developing contacts with relevant domestic constituencies within the States. For not only have other departments created their own external policy sections to guard their international interests, they are very jealous of their relationships with the State governments. Thus the elaborate network of Federal-State consultative mechanisms, focused on the domestic public service departments, is the forum in which issues related to foreign policy are raised. The DFA has only very hesitantly attempted to follow the examples of departments such as Trade and Resources which maintain regional offices in the States, by appointing Senior Foreign Affairs Officers to the State capitals. The result is a highly fragmented mode of consultation between the policy-making centre and the regions on issues affecting external relations and a lack of communication between the DFA and groups within the community whose interests are increasingly affected by international events. In turn, this means that the DFA is limited in its ability to perform the function of balancing the competing claims of such groups and projecting a foreign policy whose elements reflect that balance.

The situation is complicated by the existence of a Federal-State pattern of bureaucratic politics which supplements that existing between the public service departments in Canberra. In many areas relating to external policy, such as fisheries agreements, it is State public servants who possess the practical expertise and whose cooperation is frequently required by the Federal bureaucracy. This helps to add to the traditional tensions between the two levels of administration which are generated by differences in status, power and resources. The desire of the States, confronted with a highly centralised foreign policy process in which these interests go unheard or are regarded with disfavour, to develop their own overseas links are reinforced by bureaucratic rivalries produced by the desire of State officials to become involved in international organisations related to States' interests. Where State representatives are included in Australian overseas delegations (as is the case with UNCLOS) differences in objectives, and suspicions held by both levels of officialdom of the competence and good faith of the other, reflect these well-established bureaucratic tensions.

III—STATE INTERNATIONAL ACTIVITY
AND FOREIGN POLICY MANAGEMENT

Each of these factors has encouraged the States to become both "primary" foreign policy actors, seeking access to the international community for the promotion of their own interests and "secondary" or "mediating" actors, attempting to influence the making of foreign policy at the centre on their own behalf and on that of regional groups who see their interests affected by external policy decisions. The two are linked in as much as the inadequacies of the machinery for communicating with the centre encourage State governments to develop their own international links—such as overseas offices—and to by-pass the Federal government where possible. What is the consequence of this situation for the management of foreign policy?

In general terms, the involvement of the States in external relations has added to the unpredictability of the environment in which Australian foreign policy decision-makers are constrained to operate.[20] As the inter-actions between three levels of political activity, sub-national, national and international, increase both in scope and intensity, it becomes increasingly hard to predict who will become involved in any given policy issue and, in particular, which issues will assume a foreign policy dimension. Nor is it easy to predict which arenas will be employed in the pursuit of policy goals. Whilst State and Federal governments seek to co-opt international organisations, foreign governments and interest groups in pursuit of their own goals and as reflections of their own rivalries, so international actors recognise the need to exploit contacts at the State level and the advantages to be gained from doing so.

One consequence of this growth in unpredictability is to render it far more difficult to maintain flexibility in foreign policy: that is, the ability to link or isolate different elements in the overall pattern of foreign relations where this is seen as desirable. Pressures from both within and without the political system help to ensure that issues on the domestic and foreign-policy agendas will become intermeshed, occasionally with startling implications for those attempting to hold the reins of foreign policy. State activity in international politics may serve simply to encourage rigidity in foreign policy. The knowledge that a certain decision might excite State hostility or require (as could well be the case with accession to an international agreement) the co-operation of State governments, may discourage a Federal

---

[20] On the problems that growing "uncertainty" presents to foreign policy-makers, see M. Smith, "Foreign policy analysis and the growth of uncertainty," paper presented to British International Studies Association annual conference (December, 1982), pp. 14–16.

government from re-evaluating its external policies in particular areas. The nature of Federal-State relations also makes it harder to develop and maintain a domestic consensus with regard to the objectives desirable in particular areas of external policy and can, in turn, affect the stability of relationships with the international environment. In this sense, the States constitute an additional focus of opposition to the government in Canberra: " . . . any Australian national government has to face two sets of opposition. One is the official opposition sitting on the opposite bench in the two Houses of Parliament. The other is the unofficial opposition which consists of the states . . . it can by no means be taken for granted that a state government will support a national government merely because both happen to come from the same political party. Local consider-ations will override party ties."[21]

It is not the case, of course, that all federal systems are deficient in the qualities necessary to the successful management of foreign policy. Response to local needs can enhance the flexibility of exter-nal relations by devolving certain responsibilities, albeit under cen-tral supervision to the regions. This is most apparent where transborder relations are concerned; for example, between Canada and the United States[22] and between Yugoslavia and adjacent coun-tries where, as Duchacek has noted, "individual republics have some special problems with regard to their neighbours and have some economic interests that may not call for an overall national commitment."[23] It has also been argued (as does Akenyemi in the case of Nigeria between 1960 and 1965) that a federal structure pro-vides the opportunity for the expression of a wider range of views which may help to counter rigidity in foreign policy.[24] The problem in the Australian case is that, due to historical, political and bureau-cratic factors, the disadvantages of federalism for the conduct of foreign relations are maximised and the advantages minimised. In essence, this is because internal coherence in foreign policy, the balancing of the domestic forces impinging on foreign relations, is, for reasons identified above, frequently not achieved. Regional interests may, therefore, seek expression outside the machinery for

---

[21] C. Howard *Australia's Constitution* (1978), p. 26.

[22] See P.R. Johannson, "Provincial International Activities," 33 *International Journal* (Spring 1978), pp. 365–369, and the collection of essays in Annette Baker Fox, A.O. Hero, Jr, and J.S. Nye, Jr (Eds.), *Canada and the United States: Transnational and Transgovernmen-tal Relations* (1976).

[23] I.D. Duchacek, *Comparative Federalism: the Territorial Dimension of Politics* (1970), pp. 214–215.

[24] A.B. Akinyemi, "Federalism and Foreign Policy" in A.B. Akinyemi, P.D. Cole, and W. Ofonagoro, *Readings on Federalism*, Lagos, Nigerian Institute of International Affairs (1979), pp. 41–42.

the conduct of the nation's external policy or attempt to exert influence at the point of implementation rather than during the formulation of objectives.

Examples of situations where State governments have suddenly "emerged" as interested parties in aspects of Australia's foreign relations are not uncommon.

One such occasion occurred during the fisheries negotiations between Australia and Japan in 1979. Despite the fact that the Department of Primary Industry (DPI) had engaged in consultations with State governments and the fishing industry before negotiations with the Japanese started, as the first round of negotiations moved towards their close, major domestic dissension over the nature of the agreement developed. Particularly vociferous opposition came from Queensland game fishermen who wanted a wider exclusion zone imposed on the Japanese fishing industry than that included in the agreement, and who succeeded in pressuring the Queensland government to take up their cause. This late expression of regional concern reflected what one observer has termed "the relatively closed nature of the debates" and the fact that control of the Australian negotiations were focused at the highest levels of government, namely the Federal cabinet.[25]

Whether or not the Japanese were surprised at these developments since it was clear that they were well aware of regional interests, having used their consuls to sound out State government positions, they were certainly resentful at the intrusion of domestic politics at this late stage of the negotiations and blamed the Australian government for its apparent inability to reconcile its various domestic interests.[26] This experience encouraged the DPI to include a State observer to the second round of negotiations held during 1980, an innovation which, according to DPI officials, helped to resolve problems relating to regional interests at an earlier stage than had been the case in the previous round of negotiations.

The activities of the Japanese consuls in the State capitals during the fisheries negotiations highlights another facet of the impact of the federal structure on the conduct of foreign relations; namely, the need for foreign governments to "federalise" their diplomatic representation. Apart from their embassies located in Canberra, many governments (such as the Japanese) maintain a network of career consuls in the State capitals with their own channels of communication to the home foreign ministry. Their reasons for so doing

[25] G.W.P. George, *Linkage Diplomacy and Bilateral Economic Interdependence* Ph.D. thesis, Canberra, Australian National University (1981), pp. 188 and 263.
[26] Information supplied to author.

are to be found partly in the remoteness of the centres of economic
and commercial power from Canberra, but also in the frequently
displayed inability of Australian negotiating teams to channel information from, and speak for, domestic interests. Whilst there are no
inhibitions in international law, within the Australian Constitution
or under the Vienna Convention on Consular Relations to prevent
such contacts, Canberra has been reluctant to see foreign governments use their consular representatives in situations where sensitive issues involving Federal-State relations are related to matters of
external policy and could be exploited to the advantage of other
governments.

Such examples as this illustrate the problems of achieving internal
coherence in foreign policy where domestic interests are involved,
and the consequences of its absence. A lack of internal coherence
reduces, in turn, external coherence as negotiating partners, uncertain of the objectives being pursued by the Australian Federal
government and recognising the absence of domestic consensus,
develop contacts with the States, seeking to achieve by external
influence on the relevant interests, what Canberra has failed to
effect through internal consultation and negotiation.

IV—COPING WITH THE PROBLEM

Confronted with such difficulties, by what methods have Federal
governments attempted to reduce the potentially disruptive effects
of State international involvement? It should be emphasised at once
that since, on the whole, politicians and bureaucrats have been
unwilling to acknowledge the nature of the problem, relying on an
appeal to those sections of the constitution which vest the power to
conduct external policy in the Federal government as confirmation
of their authority, there has been no powerful impetus to devise
methods for coping with it. Nevertheless, if only on an ad hoc basis,
some attempt has, of necessity, been made to accommodate State
interests and jurisdictional concerns. Moreover, the Fraser Government's emphasis on improved Federal-State relations extended to
the realm of external policy and witnessed the introduction of new
co-operative mechanisms.

First, as noted above, the DFA has attempted to follow the policy
of seeking to develop relationships with domestic constituencies,
generally identified as one characteristic response by foreign ministries to the enhanced role of domestic ministries in the conduct of
external policy.[27] The experiment of appointing Senior Foreign

---

[27] See East and Salomonsen, *loc. cit.* (in note 6 above).

Affairs Officers (SFARs) to DFA regional offices has not been particularly successful in enhancing the extent to which regional interests are consulted on a regular basis and information channelled back to Canberra. This is partly due to lack of resources for such work but more significantly because no machinery appears to exist at the centre towards which information can be directed and within which it can be processed. There is, for example, no equivalent to the Federal-Provincial Co-ordination Bureau within the Canadian Department of External Affairs. That there is not reflects the historic remoteness of the DFA from domestic interests, rivalries within the Canberra bureaucratic machine and an inherent suspicion on the part of State politicians and public servants concerning the motives of any Federal department attempting to develop a role at the regional level.

There have also, secondly, been developments in the practice (much more widely utilised in Canada) of including State representatives in delegations to international organisations. Since the late 1940s, for example, an official from a State Department of Labour has attended ILO meetings. More recently, as mentioned above, State interests in offshore mineral resources (an area where some of the State legal officers have a recognised and respected expertise) have been reflected by representation in Australian delegations to UNCLOS. Despite reservations within the Federal Attorney-General's Department regarding the wisdom of a practice which can lead to State representatives seeking to include unrealistic federal clauses into international agreements, the process of participation was extended in 1982 with the inclusion of a State representative in the delegation to the Human Rights Commission in Geneva. The advantage of this practice in terms of both informing Canberra of legitimate State concerns and making the States aware of the constraints under which governments have to operate in the international arena appears to be self-evident.

Thirdly, in accord with the self-proclaimed desire of the Fraser Government to enhance Federal-State co-operation, new consultative procedures have been developed whereby the States are advised of potential treaty commitments which Australia might enter and opinions sought from the relevant State Public Service Departments. Irrespective of whatever ideological motivations inspired the government to introduce this system, it is a recognition of the fact that the States' responsibilities are increasingly affected through the internationalisation of public policy and that their hostility in such areas as human rights can be highly embarrassing to Canberra. In bureaucratic terms, one crucial problem with such a consultative process is that it assumes a capacity on the part of the

State Public Service Departments to participate in it. Even the large States such as Victoria and New South Wales may find it difficult to perform the necessary tasks of consultation within their bureaucratic structures and transmit the results to Canberra. In the small States such as Tasmania, however, the task may become virtually impossible as an overworked Premier's Department attempts to extract information from various areas of the State bureaucracy. In such circumstances, responses may be too late to be of use to Canberra and the whole process became a rather meaningless charade. Here, just as at the centre, consultation and co-ordination is expensive in terms of time and resources.

Fourthly and finally, the Fraser era witnessed the creation in 1978 of a special agency intended to co-ordinate Australia's relations with Japan, the Japan Secretariat. The Secretariat is intended to overcome the problems identified by the Myer Report in managing Australia's relations with Japan, particularly the fear that a lack of coherence in Australia's dealings with Japan could be exploited to the latter's advantage. As mentioned above, the report was very much concerned with the impact of the States' relationships with Japan, and one of the consultative committees which the Secretariat services brings together Federal and State public servants at regular intervals. The States' inherent suspicion of any Canberra initiative has been tempered by the recognition that the Secretariat may be positively useful to them—or, at least, presents no real challenge to State interests with regard to Japan. The paucity of such mechanisms serves to emphasise the failure to confront the problems involved in the management of foreign policy, or to define these problems in such a way as to deny their real nature.

V—Restating the Problem

In his study of the conduct of foreign relations in federal States written during the 1930s, Harold Stoke predicted that, of all the federations which he examined, Australia seemed destined, by virtue of the constitutional allocation of powers, to suffer from a high level of conflict between national and sub-national governments in the conduct of foreign policy.[28] The fact that other federations, such as Canada have been confronted with more dramatic problems indicates that constitutional documents are by no means an infallible guide in this area. It is not that such documents are unimportant; indeed, the distribution of powers between the levels of government provides the framework within which difficulties develop. But onto

---

[28] H.W. Stoke, *The Foreign Relations of the Federal State* (1931), p. 3.

this framework are pegged other factors, the changing nature of the international environment and foreign policy preoccupations, the socio-economic composition of the regions and the pattern of domestic politics, which ensure that the problem becomes one of managing foreign policy in a situation where the interface between domestic and foreign policy grows ever closer. In the Australian case the difficulty has been that the problem is debated largely in legal-constitutional terms inspired by ideological predispositions of the political parties towards the federal system itself. This has produced a sterile debate on the issue of State involvement in international affairs which bears little relationship to the real issues.

As a new ALP government under Prime Minister Hawke assumes power, there are signs that some of the problems have been recognised. During 1982 the then opposition foreign affairs spokesman indicated on several occasions that a future ALP government would adopt a more cautious approach towards the States than had been the case in the Whitlam years.[29] Some of his proposals—secondment from State governments to the DFA and the creation of a branch within that department concerned with Federal-State coordination—sounded promising. Others, such as pressuring the State governments to close their overseas offices, seemed reminiscent of earlier conflicts. The new Federal (and State) governments could do worse than re-read an extract from the Myer report which, in the context of Australia's relations with Japan, encapsulates the problem: " . . . the difficulties which arise between the Commonwealth and the States in relation to Japan will not be satisfactorily resolved by reference to the Constitution or resort to law. A practical solution, consistent with Australia's national interest, cannot be achieved unless the States respect the right of the Commonwealth to determine national policy and unless the Commonwealth in developing national policy, takes account of the particular interests of each state and the expertise in specific areas that it can bring to dealings with Japan."[30]

Recent history indicates, however, that defining "practical solutions" acceptable to both levels of government is no easy task.

---

[29] See L. Bowen, "Department's shake-up under Labor" *Canberra Times* (April 6, 1982).
[30] *Loc. cit.* (in note 7 above), p. 161.

RUSSIA AND POLAND
IN THE LIGHT OF HISTORY

By

ROBIN KEMBALL

ANY serious assessment of Russo-Polish relations demands some inquiry into the past—into the respective histories of these two Slav nations that have lived for centuries, and live to-day, on terms, at best, of sullen rivalry and suspicion and at worst, in one historian's words, of "tragic enmity."[1] A mere review of events since 1945 (or 1939) is manifestly insufficient and, even if we return, say, to the partitions of the late eighteenth century, we are still left without any knowledge of Poland's true heritage. Her great age lies further back in time, and it is one of the ironies of her fate that, for people in the West, her history tends to begin only from the moment at which she falls increasingly under foreign, especially Russian, domination. As a result, while aware of her recent misfortunes, few have any knowledge of her "centuries-old rights to life and liberty."[2] Conversely, while the main facts of modern Russian history are more familiar (at least from 1812), it is not always realised that, in Poland's finest hour, the young Muscovite State was still struggling to free itself from the Tatar yoke and to recover what it regarded as its rightful Kievan heritage from the mighty Polish-Lithuanian State on its western borders. Factors such as these, though not always appreciated at an individual level, yet live on down the ages in the collective consciousness of the peoples concerned. To ignore them is thus to ignore some of the most telling factors in the situation in which these peoples find themselves to-day. If, then, in the first part of this paper, we reach back to the very beginnings of Polish and Russian history, it is not only because they are little known but because it is there that the seeds of future misgivings and misunderstandings lie.

I—POLAND AND RUSSIA
ENTER THE CHRISTIAN FOLD

In terms of modern history (in the widest sense of the term), Poland and Russia make their entry on the European stage in the second

---

[1] N.V. Riasanovsky, *A History of Russia* (1963) p. 39.
[2] A. Coville, in the Preface to O. Halecki, *La Pologne de 963 à 1914* (1933), p. IX. (The translations from this French edition and from other non-English texts cited have been made by the author of this paper).

half of the tenth century A.D. In the year 966, Mieszko I, Duke of Poland and the fourth member of the Piast dynasty, accepts the Christian faith for himself and his people. In 988, Vladimir Sviato-slavovich, Grand-Duke of Kiev and the fourth member of the Rurik dynasty, does likewise. Yet, as a German adage has it, when two persons act alike, the outcome is not always the same.[3] It is true that both conversions fit into a broad historical pattern—Christianity was at that time spreading rapidly across Europe, with only a few remote peoples (notably the Lithuanians) offering serious resistance. Both rulers, moreover, were prompted by severely pragmatic consider-ations of national interest, Mieszko being under constant attack from the Germans, with Vladimir in similar difficulties with Byzan-tium. But there the parallel ends. Mieszko might have countered the German threat by turning to Byzantium but, anxious to forge and strengthen links with the Latin West, was ready to embrace the Roman form of Christianity, provided he did not have to accept it at German hands. In the event, he found an ideal intermediary in the neighbouring kingdom of Bohemia, to which he literally wedded his cause by marrying the Bohemian princess Dubravka prior to his con-version.[4] Vladimir's choice was more complex. Before opting for Christianity at all, he had already considered—and rejected—both Islam and Judaism, thus electing "to become the Eastern flank of Christendom rather than an extension into Europe of non-Christian civilisations."[5] But there still remained the very real choice between Western and Eastern forms of Christianity. In embracing the latter, he took a decision no less momentous than the opposite one taken by Mieszko before him.[6] As Riasanovsky rightly insists, " . . . the Russian allegiance to Byzantium determined or helped to determine much of the subsequent history of the country. It meant that Russia remained outside the Roman Catholic Church, and this in turn not only deprived Russia of what that Church had to offer, but also con-tributed in a major way to the relative isolation of Russia from the rest of Europe and its Latin civilisation. It helped notably to inspire Russian suspicions of the West and the tragic enmity between the Russians and the Poles. On the other side, one can well argue that Vladimir's turn to Constantinople represented the richest and most rewarding spiritual, cultural, and political choice that he could make at the time."[7]

---

[3] *"Wenn zwei dasselbe tun, dann ist es nicht dasselbe."*

[4] See O. Halecki, *op. cit.* (in note 2 above) p. 17.

[5] Riasanovsky, *op. cit.* (in note 1 above), p. 38.

[6] Like Mieszko, Vladimir also married a princess of the same faith—in his case, Anne, sister of the Byzantine Emperor Basil II.

[7] *op. cit.* (in note 1 above), pp. 38–39.

Not that the parting of the ways was immediately apparent. For one thing, the Great Schism between Western and Eastern Christianity (1054) was still some decades away. For another, the Kievan dynasty, socially and politically open and receptive to West as well as East, long entertained close connections with the other reigning houses of Europe, and in particular with Poland. Such connections did not preclude rivalries—it was inevitable that the border regions should be coveted by both parties, and this, as we shall see, would eventually form the tedious pattern of Russo-Polish relations in history. But at this stage there was nothing in those relations to suggest that the two peoples were in any way fated to become the seemingly irreconcilable foes they would later prove to be.[8]

II—THE MONGOL INVASIONS (1237–1242)

The crucial stage in the process of estrangement came with the Mongol onslaught led by Batu, a grandson of Genghis Khan. While this would place Russia under Tatar domination, and isolate her from the West, for two centuries and over, it would leave Poland, despite the initial devastation following the Mongol victories at Chmielnik and Lignica in 1241, relatively unaffected in the long run. Perhaps inevitably, these differing experiences lead in their turn to differing interpretations in the respective national consciousness. Poland, with some justice, sees herself hereafter as the advance bastion of Western Christianity, whose heroic resistance contributed to the retreat of the Mongols and so to saving Europe. Russia, with no less justice, feels that the West has been saved as the result of *her* efforts and at *her* expense. Despite her no less heroic resistance, her no less Christian fervour, she is forced to bow to the Tatar will—even the great Alexander Nevsky, fresh from his triumphs over the Swedes and the Teutonic Knights, is statesman enough to recognise the futility and fatality of resistance.[9] The exact role of the Mongol occupation in shaping Russian history is also the subject of some dispute—in particular, as to whether the Muscovite State that emerged from the disaster owed its inspiration and character to Mongol influences, or rather to Kievan and Byzantine trends. However that

---

[8] On the matrimonial alliances of ancient Kiev, see especially N. de Baumgarten, *Généalogies et mariages occidentaux des Rurikides russes du Xe au XIIIe siècle* (1927), *passim*. On the basis of these findings, Vernadsky calculated that Kiev *Rus* contracted 15 such alliances with Poland (cited in Riasanovsky, *op. cit.* (in note 1 above), p. 41).

[9] In 1240, Nevsky defeated the Swedes at the battle on the River Neva that gave him his surname. In 1242, he routed the Teutonic Knights at the "slaughter of the ice" fought on Lake Chud (today Lake Peipus). The concept of Russia as the West's centuries-old shield against the "yellow peril" constantly finds its reflection among Russian poets from Pushkin to Vladimir Soloviev, and most notably in *The Scythians* (1918) of Alexander Blok.

may be, liberation from the Tatar yoke was a long, arduous, and complex process. In 1380, Dmitry of the Don, Prince of Moscow, defeated the Mongols for the first time on the Field of Kulikovo. But this victory was short-lived, and another century would pass before Mongol suzerainty would officially come to an end.

III—LITHUANIA AND POLAND

By that time, the map of Eastern Europe had been radically transformed. Before the Poles, it was the Lithuanians—the "godless *Litva*" of the Russian annals—who, under Gedimin the Conqueror (1316–1341) and his son Olgerd, or Algirdas (1345–1377), had captured vast tracts of former *Rus* territory, extending Lithuanian sway from the Baltic to the Black Sea.[10] But then the Poles re-enter the scene. By the dynastic agreement of Krewo in 1385 (five years after Dmitry's victory at Kulikovo), Olgerd's son Jagellon (Jagáilo; Polish Jagiello) accedes to the crown of Poland under the title of Wladyslaw II, accepting in his turn Roman Christianity for himself and his people and sealing the Personal Union between the States by marrying the luckless 12-year-old Queen Hedwig (Jadwiga) who, against all her inclinations, accepts her barbarian husband in the desperate hope of putting an end to Polish-Lithuanian feuds.

Her sacrifice was not in vain; by common consent, the "Age of the Jagellons" is the most brilliant in Polish history. Halecki considers Hedwig's short life (she died aged 26) "the most decisive turning-point in the destinies of Poland and Eastern Europe," and the Union "the most important treaty in the whole of Polish history."[11] Even Beazley, scathing in general concerning the Poles' lack of political foresight, does not hesitate to qualify the agreement as a "master-stroke": "It creates the mighty Polish state of the Renaissance, the Reformation, and the 17th century. It holds back the Moscovite till Peter the Great. It forms a powerful and fairly effective barrier against Turkish advance beyond Hungary, Transylvania, and the Euxine steppes. It arrests and rolls back the German crusading and colonial expansion, the *Drang nach Osten* in Baltic lands. It shatters the Teutonic Order, wins Courland and Old Prussia from the German knights and settlers, commences a momentous Slavonic revival, a notable Germanic depression. . . . In the time of Charles I of England, as in that of Richard II and Henry IV, Poland-

---

[10] Lithuania's ties and affinities at this time were essentially with Russia, rather than Poland—many historians even speak of a Lithuanian-Russian State; for a time this State constituted a serious rival to Moscow for the ancient Kievan inheritance. (See Riasanovsky, *op. cit.* (in note 1 above), pp. 148–149.).

[11] *Op. cit.* in note 2 above, pp. 83–88.

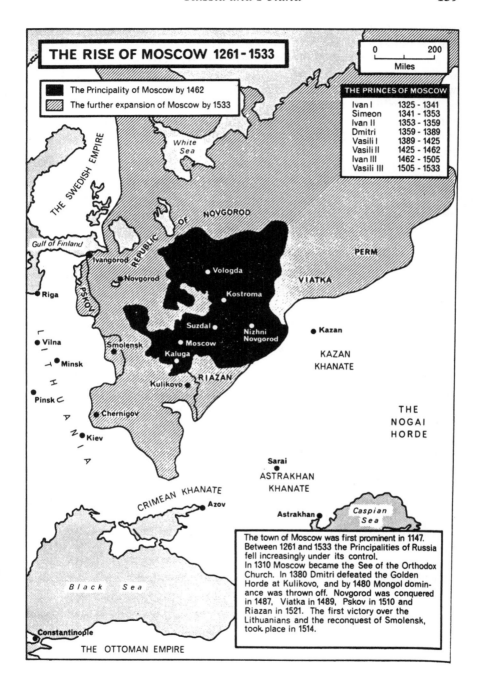

THE RISE OF MOSCOW 1261-1533

■	The Principality of Moscow by 1462
▨	The further expansion of Moscow by 1533

0 — 200 Miles

THE PRINCES OF MOSCOW

Ivan I	1325 - 1341
Simeon	1341 - 1353
Ivan II	1353 - 1359
Dmitri	1359 - 1389
Vasili I	1389 - 1425
Vasili II	1425 - 1462
Ivan III	1462 - 1505
Vasili III	1505 - 1533

THE SWEDISH EMPIRE

White Sea

REPUBLIC OF NOVGOROD

Gulf of Finland

Ivangorod

PERM

Novgorod

Vologda

VIATKA

Riga

PSKOV

Kostroma

Suzdal

Nizhni Novgorod

Kazan

Vilna

Smolensk

Moscow

KAZAN KHANATE

Minsk

Kaluga

Pinsk

RIAZAN

Kulikovo

THE NOGAI HORDE

Chernigov

Kiev

Sarai

ASTRAKHAN KHANATE

CRIMEAN KHANATE

Azov

Astrakhan

Caspian Sea

Black Sea

The town of Moscow was first prominent in 1147. Between 1261 and 1533 the Principalities of Russia fell increasingly under its control.
In 1310 Moscow became the See of the Orthodox Church. In 1380 Dmitri defeated the Golden Horde at Kulikovo, and by 1480 Mongol dominance was thrown off. Novgorod was conquered in 1487, Viatka in 1489, Pskov in 1510 and Riazan in 1521. The first victory over the Lithuanians and the reconquest of Smolensk, took place in 1514.

Constantinople

THE OTTOMAN EMPIRE

MAP I

Lithuania is mistress of all western *Rus*."[12] The Union was initially only a personal one. But from an early stage, and certainly with the death, in 1430, of Jagellon's cousin Vitovt, hero of the Polish-Lithuanian victory over the Teutonic Knights at Tannenberg (Grünwald), Lithuania passes more and more into the Polish cultural and political orbit. And when, under Sigismund II, the last of the Jagellons, the Union of Lublin (1569) creates an indissoluble political fusion of the two States, it merely confirms the long-standing fact of Polish supremacy. It also exacerbates Polish-Russian relations inasmuch as Lithuania's extensive Orthodox population, hitherto left largely unmolested, now find themselves exposed to an active policy of Polish-Catholic propaganda and pressure. Mutual resentment and suspicion are further increased with the establishment in 1596 of the Uniate Church, owing allegiance to Rome while retaining the Eastern rite.[13]

IV—THE RISE OF MOSCOW: THE "THIRD ROME"

The dimensions of Polish-Lithuanian, and hence Roman Catholic, eastward expansion may be gauged from Map I. The limit year selected—1462—falls during the reign of the great Jagellon king, Casimir IV. It also marks the accession of Ivan III (The Great) of Moscow, and a serious reassertion of a Russian presence. In 1480, Ivan publicly renounces all further allegiance to the Golden Horde[14]; in 1493, he assumes the title of Sovereign (*Gosudar*)—at times Emperor (*Tsar*)—of all Russia, a manner of laying claim to the entire Kievan heritage. Profiting from Casimir's preoccupation with central Europe, Ivan subdues the proud cities of Tver and Novgorod—both of which, significantly, appeal for Lithuanian aid in vain. With Casimir's death in 1492, Ivan attacks his son Alexander, reconquers a good third of the Ruthenian provinces and pushes back the frontier between the two States from the environs of Moscow to the gates of Kiev. To the ambassador of Hungary (and of the Pope), who complains that Moscow has robbed Lithuania of her possessions, Ivan retorts: "Wherefore do they call them their *possessions*? . . . Surely the Pope knows that the princes Vladislav and

---

[12] R. Beazley, N. Forbes and G.A. Birkett, *Russia from the Varangians to the Bolsheviks* (1918), p. 57. (A composite work in three books, each by one of the authors. Henceforth referred to as Beazley *et al.*)

[13] While the nobles and bishops mostly favoured the union with Rome, the people and many of the priests did not. See Riasanovsky, *op. cit.* in note 1 above, pp. 197–8; Beazley *et al., op. cit.* in note 12 above, p. 207.

[14] At this, Khan Ahmad characteristically allies himself with Casimir IV, but suffers defeat on the Ugra River before the promised Polish-Lithuanian help arrives.

THE EASTWARD SPREAD OF CATHOLICISM BY 1462

Simultaneously with the Mongol invasions from the east, Russia was subjected to the continual westward movement of Roman Catholicism. Under Swedish and Lithuanian pressure, Russian Orthodoxy was pushed back almost to Moscow. Roman Catholicism also made advances against the Orthodox Bulgars in the Balkans, and against the Muslim lands in the eastern Mediterranean.

LAPLAND 1300

NORWAY

SWEDEN

RUSSIA

Vyborg 1293

DENMARK

Baltic Sea

Reval 1219

Novgorod

Pskov

Tver

Moscow

Mitava 1271

PRUSSIA

Danzig 1200

Vilna 1386

Smolensk 1450

Kaluga

THE

Warsaw

LITHUANIA

POLAND

Prague

GALICIA

Kiev 1385

HOLY

BOHEMIA

Lvov 1340

UKRAINE

ROMAN

Vienna

Tana 1261

EMPIRE

HUNGARY

CROATIA

TRANSYLVANIA

Kaffa 1261

Black Sea

Rome

BALKANS

Constantinople 1261

Amastris 1310

Samsun 1310

Athens 1305

Aegean Sea

Edessa 1098

Antioch 1098

■ The Roman Catholic world in 1000 AD

▨ Conquered between 1000 and 1462 AD by Roman Catholic rulers, and forming part of Catholic kingdoms

0 — 300

Miles

MAP II

Maps I–III are reproduduced from: Gilbert, M., *Imperial Russian History Atlas* (1978)

Alexander are heritors of Poland and Lithuania from their fathers only, whereas we are heritors of the Russian land from the beginning."[15]

Prior to this, by his second marriage to Sophia Palaiologos, a niece of the last Byzantine Emperor, in 1472, Ivan had in effect laid claim also to the spiritual-religious heritage of Constantinople, with Moscow as the new guardian, in Orthodox eyes, of the only true faith—the "third Rome," a fourth of which, as the prophecy had it, would not be.[16] It is important to note that, throughout their history, Russia's rulers, no less than Poland's, saw themselves as entrusted with the divine task of defending "the" faith and, with it, an entire way of life, thought, and culture—an historical mission. As Beazley rightly emphasises, " . . . *Holy Russia* has been no empty phrase. Constantly one finds the religious element surprising one afresh by the depth, the ubiquity, and the subtlety of its action in Russian history. . . . "[17]

This action was never more evident than during the national revival which put an end to the Time of Troubles (1606–1613), that period of anarchy following the death of Boris Godunov which witnessed the occupation of Moscow by the Poles, of Novgorod by the Swedes, of numerous attempts by Sigismund III of Poland—aided and abetted by many of the Russian boyars—to secure the throne of Muscovy for his son Wladyslaw or for himself, and finally the expulsion of the invaders and the *election* of a new dynasty and a new Tsar in the person of Michael Romanov. During this time of desperate struggle, it was the Holy Trinity-Saint Sergius monastery (Sergiev: since 1930 Zagorsk) that was the rallying-point, not only of spiritual, but also of political and military, resistance.[18]

V—POLAND TO THE PARTITIONS:
CZESTOCHOWA, SOBIESKI, KOŚCIUSZKO

Some 40 years later, Poland would find herself in a somewhat similar situation. Under simultaneous attack from the Russians and Swedes, who between them occupied most of the country, including

---

[15] Cited in Beazley *et al., op. cit.* (in note 12 above), pp. 80–81. Muscovite expansion during this period is shown in Map II.

[16] Constantinople had in 1453 fallen to the Turks, who then acquired control of the Balkan peninsula. One effect of this, as Riasanovsky remarks, was to strengthen "Muscovite xenophobia and self-importance." (*op. cit.* (in note 1 above), p. 113).

[17] *op. cit.* (in note 12 above), p. 19.

[18] See Beazley *et al., op. cit.* (in note 12 above), p. 161, where Forbes adds: "The monastery had already successfully withstood a siege of sixteen months by Polish forces. . . . It was strongly fortified, and was a sort of general base of arms, money, and food for the whole people."

Vilna, Warsaw, and Cracow, she in her turn would witness a national wonder—the miraculous defence, by the prior Kordecki and a handful of men, in the autumn of 1655, of the monastery of Czestochowa (with its famous image of the Black Virgin) which for the first time forced the all-conquering Swedes to withdraw. Amid a wave of religious and patriotic fervour, the Polish King, Jan Casimir, solemnly proclaimed that the Virgin of Czestochowa should be venerated for all time as the "Queen of the Crown of Poland"; and ever since, this shrine has remained for the Polish people, in Halecki's words, "their supreme consolation in times of anguish greater than that of 1655."[19] Unlike the Russian revival of 1611, however, this Polish rebirth, while it temporarily saved the country, was not fated to produce such enduring results. True, in a further brilliant feat of arms, the great Jan Sobieski, commanding a joint Polish-Habsburg force, in 1683 drove the Turks from Vienna and delivered Christian Europe from the advance of Islam. But this memorable triumph, which seemed to herald a new great age, would in fact prove merely "one last ray of glory before the twilight . . . a symbolic memory whose worth would grow with the misfortunes that subsequently befell the country."[20] With the next Russian reign, that of Peter the Great, begins that long-term decline in Polish fortunes which would culminate in the three partitions of 1772, 1793, and 1795 that, for over a century, would effectively erase Poland from the map.[21] But not before the Poles, in the Constitution of May 3, 1791, had produced a model that would have made of Poland a true parliamentary monarchy (a fact which explains its prompt suppression with massive Russian connivance[22]) and, under the inspired leadership of Kościuszko, had rallied to a man in one last heroic, albeit vain, attempt to save their country from political extinction.[23]

---

[19] One might add, never more so than today, on the occasion of the second visit to his homeland by the first Polish Pope in history. (See Halecki, *op. cit.* (in note 2 above), p. 201).

[20] Halecki, *op. cit.* (in note 2 above), pp. 217–218.

[21] Details of the three partitions are shown in Map III *q.v.*

[22] Fearing the loss of their own privileges, Felix Potocki and other Polish magnates in 1792 formed the so-called Targovica secession, aimed ostensibly at "restoring the liberty of the people" but in fact at overthrowing the new Constitution with massive Russian assistance (100,000 Russians crossed the frontier and finally occupied Warsaw). The parallel with present-day techniques is interesting. To this day, "Targovica" in Poland remains the byword for such treachery and is the brush with which all similar collaboration is tarred.

[23] The Poles were finally defeated at Maciejowice on October 10, 1794. Kościuszko, wounded and taken prisoner, was released in 1797 under Tsar Paul. He fought in the American War of Independence and died in 1817 in Switzerland (Solothurn). His remains are buried in Cracow.

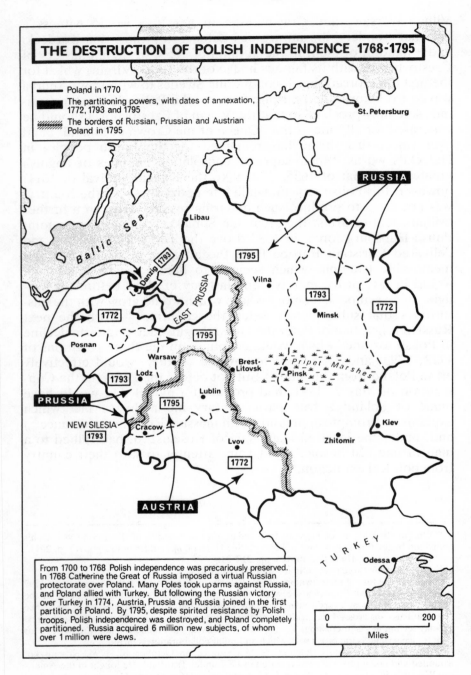

MAP III

VI—THE NINETEENTH CENTURY

1. *Russian attitudes to Poland*

With Napoleon's initial successes against the Russians and his establishment of the Duchy of Warsaw (1807), the Poles placed new hope in the lavish promises of their "enemies' enemy." Even after his defeat, at the Congress of Vienna, the partitioning Powers were at least brought to acknowledge a distinct Polish "nationality" and for the newly created Kingdom of Poland, drastically curtailed though it was, Alexander I produced a constitution rather more "liberal" than Napoleon's own.[24] But, well before his death in 1825, Alexander, like his brother monarchs, increasingly disregarded his own undertakings, and any immediate hopes of a viable solution for Poland died with the Decembrist Revolt. Not that the Poles would have done much better had the Decembrists triumphed. In the whole intellectual history of Russo-Polish relations (which now becomes our main concern), there are few more significant—and depressing—factors than the almost universal opposition of the "liberal" Decembrists to Polish independence. In view of the tenuous state of such "independence" to-day, it is pertinent to recall that Pestel, the leader of the Southern Society and the author of a projected republican constitution for Russia, while accepting the *principle* of Polish independence, made it subject to a so-called Russian "right of convenience" which stipulated that (a) the frontiers of any future Polish State must be fixed by the Russian government; (b) the two countries must be linked by a permanent alliance, in peace as in war; and (c) the new Poland must adopt the same socio-political system as Russia. Further comment is needless.[25] In their negative attitude towards Poland, the Decembrists were far from being alone. The future Slavophils, for instance (with whom they display a number of common features),[26] considered the Poles with a mixture of sorrow and anger, regarding them, in terms of their own national-religious philosophy, essentially as traitors to the Orthodox cause. In their peculiar conception of history, it was precisely this act of "treachery" that accounted for the decline of Polish culture and ultimately the collapse of the Polish State.[27]

---

[24] This is admitted by Halecki (*op. cit.* (in note 2 above), p. 285).

[25] On this (still little-known) aspect of Decembrist thought, *cf.* esp. Georges Luciani, *La Société des Slaves Unis (1823–1825)* (1963), pp. 175–181. A further irony in this story is Berdyaev's description of Pestel's character as displaying "that will to power and violence which in the twentieth century appeared in the communists" (*The Origin of Russian Communism* (1955) p. 24).

[26] On this point, *cf.* especially N.L. Brodskij, *Rannie slavjanofily* (1910) pp. XXXI–XXXV.

[27] *Cf.* esp. N.V. Riasanovsky, *Russia and the West in the Teaching of the Slavophiles* (1952) pp. 111–112, where the author cites the views of Khomiakov, Ivan Aksakov, and Samarin.

At the time of the Polish insurrection of 1830, anti-Polish feeling in Russia was almost universal. Though Pushkin's polemical poem *To the Detractors of Russia*, written on that occasion, was *primarily* directed against Western meddling in "a quarrel between Slavs," his correspondence reveals a profound contempt and aversion for the Poles (of whom Mickiewicz, he declared, was the only one to interest him). "Our old enemies will thus be exterminated," he wrote on December 9, 1830, "and thus nothing of what Alexander did can survive, for nothing is based on the true interests of Russia. . . . We can only pity the Poles. We are too powerful to hate them, the war . . . will be a war of extermination . . . or ought to be, at least." A later letter ends with the words " . . . *et delenda est Varsovia*."[28] In his polemics, Pushkin was joined by another great Russian poet—the generally apolitical, generous, and humane Zhukovsky.[29] Pushkin's poem even found approval with Chaadayev, normally regarded as a living veto of narrow Russian chauvinism and one of the very rare Russian thinkers to have castigated Russia's Byzantine heritage, contrasting it with the truly civilising mission of the Catholic West.[30] At the time, almost the only dissenting voice was that of Prince P.A. Viazemsky, who had won many friends in Warsaw during Alexander's "pro-Polish" period. Castigating both Pushkin and Zhukovsky with rare vehemence, Viazemsky acidly remarked that the real trouble was that "we have not succeeded in making the Poles like our rule." "Our actions in Poland," he wrote, "will set us

---

[28] Letters (in French) to E.M. Khitrovo of January 21, 1831, December 9, 1830, February 9, 1831 in: *Pis'ma Puškina k Elizavete Mikhajlovne Khitrovo 1827–1832* (1927), pp. 14, 11, and 17 respectively.

[29] Zhukovsky's poem "Old Song to a New Tune" appeared with Pushkin's *Detractors* . . . and "Borodino Anniversary" in a brochure (*On the Capture of Warsaw*) published on or about September 14, 1831. Warsaw had been occupied by the Russians during August 24–27.

[30] *Cf.* Chaadayev's letter to Pushkin of September 18, 1831 ("Enfin, vous voilà poète national; . . . La pièce aux ennemis de la Russie est surtout admirable; c'est moi qui vous le dis.") in: *Sočinenija i pis'ma P. Ja. Čaadaeva* (1913) I, pp. 162–166. Chaadayev's praise seemed so much out of character with his general philosophy that Lednicki interpreted it as a subtle piece of mordant satire (*Russia, Poland and the West* (1954), p. 82). But Lednicki did not know Chaadayev's recently discovered manuscript "Un mot sur la question polonaise," in which, in a narrowly Russian analysis of her history, he argues that for Poland, incapable of existence as an independent state, the only salvation lies in "sharing the destinies of her (Russian) brother nation." *Cf.* J. Brun-Zejmis, "A Word on the Polish Question by P. Ya. Chaadaev" in XI *California Slavic Studies* (1980), pp. 25–32. Chaadayev originally exposed his philosophy of history in his first *Philosophical Letter* (written in French in 1829), whose publication in October 1836 in the review *Telescope* (in Russian translation) created a vast scandal: for some nine months, the government placed him under virtual house arrest, declared him insane, and insisted he be visited each day by a doctor. His reply was his *Apology of a Madman* (1837), in which, while defending his basic position, he confessed to exaggeration, predicted a promising *future* for Russia, and paid tribute to the humility and heroism of the Orthodox Church. *Cf.* Pierre Tchaadaev *Lettres philosophiques* . . . présentées par François Roulet, Paris, 1970.

back another fifty years from European civilisation." "We act as a brake on the movements of (other) peoples striving towards gradual moral and political perfection. . . . We are outside civilised Europe, but at the same time drag on it like a weight."[31] Viazemsky was not quite alone—but almost. Alexander Turgenev, in a letter to his brother Nicolas, agreed with the latter that there was still a trace of barbarism in Pushkin (albeit "only in relation to Poland"), while adding that Viazemsky was the only person known to him who had sized up the poem correctly.[32] On the whole, the poem was accorded a favourable, even rapturous, reception. Russian opinion was almost unanimously anti-Polish and, broadly speaking, this holds true, not just for the 1830 insurrection and its immediate aftermath, but for the century in general and, as we shall see, for the second (1863) insurrection in particular.

If ever an exception may be said to have "proved" the rule, it is in the fate meted out to the only leading Russian thinker of this time to have consistently supported the Polish cause: Alexander Herzen. Leaving Russia in 1847, Herzen, by way of France and Switzerland, in 1852 settled in London where, with the help and friendship of the Polish emigration, he set up the first free Russian press in history. In 1857, he launched his famous periodical *The Bell* (*Kolokol*) which, smuggled into Russia in thousands of copies, played a vital role in the Russian "resistance" of the time (reminiscent of to-day's *Samizdat*), not only for the information it contained on events inside Russia, but for the inspiration of its message, calling for reforms, including the abolition of serfdom and censorship and the establishment of a more humane society generally. In 1861, serfdom was in fact abolished, and Herzen's fame and influence in Russia were at their height. But when, with the Polish insurrection of January 1863, Herzen—despite the warnings of friends and, be it said, his own dire forebodings—persisted on principle in continuing to support the cause of Polish independence, his following vanished almost overnight. As with the Decembrists, such support was more than the Russian "liberals" could countenance. The insurrection, like all previous ones, was brutally suppressed and, with it, even the nominal autonomy that still existed. The Poles were left once more to await a

---

[31] *Cf.* Viazemsky's diaries (note-books) for September 14, 15, and 22, 1831, in P.A. Vjazemskij, *Zapisnye knižki (1813–1848)* (1963) pp. 211–215.

[32] Letter of October 2, 1832, cited in *Pis'ma Puškina k El. Mikh. Khitrovo, op. cit.* (in note 28 above), p. 290. A detailed article in this book, by M.D. Beljaev, deals with the Polish insurrection in the light of Pushkin's letters ("Pol'skoe vosstanie po pis'mam Puškina k E.M. Khitrovo," pp. 257–300).

disaster of international proportions—in the event, the First World War—as the only means of recovering their independence.[33]

2. *Poland at home and abroad*

On January 25, 1831, at the height of the so-called "November rising," the Polish Diet (*Sejm*) had renounced allegiance to the Russian Tsar and appointed a national government headed by a man universally respected in Poland and abroad, Prince Adam Czartoryski. As the situation deteriorated, it had also passed a law enabling decisions vital to the welfare of the country to be taken, if need be, on foreign soil, subject to a *quorum* of 33 of its members. In the event, this foreign soil proved to be France, which before long found itself sheltering a type of State within the State—a Poland in microcosm, comprising the elite of an entire nation, with its soldiers, statesmen, and poets. Henceforth, and for a long time to come, Paris becomes the centre of Polish national policy and Polish culture.

Politically, this Polish emigration was marked by two broad tendencies. The first was represented by Czartoryski who, though not in charge of an official "government in exile," was regarded, at least by Polish monarchists, as "le roi *de facto*," and had his own diplomatic representatives in most European capitals from London to Constantinople. For 30 years, this great patriot worked tirelessly in Poland's cause, endeavouring by every available means to instruct and enthuse European statesmen and writers in the Polish problem and keep it alive on the international agenda. With the Crimean War, hopes rose of British and French support for a revived Poland but, in the face of Prussian and Austrian opposition, the matter was dropped. When Czartoryski died in 1861, Poland's political position seemed as desperate as ever. The other tendency, the *Democratic Society* grouped round the historian Lelewel, a hero of 1831, preferred direct action to diplomacy, appealing mainly to international solidarity. Following the failure of the Cracow rising in 1846, its followers participated in both the Prussian and Austrian insurrections

---

[33] On Herzen's life and work, *cf.* especially E. Lampert, *Studies in Rebellion* (1957) Chap. IV, pp. 171–259: this is the best general study of Herzen in English. Birkett maintains that, in 1863, "Russian opinion had for a long time been sympathetic to the Poles" and that it was the diplomatic intervention on their behalf by Britain, France, and Austria that caused "an explosion of patriotic feeling that made it easy for the Russian government to disregard the representations of the Powers" (Beazley *et al., op. cit.* in note 12 above, p. 443). The first statement seems highly questionable. As for the second: the Russians mainly reproached the Poles with "rocking the boat" just when Alexander II was embarking on his great reforms. These included some concessions to Poland, though hardly the restoration of "much of the former Polish autonomy" claimed by Riasanovsky (*op. cit.* (in note 1 above), p. 420).

of the revolutionary year 1848. But all to no avail; their efforts for Poland proved no more successful than Czartoryski's diplomacy.

With the accession, in 1855, of the more liberal Alexander II, a new attempt at a *modus vivendi* with Russia was attempted in Poland by the marquess Alexander Wielopolski; but his general concept of the old "autonomy" could not satisfy those "extremists" who aspired to complete independence. Patriotic demonstrations flared sporadically during 1861 and 1862 and, when the Russians started enrolling in their army the agitators denounced by the police, open insurrection broke out on a nationwide scale (January 22, 1863). Despite the sympathy and moral backing of Napoleon III and Pius IX, of Britain and Austria, no one was prepared to risk war on behalf of the Poles, who again found themselves abandoned to their fate. Yet for them, the insurrection, an act of sheer despair, remains to this day a sacred memory; for, as Halecki stresses, " . . . no sacrifice in the national cause had ever been more disinterested or more moving."[34]

Against this dismal background of military and diplomatic failure, however, there shines like a beacon the most brilliant and original age in Polish intellectual and cultural history—an age which, against all the laws of history, grew and thrived on foreign soil. As a young student in his native Vilna, Adam Mickiewicz had been deported to Russia—an event to which he owed his close friendship with Pushkin. On the eve of the 1830 rising, he had already stirred the national ardour of his countrymen with his drama of *Konrad Wallenrod*, the prototype of the persecuted patriot who bears his cross for millions of his fellow-men. From his exile in Paris, he continued, in a variety of *genres*, on the path that was to establish him as Poland's national poet. In *Pan Tadeusz*, he evoked, in twelve cantos, the great events of Poland's glorious past. In his *Book of the Polish Pilgrims*, couched in Biblical style and ending with the Prayer of the Pilgrim ("God of the Jagellons, God of Sobieski, God of Kościuszko! Have mercy upon our country, have mercy upon us!"), he produced a literary rendering, as Halecki puts it, of "the confused feelings of the insurgents of 1830, (of) what alone was capable of uniting the emigré politicians and so keeping alive, beyond all possibility of success, the conspiracies and insurrections of the succeeding generation."[35] Over and beyond the hearts of his compatriots, Mickiewicz saw it as his mission to enlighten the West. In this sense,

---

[34] *Op. cit.* (in note 2 above) p. 302. On Russian reactions to these events, *cf.* note 33 above; in some views, Western diplomatic intervention did the Poles more harm than good.

[35] *Op. cit.* (in note 2 above), p. 306. On the *Book of the Polish Pilgrims, cf.* also E. Privat, *L'Europe et l'Odyssée de la Pologne au XIXe siècle* (1918), pp. 175–180.

his supreme achievement will always remain the lectures on *The Slavs* which he read at the Collège de France in 1840–44. These lectures aroused an enthusiastic response in the generous heart of Jules Michelet, who, in his *Legend of Kościuszko* and other *Democratic Legends of the North*, took up the Polish cause with single-minded idealism—but also a blatant anti-Russian partiality that would provoke an impassioned response from Herzen, in defence of the Russian *people* (whom Michelet found it hard to distinguish from their rulers!).[36] When, in his lecture of June 27, 1843, Mickiewicz—with a magnanimity that puts Pushkin to shame[37]—makes his impassioned plea for inter-Slav reconciliation, Michelet's immediate reaction is one of stunned indignation: "Prodigieuse abnégation! Monstrueuse clémence!" But later, composing his *Legends*, he warms more and more to Mickiewicz' grandiose—by then Messianic—conception of a Poland which, with Christian abnegation and humility, patiently bears her cross in atonement for the violence of sinful humanity. "Magnanimous instincts of generosity and grandeur, heroic impulses of the heart, to love those who have made us suffer. . . . It is the mystery of the white eagle which sheds its blood, and (thereby) saves the black (one)."[38] In his *Legends*, Michelet returns many a time to this idea, clearly inherited from Mickiewicz, that Russia can only be saved "by the fraternity of Poland—Without her, without that luckless Poland whom people believe dead, Russia would have no chance of resurrection."[39]

In his devotion to the Polish cause, Mickiewicz did not confine himself to literature or lecturing. It was while on a diplomatic mission to Constantinople aimed at raising a Polish legion to fight

---

[36] *Le Peuple russe et le socialisme. Lettre à Monsieur J. Michelet*, Professeur au Collège de France, par Iscander (A. Herzen), Paris, 1852: On Michelet, Mickiewicz, and Herzen, *cf.* esp. the excellent edition annotated by M. Cadot: J. Michelet, *Légendes démocratiques du Nord* (1968), *passim*; also our article: "Mickiewicz, Herzen et l'image du monde slave dans la pensée historique de Michelet" in 7 *Slavica Helvetica* (1973), pp. 75–92. In English: Waclaw Lednicki, "Mickiewicz at the Collège de France," in *Bits of Table Talk on Pushkin, Mickiewicz, Goethe, Turgenev, and Sienkiewicz* (1956) pp. 132–156. For Mickiewicz' lectures, *cf. Les Slaves* Cours professé au Collège de France par A. Mickiewicz, Paris, 1849, tt. I–V. (Vols. I–III contain the lectures for 1840–42, Vols. IV and V those for 1842–44.)

[37] Pushkin's strong anti-Polish views—and poems—have already been discussed. Mickiewicz attacked the poems in a satirical one of his own *To my Moscow Friends*. Pushkin's reply (a poem beginning "He once lived among us") showed a complete inability, or unwillingness, to accept Mickiewicz' own patriotism, and included the lines: "Our peaceable guest has become our foe—and, to please the turbulent crowd, he instils his poems with venom." Mickiewicz, to our knowledge, never changed his personal feelings towards Pushkin. A questionable legend even has it that, on Pushkin's death, he challenged Dantes, his assassin, to a duel. *Cf.* in general W. Lednicki, "Ex Oriente Lux (Mickiewicz and Pushkin)," *op. cit.* (in note 36 above), pp. 157–179.

[38] Michelet, *op. cit.* (in note 36 above), pp. X, 23–24, and 264.

[39] Michelet, *op. cit.* (in note 36 above), p. 17.

the Russians that, in 1855, he died of cholera. His life's work for Poland, and the doctrine that inspired it, is well summarised by Lednicki: "Mickiewicz led Poland into the broad fields of Europe and he assured her of an undying prestige on the continent. His conception of an independent Poland was closely bound up with his idea of the moral regeneration of Europe and Poland. . . . In suffering Poland awaited and prepared the coming of the reign of the New Testament, and prepared herself for it. And that was the theodicy of her martyrdom; that is the essence of Polish Messianism." Mickiewicz' brand of Messianism, despite (or because of?) a definite mystical component, inspired mainly by Towiański, was never more powerful or more relevant than in Poland to-day. If his teaching, in a certain sense, is "aristocratic," it is first and foremost deeply Christian. As Lednicki reminds us in another passage: "He also taught love and respect for the suffering masses. He shows the revolutionary truth that the real creative power of human comprehension and love, the factor of international understanding, is to be found in the hearts of the common people. He showed how the faith and prayer of the Polish common people stopped Russian officers and soldiers whom Polish guns could not stop . . . 'The common people are those who suffer, those who yearn, those who are free in spirit, who do not come with a sheaf of ready-made systems'. . . . "[40]

Mickiewicz is the greatest name in Polish literature—but the same golden age produced many other writers whose spiritual heritage lives on, a source of pride and inspiration, in Poland today: Krasiński, author of a remarkable *Undivine Comedy* which contains a prophetic vision of the excesses of the coming revolution, but notably, too, the creator of a Polish philosophy of history, also Messianic in conception—a Christian transformation of Hegelian doctrine, at times reminiscent of Chaadayev, in its search for "the kingdom of God on earth," and, *mutatis mutandis*, of the (Russian) Slavophils, in the missionary role assigned to Poland in the divine order of things; and Słowacki, the third great poet of this period, who may be described as the poet of historical symbols; at times in disagreement with Mickiewicz or Krasiński, he was at one with them in his mystical interpretation of Poland's sufferings. These three poets, the intellectual leaders of their generation, were surrounded by many others: Cieszkowski, friend and disciple of Krasiński, who contributed his share to Poland's spiritual rebirth with his remarkable commentary of the *Paternoster*, and Norwid, the solitary, duty-

---

[40] Lednicki, *op. cit.* (in note 36 above), pp. 153–154.

conscious author of *Vade-mecum*; historians—Lelewel (already mentioned), whom Halecki called the "Polish Michelet," and Szajnocha; painters—Chelmonski, Kossak, Matejko, Michalowski and Grottger; and finally, the best-known name of them all—the immortal Chopin. That these, and other, men of genius should have created, far from their native soil, another Poland—living, spiritual, timeless, indestructible—is one of the more astounding and inspiring paradoxes of history.[41]

VII—THE TWENTIETH CENTURY: POLAND AND RUSSIA TODAY

Out of this prodigious achievement, Poland emerged as a living symbol: not only of liberty, in the face of an order based purely on force, but also, as Halecki rightly stresses, of *nationhood*, which could survive independently and outside of the all-powerful State.[42] In 1918, this nationhood would at last rejoin its own, independent, State. In the war against the Bolsheviks (1920), the ancient feud resumed once more, ending, after several reversals of fortune, in favour of the Poles who, by the Treaty of Riga (1921), took their brief revenge and, with it, extensive territories to the East.[43] By a further paradox of history, the period of new Polish independence up to 1939 adds little that is of relevance to our problem. For most of this time, the new Soviet State was virtually sealed off from Western contact, and in any case the Poles were busy setting their own new house in order. Polish suspicions of Soviet intentions were revealed when, in the face of the Nazi threat, they consistently refused any defensive alliance that would entail the presence of Soviet troops on their soil.[44] The rest of the story is too well known to require detailed treatment here: the 1939 Nazi-Soviet pact; the invasion and occupation of Poland, first, by Nazi Germany and then by Soviet Russia (*cf.* Map IV); the liberation from the former and, in the wake of Yalta, under the iron heel and watchful eye of the latter, the travesty of "socialist" independence that has persisted, albeit with many vicissitudes (1956, 1970, 1980–81) to the present day. (*cf.* Maps V & VI). The period of the Second World War also includes the Katyn massacres and the betrayal of the Warsaw rising

---

[41] For a general account of this period, *cf.* especially Privat, (*op. cit.* (in note 35 above), Chaps. XII, XV, and XVI) and Halecki (*op. cit.* (in note 2 above), Chaps. XXI and XXII), on which this section is largely based.

[42] *Op. cit.* (in note 2 above), p. 316.

[43] Territories which, if not ethnically Polish, were no more ethnically Russian, but rather Ukranian or White-Russian.

[44] For this, the Poles were frequently criticised in the West for their "stubborn intransigence." In the light of subsequent events, their misgivings are better understood today.

The destruction of Poland was principally a German action. 1,700,000 German troops soon defeated the 600,000 Polish soldiers. German air attack destroyed the centres of the main Polish cities. The Poles hoped to make a final stand in the Pripet marsh area, but the Russian advance destroyed all chance of further Polish resistance

THE PARTITION OF POLAND 1939

German advance against Poland from 3 September 1939

Russian advance against Poland from 17 September 1939

Dividing line between the German and Russian zones of occupation, agreed upon in advance by the Russo-German Pact of 23 August 1939

Annexed by the Soviet Union in October 1939

Annexed by Germany

Annexed by Lithuania

0   100
Miles

MAP IV

Maps IV–VI are reproduduced from: Gilbert, M., *Soviet History Atlas* (1978)

MAP V

against the German invader in August 1944—both factors of immense psychological importance for an understanding of the climate today.

Compared with previous Russo-Polish settlements throughout history, that of 1945 was branded with one vital new factor: the birth and survival in Russia of Soviet Communism. This factor removes, on the face of things, the traditional Orthodox-Catholic bone of contention. In fact, in Russia, the same old "siege mentality," the same mistrust of a Catholic Poland, persists, and has since been fanned by the presence of a Polish Pope in Rome. In any case, the old feud is henceforth replaced by a new one, infinitely more fateful—the presence of a new ideology (materialist and atheist to boot) totally foreign to the entire Polish tradition; an ideology, moreover, which no significant body of Poles desired in 1945, and still less today. After nearly 40 years of "socialist independence," few Poles would quarrel with the account of this ideology given in the earliest years of Communist rule by a Polish statesman who staked his all in an effort to reach a decent solution for his people: "History has never known a better organised attempt to corrupt men and entire nations than that currently under way in the countries dominated by the Communists. The people living there are obliged to lie in order to survive, to hate instead of loving, to condemn the most patriotic of their countrymen, their natural leaders, even their own ideas. The outside world allows itself to be taken in by the manner in which the communists abuse the organs of true democracy, of true patriotism, and even, when needed, of true Christianity."[45]

In assessing how such an alien doctrine came to be imposed on the Polish people, it is customary to blame the Yalta Agreement (February 11, 1945). It would be more accurate to blame the deliberate failure of the Soviets, to this day, to honour that Agreement, which includes the following clause:

"The Provisional Government which is now functioning in Poland should . . . be reorganised on a broader democratic basis, with the inclusion of democratic leaders from Poland itself and from Poles abroad. This new Government should then be called the Polish Provisional Government of National Unity. . . . This Polish Provisional Government of National Unity shall be pledged to the holding of free and unfettered elections as soon as possible on the basis of universal suffrage and secret ballot."[46] In the event, of course, no

---

[45] Stanislas Mikolajczyk, *The Rape of Poland* (Our citation is retranslated from the French edition, *Le Viol de la Pologne* (1949), p. I).

[46] *Cf.* Winston Churchill, *The Second World War*, Vol. VI (1954), pp. 338–9, where the full text of the Yalta Agreement is given.

MAP VI

such elections were held, then or since. At the time, the Western Powers protested but, not having the will to intervene effectively (as Churchill admitted to Mikolajczyk),[47] they claimed not to have the means either—and the Soviet take-over was complete.

Everything that has happened in Poland since stems from this simple fact, mention of which, for totally inexplicable reasons, remains a virtual taboo even in the free West. Similar Western protests to Tsarist governments may not have achieved much for Poland, but at least they exposed the former to international opprobrium and kept the Polish problem alive in world opinion. Yet, since 1947, when the Soviets took full charge of Poland's destinies *via* a series of puppet governments, no protest has been raised, to our knowledge, either by the Great Powers or by the United Nations (otherwise so avid in invoking self-determination) against this flagrant breach of a solemn undertaking. If anyone, in West or East, hoped that in this way the Polish problem would disappear, they have been sadly disillusioned; the Polish nation has seen to that. *Solidarność* (to take only the latest and most spectacular demonstration of Polish *nationhood*) is something far more than a trade union that attracted ten million members overnight. It is yet one more of the great *symbols* of which Polish history is made—the symbol, as its name implies, of the solidarity of all those Poles, be they workers or writers, judges or journalists, priests or professors, surgeons or students, who, together with their families, are united in cherishing the most modest of human aspirations imaginable: the simple right to live their own lives in dignity and freedom—freedom, above all, from the eternal, ubiquitous "big lie," which is, in effect, the counter-symbol of a system which by definition lives, and must always live, in constant fear of the truth.

More specifically, the big lie in present-day Poland is the steadily cultivated fiction that the country is by its own choice a "real-socialist" State, whose leaders represent the true aspirations of their people, among whom a handful of counter-revolutionary trouble-makers in league with the CIA are trying to "destabilise" the peaceful post-war settlement in Europe.[48] *Solidarność* the free trade union has been suppressed by decree (as it was bound to be from the

---

[47] Mikolajczyk, *op. cit.* (in note 45 above), pp. 144–5.

[48] One of Warsaw's innumerable anecdotes from the martial-law period takes the form of a questionnaire. "Three men are found talking in the street: what does that represent?—An illegal meeting. When five men meet?—An illegal demonstration. And when ten million gather?—Just a handful of counter-revolutionary extremists."

start),[49] but *Solidarność* the symbol of Polish nationhood burns brighter than ever in Polish hearts, and no measures General Jaruzelski or Moscow can think up can alter this fact of life. The situation is thus one of utter deadlock: the Polish government cannot (even if it wished to) go far to meet popular aspirations without falling foul of the Kremlin (Mr. Rakowski has warned that there is no "more liberal" alternative to Jaruzelski, but only a "harder" one). But without a minimum of popular support (which, in the absence of dialogue, is inevitably lacking) it can do nothing to restore the country's economy or improve the political and social climate. To the extent that it disposes of overwhelming physical force, the régime can, in the short term, maintain a semblance of law and order; but, beyond this purely negative policy of repression, it has nothing constructive to offer whatever. Therein lies the supreme danger, for it is as idle as it is unintelligent to imagine that the Polish people, having savoured the heady draught of 18 months' relative freedom and dignity, will ever again submit passively to the dictates of Jaruzelski's "barrack-square socialism," as one perceptive observer has termed it.[50] This is the deeper meaning behind the oft-heard dictum that "after *Solidarność*, things will never be the same again," which is far more than a mere catch-phrase to keep up morale.

Jaruzelski's true motives are, understandably, the subject of conflicting assessments. His abiding tragedy is that, at the crucial moment, he could, with a little more imagination (he does not lack courage), have rallied the entire nation behind him and, with the support of the army, have faced the Soviets with a united, instead of a bitterly divided, people. His Kremlin masters would have plotted his downfall, but the task might well have defeated them, and it is unthinkable that under such circumstances they would have risked direct military confrontation. But this was not to be. Jaruzelski makes much play of his Polish patriotism and of the "enemies" that confront him, but his patriotism is of the insidious kind inculcated by his Soviet masters, and his "enemies," if the truth be told, are the

---

[49] Moscow's decision to crush *Solidarność* at all costs is convincingly demonstrated in the penetrating analysis by M. Heller, *Sous le regard de Moscou: Pologne (1980–1982)* (1982). Born in the U.S.S.R. in 1922, Heller spent many years in Poland before settling in Paris in 1969. These brilliant, well-informed articles originally appeared in the Polish review *Kultura* (Paris) under the pen-name A. Kruczek.

[50] The term (in German *Kasernensozialismus*) was coined by Bogdan Osadczuk, whose exceptionally well-informed articles on Poland in the *Neue Zürcher Zeitung* (under the signature: *ok*) constitute one of the finest sources of day-to-day information available. A selection of his articles covering the period 1956–1982 was recently published under the title *Weisser Adler, Kreuz und rote Fahne* (White Eagle, Cross, and Red Flag) by the Verlag NZZ (Zurich, 1982).

Polish people whom he claims to serve. Like most others around him, he is ultimately a product—one might say a creature—of Soviet indoctrination, deported as he was to the Soviet Union (where his parents "disappeared") in order to prepare him, like thousands of his countrymen, for just the sort of task that has now come his way. Basically, nothing has altered since the situation of October 1947 described by Mikolajczyk: " . . . All the control levers were—and remain—in the hands of the Russians. Their orders, even the most barbaric, were and still are carried out by Poles. The latter are either communists, or men of good faith whose minds have long since been circumvented. For the most part they were selected from the 1,500,000 Poles that Stalin had transported to Russia in 1939, and carefully 'prepared' to play their part."[51] Such a "man of good faith," once, was Jaruzelski, a son of the Polish *petite noblesse* who in his youth went to a Jesuit college. Such is the system, fiendish in its capacity for human depravation and corruption, that produces the modern version of the men of Targovica. . . .

It remains to say a word about the Catholic Church, whose survival, let alone its active role, in the life of contemporary Poland is yet another paradox, and one, no doubt, the Soviets would gladly do without. Having survived, under the inspired and resolute leadership of Stefan Wyszyński, the worst that Stalinist oppression could do, it received an unexpected boost with the election of his disciple, Karol Wojtyla, to the papal throne.

If the election alone fired the imagination of the Poles, it is no exaggeration to say that John Paul's first visit to his homeland set in motion a thorough-going spiritual revival of the entire nation. It is of this spiritual revival that *Solidarność* was born—not only the trade union, with its basic doctrine of non-violence, rooted in Polish history, its calm dignity in the face of insult and oppression (who can forget the Gdansk shipyards in August 1980?), but also *Solidarność* the symbol of nationhood, which, in a sense, carries on, in "internal emigration," the role of the ("external") emigration of the nineteenth century in France. While the influence of the Church on hearts and minds in Poland today is immensely powerful, its position is not an envious one. The Church strives to remain aloof from "politics," but what things are ultimately non-political in a Communist society? The poor, the hungry, the oppressed, often even the bereaved, the injured, and the unemployed, owe their misfortunes to the political dictates of the regime. The Church, in common with other free intellectual circles, is also concerned with the vital task of

---

[51] *Op. cit.* (in note 45 above), p. II.

educating (or re-educating) young Poles in the true history and morality of their country, countering the organised disinformation put out at all levels by the communist "educational" machine. The Church, like the citizen, is hugely concerned with the big lie, as with all those other elements of human demoralisation inseparable from the communist State. Despair sometimes overcomes even the bravest: to the long-standing problem of alcoholism is now added that of drugs.

As these lines are written (May 1983), the Jaruzelski régime is setting high hopes on the Pope's forthcoming second visit, partly for the aura of legitimacy and respectability it hopes to draw from it, but partly, as it affirms, in the hope that it will contribute to "national reconciliation." Karol Wojtyla knows his countrymen, and he has his own methods of getting his message across. That he will bring them new hope, new inspiration, and sound guidance, is beyond doubt. But it is hard to see what real reconciliation there can be between a nation attached to Western ideals of truth, human dignity, and freedom, and a régime which ultimately gets its orders from Moscow and which (perhaps for this very reason) has so far steadfastly turned down every appeal for an amnesty and refused all dialogue, with an obstinacy that smacks of a death-wish. When, in days to come, the story of the collapse of Soviet Communism comes to be written, the turning-point will be seen to have been the moment at which, before the eyes of the world, the workers of a Communist-ruled country rose to a man in peaceful protest against their government, and that government, after a protracted show of reasonableness designed in fact only to gain time, ultimately found no better solution than to resort to the mass arrest, imprisonment, "trial," and punishment of those same workers who, until the very day before, had been negotiating with them in good faith. With this, what little was left of the myth of Communism as the representative and defender of the workers' interests, was exposed, lock, stock, and barrel, once and for all.

As in the nineteenth century, the heart of the true Polish nation will continue to live in a "State within the State," this time in internal emigration. But *a valid political solution* can only be brought about by the final implementation—or, failing this, the revision—of the Yalta Agreement. The claim that the Soviet Union is entitled, for reasons of its own security, indefinitely to impose its will on 30 million Poles is without precedent in modern history, and totally unacceptable. As long as it continues to do so, as long as it fails to arrive at a working relationship based on something more viable than brute force, so long will Poland—through no fault of the Poles—remain a permanent focus of disaffection and a constant danger to world peace. Those who claim to be anxious to "reduce the causes of tension in Europe" would do well to give first attention to this first of causes. As for the Soviets, they would be wise, not least in their own long-term interests, to ponder the lesson drawn over 150 years ago by one of the most intelligent Russians of his time, Pushkin's friend Prince Viazemsky: "At the first (sign of) war, the first movement inside Russia, Poland will rise against us, or else we shall have to find a Russian sentry for every Pole alive. There is one solution: let go of Poland . . . Let Poland choose her own way of life."[52] Then, but only then, might there be some hope, if not of burying, at least of surmounting, the tragic suspicions and hatreds of a millenium.

---

[52] *Op. cit.* (in note 31 above), p. 212 (diary entry for September 14, 1831).

THE SOUTHERN AFRICAN DEVELOPMENT CO-ORDINATION CONFERENCE

By

P. E. SLINN

THE history of attempts at effective sub-regional economic co-operation in Africa south of the Sahara in the post-independence era is not a happy one. The Economic Community of West African States survives, but cannot yet be regarded as having achieved effective levels of co-operation between States. The most sophisticated and, for a time, the most successful attempt at sub-regional economic integration, the East African Community of Kenya, Uganda and Tanzania, proved only to have a ten-year life.[1] There are complex political and economic explanations for such failures. Perhaps the root cause lies in the over-ambitious nature of attempts at economic integration between countries of diverse political and economic outlook; the rhetoric of co-operation has not been matched by deeds and the political will has been lacking to overcome crises provoked by clashes of interests between member States, as between Kenya and Tanzania in the case of the East African Community. However, this is a problem common to all such organisations and is not confined to Africa, as the stormy history of the European Community demonstrates only too clearly. Africa and other regions of the developing world do however have special problems in the weak state of most of the economies involved in the process of co-operation. Perhaps too, it is particularly difficult for the political leadership of countries which have only relatively recently attained national independence to abandon some element of sovereignty in the interests of regional solidarity.

In the light of precedent, therefore, the prognosis for the latest African venture in sub-regional co-operation, the Southern African Development Co-ordination Conference (referred to hereafter as SADCC), may not seem too hopeful. However, as Dr. Fred Parkinson has reminded us, where regional economic organisations are concerned, it is the late bird which catches the worm.[2] The fact that

---

[1] The Community was established by Treaty in 1967, and effectively ceased to function from July 1, 1977.

[2] F. Parkinson, "The Law of Regional Communities for Economic Development," address to British Branch of International Law Association, London (October 20, 1981).

the inaugural meeting of what was to become SADCC was held in July, 1979, in Arusha, the former headquarters of the East African Community, may symbolise a willingness to learn from past mistakes and a determination to devise a new formula for sub-regional co-operation which will provide a secure and permanent environment for the achievement of regional development goals. Certainly, SADCC does present some interesting features for the student of international economic institutions, particularly, in Dr. Parkinson's phrase, "regional development communities." SADCC may also be seen as a phenomenon illustrative of the implementation of the evolving principles of the international law of development, including regionalism, solidarity and interdependence. The purpose of this article, therefore, is to offer a legal analysis of the structure and *modus operandi* of SADCC in order to evaluate the claims made on its behalf to innovation in the legal techniques used to provide a framework for co-operation between the member States.

I—THE HISTORICAL BACKGROUND

The Declaration by the Governments of Independent States of Southern Africa made at Lusaka, April 1, 1980—the "Lusaka Declaration" which may be regarded as the founding declaration of SADCC—was signed on behalf of nine States—Angola, Botswana, Lesotho, Malawi, Mozambique, Swaziland, Tanzania, Zambia and Zimbabwe.[3] No common denominator of previous regional co-operation linked all these States, but, within the group, there was considerable historical experience of various forms of co-operation in the economic sphere, both amongst themselves and involving outside countries. In particular, Tanzania, as mentioned above, had been a member of the East African Community; Zambia, Zimbabwe and Malawi had been members of the Federation of Rhodesia and Nyasaland, and rail, air and electric power common services between Zambia and what was then Southern Rhodesia survived the demise of that Federation in 1963; the three former High Commission territories of Botswana, Lesotho and Swaziland are members of the Southern African Customs Union, an association with the Republic of Southern Africa which has its origins as far back as the creation of the then Union of South Africa in 1910.

In the wider sphere, all members of SADCC, except Angola and Mozambique (itself once a candidate member of the Council for Mutual Economic Assistance—CMEA) are partners in the ACP (Africa Caribbean Pacific) Group and under the Lomé Convention

---

[3] *Southern Africa*: *Towards Economic Liberation*, London, 1981, p. 2.

régime established with the European Community; again with the exception of Angola and Mozambique, SADCC countries have experience of functional co-operation for development in the Commonwealth association.[4] As an example of experience at the bilateral level, the crisis provoked by the illegal declaration of independence in Southern Rhodesia in 1965 pushed Zambia and Tanzania into close co-operation in the field of road and rail services, including the remarkable Tanzara Railway, built in co-operation with the People's Republic of China. However, although it can be seen that some SADCC countries have experience of co-operation with one another in economic matters, it is also true that the SADCC grouping cuts across many former linkages, such as that of Tanzania with her former East African partners and those of Swaziland, Lesotho and Botswana with the Republic of South Africa, and involves countries with widely differing ideological approaches to economic development.

For SADCC planners, there was the memory of two major exercises in regional economic integration, the institutions created for the Federation of Rhodesia and Nyasaland and for the East African Community. Each involved formidable and complex legal arrangements, which this is not the place to analyse in detail. However, as we shall see, the focus of SADCC functional co-operation is in fields such as transport and energy, in which the experience for the Central and East African institutions illustrates the problems of jointly-owned inter-state corporations. As Reginald Herbold Green, who has had an important influence in shaping the structures of SADCC, commented, these " . . . have often been a source of discord outweighing any potential gain."[5]

In the case of Central Africa, the jointly-owned corporations were designed to preserve, after the demise of the Federation in 1963, interterritorial co-operation in the fields of electric power, civil air transport, railways and agricultural research.[6] The independence of the three territories and the stresses caused by the illegal declaration of independence in Southern Rhodesia soon brought these experiments to an end with the remarkable exception of the

---

[4] The historical background to SADCC is helpfully summarised in R. Hofmeier, "Die Southern Africa Development Conference (SADCC)" in *Africa Spectrum* (1981) pp. 245–264. I am most grateful to Dr. F. Parkinson for drawing my attention to this article, and supplying me with a summary in English of its contents. For the Commonwealth, see D.O. Judd and P.E. Slinn *The Evolution of the Modern Commonwealth 1902–1950* (1982) pp. 138–142.

[5] "Towards Southern Africa Regionalism: The Emergence of a Dialogue," *Africa Contemporary Record* (1978–79), p. A44.

[6] Federation of Rhodesia and Nyasaland, (Dissolution) Order in Council, 1963 (S.I. 1963 No. 2085).

Central African Power Corporation. Jointly-owned by Zambia and Zimbabwe, this body has been responsible for the Kariba hydro-electric power complex for nearly twenty years. As part of the elaborate institutional structure of the East African Community, corporations constituted as institutions of the Community were created to operate, jointly on behalf of the partner States, railways, harbours, airways, posts and telecommunications. These bodies did not survive the collapse of the Community itself.[7]

Both the East Africa Community and the Central African common services may be seen as legacies of the British colonial past in the sense that they reflect patterns of co-operation before independence. In political terms, this legacy may be seen as a liability. The roots of SADCC, however, do not lie in the colonial past but in the response of the newly independent countries of Southern Africa to the problem of confrontation with the remaining white-ruled States of the sub-region. After the independence of Mozambique and Angola in 1975, informal co-operation between the five "Front-Line" States—Angola, Botswana, Mozambique, Tanzania and Zambia—intensified at the political level in pursuit of the goal of the independence of Zimbabwe. It was also recognised, however, that economic as well as political co-operation had a key role to play in the consolidation of freedom in South Africa. At a meeting of the foreign ministers of the Front-Line States, held in Botswana in May, 1979, it was decided to convene a conference of economic ministers to devise a programme of action for the promotion of regional economic co-operation. It was decided also to take the initiative and invite representatives of bilateral and multilateral external co-operating agencies and institutions to discuss the proposed programme. Both these meetings took place at Arusha, Tanzania, in July, 1979, a gathering which came to be known as SADCC 1, the first Southern African Development Co-ordination Conference.[8]

II—SADCC: Objectives
Institutions and Procedures

The way in which SADCC took shape after the Arusha Conference certainly demonstrates the flexible and pragmatic approach by which the planners set such great store: the first priority was to identify development objectives and needs and to create only those institutional structures which were essential to service the oper-

---

[7] Treaty for East African Co-operation 1967, Chap. XIX arts. 71–79, Ian Brownlie (Ed.) *Basic Documents on African Affairs* (1971) p. 63.

[8] *Op. cit.* (in note 3 above), pp. x–xii.

ations required.[9] From a legal point of view, therefore, the creation
of SADCC appears a rather haphazard and untidy process, with a
number of carts appearing before the horse. This, however, is a
source of pride to SADCC itself: the Vice-President of Botswana
has described it as " . . . a rather unconventional regional economic
co-operation grouping in its sectoral priorities . . . its stated goals,
its institutional structure and its operating procedures."[10]

The development objectives and a programme of action emerged
from a 'summit' meeting held in Lusaka on April 1, 1980. This was
attended not only by the Front Line participants in the Arusha
meeting, but also by Lesotho, Malawi, Swaziland and Zimbabwe,
the latter (strictly still "Southern Rhodesia" as independence was
still just over two weeks away). The Lusaka Declaration, signed by
or on behalf of the Heads of Government of all nine countries, set
out the following development objectives to be pursued through co-
ordinated action: (a) the reduction of economic dependence, particularly, but not only, on the Republic of South Africa; (b) the
forging of links to create a genuine and equitable regional integration; (c) the mobilisation of resources to promote the implementation of national, inter-State and regional policies; (d) concerted
action to secure international co-operation within the framework of
a strategy for economic liberation.[11]

The Declaration identified transport and communications as the
key to economic liberation from dependence upon South Africa and
contained a commitment to create a Southern African Transport
and Communications Commission (SATCC) "to co-ordinate the
use of existing systems and the planning and financing of additional
regional facilities."[12] However, the principle on which action would
be taken regarding transport, communications and other key areas
of activity was that of *sectoral responsibility*. Thus responsibility for
transport and communications, and therefore for the establishment
of SATCC, was allocated to Mozambique; responsibility for industrial development projects was assumed by Tanzania, for food
security by Zimbabwe, for animal disease control and crop research
by Botswana, for energy by Angola, for manpower development by
Swaziland and from Zambia for the preparatory studies for the
establishment of a Southern African Development Fund. Subsequently, other sectoral responsibilities were assumed: soil conser-
vation, Lesotho; mining, Zambia; fisheries, wild life and forestry,

[9] *From Dependence and Poverty Toward Economic Liberation*, SADCC (1981), p. 8.
[10] Opening statement by Hon. P.S. Nmusi, SADCC Maseru, January 27, 1983.
[11] *Loc cit.* (in note 3 above).
[12] *Ibid.*

Malawi; security printing, Zimbabwe.[13] The application of the principle of national responsibility was designed to avoid the need for
the elaborate institutional structures and large centralised bureauc-
racies which have characterised the East African Community and
other regional economic communities such as the EEC.

Significantly, the Lusaka Declaration was addressed not only to
the peoples of Southern Africa but also to international bodies and
States outside Southern Africa; these were invited to co-operate in
implementing programmes towards economic liberation and development in the region. However, from the beginning the emphasis
was on co-operation with international partners, rather than on aid.
"Ours is not a begging bowl," as Prime Minister Mugabe of Zimbabwe put it.[14] Annual conferences would be held between the
SADCC states and the co-operating governments, international
organisations and development agencies in order to review and evaluate projects and plan future investment. Thus there would be a
regular "dialogue" between the SADCC States and their international partners in development, though not one involving the creation of elaborate institutions on the lines of those involving the
EEC and ACP States in the Lomé Convention machinery.

During the course of the year following the Lusaka Summit, a
series of institutional arrangements evolved, as a SADCC document
rather ponderously put it, "in response to perceived needs of ongoing substantive operations."[15] A ministerial meeting took place in
Salisbury in September, 1980, to prepare for a second major Conference involving international partners which took place in Maputo
in November, 1980 (SADCC 2). Although SADCC itself was still
constituted on an entirely informal basis without any governing
between the member States, the latter proceeded to adopt a *Convention on the Establishment of the Southern Africa Transport and
Communications Commission*, (SATCC), the text of which was
approved by ministers at the September 1980, meeting.[16] Eventually, at a second Summit meeting, held at Salisbury, Zimbabwe,
on July 20, 1981, Heads of State and Governments signed a *Memorandum of Understanding on the Institutions of the Southern African
Development Co-ordination Conference*, codifying, in the words of
the communiqué "all SADCC decisions relating to institutional
arrangements." These were designed to "provide SADCC with an

---

[13] Agenda of SADCC Council of Ministers meeting, Maseru, January 26, 1983 recorded a
review of progress regarding members' sectoral responsibilities.
[14] Address to Salisbury Summit, July 20, 1981.
[15] *Loc. cit.* (in note 9 above).
[16] Below, Section II, *Sectoral Commissions* (Article IV).

effective and flexible mechanism for regional consultation and decision making" while eschewing "the creation of a large and unwieldy bureaucracy in favour of a system which places responsibility for the implementation of its programme on the Governments of Member States."[17]

Although styled a "memorandum of understanding," the formula usually employed when an international instrument does not create binding obligations, the text sets out the agreement of the parties and refers to obligations assumed thereby. It would appear therefore that the memorandum does constitute an agreement registrable under Article 102 of the United Nations Charter, although it does not appear having been so registered. The memorandum recites the development objectives annunciated in the Lusaka Declaration and provides for five SADCC institutions. These are (a) the Summit of Heads of State or Government, (b) the Council of Ministers, (c) Sectoral Commissions, (d) the Standing Committee of Officials, and (e) the Secretariat.

The Summit (Art. II), which consists of the Heads of State or Government of all member States, is "the supreme institution of SADCC" and is "responsible for the general direction and control of the functions of SADCC and the achievement of its objectives." The Summit meets at least once a year and takes decisions by consensus. The *Council* (Art. III) is the executive organ of SADCC and consists of one Minister from each member State. The Chairman of the Council of Ministers is appointed by the member State holding the Chairmanship of the Summit. The Vice-Chairman is elected from among the members of the Council and holds office for two years. This provision is as amended by the Summit held at Gaborone, Botswana in July 1982.[18] The Council is required to meet at least once a year: in practice it meets three times a year, including one meeting before the annual Summit and one before the annual SADCC meeting, which it is the Council's responsibility to convene, with co-operative governments and agencies. The Council is responsible to the Summit and takes its decisions also be consensus. It has discretion to appoint Ministerial Committees for programmes in functional areas.

Sectoral Commissions (Article IV). The Summit is authorised to establish, in addition to SATCC, other *Sectoral Commissions* for

---

[17] SADCC Communiqué July 20, 1981 in "From Dependence and Poverty," *loc. cit.* (in note 9 above), Appendix A. The Memorandum itself is at Appendix B. Curiously, although the organisation is styled "Conference" in the title of the Memorandum, the Conference is not itself an institution of SADCC. References to SADCC 1, SADCC 2, SADCC 3, and SADDC 4 refer to the meetings with the co-operating partners.

[18] *Record of Gaborone Summit*, July 22, 1982, SADCC.

programmes in functional areas, each such commission to be governed by a convention to be adopted by the Council and ratified to by member States. So far SATCC is the only commission to have been created under this provision. A new Convention was adopted by the Gaberone Summit in July 1982 to replace the original 1980 convention which lacked provision regarding entry into a force, amendment, and settlement of disputes. The convention is a binding and registrable international agreement between the SATCC States and provides that the commission shall consist of three organs, a Committee of Ministers, a Co-ordinating Official Committee and a Technical Unit, in accordance with sectoral responsibility. The Chairmanship of the ministerial and of the co-ordinating committees rests with Mozambique, where the headquarters of the commission are situated. Article II of the Convention provides that one representative each of the liberation movements of Southern Africa recognised by the Organisation of African Unity (OAU) shall be accorded observer status at meetings of the Committee of Ministers and the co-ordinating Committee. The Technical Unit which has a key role in the preparation, presentation of policy and programmes relating to transport and communications is financed until the end of 1983 by the Nordic Countries—Denmark, Finland, Norway and Sweden. At the time of the SADCC 3 meeting at Maseru in January 1983, the SATTC programme consisted of over 106 projects with a total cost of 2·54 billion dollars, for about a quarter of which financial assistance was said to be pledged.[19] Truly the performance of SATCC in the designated priority field of transport and communications will be an important test of the effectiveness of the SADCC arrangements as a whole. It is intended that SATCC play a role in the co-ordination, planning and financing of projects which will be implemented by the member States rather than attempt to undertake multi-national projects. SATCC may also perform a useful international role in representing the member States in respect of the co-ordination and development of the region's transport and communications programme.

A *convention on the establishment of the Southern African Energy Commission* also reached the draft stage in 1982. However, the Council of Ministers at its Luanda meeting in June 1982 decided to postpone the establishment of the commission "dependent upon the development of a programme of concrete regional energy projects."[20] This decision does appear to reflect SATCC's determination not to create institutional structures prematurely.

---

[19] "SADCC 4 meets in Masseru" *The Courier*, N. 78 (March-April 1983), p. XII.
[20] *Record of Council of Ministers Meeting, Luanda* June 25/26, 1982 Vol. 1, p. 10.

At the official level, the Memorandum of Understanding provides for a *Standing Committee of Officials* responsible to the Council, which may also appoint sub-committees of officials for programmes in functional areas convened and co-ordinated by the governments. *The Secretariat* is headed by an Executive Secretary and his Deputy. It is perhaps significant that SADCC managed for over two years without a Secretariat, the office of which was not opened in Gaborone until October 1982. The office of Executive Secretary was then assumed by F.A. Blumeris, a Zimbabwean Diplomat who had experience as Ambassador to the European Community and before that in UN agencies. Again it is intended that the Secretariat will have a limited liaison and co-ordinating role responsible to the Council of Ministers. Functional sectoral programme responsibility will remain with the commissions and the sectoral co-ordinating States. No doubt, however, the role of the Executive Secretary and the Secretariat will evolve as the needs of SADCC require. It will be recalled that the role of the Commonwealth Secretary General was envisaged in very restricted terms when the Secretariat was first established in 1965. Since then, however, the Commonwealth Secretariat has assumed important functions and the Secretary General himself has emerged as a key spokesman for the organisation.[21]

The Memorandum of Understanding also contains general provisions which are of interest in establishing the legal character of the SADCC organisation. Article IX provides that SADCC itself shall have in the territory of each member State, to the extent consistent with its laws, such legal capacity as may be necessary in the exercise of its functions. The Executive Secretary, his Deputy and other staff enjoy in the territories of member States privileges and immunities as are necessary for the fulfilment of their functions. Article XI is designed to protect the international character of the Secretariat. The Executive Secretariat may not seek or receive instructions from any member State or from any authority external to SADCC. They are designated as international officials responsible only to SADCC, a status which each member State is bound to respect. As far as new membership is concerned, any State may notify the Chairman of the Summit of its desire to become a member (Art. XIII). Admission of a state to SADCC shall be by consensus of the existing member States. The reference to consensus with regard to new membership and indeed the general reliance on consensus for the decision making process in SATCC institutions again recalls the Commonwealth

---

[21] A. Smith (with C. Sanger) *Stitches in Time: The Commonwealth in World Politics* (1981), pp. 38–43. Smith was Secretetary-General of the Commonwealth, 1965–75.

precedent.[22] As far as new membership is concerned it is unlikely that it will be extended beyond Namibia, to the plight of which express reference is made in the Lusaka Declaration. However, there is also a distant prospect of the accession of a South African state in which majority rule has been achieved.

The Memorandum contained provisions for amendment and settlement of dispute (Art. XIV and XV). The Summit is empowered to amend the Memorandum by consensus. This procedure has already been followed by the Gaborone Summit of July 22, 1982, which amended the provisions of paragraph 2 of Article III relating to the appointment of the Chairman and Vice-Chairman of the Council of Ministers. As far as disputes are concerned, those arising from the interpretation or application of the Memorandum and which cannot be settled by negotiation, conciliation or other means may be referred to the Summit by any Party to the dispute for decision. The Memorandum provides that the decision of the Summit shall be "final and binding" a provision which emphasises the obligatory character of the document. No dispute leading to the invoking of this article has, as yet, arisen.

The Memorandum of Understanding contains no reference to the Southern African Development Fund, the creation of which was provided for in the Lusaka Declaration in order to finance priority sectors such as transportation, mining, energy, agriculture and industry.[23] The Government of Zambia undertook the task of preparing a draft agreement between the member states for the creation of the Fund. A draft was considered by the ministerial meeting which took place in Salisbury in September, 1980, and the matter was referred back for further study with the assistance of the UN Economic Commission for Africa. Although a further report clearly identified the need for a sub-regional development institution in Southern Africa, ministers remained cautious. At the Maseru Council of Ministers in January, 1983, it was agreed to postpone any decision on the setting up of the Fund in view of currently unfavourable general economic conditions and doubts about financial support for the proposed institution.[24]

---

[22] Commonwealth Heads of Government meetings reach agreement by consensus which "involves the support of a significant majority sufficient to make the action under consideration practicable," Smith, *op. cit.* p. 44.

[23] Note 3 above.

[24] *Record of Council of Ministers*, Meeting, Maseru, January 26, 1983, SADCC.

III—SADCC: THE INTERNATIONAL DIMENSION

As noted above, the SADCC Memorandum provides that the Council of Ministers shall convene annually consultative meetings with co-operating governments and agencies. These meetings are not part of the formal SADCC decision-making machinery and there are no formal institutional arrangements which govern relations between the members of SADCC and the co-operating governments and agencies. However, this consultative process must be regarded as essential to the achievement of SADCC's development objectives, what the communiqué issued after SADCC 3 at Maseru in January 1983, referred to as the strengthening of "the community of interest between SADCC and its partners in development." Clearly these annual conferences play a key role in the procurement of outside financial commitment to SADCC programmes.[25] The outside participants in the annual conferences may be seen as committing themselves to the broad objectives of SADCC and participating in another element in the North-South dialogue and in part of the process designed to achieve a more equitable New International Economic Order. This "dialogue" between SADCC and its international partners is not a new phenomenon in international economic relations: one obvious precedent is the Euro-Arab dialogue.[26] The list of SADCC's "international co-operating partners" is an interesting one. It includes countries, both developed and developing, from most of the major world groupings: Algeria, Australia, Brazil, Canada, Egypt, both Germanies, India, Nigeria, the United Kingdom, the United States, Hungary and Yugoslavia. The significant absentees are the Soviet Union and the People's Republic of China. The international institutional participants include the Commonwealth Secretariat and the EC Commission (both of which have been closely involved with the birth of SADCC), the Council for Mutual Economic Assistance (CMEA), OPEC, UNCTAD, UNDP, the IBRD, and a number of regional and development banks and development agencies. The dialogue therefore does not involve a "confrontation" between a group of developing countries, on the one hand, and a group of developed countries on the other, as is the inevitable tendency of the Lomé arrangements. It is rather a development dialogue between the SADCC countries and the rest of the world community.

Another step in the process of the recognition of SADCC's international position was taken by the adoption, in December 1982, of a

---

[25] SADCC Maseru, Communiqué, Maseru, Lesotho (January 28, 1983).
[26] J. Bourrinet (Ed.), *Le Dialogue Euro-Arabe* (Paris, 1979).

UN General Assembly Resolution on *Co-operation between the United Nations and the Southern African Development Co-ordination Conference.*[27] The Resolution was adopted after a statement by Botswana, as current Chairman of SADCC, an approach which had been endorsed by the SADCC Council of Ministers in July 1982. The objective of the Resolution was to achieve formal recognition of SADCC by the UN and thus to facilitate increased support of SADCC by the United Nations agencies. Accordingly, the Resolution recognised SADCC "as a sub-regional organisation whose work is consistent with the objectives and principles of the UN Charter." The Resolution further recognised that SADCC has been mandated by the States concerned to co-ordinate projects and programmes falling within its competence and requested the UN Secretary-General to take appropriate measures to promote co-operation between United Nations bodies and SADCC. The United Nations therefore, in recognising SADCC, has accepted the organisation's role relating to matters within its competence.

The UN Resolution contained no explicit reference to SATCC, but clearly the Commission, and any others which may be established, also have an international role to play. SATCC has achieved already a measure of recognition by the international community as an institution which can represent the member states in respect of areas within its competence relating to the co-ordination and development of the sub-region's transport and communications programme. Thus, in 1982, the Chairman of the SATCC Committee of Ministers visited Norway for discussions with the Nordic development agencies.

What, then, is the status of SADCC in international law? Sir William Dale has recently published a perceptive analysis of the Commonwealth, an organisation the members of which, as those of SADCC, are at pains to stress the informality and flexibility of their association.[28] Dale arrives at a definition of an international organisation as "an association of States or their governments having agreed purposes, and one or more organs for carrying these out." Clearly, in the light of the analysis of SADCC's structure and institutions offered in the above pages, the organisation passes this test. SATCC, constituted by a formal agreement between the member States, also is entitled to be regarded as a separate international organisation. An organisation, however, does not necessarily possess international legal personality, the criteria for which have been

---

[27] Resolution 37/248, (December 21, 1982). The Resolution was adopted without a vote.
[28] "Is the Commonwealth an International Organisation?" 31 *International and Comparative Law Quarterly* (1982), pp. 451–473.

summarised by Professor Ian Brownlie as follows: (a) a permanent association of States, with lawful objects, equipped with organs; (b) a distinction, in terms of legal powers and purposes, between the organisation and its member States; (c) the existence of legal powers exercisable on the international plane and not solely within the national systems of one or more States.[29] These criteria should not be applied too rigidly, as elements of international personality are likely to be present in some measure in most international organisations.

SADCC clearly satisfies the first criterion in that it is an association of States with defined objects and a number of organs, including a Secretariat, on which specific powers have been conferred. The provisions of articles IX, X and XI of the Memorandum of Understanding, relating to the legal capacity of SADCC, immunities and privileges and the international character of the Secretariat would also seem to point to the existence of the distinction required by the second of Brownlie's criteria.[30]

The third criterion, however, raises more problems. SADCC, as we have seen, has been accorded a degree of international recognition as an organisation distinct from its members; the UN Resolution of December, 1982, is evidence of this. However, it cannot yet be said to function as an independent entity on the international plane as a fully-fledged regional economic organisation such as the European Community, which is recognised by the international community as having competence in certain matters. It is possible that SADCC may develop into an institution with a greater measure of legal personality as a result of powers conferred upon it by member States and of the acceptance of its competence on the international plane by the international community.

PROSPECTS

It is far too early to make an assessment of the operational effectiveness of SADCC, but it appears from the above account that a cautious and pragmatic approach has been adopted to the evolution of institutional structures appropriate to the emphasis on functional co-operation. This approach may lead to the establishment of a habit of consultation and co-operation between the member States, at both the bilateral and multilateral level, which may in the long run prove more valuable than the hasty creation of complex structures and the imposition of a regulatory trading régime in a way

---

[29] Brownlie, *Principles of Public International Law* (3rd ed., 1979), p. 679.
[30] These provisions are discussed above.

which tends to exacerbate conflicts of economic interest within a community. A precedent may be seen in the development of the Association of South-East Asian Nations (ASEAN), generally accepted as one of the most effective of the regional development communities so far established. Like SADCC, ASEAN began life with a declaration of common principles and objectives, the Bangkok Declaration of 1967. Within the framework of this Declaration, the following decade saw the slow evolution of bilateral and multilateral agreements in various spheres of functional co-operation, and it was not until 1976 that the association was formalised by a Treaty of Amity and Co-operation, a further Declaration of ASEAN Accord and an agreement establishing an ASEAN Secretariat in Djakarta.[31]

SADCC may be saved from over-ambitious institution building by the existence of the *Preferential Trade Area for Eastern and Southern African States*. The Treaty establishing this organisation was signed in Lusaka in December, 1981. The potential membership embraces all the SADCC states as well as Burundi, the Comoros, Djibouti, Ethiopia, Kenya, Madagascar, Mauritius, Rwanda, Seychelles, Somalia, Uganda and Zaire. The Treaty is a formidable document consisting of 51 articles and XI protocols, creating a Preferential Trade Area (PTA) with an Authority, a Council of Ministers, a Secretariat, a Tribunal and Intergovernmental Commission. The establishment of an Eastern and Southern African Development Bank is envisaged, and the Treaty looks forward to the gradual establishment of a Common Market and Economic Community for Eastern and Southern African States.[32] The first positive step appears to have been the establishment of a substantial secretariat in Lusaka.

Membership of SADCC is not inconsistent with that of the PTA or indeed of any other bilateral or multilateral trade agreements, of which Lomé is an important example. SADCC's objectives may be stated in modest terms—the promotion of functional co-operation in certain key sectors for which individual members assume operational responsibility. SADCC members appear to have no ambition to convert the organisation into a free-trade area, an aspiration which, as explained above, rests with the PTA in Lusaka.

Modest objectives may yield modest achievements. Critics may

---

[31] For a helpful summary of the development of ASEAN, see M. L. Marasinghe, "A review of Regional Economic Integration in Africa and Other Developing Countries," paper presented to International Conference on Law and Economy in Africa, University of Ife, Nigeria, (February 15–22, 1982).
[32] *Treaty for the Establishment of the Preferential Trade Area for Eastern and Southern African States*, UN Economic Commission for Africa, (1982).

argue that, by denying itself effective institutions and by relying on a complex structure of consultative bodies, SADCC exists merely as a forum for endless discussion rather than for effective decision making and that most of the "SADCC projects" would have been launched if SADCC had never been created. However, the SADCC 4 meeting at Maseru in January 1983, showed strong international support for SADCC as a body with which the international donors are keen to co-operate, a willingness reflected in the warmth of the commendations conferred upon the organisation by the participating delegates—the Danish foreign minister, on behalf of the Nordic countries, spoke of a pace of progress virtually unique among South-South regional co-operation groupings—and in the relative generosity of the aid pledges totalling some $200 million. However, only time will tell whether SADCC will sustain the role, in Maseru Chairman Peter Mmusi's words, of a "practical tool of co-operation not deteriorating into a talking shop."[33]

---

[33] *Loc. cit.* (note 19 above), p. xiii. A full record of SADCC 4 was published in Autumn, 1983.

EQUALITY AND DISCRIMINATION IN INTERNATIONAL ECONOMIC LAW (XII):

THE PROPOSED GLOBAL SYSTEM OF TRADE PREFERENCES AMONG DEVELOPING COUNTRIES

By

B.G. RAMCHARAN

THIS is the twelfth contribution to the series on *Equality and Discrimination in International Economic Law*, initiated by Professor Schwarzenberger's paper under this title in the 1971 Volume of this Annual, and continued in the 1972 Volume by G.G. Kaplan on *The UNCTAD Scheme for Generalised Preferences* and B.G. Ramcharan on *The Commonwealth Preferential System*, in the 1974 and 1975 Volumes by P. Goldsmith and F. Sonderkötter on *The European Communities* and *The European Communities in the Wider World*, in the 1977 Volume by A. Sutton on *Trends in the Regulation of International Trade in Textiles* and C. Stoiber on *The Multinational Enterprise* and by B.G. Ramcharan in the 1978 Volume on *The United Nations Economic Commissions*, the 1980 Volume on *The Council for Mutual Economic Assistance*, and the 1981 Volume on *Development and International Economic Co-operation* and in the 1983 Volume on *The General Agreement on Tariffs and Trade* by John H. Jackson—*Managing Editor*, Y.B.W.A.

Two earlier papers in the present series have examined the Generalised Scheme of Trade Preferences (GSP)[1] and the Commonwealth Preferential System.[2] While the Global System of Trade Preferences Among Developing Countries (GSTP), is still in the process of elaboration, the basic principles on which it is to be based have been enunciated and merit examination in view of various novel

---

[1] See G.G. Kaplan, "Equality and Discrimination in International Economic Law (II): the UNCTAD Scheme for Generalised Preferences," in Y.B.W.A., Vol. 26 (1972), pp. 267–285. By a resolution adopted on June 4, 1980, the UNCTAD Special Committee on Preferences agreed upon the extension of the GSP. While the agreement reached by the 80 countries participating in the meeting did not specify the date beyond which the prolongation should extend, the initial 10 year duration (which would have ended for most preference-giving countries in 1981), the decision contained provision for another comprehensive review of the GSP in 1990. See UNCTAD press release TAD/INF/1179 (June 5, 1980).

[2] See B.G. Ramcharan, "Equality and Discrimination in International Economic Law (III): The Commonwealth Preferential System," in Y.B.W.A., Vol. 26 (1972), pp. 286–314.

characteristics which are involved in the proposed system. While preferential arrangements such as the GSP operated *de jure* and *de facto* as exceptional régimes to the principle of most-favoured-nation treatment provided for under Article 1 of the GATT, the GSTP as presently conceived would go beyond an exceptional arrangement and would represent in fact "régimes within régimes," that is to say, the GSTP régime would be an inner régime operating within the GATT-GSP régime and would itself encompass further sub-régimes such as regional or sub-regional economic integration groupings. This would raise complex questions of the interrelationships of regulatory or preferential régimes in international economic law as well as issues of equality and discrimination within as well as among régimes.

I—THE ORIGINS OF THE GSTP

In a report on Economic co-operation among developing countries which it submitted in 1976 to the fourth UNCTAD conference in Nairobi, the UNCTAD Secretariat proposed the idea of trade expansion among developing countries by three major and complementary sets of instruments: first, a system of preferences among developing countries which would set in motion the process of liberalising access to markets; secondly, a system of devices to promote trade actively and to improve the trading position of the developing countries and thirdly, a system of payments.[3] The UNCTAD Secretariat was motivated by concern that the share of developing countries in world trade is small, less than one-fifth of the total. About 80 per cent. of their exports consist of primary commodities and agricultural products. The share of their industrial exports in world industrial trade is marginal: 6–7 per cent. In contrast, industrial products represent more than two-thirds of total imports into developing countries and about one-fifth of world trade in these products. Developing countries exchange among themselves only about 20 per cent. of their total exports and imports. Developed market economy countries take about three-fifths of developing countries' exports and supply some 70 per cent. of their imports. Socialist countries account for 6 per cent. of developing countries' exports and supply nearly 9 per cent. of their imports. Dependence on the markets of these two groups of countries is striking in the imports of developing countries of industrial products. Developed market economy countries accounted in 1973 for about 84 per cent. of these imports and

---

[3] TD/192.

for nearly 90 per cent. of total developing countries' imports of capital goods which are vital for the industrialisation and economic development of these countries. The corresponding percentage shares of industrial imports from socialist countries were 14 and 6 per cent. respectively. Capital goods represent more than half the total imports of industrial products into developing countries.[4]

The basic objectives of the third-world preference scheme as proposed by the UNCTAD Secretariat were (a) to provide a limited advantage in favour of developing country suppliers vis-à-vis imports from developed countries, and (b) to ensure an equitable distribution of the costs and benefits of the scheme among the individual participating countries. It was suggested that the proposed preference system could follow three interrelated approaches. One would consist of negotiations within existing and emerging sub-regional co-operation or integration groupings. Another would involve the formation of regional schemes covering the main geographical areas, which would not only ensure the outward-orientated development of integration groupings but also permit their harmonious co-operation with non-member countries of the same region. Over and above these two approaches a Third-World scheme could be applied; thus, interregional preferences would form part of regional preferences and both would be included as part of sub-regional co-operation or integration schemes.[5]

The Arusha Programme for Collective Self-Reliance and Framework for Negotiations, adopted by the Fourth Ministerial Meeting of the Group of 77 at Arusha, Tanzania, in February, 1979, recommended the establishment of a Global System of Trade Preferences Among Developing Countries (GSTP) as a major instrument for the promotion of trade, production and employment among developing countries. The Ministers foresaw that the GSTP would need to be based on the principle of mutuality of advantages, so as to yield benefits to all participants. In addition to non-reciprocal trade preferences, effective special treatment was envisaged in favour of products of export interest to least-developed countries, landlocked and island developing countries on a non-reciprocal basis. The gradual establishment of a GSTP was seen as being accompanied by a parallel strengthening of sub-regional, regional and inter-regional integration groupings.

The Ministers recommended that the GSTP should be open to the participation of all interested developing countries and that product

---

[4] These statistics are taken from TD/192/Supp. 2, paras. 6 and 7. See also, TD/B/C.7/36: Statistics of Trade Among Developing Countries by Country and Product.

[5] TD/192: Economic Co-operation Among Developing Countries, pp. 7–9.

coverage should include not only manufactures but also commodities and agricultural products in their raw and processed forms. Moreover, the GSTP should not rely only on traditional tariff concessions but in addition to covering non-tariff barriers it ought to be progressively interrelated with other measures in the field of production, marketing, payments, finance and transport. Finally, the Ministers recommended that the GSTP should consist of a coherent set of closely related components, including such elements as the adoption of indicative targets for increasing mutual trade, special techniques and modalities on preferential negotiations and for concessions on quantitative restrictions, agreements on direct trade measures and the use of long-term contracts, recourse to sectoral negotiations when appropriate, provisions on rules of origin and safeguards, and other essential provisions of preferential trade arrangements. The GSTP should furthermore incorporate appropriate mechanisms and regular medium-term reviews for evaluating progress. While the initial duration of trade concessions may be limited in time it was expected that the systems as a whole should provide a framework for lasting, trade and economic co-operation among developing countries.[6]

Preparatory work on the establishment of the GSTP has been carried out since then, *inter alia*, in Meetings of Governmental Experts of Developing Countries on the GSTP held within the framework of UNCTAD.[7] On October 8, 1982, the Ministers for Foreign Affairs of the Group of 77, at their sixth annual meeting, adopted a Ministerial Declaration on the Global System of Trade Preferences Among Developing Countries (GSTP). This recognised that a global system of trade preferences would constitute a major instrument for the promotion of trade among developing countries and increase production and employment in those countries. Conscious of the need to create an appropriate framework for a global system of trade preferences among the developing countries members of the Group of 77 decided "to commence negotiations for the establishment of a global system of trade preferences among developing countries" in accordance with certain principles, rules and a stated time-table.

The Declaration provided that the principles contained in para-

---

[6] Arusha Programme for Collective Self-Reliance and Framework for Negotiations, reproduced in TD/236, pp. 9–11. See also the Caracas Programme of Action on Economic Co-operation Among Developing Countries (1981), U.N. doc. A/36/333.
[7] See J.P. Barnouin "Trade and economic cooperation among developing countries," 19 *Finance and Development* Nr. 2, (June, 1982) pp. 24–27. See also, A/37/544, Annex II.

graph 5(iii)[8] of the Arusha Action Plan, and in particular the following specific principles, shall provide the basic guidelines for the
GSTP: (a) The GSTP shall be reserved for the exclusive participation of developing countries members of the Group of 77. The Rules of
origin should be devised to ensure that the benefits of the GSTP
accrue only to participating countries; (b) The GSTP shall be negotiated step by step, improved and extended in successive stages,
with periodic reviews; (c) The GSTP should be based on the principle of mutuality of advantages in such a way as to benefit equitably
all participants, taking into account their respective levels of economic and industrial development, the pattern of their external trade
and their trade policies and systems; (d) The GSTP should not
replace but supplement and reinforce present and future sub-
regional, regional and interregional economic groupings of developing countries and shall take into account the concerns and commitments of such economic groupings; (e) The special needs of the
least-developed countries should be clearly recognised and concrete
preferential measures in favour of these countries should be agreed
upon; the least developed countries will not be required to make
concessions on a reciprocal basis; (f) All products, manufactures,
and commodities in their raw and processed forms should be
covered in the negotiations; (g) Intergovernmental sub-regional,
regional and interregional groupings for economic co-operation
among developing countries members of the Group of 77 may participate, fully as such, if and when they consider it desirable, in any
or all phases of the work on the GSTP; (h) In negotiating tariff concessions, reduction of non-tariff barriers, etc., participants may
explore various approaches, including linear, product-by-product,
sectoral, or a combination thereof, or combinations of tariff concessions, non-tariff concessions, para-tariff concessions and direct
trade measures, including long-term contracts, as appropriate; (i)
The GSTP participants may consider all other measures likely to
increase trade, including possibilities for expanding, where appropriate, the scope of bilateral arrangements as agreed by the parties
thereto.[9]

It is intended that the first phase of the negotiations should
include a limited number of components such as tariff concessions,
non-tariff barriers, in particular major ones, and para-tariff barriers,

---

[8] See "Proceedings of the United Nations Conference on Trade and Development, Fifth
Session," Vol. I, Report and Annexes (TD/269), Annex VI, "First Short Medium-term
Action Plan for Global Priorities on Economic Co-operation Among Developing Countries,"
para. 5(c).
[9] A/37/544, Annex II, para. 1.

direct trade measures, including long-term contracts, rules of origin and safeguards. Participants are expected to establish, at the national level, non-binding indicative targets for the expansion of their trade with other developing countries over a given period. Such targets would include all trade increases within subregional, regional and interregional groupings of developing countries.

A GSTP Negotiating Committee was established by the Ministerial Declaration open to Governments of developing-country members of the Group of 77 desirous of participating in the negotiations. It is also open to sub-regional, regional, and interregional groupings of developing countries for participation in the work of the Committee whenever they consider it desirable.

The Negotiating Committee has authority to take all the necessary steps, in keeping with the principles mentioned above, for the establishment of the GSTP and for the negotiations therefor. It was decided that the GSTP Negotiating Committee shall hold its opening meeting not later than April 30, 1983, and it is intended that the first phase of the negotiations should be concluded by 1985.

The UNCTAD Secretariat has been requested to provide technical secretariat and other support to the Committee and generally for the conduct of negotiations and for the implementation of the GSTP. Other competent organisations and bodies, such as GATT, ITC, UNDP, UNIDO, FAO, the Customs Co-operation Council and the regional economic commissions may also be requested to provide their support for the negotiations.

II—LEGAL BASIS

It has been argued that "Preferential treatment among developing countries should be a recognised principle, rather than a derogation from or exception to the MFN principle. The developing countries should have the right to accord preferential trade treatment among themselves and the developed countries should not invoke their rights to most-favoured-nation treatment with a view to obtaining such preferential treatment, in whole or in part. With the exception of special measures in favour of the relatively less advanced countries, it would be important for developing countries to agree that preferential treatment granted by individual developing countries in the context of the system should be extended to all developing countries without discrimination. However, the preferential concessions granted under this system would have to be dovetailed with those granted under sub-regional or regional preferential arrangements of developing countries. Moreover, no developing country should grant to developed countries (individually or collectively) treatment more favourable than that which it grants to all other developing countries."[10]

It may be recalled in this regard that decision L/4903 on "Differential and more favourable treatment, reciprocity and fuller participation of developing countries" adopted by the Contracting Parties of GATT on November 28, 1979, provided that notwithstanding the provisions of Article I of the General Agreement, Contracting parties may accord differential and more favourable treatment to developing countries without according such treatment to other Contracting parties. This would apply, *inter alia*, in the cases of "regional or global arrangements entered into amongst less-developed contracting parties for the mutual reduction or elimination of tariffs and, in accordance with criteria or conditions which may be prescribed by the Contracting parties, for the mutual reduction or elimination of non-tariff measures, on products imported from one another." It would also apply in cases of special treatment of the least-developed among the developing countries in the context of any general or specific measures in favour of developing countries.[11]

The GSTP would seem to be covered by GATT decision L/4903 inasmuch as it is a global arrangement entered into amongst less-developed contracting parties for the mutual reduction or elimination of tariffs as well as for the mutual reduction or elimination of non-tariff measures, on products imported from one another. It is significant, however, that the developing countries are proceeding with their proposed preferential system without any prior blessing by GATT contracting parties regarding the criteria or conditions for the mutual reduction or elimination of non-tariff measures, which is called for by GATT decision L/4903. Inasmuch as the GSTP would involve special treatment for the least-developed among the developing countries, it would also seem to be covered by GATT decision L/4903.

III——MUTUALLY EQUITABLE ADVANTAGES

As has been seen earlier the GSTP would be based on the principle of mutuality of advantages, in such a way as to benefit equitably all participants, taking into account their respective levels of economic and industrial development the pattern of their external trade and their trade policies and systems. It is understood that evaluations of

---

[10] TD/192/Supp. 2, para. 26.

[11] See GATT, "Basic Instruments and Selected Documents," Twenty-Sixth Supplement 1978–79 (1980), pp. 203–205. See also R.G. Berger, "Preferential Trade Treatment, For Less Developed Countries: Implications of the Tokyo Round," 20 *Harv.Int.Law Jnl.* (1979), pp. 540–582.

the benefits offered by GSTP to participating countries, especially to least developed countries should be carried out at regular intervals.

From the outset the UNCTAD Secretariat envisaged that preferential tariff concessions among the developing countries should be exchanged on the basis of mutual and equitable trade advantages for all developing countries, taking into account the level of industrial and economic development of each country and its actual trade, financial and development needs. It also envisaged that since the developing countries are at various levels of economic development the system should in particular ensure trade advantages for the relatively less advanced countries.

The approach of the UNCTAD Secretariat was that: "The contribution that can be expected from each developing country within the preferential system would have to be commensurate with its level of economic development so that all developing countries can obtain equitable advantages from the system. Since there appear to be no objective criteria by which the contribution of each country could be precisely determined, a pragmatic approach would probably have to be adopted within general guidelines which the developing countries would need to work out. This would assume a high sense of solidarity on the part of all developing countries, in particular of the industrially more advanced among them. Successful co-operation among developing countries hinges on a fair and equitable solution of this issue.

"In order to enable the relatively less advanced countries to benefit equitably from the new system, consideration would need to be given to the adoption of special measures in their favour within the framework of the system. These measures would need to be supplemented, within a comprehensive programme of co-operation among developing countries, by technical and financial assistance. Irrespective of the scope and nature of the contributions of the relatively less advanced countries within the system, it is important that these countries should extend to other developing countries a more favourable trade treatment than the treatment they extend to developed countries."[12]

An equitable distribution of costs and benefits among the participants is seen as presupposing that the major export products of all of them would find access possibilities in the partner countries, which in turn would require the relaxation of import barriers precluding

---

[12] TD/192/Supp. 2, paras. 28–29. See also North-South: A Programme for Survival. The report of the Brandt Commission (1980), Chap. III: Mutual Interests: "This principle of mutuality of interest has been at the centre of our discussions," p. 64.

such access. Countries protecting their domestic production by means of tariffs should be no worse off than countries resorting to other important restrictions for the same purpose. Even beyond that type of balancing action, additional measures may be needed to ensure that individual countries can both participate with their exports and with their imports in the scheme so as to avoid imbalances in preferential trade leading to a net cost of their participation in the form of higher import prices and worsened terms of trade, reduced budgetary revenue or declining development perspectives. It has been pointed out that while this needs to be a general concern of any preference scheme with respect to all its various member countries, special provisions would need to be included with respect to both advantages and exceptions from commitments in favour of the relatively less advanced developing countries wishing to participate in such a Third-World preference scheme.[13]

IV—LEAST-DEVELOPED COUNTRIES

Resolution 98 (IV) adopted by the fourth UNCTAD conference requested developing countries in a position to do so to provide preferential treatment, as far as possible, to imports of goods produced by the least-developed countries. The Arusha Programme for Collective Self-Reliance and Framework for Negotiations provided that within the context of a global system of trade preferences among developing countries, "in addition to non-reciprocal trade preferences, effective special treatment would be required in favour of products of export interest to least-developed countries, landlocked and island developing countries on a non-reciprocal basis." In a report on "special, differential and non-reciprocal measures in favour of least-developed countries within a GSTP" the Secretariat of UNCTAD suggested that the following objectives and principles could determine the application of differential measures.[14]

(a) The GSTP should contain within its various components and areas adequate sets of special differential and non-reciprocal measures which developing countries should adopt as far as possible in favour of their least developed partner countries. To the extent possible, such special measures should be of a uniform nature and be applicable to all least developed countries alike.

(b) Certain developing countries have already adopted tariff preferences without reciprocity as a differential measure within the GATT Protocol Relating to Trade Negotiations among Developing

---

[13] TD/192/Supp. 1, para. 3.
[14] TD/B/C.7/35, para. 91.

Countries. Within the GSTP equally simple differentials could be conceived with respect to non-tariff preferences, and preferential protective measures allowed to least developed countries.

(c) Differential measures for the least-developed countries at the interregional, regional and sub-regional levels should run parallel with and reinforce each other. The interregional measures should, however, in some areas and respects, be consequent upon and succeed more, intensive sub-regional integration efforts. In the latter sense only the measures/mechanisms whose efficiency has been established within the sub-regional frameworks should be initiated at the interregional level and the technical feasibility of the measures proposed for application within interregional arrangements should first be thoroughly studied.

More specifically, it has been suggested that in terms of an adjusted linear approach, the special treatment in favour of least developed countries could, for example, be translated into the following individual or combined measures: (a) The application of a lower percentage reduction of MFN tariffs by least-developed countries (for example 10 per cent. instead of a general 20 per cent. rate), with the possibility of a higher number of exceptions, if required; (b) The granting of deeper than general tariff cuts in their favour (for example a 30 per cent. reduction of the MFN rate instead of a general 20 per cent. rate); (c) The granting of supplementary special concessions, on a non-reciprocal basis, in favour of products of special export interest to LDCs.[15]

As we have seen above, the Ministerial Declaration of the Group of 77 expressly recognised that "The special needs of the least-developed countries should be clearly recognised and concrete preferential measures in favour of these countries should be agreed upon; the least-developed countries will not be required to make concessions on a reciprocal basis."

With regard to the question as to whether the less advanced countries should also be expected to give concessions to other developing countries, it has been suggested that in principle, they should grant more favourable treatment to other developing countries than that which they apply to developed countries. The less advanced countries would probably need to have longer lists of exceptions and smaller tariff cuts, which would ensure the necessary protection of their national economies against competition from imports. They may need special protection not only for nascent industries but also for their agriculture. However, since in the international trade in

---

[15] See TD/B/C.7/42, para. 54.

sophisticated industrial goods the developed countries have generally a competitive edge over similar goods produced in developing countries, the actual protection in the latter countries may be set at a level which provides protection against the most competitive imports, namely those from developed countries. If so, any developing country, including the less advanced, may, as far as imports of sophisticated industrial products from other developing countries are concerned, reduce the actual level of protection and thus provide "preferential," in fact equal, treatment to developing countries, while still preserving sufficient protection for the domestic industry in question, or for the development of such an industry. This approach, it has been said, could lead to an initial wide preferential reduction of protection on most industrial products currently imported from developed countries.[16]

V—SUB-REGIONAL AND REGIONAL ECONOMIC GROUPINGS

Among the principles set out for the GSTP is that it should be consistent with, and indeed be accompanied by, a parallel strengthening of existing sub-regional and regional integration groupings of developing countries. Insofar as existing sub-regional and regional integration groupings are concerned it has been pointed out that given the level of trade liberalisation already achieved within such groupings, the extension of tariff preferences by individual members of such groupings to third developing countries will result in an erosion of the levels of preferences obtaining within the groupings. Hence it has been suggested that to maintain the same level of such preferences after the extension of preferences to third developing countries, the groupings would need to deepen the existing levels of intra-group preferences. In this respect three categories of integration groupings have been distinguished: (a) those that have already fully eliminated all tariffs on intra-group trade; (b) those in which tariff liberalisation on intra-group trade has proceeded beyond the levels being proposed for an across-the-board tariff cut; and (c) those in which tariff liberalisation has not yet reached the level being proposed for the across-the-board tariff cut.[17]

In respect of groupings falling under (a), it has been said that the implementation of an across-the-board tariff cut applicable to imports from all developing countries would have the effect of eroding the existing levels of preferences enjoyed by regional partners vis-à-vis other developing countries, and that this erosion could only

---

[16] TD/192/Supp. 2.
[17] TD/B/C.7/47, para. 26.

be avoided if the level of tariffs from non-preferred, *i.e.* developed country sources, were correspondingly increased to create the margin of preferences to be extended to third developing countries. In respect of (b), preferences granted to third developing countries would also erode existing intra-group preferences, but the level of such preferences could be maintained by deepening the process of intra-group trade liberalisation. In respect of (c), an across-the-board tariff cut would more than offset existing intra-group preferences, and would require a substantial deepening of the trade liberalisation process within such groupings in order to maintain some level of distinctive intra-group preferences.[18]

It may thus be seen that complex questions of equality and discrimination are involved including: the possibility of discriminatory treatment against developed countries; potential inequalities between countries which are members of regional or sub-regional groupings and those which are not, as well as the possibility of discriminatory treatment against the former. The precise impact of the GSTP must await the outcome of the negotiations.

VI—Future Negotiations

As we have seen above, the Ministerial Declaration of the Group of 77 has envisaged that the first phase of the negotiations should include a limited number of components such as tariff concessions, non-tariff barriers, in particular major ones, and para-tariff barriers; direct trade measures, including long-term contracts; rules of origin and safeguards. It would be speculative to dwell on the possible outcome of the negotiations but some guidance may be obtained from the preparatory work which has so far been done.

It has been suggested that recognition of the existing disparities amongst developing countries would appear to advocate the adoption of preferential targets of more limited depth during the initial stages of the establishment of the GSTP: "Such preferential objectives could include the establishment of an effective margin of tariff preference in favour of products originating in other developing countries; the provision of commercially viable quotas and licensing opportunities in favour of such products or an increase of their size; the negotiation of long-term contracts and other direct trade measures with regard to a proportion of the import requirements and export supplies. Depending on the areas of negotiation, similar limitations may also be applied with regard to product coverage; in

---

[18] *Ibid.* para. 27.

some areas negotiations may be limited to certain products or certain sectors.

"Parallel progress in all main areas of the negotiations should be considered as more important than committing countries from the very outset to total removal of trade barriers in one single area, such as tariffs. As global negotiations imply participation of all countries of the Group of 77, all these countries need to find a place within the modalities of the negotiations, regardless of whether a country relies relatively more on tariffs, or on non-tariff barriers, or on State trading, long-term contracts or similar measures for regulating its foreign trade."[19]

It has also been pointed out that unless negotiations cover a wide range of products, including agricultural and other basic commodities in their raw and processed forms along with industrial products, it would be difficult to provide a substantial trade interest to the majority of developing countries. Only a broad product coverage of GSTP instruments is likely to take account of the widely differing commodity patterns of developing countries' imports and exports, the high concentration of industrial exports in a small number of them, and the overriding importance of agricultural products for the large majority of these countries.

It is argued that preferential targets of a limited size would have the advantage of comprising relatively limited and calculable risks of eventual undesirable effects on domestic production, budget and foreign exchange. They would be matched by appropriate and sufficiently flexible safeguards and exceptions which should form part of the final GSTP Agreement. The step-by-step increase in the depth of commitments would, it is said, enable each country to evaluate carefully the experiences made with the application of preferences resulting from preceding rounds of negotiations. Regular medium-term reviews would enable adjustments to be made in the GSTP arrangements instead of relying too heavily on *ex ante* evaluation and expectations. Corrective measures could be taken in the light of actual experiences with regard to the balance of advantages deriving from the working of the agreement.

The inclusion of quantitative restrictions and direct trade measures within the ambit of the negotiations from the beginning is said to be a basic requisite for balancing of advantages, the attraction of the interest of a maximum of countries and the participation of a maximum of interested developing countries in all the various areas of the GSTP negotiations.

It has been suggested that the results of the first stage of negoti-

---

[19] TD/B/C.7/42, paras. 17–18.

ations should be incorporated into an over-all framework agreement, which would embody the concessions negotiated and provide the provisions for their application, including the rules of origin, safeguards, rules of competition and rules for the multilateral extension of concessions as well as the exceptions thereto. Such an agreement could furthermore lay out the main features and components of a medium-term action programme to maintain the dynamics of the process towards accomplishing the GSTP. Medium-term reviews are said to have an essential role to play as part of such a programme in order to evaluate on the basis of actual trade results the degree to which development objectives and targets have been met and to identify any further balancing requirements to be taken into account during the following stages of negotiations. Finally, such a framework agreement would need to contain certain institutional and legal provisions for assuring appropriate guidance and supervision of its functioning and for its articulation within the international trading framework.[20]

As regards negotiating objectives in the area of tariffs the UNCTAD Secretariat has advanced the idea that the main aim of the tariff negotiations for a first phase of the GSTP could be the establishment of an affective margin of preference for mutual trade among developing countries. The initial commitment could be limited in depth. Further progressive commitments would then be subject to further rounds of negotiations.[21] Concretely, it has suggested that consideration be given to the following elements as a framework for the first stage of the GSTP negotiations: (i) A modest, across-the-board tariff cut of, say, 10 per cent. applicable to the whole range of traded products, including agricultural products, processed commodities and manufactures. For the least developed countries the cut could be limited to 5 per cent. (ii) Provision for limited preferential liberalisation of non-tariff barriers in selected, clearly defined areas; (iii) Creation of a special fund for the benefit of countries, particularly the least developed countries, whose exports are least likely to enjoy immediate benefits from trade liberalisation.[22]

As regards negotiating objectives in the field of non-tariff barriers it has been suggested that negotiations on non-tariff barriers should aim directly at their progressive reduction on intra-developing country trade. They should be closely interrelated with tariff negotiations and negotiations in other GSTP areas, and they should par-

---

[20] *Ibid*. paras. 20–22.
[21] TD/B/C.7/42, para. 33.
[22] TD/B/C.7/47, para. 4.

ticularly explore special techniques and modalities for preferential negotiations and for concessions on quantitative restrictions.

Specific negotiating objectives in the area of non-tariff barriers which have been suggested are: (i) Generalised principles for preferential relaxation of quantitative restrictions (QRs), import prohibitions and other NTBs with regard to the products covered by tariff preferences, so as to render such concessions effective; (ii) Specific negotiations on preferential relaxation of QRs, import prohibitions and other NTBs on individual products on the basis of bilateral negotiations procedures, and mutual request and offer lists; (iii) The elaboration of certain rules regarding the application of licensing and other administrative procedures in a non-restrictive manner; (iv) Non-tariff concessions applicable on a MFN basis.[23]

Bearing in mind the multifaceted character and individualised nature of NTBs, a modest approach to the inclusion of NTB measures in the first stage of the GSTP negotiations has been advocated along the following lines: It would focus first on quantitative restrictions, omitting for the time being consideration of other NTBs. The advantage of focusing at the initial stage on quantitative restrictions is said to be that these are an easily identifiable NTB mechanism, that their use is fairly widespread, if not universal, among developing countries, and that they are used for broadly similar purposes in all countries. In respect of quantitative restrictions, two general principles have been offered to provide the basis for the initial stage of the GSTP negotiations. The first principle could be that, as a general rule, wherever quantitative restrictions exist, developing country exporters should be given preference in the filling of quotas and when appropriate, a certain share of existing or future quotas should be reserved for these countries. The second principle could be that the exchange of quota preferences should be linked to existing and potential performance in taking advantage of tariff perferences under the GSTP. This principle would imply that countries whose markets are most open to penetration from tariff preference-receiving countries relative to their own ability to take advantage of such preferences should be least obliged to extend quota preferences, and, conversely, those countries with the greatest propensity to take advantage of tariff perferences relative to the operation of their own markets should accept the greatest obligation to extend quota preferences.[24]

Approaching the question of quantitative restrictions in this way would, it is said, ensure that concessions in this area are linked to

---

[23] TD/B/C.7/42, paras. 63–64.
[24] TD/B/C.7/41, para. 13.

tariff concessions in a wider framework designed to facilitate the achievement of a broad balance in the distribution of costs and benefits from the package of preferences envisaged for the first stage of the GSTP. The linking of quantitative restrictions and tariff preferences could, it is further argued, also serve a useful purpose in linking up trade in manufactures and agricultural products within the preference scheme. Thus quantitative restrictions are particularly widespread in respect of trade in agricultural products, and many countries, particularly the least industrialised, which may be unable to achieve immediate benefits from tariff preferences in respect of manufactures could gain advantages by finding markets for their agricultural exports in countries that would be obliged, within the framework of this approach, to extend quota concessions in respect of these products.[25]

Inasmuch as the thinking of the UNCTAD Secretariat has obviously influenced the origin, launching and shape of the GSTP so far, it may be expected that the first phase of the negotiations would be influenced to a considerable degree by the thinking which has been described above. However, we must await the outcome of the negotiations to see how they fare in the hard bargaining ahead.

CONCLUSIONS

The following conclusions may be suggested from the above review of issues of equality and discrimination involved in the proposals for the establishment of the GSTP:

(1) The GSTP represents an attempt by a group of historically disadvantaged countries to assist themselves through the practice of intra-group solidarity and mutual self-help.

(2) The GSTP also forms part of schemes of global solidarity which have been recognised in principle within the GATT as being consistent with the principle of most-favoured-nation treatment.

(3) The GSTP is designed to contribute towards redressing historical inequalities and inequities between individuals and peoples of the developing countries and the developed countries. It is also designed to redress a specific inequality namely the paucity of the share of developing countries in world trade.

(4) Insofar as participating countries of the GSTP are involved the GSTP would be based on the principles of mutuality of advantage and of equitable treatment.

(5) Special and non-reciprocal preferential measures would be

---

[25] *Ibid.* para. 14.

applied in favour of least developed countries, as well as in favour of land-locked and island developing countries.

(6) Insofar as existing regional groupings are concerned, the GSTP would seek to incorporate them in a pragmatic way and to enhance and strengthen them. While some inequality of treatment may be involved as between participating countries in the GSTP which are members of such groupings and those which are not, the participating countries as a whole understand and accept that such groupings are beneficial and wish to see them reinforced.

(7) Some measure of discriminatory treatment against developed countries is theoretically possible, but it is difficult at this stage to predict whether this will actually materialise and to what degree.

THE NEW INTERNATIONAL
ECONOMIC ORDER
(PART TWO)

By

D.H.N. JOHNSON

I—ARBITRATIONS WHERE NIEO
HAS BEEN AN ISSUE

IN at least two recent arbitrations NIEO has been an issue.* The arbitrations were *Texaco Overseas Petroleum Company/California Asiatic Petroleum Company* v. *Government of the Libyan Arab Republic*[1]; and *Libyan American Oil Company* v. *Government of the Libyan Arab Republic.*[2] The facts in the two cases (which will be referred to as *Texaco* and *Liamco*) were similar.

In Texaco an oil concession was granted to the two American companies in 1955 under the Libyan Petroleum Law, also of 1955. The terms of the concession were amended from time to time by agreement. The most important provisions were Clause 16, which read as follows: "The Government of Libya will take all steps necessary to ensure that the Company enjoys all the rights conferred by this Concession. The contractual rights expressly granted by this concession shall not be altered except by mutual consent of the parties," and Clause 28 which read as follows: "This concession shall be governed and interpreted in accordance with the principles of the law of Libya common to the principles of international law and, in the absence of such common principles then by and in accordance with the general principles of law, including such of those principles as may have been applied by international tribunals."

Clause 28 also provided that, in the event of a dispute between the Petroleum Commission—later Petroleum Ministry—and the concessionaires, either side could appoint an arbitrator, and the two arbitrators thus appointed would appoint an umpire. In the event of a failure to agree on the umpire, either party could request the President of the International Court of Justice to make the appoint-

---

* Part One of this paper was published in the 1983 Volume of this *Year Book*. Professor Johnson, who has been ill, acknowledges the assistance of Mr. David Flint, Senior Lecturer in Law at the New South Wales Institute of Technology, in the completion of this paper. However, the views expressed in it remain Professor Johnson's own views.
[1] 17 ILM 1.
[2] 20 ILM 1.

217

ment. Further, in the event of one party failing to appoint an arbitrator, the other party could request the President of the Court to appoint a sole arbitrator.[3]

By laws of 1973 and 1974 the properties, interests, rights and assets of the concessionaires were nationalised, at first partially, and later totally. The Nationalisation Laws provided for compensation on a scale to be determined by a committee of three Libyan nationals appointed by the Ministry of Petroleum. It appears, however, that this committee never functioned.

The companies appointed an arbitrator, but as the Government of Libya did not do so, the companies approached the President of the International Court of Justice, who at that time was Judge Manfred Lachs (Poland). He appointed as sole arbitrator Mr. R.J. Dupuy, Secretary-General of the Hague Academy of International Law and Professor of Law at the University of Nice. Before making this appointment the President considered and rejected a submission from the Government of Libya that, since nationalisation was an act of sovereignty, the arbitration should not proceed.

Professor Dupuy first invited the parties to consider the question whether he had jurisdiction. The companies submitted that he had. The Government of Libya made no submission on this point, but the arbitrator considered, and likewise rejected, the submission that the Libyan Government had made to the President of the International Court. Having looked yet again at the Libyan submission when considering the merits of the case, the arbitrator eventually, on January 19, 1977, delivered an Award in which he held (i) that the concession was binding on the parties; (ii) that the Government of Libya had breached it; and (iii) that the Government of Libya was bound to give full effect to the concession in accordance with the principle *restitutio in integrum*. The arbitrator gave the Government of Libya a period of five months "in order that it may bring to the notice of the Arbitral Tribunal the measures taken by it with a view to complying with and implementing the present Arbitral Award." The conclusion of the case was that, eight months after the delivery of the Award, an agreement was reached under which Libya agreed to provide the companies over the next 15 months with $152 million of Libyan crude oil and the companies agreed to terminate the arbitration proceedings.

The attempt therefore to use NIEO as a bar to arbitral proceedings, where there had been an agreement to arbitrate between the

---

[3] It was further provided that, if the President of the International Court of Justice happened to be a national of Libya or of the country where the concessionaires were incorporated, the appointments should be made by the Vice-President of the Court.

Government of a developing country and foreign companies, failed. More interesting, however, are the conclusions reached by the arbitrator on the merits of the case.

The first question to which Professor Dupuy addressed himself was the legal nature of the concession agreements between the Government of Libya and the companies. He held that these agreements were of a contractual nature. The second question the arbitrator considered was what was the applicable law of the contracts; on this question Professor Dupuy held that the applicable law was not Libyan law, or more precisely it was not Libyan law alone. Had it been Libyan law alone, "the result would have been that their binding nature would be affected *a priori* by legislative or regulatory measures taken within the Libyan national legal order (quite apart from the questions of responsibility which the adoption of such legal measures might, should the case arise, entail in conformity with Libyan municipal law)."

Professor Dupuy then stated: "It is incontestable that these contracts were international contracts, both in the economic sense because they involved the interests of international trade and in the strict legal sense because they included factors connecting them to different States."

It is indeed incontestable that these were international contracts "in the economic sense." To say, however, that they were international contracts "in the strict legal sense" raises difficult issues. If it is maintained that they were governed by public international law, such a proposition runs counter to the statement of the Permanent Court of International Justice in the case relating to the *Serbian and Brazilian Loans*, where the Court said: "Any contract which is not a contract between States in their capacity as subjects of international law is based on the municipal law of some country."[4]

Professor Dupuy's statement also appears to be incompatible with the finding of the International Court of Justice in the *Anglo-Iranian Oil Company* case, where the Court held that the concession granted to the Company by the Government of Iran was "nothing more than a concessionary contract between a government and a foreign corporation" and as such was governed entirely by Iranian law.[5] Of course, Professor Dupuy was well aware of this, and much interest lies in the argumentation by which he held himself not bound by those precedents. He said: "However, because it is a long time since the Permanent Court of International Justice delivered its

---

[4] P.C.I.J. Series A, Nr. 20 (1929), p. 41.
[5] *I.C.J. Reports 1952*, p. 93 at p. 112.

judgments in the cases relating to the *Serbian and Brazilian Loans*, juridical analysis has been much refined in this field, in particular under the influence of contractual practice. This tends more and more to "delocalise" the contract or, if one prefers, to sever its automatic connections to some municipal law; so much so that today when the municipal law of a given State, and particularly the municipal law of the contracting State, governs the contract, it is by virtue of the agreement between the parties and no longer by a privileged and so to speak mechanical application of the municipal law as at a certain time was believed. Under the pressure of the needs of international trade, the principles of the autonomy of the will of the parties appears today to be much more significant than at the end of the 1920s."

This is a very revealing statement: it almost amounts to saying that the principle of *pacta sunt servanda* applies to contracts between governments and private foreign parties. In the present context it appears to indicate that "the needs of international trade" under the existing economic order are more potent than the principles of NIEO.

In a subsequent passage Professor Dupuy was even more explicit. He said that "while the old case law viewed the contract as something which could not come under international law because it could not be regarded as a treaty between States, under the new concept treaties are not the only type of agreements governed by such law. And it should be added that, although they are not to be confused with treaties, contracts between States and private persons can, under certain conditions, come within the ambit of a particular and new branch of international law: the international law of contracts." From this it followed that "the Deeds of Concession in dispute are within the domain of international law." By saying this, the arbitrator did not mean to infer that all contracts between governments and foreign private parties are within the domain of international law. In order to achieve this result there must be an "element of the internationalisation of the contracts in dispute," for example, a provision for arbitration along the lines of clause 28 in the present case.

Space does not permit of a full analysis of Professor Dupuy's interesting award. Suffice it to say that he did not adopt an extreme position. He was careful to point out that "to say that international law governs contractual relations between a State and a foreign private party neither means that the latter is assimilated to a State nor that the contract entered into with it is assimilated to a treaty." It only means that 'for the purposes of interpretation and performance of the contract, it should be recognised that a private contracting party has specific international capacities. But unlike a State, the private person has only a limited capacity and his quality as a subject of international law does enable him only to invoke, in the field of international law, the rights which he derives from the contract."

The next major question considered by Professor Dupuy was whether, as claimed by Libya, nationalisation terminated not only the agreement which linked the companies to the Libyan State but also their legal status. He had little difficulty in rejecting the latter part of this contention since, although nationalisation measures "concern the total assets of the companies located within the territory of the State which nationalises, such nationalisations cannot purport to destroy the existence of these companies as legal entities." Here there is a certain amount of common ground. Professor Dupuy accepts that sovereign States have, in principle, the right to nationalise foreign assets, and probably most apologists for NIEO would accept that nationalisation measures do not have extraterritorial effect. Where views diverge is on the question whether a State can nationalise an "internationalised contract." Professor Dupuy says "No," because "where the State has concluded with a foreign contracting party an internationalised agreement . . . the State has placed itself within the international legal order in order to guarantee vis-à-vis its foreign contracting party a certain legal and economic status over a certain period of time."

The State has made what might appear at first sight a surrender of its sovereignty, says Professor Dupuy, because such internationalised contracts "tend to bring to developing countries investments and technical assistance, particularly in the field of research and exploitation of mineral resources" and "assume a real importance in the development of the country where they are being, performed." As for the argument that a State cannot be presumed to make such a surrender of its sovereignty, Professor Dupuy relied on the well-known passage in *The Wimbledon*, where it was said in respect of a treaty obligation entered into by Germany, that "The Court declines to see in the conclusion of any Treaty by which a State undertakes to perform or refrain from performing a particular act an abandonment of its sovereignty. No doubt any convention creating an obligation of this kind places a restriction upon the exercise of the sovereign rights of the State, in the sense that it requires them to be exercised in a certain way. But the right of entering into international engagements is an attribute of State sovereignty."[6] Professor Dupuy commented: "This observation has logically the same scope and significance in the case of an agreement entered into by a

---

[6] P.C.I.J. Series A, Nr. 1 (1923), p. 25.

given State with a foreign private company. Of course, this agreement is not a treaty commitment because a treaty can be entered into only as between States, but it is an agreement which falls within the international legal order since the contracting State agreed to submit the agreement not to the exclusive, and unlimited in time, application of its municipal law, but to rules falling at least in part within the framework of international law or of general principles of law."

It remained for Professor Dupuy to consider the argument that "the exercise by a State of its rights to nationalise, places that State on a level outside of, and superior to, the contract, and also to the international legal order itself" and moreover that this proposition amounts to "a mandatory rule of general international law (*jus cogens*)." This in effect is the proposition contained in Article 2(2)(*c*) of the Charter of Economic Rights and Duties of States and is the very kernel of the theory of "permanent sovereignty over natural resources." The arbitrator dealt with this proposition by holding that "the notion of permanent sovereignty can be completely reconciled with the conclusion by a State of agreements which leave to that State control of the activities of the other contracting party" and that, in the present case, "the Libyan State did not alienate but exercised its sovereignty and ensured that it would not be affected in principle, the limitations accepted by it in respect of the exercise of certain of its prerogatives having been accepted only in particular areas and *for a specific period of time.*"[7]

Professor Dupuy admitted that there were "some tendencies to separate completely nationalisation from international law, tendencies which, if they were to be confirmed by positive law, would result in restricting to the framework of the national law of the State all its relations with foreign private companies." In that context he referred to the statement of the International Court of Justice in the *Fisheries Jurisdiction* case that "the Court, as a court of law, cannot render judgment *sub specie legis ferendae*, or anticipate the law before the legislator has laid it down."[8] This raised the very question which has been so much discussed in this article, namely are the principles of NIEO legally binding?

Professor Dupuy's approach to this question was to contrast Resolution 1803 (XVII) of 1962 with the NIEO Resolutions of 1974 and to hold that the former reflected "the state of customary law existing in this field" whereas the latter did not. The former resolu-

---

[7] Italics added.
[8] *I.C.J. Reports 1974*, p. 3 at p. 23.

tion had been adopted by 87 votes to 2,[9] with 12 abstentions, and, in his view, "the principles stated in this Resolution were therefore assented to by a great many States representing not only all geographical areas but also all economic systems," whereas Article 2 of CERDS "must be analysed as a political rather than as a legal declaration concerned with the ideological strategy of development and, as such, supported only by non-industrialised States." The basis of the disinction between the resolutions lay, in the view of the arbitrator, both in the circumstances in which they were adopted and in the role they respectively allotted to international law in the exercise of permanent sovereignty over natural resources, Resolution 1803 (XVII) providing for such a role and the NIEO Resolutions not doing so.

The facts in *Liamco* were similar to those in *Texaco*. An oil concession similar to that in *Texaco* was granted in 1955, and in 1973 this concession was nationalised, 32 years before the expiry period of the concession. The Libyan Government declined to arbitrate and, as in *Texaco*, the company applied to the President of the International Court of Justice for the appointment of a sole arbitrator. The President (Judge Lachs from Poland) appointed Dr. Sobhi Mahmassani, Counsellor-at-Law of Beirut, as sole arbitrator. The Government of Libya took no part in the proceedings and in an Award delivered on April 12, 1977 the arbitrator held (i) that the proper law of the contract was "in the first place Libyan law when consistent with international law and subsidiarily the general principles of law"; (ii) the arbitration clause "is valid and remains binding even after the nationalisation of the concession rights"; (iii) that "the right of a State to nationalise its wealth and natural resources is sovereign, subject to the obligation of indemnification for premature termination of concession agreements"; (iv) that "nationalisation of concession rights, even before the expiration of the concession term, if not discriminatory and not accompanied by a wrongful act or conduct, is not unlawful as such, and constitutes not a tort but a source of liability to compensate the concessionaire for said premature termination of the concession agreements"; (v) that in this case there was no conclusive evidence that the nationalisation measures were of a discriminatory character; (vi) that the claims by Liamco for *restitutio in integrum* and an award declaring the

---

[9] The two States voting against were France and South Africa and those abstaining were Bulgaria, Burma, Byelorussian SSR, Cuba, Czechoslovakia, Ghana, Hungary, Mongolia, Poland, Romania, Ukrainian S.S.R., U.S.S.R. It is a tribute to Professor Dupuy's integrity as an arbitrator that he was prepared to place such reliance on resolution 1803 (XVII), notwithstanding that his own country (France) had voted against it.

invalidity of Libya's title to Liamco's nationalised rights "are to be rejected in accordance with prevalent international practice"; (vii) but that nevertheless Liamco was "entitled to *damnum emergens,* which represents the value of the nationalised physical plant and equipment that Liamco owns and has the right to recover at the termination of the concession"; (viii) however, that Liamco was not entitled to the value of the nationalised concession rights, representing the loss of profit (*lucrum cessans*), but only to "equitable compensation as a measure for the assessment of damages in the present dispute, with the classical formula of 'prior, adequate and effective compensation" remaining as a maximum and a practical guide for such assessment."[10] Applying these principles the arbitrator ordered Libya to pay $13,882,677 as indemnification for loss of physical plant and equipment; $66,000,000 as "equitable compensation" for loss of concession rights; $203,000 "as contribution by the Respondent towards the arbitration costs and expenses of the Claimant"; and a "compensatory indemnity in lieu of interest at the rate of 5 per cent. on the above-mentioned sums to be added from the date of this Award till the date of their payment in full."[11]

It is unfortunate that, notwithstanding some common features, the Awards in *Texaco* and *Liamco*, delivered on similar facts within three months of each other, exhibit considerable differences in approach, thus indicating that there is still much truth in the statement made by the Supreme Court of the United States in 1964, that "there are few if any issues in international law today on which opinion seems to be so divided as the limitations on a State's power to expropriate the property of aliens."[12] Whereas Professor Dupuy considered that Libya's conduct warranted the application of the principle *restitutio in integrum*, Dr. Mahmassani specifically rejected the application of that principle, saying of that principle that it has "been considered in international law as against the respect due for the sovereignty of the nationalising State." In his view the question resolved itself into one of deciding the "appropriate compensation"[13] that should be paid, and here he decided that by "appropriate" was meant "equitable." The arbitrator thus put himself in line with the International Court of Justice and other international arbitrators who have found the notion of "equity" a convenient one for

---

[10] The formulation is usually "prompt, adequate and effective" and is taken from the Note of Secretary of State Cordell Hull to the Mexican ambassador in Washington, dated August 22, 1938. See 3 Hackworth, *Digest of International Law* 655–665 (1942).

[11] Liamco had claimed a total of $207,652,667 and also interest at 12 per cent. as from January 1, 1974.

[12] In *Banco Nacional de Cuba* v. *Sabbatino*, 376 U.S. 398 at p. 428 (1964).

[13] These were the words used in Resolutions 1803 (XVII) and 3281 (XXIX).

resolving disputes where the rules of international law are uncertain.[14]

The formula of "equitable compensation," said Dr. Mahmassani, is "in complete harmony with the general trend of international theory and practice on the concepts of sovereignty, destination of national wealth and natural resources, nationalistic motivations in the attitude and behaviour of "Third World" nations, the lawfulness and frequency of nationalisation, and the recent declarations affirmed in successive United Nations Resolutions by the majority members of the General Assembly." The arbitrator made passing references to Resolutions 1803 (XVII) and 3281 (XXIX), but did not expatiate on the principles of NIEO, preferring to rely on earlier international practice such as the lump-sum awards paid subsequent to the post-war nationalisations and also in the case of the nationalisation of the Suez Canal Company in 1956. He referred specifically to the Award of Judge Lagergren, President of the Court of Appeal for Western Sweden, as sole arbitrator in *BP Exploration Company (Libya) Limited* v. *Government of the Libyan Arab Republic*.[15]

The *BP Exploration* case was yet another dispute arising out of the nationalisation by Libya of a foreign oil company and was referred to an arbitrator appointed by the President of the International Court of Justice—at that time Sir Muhammad Zafrullah Khan (Pakistan)—because of the Libyan Government's refusal to appoint an arbitrator. In the Award, delivered on October 10, 1973, the arbitrator found that the relevant Libyan Nationalisation Law of 1971, through a breach of the concession agreement, was effective to terminate that agreement; and Judge Lagergren was emphatic in holding (i) that "there is no explicit support for the proposition that specific performance, and even less so *restitutio in integrum*, are remedies of public international law available at the option of a party suffering a wrongful breach by a co-contracting party"; (ii) that "the case analysis also demonstrates that the responsibility incurred by the defaulting party for breach of an obligation to perform a contractual undertaking is a duty to pay damages, and that the concept of *restitutio in integrum* has been employed merely as a vehicle for establishing the amount of damages"; and (iii) that "*restitutio in integrum* is not to be understood in its literal sense of being a remedy for physical reinstatement of a concessionaire party into a

---

[14] See *North Sea Continental Shelf* cases, *I.C.J. Reports 1969*, p. 3, especially at pp. 48–54; *Fisheries Jurisdiction* case, *I.C.J. Reports 1974*, p. 3, especially at pp. 33–35; and *Arbitration between the United Kingdom of Great Britain and Northern Ireland and the French Republic on the Delimitation of the Continental Shelf*, June 30, 1977 and March 14, 1978, *Cmnd.* 7438 or 18 ILM 397.

[15] 53 I.L.R. 297.

position from which it has been effectively and definitively removed by the other, sovereign party."

There is thus a complete divergence, especially on the issue of *restitutio in integrum*, between the pre-NIEO Award of Judge Lagergren and the post-NIEO Award of Professor Dupuy. The other post-NIEO Award of Dr. Mahmassani sides with that of Judge Lagergren, but, in order to complete the picture, reference should be made to the case of *Revere Copper and Brass Inc.* v. *Overseas Private Investment Corporation*[16] decided on August 24, 1978, *i.e.* another post-NIEO case. This was not an international arbitration in the ordinary sense, though issues of international law were raised and pronounced upon. It was a dispute under the Investment Guaranty Program of the Government of the United States, this being a system whereby that Government, through its Overseas Private Investment Corporation (OPIC), extends certain guarantees to American firms investing in developing countries. The guarantees are against certain kinds of "expropriatory action" taken or condoned by the Government of the Project Country, including action which prevents the foreign enterprise "from exercising effective control over the use or disposition of a substantial portion of its property or from constructing the Project or operating the same." In other words the guarantees, which are not extended to the American firm concerned unless the Government of the Project Country agrees to such extension, can cover what has come to be known as "creeping nationalisation" as well as outright nationalisation, and it is provided in the Guaranty Agreements between the United States and the Project Countries that if OPIC pay out on a claim, the United States Government itself can pursue the claim against the Project Country under international law. So, in an arbitration between a claimant firm and OPIC, the latter may find itself arguing against the American firm concerned that the measures taken by the Project Country did not constitute "expropriatory action." Moreover, it is provided that the term "expropriatory action" does not include action resulting from "any law, decree, regulation or administrative action of the Government of the Project Country which is not by its express terms for the purpose of nationalisation, confiscation, or expropriation (including but not limited to intervention, condemnation or other taking), is reasonably related to constitutionally sanctioned governmental objectives, is not arbitrary, is based on a reasonable classification of entities to which it applies and does not violate generally accepted international law principles." So international law is inserted somewhat indirectly into the

---

[16] 17 ILM 1321.

Guaranty Program, the main purpose of which is to assist developing countries, as well as American investors, and to achieve a fair
balance between potentially conflicting interests.

In *Revere*, a Maryland corporation, Revere Copper and Brass
Inc., made an investment in its wholly-owned subsidiary, Revere
Jamaica Alumina, Limited (R.J.A.), another Maryland corporation, for the purpose of financing R.J.A.'s construction and operation of a bauxite mining operation, a plant to convert the bauxite
into alumina and related facilities in Jamaica. This investment was
made pursuant to an Agreement between R.J.A. and the Government of Jamaica (G.O.J.) on March 10, 1967. The Agreement provided that it should remain in force for 25 years and contained a
clause (clause 12) which provided that no further taxes, burdens and
levies should be imposed, except as stated. The operation went
ahead, bauxite was mined and an alumina plant was constructed.
However, in 1972 there was a political change in Jamaica and the
People's National Party came to power. Soon after the election, the
PNP leader, Mr Michael Manley, told the General Assembly of the
United Nations: "The time has come to reconstruct the basis on
which the gains arising from the exploitation of . . . resources are
shared between those . . . who provide the capital and technical
know-how for the process of exploitation . . . and those . . . who
own the resources and provide essential infrastructure and the
labour force."

Mr Manley lost little time in implementing his plans which were
precisely stated as follows: (i) a drastic increase in revenues from
bauxite mining and alumina production; (ii) recovery of bauxite ore
leased to the mining companies; (iii) reacquisition of all land owned
by such companies; and (iv) national majority ownership and control of the bauxite industry. On May 15, 1974, shortly after the
adoption of the first two NIEO resolutions, he announced: "the
renegotiation of contracts with the aluminum companies is not only
a necessity and the right of a sovereign nation, but an obligation to
the people. These considerations outweigh the sanctity of contractual agreements." Mr. Manley also made the point that, when the
bauxite contracts were signed, the cost of the oil which Jamaica had
to import was $2·00 per barrel; now it was $14·00 per barrel.

There then followed a series of unsuccessful negotiations between
GOJ and the bauxite companies, accompanied by the imposition by
GOJ of various imposts. Despite the existence of clause 12 in the
original agreement, the bauxite production levy was raised, and Section 4 of the Bauxite (Production Levy) Act, 1974, prescribed minimum quarterly quantities of bauxite which each producer was
deemed to have produced whether he had produced bauxite or not.

Mining royalties were also increased and the Mining Act was amended so as to empower the Minister to order holders of mining leases to produce not less than a minimum amount of bauxite. The result was that Revere reported a loss for the first quarter of 1975 of 26 cents a share, as compared wih a profit of 60 cents a share in 1974, and decided to close down its operation in Jamaica. On January 13, 1976 RJA instituted proceedings against GOJ in the Supreme Court of Jamaica for a determination that the bauxite production levy was a breach of the agreement. However, Smith, C.J. held that clause 12 of the 1967 agreement was void *ab initio* because Ministers could not fetter the sovereign power of Parliament to legislate with respect to taxation and that the agreement "did not create any right in RJA as against future taxes." On April 14, 1976 Revere submitted to OPIC an application for compensation.

In the ensuing arbitration, the majority (G.W. Haight and C.R. Wetzel) upheld Revere's claims, whilst the third arbitrator, F. Began, dissented. The majority considered that the bauxite production levy, the increase in royalties and the amendment of the Mining Law all constituted breaches of the 1967 agreement. The Jamaican court had found that there had been no breach of Jamaican law, so the question was whether the law of Jamaica was the only law to be considered. The two arbitrators forming the majority thought not, saying: "Although the Agreement was silent as to the applicable law, we accept Jamaican law for all ordinary purposes of the Agreement, but we do not consider that its applicability for some purposes precludes the application of principles of public international law which govern the responsibility of States for injuries to aliens. We regard these principles as particularly applicable where the question is, as here, whether actions taken by a government contrary to and damaging to the economic interests of aliens are in conflict with undertakings and assurances given in good faith to such aliens as an inducement to their making the investments affected by the action."

Having thus given themselves an entry into international law, the majority were content largely to follow the reasoning of Professor Dupuy in *Texaco*. In fact they went further than Professor Dupuy because, whereas the latter had listed a number of elements as justifying the "internationalisation" of a contract which on the face of it is an ordinary municipal law contract, *e.g.* a reference to "general principles of law" as the applicable law; the inclusion of a clause providing for international arbitration of disputes; and the fact that the contract constitutes an economic development agreement—the two majority arbitrators seemed to regard the fact that the contract between RJA and GOJ was an economic development agreement was in itself sufficient. The reasoning by which they evaded the principle of permanent sovereignty over natural resources was ingenious, consisting of the following: "If the sovereign power of a State cannot be fettered in this manner by entering into binding contracts, the State would be deprived of the power by such contracts to meet essential needs. Inevitably, in order to meet the aspirations of its people, the Government may for certain periods of time impose limits on the sovereign powers of the State, just as it does when it embarks on international financing by issuing long term government bonds on foreign markets. Under international law the commitments made in favour of foreign nationals are binding notwithstanding the power of Parliament and other governmental organs under the domestic Constitution to override or nullify such commitments. Any other position would mean in this case that Jamaica could not in the exercise of its sovereign powers obtain foreign private capital to develop its own resources or attract foreign industries. To suggest that for the purpose of obtaining foreign private capital the Government could only issue contracts that were non-binding would be meaningless."

It is certainly desirable that the government of a developing country should be able to attract foreign private capital, but there are several objections to the thesis of the majority in this case. First, it is difficult to see why, if the sanctity of contracts and good faith are important principles—as certainly they are—a distinction should be drawn between "economic development agreements" and other contracts. Secondly, the object which the majority consider desirable could be achieved by other means which do not involve the intrusion of international law (which despite recent changes remains essentially a system regulating relations between sovereign States) into dealings between governments and foreign private parties. All that would be necessary—and this is sometimes done—would be for the government to enter into a treaty with the government of which the foreign private parties are nationals, in which both governments pledge themselves not to expropriate the interests of such foreign private parties in a manner contrary to international law.

The third arbitrator in the *Revere* case dissented on the ground that it was unnecessary to bring international law into consideration at all and that the measures taken by GOJ, although making things awkward for RJA, did not amount to "expropriatory action" in the meaning of OPIC's contract with Revere.

II—THE RECORD OF NIEO SINCE 1974

In this section the fate of NIEO since 1974 will be briefly traced. The blunt fact is that very little progress in implementing NIEO has been made, justifying the view expressed by the French representatives at the United Nations in May 1974 that "the structures that serve as the framework for trade among States and economic entities are only what they are—they cannot be changed by simple votes." Yet it was by "simple votes" that NIEO was brought into existence, and it has largely been by "simple votes" that the effort has been made to implement the principles of NIEO.

In 1975 the General Assembly held another special session devoted to economic questions, and on September 16 of that year adopted unanimously Resolution 3362 (S–VII). This was a very long resolution restating the general philosophy of NIEO. Among its more important provisions were the following: (i) "Developed countries should fully implement agreed provisions on the principle of standstill as regards imports from developing countries, and any departure should be subjected to such measures as consultations and multilateral surveillance and compensation." (ii) "Developed countries should exercise maximum restraint within the framework of international obligations in the imposition of countervailing duties on the imports of products from developing countries." (iii) "Developed countries confirm their continued commitment in respect of the targets relating to the transfer of resources, in particular the official development assistance target of 0·7 per cent. of gross national product, as agreed in the International Development Strategy for the Second United Nations Development Decade, and adopt as their common aim an effective increase in official development assistance with a view to achieving these targets by the end of the decade."

The resolution continued with one obligation after another being placed upon the developed countries. This led the delegate of the Soviet Union—and in this he was joined by the delegate of the German Democratic Republic speaking on behalf of the Comecon group—to object that he "could not accept the notion whereby the socialist countries of Eastern Europe were placed on an equal footing with the developed capitalist countries with regard to historical responsibility for the backwardness of the developing countries and for their state of poverty in the economic crisis which had gripped the capitalist world."

In Resolution 31/178, adopted on December 21, 1976 by 128 to 1 (United States) with 8 abstentions (Belgium, France, Federal Republic of Germany, Israel, Italy, Japan, Luxembourg and the United Kingdom), the General Assembly noted "the regret expressed by the developing countries that the developed countries have yet to display the necessary political will to implement these fundamental decisions of the United Nations and fulfil their commitments and obligations and to adjust their policies for this purpose,'' and expressed itself "deeply concerned that during the current Second United Nations Development Decade the terms of trade of the majority of developing countries have deteriorated, together with unprecedented and growing balance-of-payments deficits, that the burden of debt has reached unmanageable proportions in many developing countries and growth in the developing countries is expected to fall short not only of the 6 per cent. target of the International Development Strategy but also of the rate of growth achieved in the First United Nations Development Decade and that, for many developing countries, particularly among the least developed, landlocked, island and most seriously affected developing countries, real *per capita* income could, if present trends persist, be lower in 1980 than at the start of the Decade." This being so, the General Assembly urged "the international community, particularly the developed countries, to display the necessary political will in the ongoing negotiations in different United Nations forums and elsewhere so as to reach the concrete and urgent solutions necessary to promote the establishment of the new international economic order."

In Resolution 32/174, adopted without vote on December 19, 1977, the General Assembly, being thus disappointed with the results achieved so far, decided to convene yet another special session, in 1980, "at a high level, in order to assess the progress made in the various forums of the United Nations system in the establishment of the new international economic order." Before the special session was held, the General Assembly, again under pressure from the developing countries, adopted without vote on December 14, 1979 Resolution 34/138 entitled "Global Negotiations relating to International Economic Co-operation for Development"; the emphasis on "global negotiations"—the phrase has since become a slogan—was significant. By now some of the developing countries had begun to suspect that it was the tactics of the developed countries not only to divide the so-called Third World against itself, but also to split the debate up into as many forums as possible. Moreover, in some of these forums, such as the World Bank and the International Monetary Fund, the developing countries were aware that they would be at a disadvantage because the weighted voting system employed in those organisations favours the richer nations. Hence, the Resolution stressed that there must be "new, concrete, comprehensive and global solutions going beyond limited efforts and measures intended to resolve only the present economic difficulties"; emphasised that "such global negotiations must take place within the United Nations system"; and decided that at the special session in 1980 the General Assembly should launch "a round of global and sustained negotiations on international economic co-operation for development, such negotiations being action-oriented and proceeding in a simultaneous manner in order to ensure a coherent and integrated approach to the issues under negotiation."[17]

However, neither at the eleventh special session held in August/ September 1980, nor at the ensuing regular session (the 35th), were the "global negotiations" successfully launched. The stumbling-block was, as it so often is, procedural. The developed countries were anxious lest the central negotiating forum that was proposed should derogate from the authority of the specialised agencies, especially the International Monetary Fund, whilst the Arab oil producers were anxious lest so many matters might be hived off to specialised bodies that the only serious question left for the central negotiating forum might be one which for them was particularly sensitive, namely the price of oil.

Towards the end of 1981 things took a slight turn for the better. After a lot of hesitation even such reluctant world leaders as President Reagan and Mrs Thatcher decided to go along with the suggestion, emanating from the Independent Commission on International Development Issues under the Chairmanship of Willy Brandt,[18] that there should be a summit meeting "limited to some twenty-five world leaders who could ensure fair representation of major world groupings, to enable initiatives and concessions to be thrashed out with candour and boldness."

Eventually the summit proposed by the Brandt Commission was held at Cancun in Mexico on October 22 and 23, 1981. It was however, hardly the sort of summit envisaged by Willy Brandt. Two days was obviously not enough for "initiatives and concessions to be

---

[17] UN document SEA/457, August 31, 1981, pp. 6–7.

[18] *North-South: A Programme for Survival*. The Report of the Independent Commission on International Development Issues under the Chairmanship of Willy Brandt (Pan Books, 1980). The so-called "Brandt Commission" consisted of 18 members drawn from five continents. Apart from the chairman, who had been Chancellor of the Federal Republic of Germany from 1969–74, other prominent members included Mr. Edward Heath (Prime Minister of the United Kingdom from 1970–74); Mr. Lakshmi Kant Jha (Governor of the Reserve Bank of India 1967–70; Indian ambassador to the United States, 1970–73; and Chairman of the U.N. Group of Eminent Persons on Multinational Corporations, 1973–75); Mr. Adam Malik (Minister for Foreign Affairs of Indonesia from 1966–77); and Mr. Shridath Ramphal (Secretary-General of the Commonwealth). An original member of the Commission was Mr. Pierre Mendes-France, former Prime Minister of France, but he was replaced in 1978 by Senator Edgard Pisani, a French member of the European Parliament. The Commission was officially independent, although it received financial support from many governments, especially the Government of the Netherlands, and also from regional organisations and Funds and various foundations and other private sources.

thrashed out with candour and boldness" by leaders who in any case had no authority to commit countries other than their own. Also, President Brezhnev, still taking the view that his country had no responsibility for the plight of the developing nations, held aloof. Even so, according to the communiqué issued by the co-chairmen (President Portillo of Mexico and Prime Minister Trudeau of Canada), "the very fact that 22 leaders from some of the world's most influential yet diverse countries were prepared to come to Cancun and discuss these issues clearly demonstrated the importance and gravity that they attached to them."

It is understood that President Reagan only went to Cancun on the understanding that there would be no negotiations, let alone "global negotiations." So it is not surprising that the communiqué on that subject was non-committal, simply stating: "The Heads of State and Government confirmed the desirability of supporting at the United Nations, with a sense of urgency, a consensus to launch global negotiations on a basis to be mutually agreed and in circumstances offering the prospect of meaningful progress. Some countries insisted that the competence of the specialised agencies should not be affected."

Nevertheless there is a widespread belief that, as a result of the Cancun summit, some sort of "global negotiations" will eventually be held. What effect these negotiations will have on the drive for a "new international economic order" remains to be seen.

The Future Prospects for NIEO

The future prospects for NIEO do not look bright. True, as already stated, some sort of global negotiations will probably be held. But it is doubtful if they will lead to any real consensus, or yield any more benefit for the developing nations than the successive resolutions passed by the General Assembly since 1974, and similar resolutions passed by successive meetings of UNCTAD, (*e.g.* UNCTAD IV, Nairobi, 1976; UNCTAD V, Manila, 1979).

A key factor affecting the prospects for NIEO has undoubtedly been the advent to power in Washington of the Reagan Administration early in 1981. So far this has been almost entirely a negative factor. An early indication of the changed attitude prevailing in Washington was provided by a report entitled "Foreign Aid Retrenchment" emanating from the Office of Management and Budget under its new Director, Mr. David Stockman. This report called for a reduction of one third in the foreign aid proposals of former President Carter and was particularly severe on the International Development Association, the World Bank's "soft-loan agency." IDA was accused of having "supported State planning efforts in some countries" and of having "placed a major emphasis on programmes fostering income redistribution." Also IDA was stated not to have been "vigorous in using leverage inherent in its large lending programme to press recipients to redirect the economies toward a market orientation."[19] Mr. Stockman insisted that the United States should revoke its commitment to the sixth IDA replenishment agreement which had already been negotiated in 1980. Later, under pressure from Secretary of State Haig, a compromise was worked out, but a considerable shock had been administered.

On March 3, 1981 Mr. Haig was to administer an even greater shock himself when he instructed the United States delegation at the Third United Nations Conference on the Law of the Sea (UNCLOS III) "to seek to insure that the negotiations do not end at the present session . . . pending a policy review," which, it was made clear, would last for several months. Moreover the composition of the United States delegation was substantially changed. The negotiations referred to had been going on since 1973 and it had been expected, at least by some Third-World delegations, that they would result in the conclusion of a Convention by the end of 1981, or at least early in 1982. A key feature of the expected Convention was that it would provide that the resources of the ocean floor beyond the limits of national jurisdiction (in most cases 200 nautical miles) would constitute "the common heritage of mankind" and would be exploited, at least in part, on behalf of developing countries by an international Enterprise over whose activities the developing countries would have a controlling influence.

When the "policy review" was completed, the United States delegate, Mr. James L. Malone, informed the Conference at a closed meeting on August 3, 1981—though his remarks were subsequently made public—in somewhat laconic terms that "our review of the draft convention has revealed that Part XI of the text [which deals with deep-sea mining] would, in its present form, be a stumbling block to treaty ratification." In particular there was a "lingering impression" that the draft convention would run counter to a policy of encouraging and promoting seabed resource development and "might create a situation in which the Enterprise, using funds provided in part by the United States Government, eventually would eclipse mining activity by private companies."[20]

In the meantime the United States, the Federal Republic of Germany, France and the United Kingdom had passed legislation auth-

---

[19] R. Nations, *Far Eastern Economic Review* (February 20, 1981), p. 70.
[20] United Nations Press Release, SEA/457 (August 31, 1981), p. 6.

orising seabed mining. On September 2, 1982, these countries entered into an "Agreement Concerning Interim Arrangements Relating to the Polymetallic Nodules of the Deep Sea Bed."[21] This was criticised as the forerunner of a Western "mini-treaty" which would replace or run counter to the United Nations Convention. President Reagan had already announced on January 29, 1982 that the United States was ready to resume participation in the negotiations suspended in 1981. On March 8, 1982, at the 11th session in New York, the United States delegation demanded 230 changes to the draft. These related to seabed mining, so that the Western industrialised powers would have had a decisive voice in the deliberations of the International Seabed Authority, which in granting contracts "would at all times be guided by the objective of developing the resources of the area." The proposals also envisaged that revisions to the Treaty could only be taken with the consent of those powers, and that there would be no compulsory transfer of technology. Attempts at compromise, however, failed, and on April 30, 1982 the Convention was adopted by 130 votes in favour and four against (United States and for other reasons Israel, Turkey and Venezuela). There were 17 abstentions, and 17 countries were absent. On July 9, President Reagan announced that the United States would not sign the Convention as it did "not meet U.S. objectives." He observed that those States which had abstained or voted against the adoption of the Convention produced more than 60 per cent. of the world's GDP and provided more than 60 per cent. of U.N. contributions. The concluding session was held at Montego Bay, Jamaica on December 6–10, 1982, when the Convention and the Final Act were opened for signature. One hundred and seventeen States signed the Convention, which allowed the International Seabed Preparatory Commission to meet on March 15, 1983, and a total of 150 delegations signed the Final Act; a number of major Western industrialised countries failed to do so. The Convention will come into force 12 months after instruments of ratification have been deposited by 60 countries.

Thus there is a potential conflict between the two régimes which may claim to cover seabed mining. The President of the U.N. Conference, Mr. T. Koh, had already foreseen this when he indicated he would subsequently attempt to persuade the General Assembly to ask the International Court of Justice to say whether the West's national legislation, and presumably the agreement between the Western nations previously referred to, and any subsequent West-

---

[21] The U.S.S.R. and Japan also subsequently adopted national legislation. (1982) 21 I.L.M. 950.

ern "mini-treaty," were contrary to international law. In such a
reference, it would no doubt be argued that the West, expressly or
by acquiescence, has already acknowledged that the proposition
that the deep seabed is part of the "common heritage of mankind"
has become part of international law, and perhaps even part of *jus
cogens.*

Perhaps even more decisive than these specific acts of the
Government of the United States was the general attitude adopted
by that Government, and particularly by its Chief Executive,
towards NIEO. Addressing the Annual Meeting of the Board of
Governors of the World Bank and the International Monetary Fund
in Washington on September 29, 1981, Mr. Ronald Reagan said:
"The international political and economic institutions created after
1945 rested upon a belief that the key to national development and
human progress is individual freedom, both political and economic.
The Bretton Woods institutions and the GATT established generalised rules and procedures to facilitate individual enterprise and an
open international trading and financial system. They recognised
that economic incentives and increasingly commercial opportunities
would be essential to economic recovery and growth. We who live in
free market societies believe that growth, prosperity and ultimately
human fulfilment, are created from the bottom up, not the government down . . . . The societies which have achieved the most spectacular, broad-based economic progress in the shortest period of
time are not the most tightly controlled, nor necessarily the biggest
in size, or the wealthiest in natural resources. No, what unites them
all is their willingness to believe in the magic of the market
place . . . . Governments that set out to regiment their people with
the stated objective of providing security and liberty have ended up
losing both. Those which put freedom as the first priority also find
they have also provided security and economic progress."

The President continued: "By reducing the rate of Government
spending, honouring our commitment to balance the budget, reducing tax rates to encourage productive investment and personal sav-
ings, eliminating excessive Government regulation, and maintaining
a stable monetary policy . . . we are convinced we will enter a new
era of sustained, noninflationary growth and prosperity, the likes of
which we have not seen for many years . . . . No American contribution can do more for development than a growing, prosperous
U.S. economy. The domestic policies of developing countries are
likewise the most critical contribution they can make to development. Unless a nation puts its own financial and economic house in
order, no amount of aid will produce progress. Many countries are
recognising this fact and taking dramatic steps to get their econom-

ies back on a sound footing. I know it's not easy—but it must be done."

To the Bank and Fund governors from inflation-ridden, deficit-financing, one-party States, these words must have come across as an unpleasant, almost impertinent, lecture. Moreover, according to one commentator who apparently has considerable acquaintance with the Washington scene, and not a little sympathy with the approach of the Reagan Administration, "The North-South dialogue is dead. It passed away peacefully on the beach of Cancun, a victim not so much of the indifference of United States President Ronald Reagan and other leaders of the North but of its own irrelevance to the economic problems which confront nations north and south, east and west, market and socialist. Meanwhile, however, a new international economic order goes marching on."[22]

However, the new international economic order that this commentator had in mind was "not the NIEO, that triumph of diplomatic sloganeering godfathered by OPEC cash, Western guilt, South Asian rhetoric and Sino-Soviet cynicism." It was rather the simple fact that some nations were gaining in economic strength whereas others were declining. The commentator then proceeded to develop his theory that NIEO has become irrelevant because some developing countries are doing very well without it, and he mentioned in particular South Korea; the ASEAN group; Sri Lanka; China, which, although it "has a very long modernisation road ahead," is also said to have "most of the ingredients of gradual progress"; and Latin America which "for all its history of misgovernment and entreprenurial skills and influx of ideas had money from the so-called North to keep transforming its large endowment of natural resources and fast-growing human ones to maintain the momentum it has achieved, after many false starts, in recent years." These promising members of the class, so to speak, were contrasted with those who were doing less well; namely the United States east of the Mississippi; Africa; the Indian Sub-continent (other than Sri Lanka); Western Europe where the workforce is ageing rapidly, consumption is rising, investment is falling, and which is "increasing its dependence on trade with the economically arthritic East European bloc, thereby reducing its ability to compete in the rest of the world"; and finally "the economically arthritic East European bloc" itself. This rise and fall of nations was said to be "the natural order of things" whereas "the official NIEO of United Nations forums has been a fiasco."[23]

---

[22] P. Bowring, *Far Eastern Economic Review* (November 6, 1981), p. 103.
[23] *Ibid.*

It is fitting that the last word on the Cancun summit should be left to the originator of the idea, Willy Brandt himself. He said that the Cancun summit was "an extraordinary event and a great opportunity" which he admitted had produced "rather ordinary results." He shared the disappointment which many people had felt about the result, but he thought there was "still hope." There had been "some progress," but it had been "progress by the millimetre." However it was sometimes said that "the first millimetres are the most important." Closing his statement, Willy Brandt said: "I had expected more from the summit but, of course, the outcome could have been worse. . . . We will continue to press for action and we will help to define possible steps. Early in January my fellow commissioners and I will meet again to do just that."[24]

So the pressure for NIEO will continue, coming from a variety of sources such as the Brandt Commission, which remains in existence; from Third World governments; from international bodies such as UNCTAD and the United Nations; from religious organisations and from influential private foundations and individuals. Against this array of forces will be set those of Western governments struggling with acute domestic problems, and powerful transnational corporations, inspired in part at least by the philosophy of the "New Right," as evinced most notably by members of the Reagan Administration, including the President himself. Given this background it is not too difficult to forecast the outcome, at least in the near future. There probably will be "global negotiations," although these will be on a more restricted basis and will drag on for longer than many had hoped. There will also most likely be action of a sort, especially in relation to the "least developed countries." Just as in the Western countries, where cost-cutting governments have tended to say that in future welfare aid should be restricted to those who really need it, so upon the international scene the cry will go out that the "welfare dollar" is being too thinly spread and that it is too much to expect that a score of "developed countries" should go on supporting well over a hundred "developing" countries who in many cases are endowed with resources far in excess of those in the "developed" countries.

There are already signs of development along these lines. Although it attracted much less attention than the Cancun summit, there was held in Paris between September 1 and 14, 1981 a conference which has been hailed as relatively successful. This conference was the United Nations Conference on the Least Developed Coun-

---

[24] *The Economist* (November 28, 1981), p. 21.

tries—the LLDCs as they are now known—and was organised by UNCTAD. The chairman was Mr Jean-Pierre Cot, Minister for Co-operation and Development in the new French administration of President Mitterand, which has already shown a constructive and practical interest in problems of world economic development. The conference adopted the Substantial New Program of Action (SNPA), which includes international recognition of the special status and development needs of the LLDCs, and an undertaking on the part of donor countries to make a special effort, in respect of the LLDCs, to increase aid to 0·15 per cent. of gross national product and to double aid to LLDCs by 1985, compared to the period 1975–80. Other ideas included in SNPA, though not yet finalised, included special treatment for LLDCs in relation to trade, food security, access to new financing mechanisms and the possibility of extending existing mechanisms to compensate LLDCs for shortfalls in the earning of their exports. A major problem will be the identification of the least developed countries, so as to keep SNPA within reasonable limits, and to adjust the list of LLDCs in accordance with changing circumstances.[25]

Early in 1983, the Brandt Commission issued a further report entitled "Common Crisis."[26] Arguing the interdependence of the industrialised and developing countries, this report contains proposals for the provision of substantial new funds to the IMF, the World Bank and other world financial institutions, as well as reforms which would mean some surrender of power by the West. The title of this report is relevant, for there is a growing realisation, even in ideologically market oriented circles in the United States, that, in the current economic recession, there is a point at which the financial collapse of important developing countries could well trigger the collapse of the international monetary system itself. Hence the United States authorities hastened to support Mexico when her financial system underwent great strains in 1982. The United States was also prepared to join in proposals to enhance the availability of

---

[25] As of September 1981, the 31 LLDC's were Afghanistan, Bangladesh, Benin, Bhutan, Botswana, Burundi, Cape Verde, Central African Republic, Chad, Comoros, Democratic Yemen, Ethiopia, Gambia, Guinea, Guinea-Bissau, Haiti, Laos, Losotho, Malawi, Maldives, Mali, Nepal, Niger, Ruwanda, Samoa, Somalia, Sudan, Uganda, Tanzania, Upper Volta and Yemen Arab Republic. The criteria for establishing LLDC status at present employed by the General Assembly of the United Nations are threefold, consisting of a low share of manufacturing in GNP (10 per cent. or less); low *per capita* income (less than $280 in 1978); and a low literacy rate (20 per cent. or less for persons over 15 years of age). These criteria are somewhat arbitrary and have so far produced the surprising result that only one Pacific island country (Samoa) is regarded as a LLDC. Three other Pacific island countries—Tonga, Kiribati and Tuvalu—were assessed but were deemed not to satisfy these criteria.

[26] *Common Crisis North-South*, The Brandt Commission (1983).

finance to the world. On January 18, 1983, the Group of Ten decided to increase the aggregate credit commitments under the General Agreement to Borrow (GAB) from SDR 6·4 billion to SDR 17 billion. Further it was agreed that access to the GAB should be available to other members of IMF for conditional financing. In February 1983, the Interim Committee of the Board of Governors of the IMF agreed to increase Fund quotas from SDR 61·03 billion to SDR 90 billion. Another aspect of this realisation of the interdependence of the world is the importance of trade as a generator of recovery. Thus those who argue against "short-term" protectionist measures being adopted as defences against unemployment by Western countries stress that a good proportion of the exports of Western countries can only be sold if the West's customers in the developing world can continue to maintain, and even to increase, access to the markets of Europe and North America.

This awareness in Western circles of the interdependence of the world in the current crisis is being matched by a new pragmatism among developing countries. The fall in oil prices, and the loss of much of OPEC's former power, have weakened hopes among developing countries that the answer to their problems lies in creating cartels antagonistic to the West. It is reasonable to expect, therefore, that practical proposals, along the lines of those adopted at the U.N. Conference in 1981 on the Least Developed Countries, referred to above, will incur less hostility in the West than the adoption of ideological positions based on "permanent sovereignty over natural resources," or supposed monopoly positions in relation to commodities.

There were hopes that this recognition by both developed and developing countries of their interdependence would produce concrete results at UNCTAD VI held in Belgrade in June 1983. These hopes were realised only to the extent that some compromise resolutions were adopted. However, the United States dissociated itself from the Conference's final declaration, which was only adopted after the Conference had been extended for two days and which displayed a fundamental difference of approach between the two groups. The Western countries seem to regard the present world economic crisis as a temporary phenomenon which will solve itself in the wake of recovery in the United States, whereas the Group of 77 tend to see it as something which has structural causes and will not be solved without structural alterations in the world economic order.

In preparation for UNCTAD VI the developing countries had held a meeting at Buenos Aires in April 1983 at which they put forward their familiar demands for greater stability in commodity prices, relief from their debt burden, more aid, reform of the world financial institutions, less protectionism in the West and so on. Lip service to some of these demands was paid by the Western countries at Belgrade, but for their part these countries suggested that the developing countries should begin to show a greater readiness to open up their own markets. The latter retorted by saying that they could not liberate their trade until their development had made much more progress than it has so far. In these circumstances it is not surprising that the final Belgrade declaration neatly stated that the world economic crisis was due to structural causes aggravated by temporary cyclical factors, and that nothing really concrete emerged.

LIMITED NUCLEAR WAR?

By

IAN CLARK

SPECULATION about the nature of war in the nuclear age has become increasingly atavistic in recent years. For so long have we been accustomed to discussing the revolutionary dimensions of nuclear strategy that the inherent conservatism of the philosophy of war, even of nuclear war, has insinuated itself almost unnoticed into the present dialogues and has achieved the status of an established, albeit subordinate, orthodoxy: nuclear war may not yet have been "conventionalised" but philosophical discussion of it, and strategic planning for it, is proceeding apace along conventional lines. To that extent, Morgenthau is correct to indicate the persistent tendency in post-1945 strategy "to find a way by which a nuclear war can be fought in a conventional way, that is, to conventionalise nuclear war in order to be able to come out of it alive."[1]

Such conventional thinking has occurred *pari passu* with the growing tendency to theorise not only about the deterrence of nuclear war but also about its actual conduct. Bernard Brodie had earlier insisted that the sole purpose of strategic nuclear forces was to avert war and a lingering consensus had endured into the 1970s that this was so. With the prevalence of nuclear war-fighting scenarios in the latter 1970s, however, this consensus began to disintegrate.[2] The emerging perspectives reflected the general atavism of nuclear thought: the outbreak of nuclear war would be bad, but losing one would be worse. In the words of one writer "fear of defeat has come to surpass fear of nuclear war."[3]

If a nuclear war was to be fought with some semblance of political purpose, the new consensus was that such a war must be a limited one and the principal thrust of strategic theorising in recent years has been directed at the forms such limitation might take and at the desirability of planning for such limited forms of nuclear war.

On these issues, the lines of debate are clearly drawn: it is easier to demarcate the respective positions than it is to attempt an overall balance or to weigh the force of some arguments against others. As

---

[1] H. Morgenthau, "The Fallacy of Thinking Conventionally about Nuclear Weapons" in D. Carlton and C. Schaerf (Eds.) *Arms Control and Technological Innovation* (1977), pp. 255–264.

[2] See M. Howard, "On Fighting a Nuclear War," 5 *International Security* (1981), pp. 3–17.

[3] N. Calder, *Nuclear Nightmares* (1979), p. 27.

the author has maintained elsewhere, neither side has a monopoly on virtue.[4]

I—COMPETING STRATEGIC PHILOSOPHIES

The arguments, both official and non-official, in favour of a trend towards limited nuclear options or—as it has most recently been depicted—a countervailing strategy, are many and various. Five in particular are worthy of mention: if they do not exhaust the doctrinal case in support of limited nuclear war strategies, they at least sketch out the main contours of this intellectual terrain.

First, and in denial of the view that we are now in a post-deterrence nuclear world preoccupied with war-fighting, limited nuclear war has been presented as a more effective deterrent. As other, more massive, options have lost credibility, limited ones are seen as having greater deterrent capacity because it is more credible that they would, in the event, be employed. At the very least, limited counterforce postures are seen as overcoming the problems of self-deterrence and, because the United States can have greater faith in its own likelihood of resorting to these options, it follows that the Soviet Union, impressed by the sincerity of United States declared intent, will avoid hostile action.

Secondly, and as a backstop to the argument just presented, it is claimed that deterrence is not infallible and that, were a nuclear war to break out, it is only sensible from a military, political or moral point of view that the level of hostilities be contained, that the extent of damage be limited and that the mechanisms be in existence to provide for the termination of war, sooner rather than later. Limited nuclear war, according to this perspective, may not be preferable to no war at all but it is measurably preferable to a total nuclear war in which there is no limitation by way of targets, weaponry, geographical scope or sequence of action.

Thirdly, and from the official American point of view, it has been asserted that the United States must avoid the dangers of strategic onanism: deterrence is, after all, a social activity and the very best of intellectual theories are of no avail if not reciprocated by the Soviet Union. The claim, in other words, is that it would be folly for the United States to persist with a war-avoidance strategic theory predicated on assuring destruction for the Soviet Union but, incidentally, also for itself, when the Soviet Union is manifestly uninterested in accommodating its strategic posture to such a rationale. Such an

---

[4] I. Clark, *Limited Nuclear War: Political Theory and War Conventions* (1982), p. 2.

asymmetry in strategic cultures between the two super-Powers would eventually have disastrous consequences for United States policy. To that extent, the re-orientation of United States doctrine towards concepts of nuclear war-fighting has been seen as no more than a realistic adjustment to the exigencies of perceived Soviet behaviour.[5]

Fourthly, there has been the view that the adoption of a genuine war-fighting strategy would permit a nuclear belligerent to win a nuclear war or, in more modest versions, at least to avoid losing one.[6] In no case is the atavistic element in the philosophy of nuclear war more apparent than where the usage of nuclear force is geared to the attainment of traditional military objectives and, in turn, to the realisation of a politically-recognisable concept of victory.

Fifthly and finally, it deserves passing mention that there have been those who have been attracted to limited nuclear options, especially of a counterforce nature, for the reason that such a mode of conducting military operations is most in keeping with classical notions of just war. Nuclear strategies that seek to maintain a meaningful distinction between "counterforce" targeting and "countervalue" targeting and that seek to develop "clean" and "discriminating" weapons are commended because they preserve the traditional *ius in bello* restrictions on immunity for innocent civilians and upon violence of an indiscriminate nature.[7]

Elaboration of the intellectual supports of limited nuclear war, along the above lines, has not, however, silenced the sceptics.[8] Their arguments, in turn, can be presented only in selective and summary fashion.

---

[5] On Soviet thinking about nuclear war, see R.L. Arnett, "Soviet Attitudes towards Nuclear War: do they really think they can win" 2 *Journal of Strategic Studies* (1979), pp. 171–191; J.L. Snyder, *The Soviet Strategic Culture* (1977); L. Gouré, "The U.S. Countervailing Strategy in Soviet Perception" *Strategic Review* (1981) pp. 51–64.

[6] Such notions are most closely associated with the name of Colin Gray. See, for example, C. Gray, "Nuclear Strategy: the Case for a Theory of Victory" 4 *International Security* (1979), pp.54–87. C. Gray and K. Payne, "Victory is Possible" *Foreign Policy* Nr. 39 (1980), pp. 14–27.

[7] An expression of this point of view can be found in P. Ramsey, *The Just War* (1968). More recently, US Defense Secretary, Caspar Weinberger, has argued that the virtue of the neutron bomb lies in its potential for "dramatically reducing the number of civilians who would be killed" and for sparing "many thousands of innocent lives." See *The Deterrent Value of the Enhanced Radiation Weapon* (1981), p.1. In a similar vein, see S.T. Cohen, "Whither the Neutron Bomb: A Moral Defense of Nuclear Radiation Weapons" XI *Parameters* (1981), pp. 19–27.

[8] As a sample, see S.M. Keeny Jr. and W. Panofsky, "MAD vs NUTS: The Mutual Hostage Relationship of the Superpowers" 60 *Foreign Affairs* (1981/2); L.R. Beres, *Nuclear Strategy and World Order: The United States Imperative* (1982); *op. cit.* in note 4, above; D. Ball, "Counterforce Targeting: How New? How Viable?" 11 *Arms Control Today* (1981), pp. 1–2, 6–9, and *Can Nuclear War be Controlled?* (1981).

First, and underlying much of the debate, is the pervasive concern that there is a very fine line between making nuclear strategy more realistic and making it more thinkable and, in consequence, another fine line between making it more thinkable and making it more likely. The proponents of limited nuclear war may well be correct that it embodies a more effective deterrent strategy. But at what cost? If there is greater deterrent power associated with limited-nuclear war doctrines, then it is for no other reason than the greater reality of the threat they bring to bear. Whether one concludes that limited-nuclear war theories make the outbreak of nuclear war more or less likely depends on whether one chooses to emphasise the enhanced deterrent effect or the augmented credibility of the threat. In either case, surely no one can deny the inextricable association between the two. Indeed such a paradoxical association is implicit in all deterrence theory: we can only make the world safer by acting (credibly) in such a way as to make it more dangerous.

Secondly, even if the intention behind the development of nuclear strategies and weapon systems for the conduct of limited nuclear operations be simply to minimise damage after war's outbreak, it may not look like that from the other side of the fence. A controlled counterforce capability may, through the fog of mutual suspicion, resemble the spectre of a first-strike capacity. In such a situation, the danger is thought to lie in the incentives for pre-emption in a crisis. In other words, there has been widespread condemnation of the limited nuclear warriors on the grounds that they are "destabilising" the strategic balance by acquisition policies that make sense only if the weapons are to be used first.

Thirdly, it can be asked if a limited nuclear war in the beginning will remain a limited nuclear war in the end. This is partly a question of mechanics: will the systems survive by means of which hostilities can be controlled? It is partly a question of psychology: how will national leaders, assuming they have survived thus far, behave under the emotional stresses of piecemeal holocaust? It is partly also a question of rational bargaining behaviour: will a political leader, having suffered some nuclear punishment, decide to desist at that point, or seek some advantage in a further roll of the cosmic dice?

Fourthly, and as if to rub salt into already exposed wounds, the proponents of Mutual Assured Destruction (MAD), having been told that the Soviets do not accept the US concept of deterrence, now eagerly retort that the Soviets do not believe in limited nuclear war either: the United States has abandoned one solipsism merely to embrace another. If it takes two parties to deter each other, it equally takes two parties to fight each other within mutually-agreed conventions. What value is there in US-centred ideas for limited,

selective, controlled and slow-motion nuclear operations if, in Pav-
lovian fashion, the Soviet military will respond with all necessary
military force? Can American theorists persist in the face of dis-
claimers, such as Brezhnev's, that "there can be in general no
'limited' nuclear war . . . it would inevitably and unavoidably
assume a world-wide character"?[9] More fully, Soviet Defence
Minister Ustinov has denounced the very basis of limited nuclear
war theory: "How should one seriously consider the possibility of
some kind of limited nuclear war? After all, it is clear to everyone
that the actions of an aggressor will inevitably and swiftly call forth a
destructive retaliatory strike from the side which has been subjected
to aggression. Only completely irresponsible people can claim that
nuclear war can be waged in accordance with some prearranged
rules, according to which nuclear missiles are to explode 'in a gentle-
manly fashion' on specific targets alone, without killing the population in the process."[10] Even more to the point, the Soviets may
believe in MAD after all. Thus Trofimenko explained his country's
agreement to SALT II on the grounds that it stabilised the strategic
balance "even if it is based on the MAD principle."[11]

II—RECENT AMERICAN STRATEGIC DOCTRINE

This strategic debate reached its crescendo in the aftermath of President Carter's Presidential Directive 59 of July 1980.[12] That document was taken as the consolidation of US nuclear thinking during
the 1970s and as providing a bench-mark of the gradual movement
in ideas that had taken place. No particular element of the new
countervailing package represented radical innovation in American
strategic ideas. Collectively, however, a series of nuances conveyed
the impression that things had moved significantly since the 1960s:
as regards the range of nuclear options required; as regards the refi-
nement of target sets and the new emphasis on targeting the Soviet
political and military control systems; as regards the envisaged
duration of a nuclear war; as regards the command and control systems necessary to sustain prolonged nuclear operations; and as
regards the military detail of projected nuclear action. Individually,
many of these elements had been present in United States policy for

---

[9] Interview, reproduced in XXIV *Survival* (1982), p. 32.
[10] *Pravda* (July 24, 1981), reproduced in XXIII *Survival* (1981), p. 274.
[11] H. Trofimenko, "Counterforce: Illusion of a Panacea" 5 *International Security* (1981), p. 39.
[12] See *e.g.* the exchange between L.R. Beres and C. Gray in XI *Parameters* (1981), pp. 19–37.

a long time and it is certainly spurious to argue the stark proposition that PD59 constituted a revolution in American thinking, representing the abandonment of the countervalue dimensions of assured destruction for the adoption of a counterforce doctrine of war-fighting.[13] Nonetheless, the cumulative impact of altered nuances suggests the emergence of a revised official orthodoxy[14] that does represent an important transformation in attitudes to nuclear war and to the relationship between nuclear strategy and policy.

There can be little doubt about the basic continuity between the strategic philosophies espoused by the Carter Administration and those expounded by its Reagan successor. Insofar as this continuity presses the United States strategic posture in the direction of limited nuclear war attitudes, it is said (by many) that the only significant difference between the two Administrations has been that the Carter people did not really believe in their own nuclear strategy whereas the Reagan men do.

The United States has had a nuclear policy, in the sense of a set of ongoing activities, ever since 1945. Only periodically has the rationale underlying that policy received public affirmation and it is a truism that the correspondence between declaratory policy and actual policy has been slight, subject to all the vagaries of strategic competition, domestic political debate and bureaucratic sparring. The latter year or so of the Carter Presidency produced an unusual emphasis on strategic declaratory policy and it was to be expected that, under Reagan, the broad conceptual framework of nuclear deterrence and/or war-fighting would be retained and the emphasis revert from public pronouncements on strategic philosophy to the mundane workaday world of weapon and system acquisition. As its policy on MX reveals, the Administration has been more than prepared to press ahead with production of hardware even in the absence of a convincing strategic doctrine governing its deployment.

This is not to claim that the triumvirate of Reagan, Haig (until mid-1982) and Weinberger maintained a stubborn silence on the underlying purposes of its nuclear weapon policy but rather to suggest that those who would seek light on the strategic directions of the current Administration must look beyond such public avowals of intent. Accordingly, Defence Secretary Weinberger is on record, on

[13] On the continuities in the U.S. policy, see M. Leitenberg, "Presidential Directive (PD) 59: United States Nuclear Weapon Targeting Policy," XVIII *Journal of Peace Research* (1981), pp. 309–317; A.L. Friedberg, "History of US Strategic 'Doctrine'," 3 *Journal of Strategic Studies* (1980), pp. 37–71.

[14] "PD59 . . . may fairly be characterised as reflecting a consensus of informed opinion among defense professionals"; C. Gray in "Presidential Directive 59: Flawed But Useful" XI *Parameters* (19819), p. 31.

the one hand, as lamenting that "in spite of budgets that reveal our priorities clearly, we still hear it said that we are preparing for limited strategic nuclear war . . . "[15] while, on the other, he has asserted unequivocally that "our top priority is on doing whatever is necessary to ensure nuclear force parity, *across the full range of plausible nuclear warfighting scenarios*, with the Soviet Union."[16] The analyst who wishes to discover to what extent Reaganite strategic philosophies are predicated on ideas of limited nuclear war must ascertain the area of overlap between these two Weinberger claims and the points on which they contradict each other.

Doctrinal statements are one source for understanding a nation's strategic policy. Another is provided by the examination of policy on specific weapon systems and by the acquisition policies actually being pursued. In the following section, specific aspects of the Reagan Administration's strategic "modernisation" programme will be explored with a view to eliciting further information on the state of the nuclear art and its attraction to ideas of limited nuclear war.

The precise nature of the relationship between strategic doctrine and weapon development is of major significance. To an extent, the relationship is that of chicken and egg and it is virtually impossible to break into the causal sequence. On specific occasions, however, analysts have maintained that it is the tail of technological development (*e.g.* MIRVs) that is wagging the doctrinal dog (*e.g.* limited counterforce targeting). Insofar as this is so, strategic doctrine becomes mere *ex post facto* rationalisation for extant weapon programmes. Alternatively, changes in the requisite military missions to be performed can lead to demand for weapons with specific characteristics. It is interesting that there are critics of *either* relationship. To some, it is unseemly that the state of our thinking about nuclear war should be determined by an out-of-control technological momentum; to others, it is equally unacceptable that doctrines should be developed which legitimise new acquisition policies, as when Daniel Ellsberg denounced the revised countermilitary content of US declaratory policy because of its effect of "legitimizing tremendously expensive weapons systems like the Trident II, MX and cruise missiles."[17] Specifically, therefore, there have been many critics who have decried the new limited war doctrines precisely because they are open-ended in their weapon requirements. Nonetheless, whether as cause or as effect, weapon policy provides some insight into trends in strategic thinking.

---

[15] *Chicago Tribune*, March 1, 1982.
[16] *Defense/81*, December 1981.
[17] Interview, in *WIN* (November 1, 1980), p. 6.

III—THE DIMENSIONS OF LIMITED NUCLEAR WAR

1. *War-fighting*

The Administration has insisted that its strategic policy has the sole objective of deterring the Soviet Union and thereby avoiding nuclear war. Speaking at an army college in Pennsylvania in June 1982, Weinberger reiterated that "nowhere do we mean to imply that nuclear war is winnable. This notion has no place in our strategy. We see nuclear weapons only as a way of discouraging the Soviets."[18] However, other official statements had previously given a more ambiguous account of the Administration's view of the relationship between strategic forces and nuclear war. Asked during his confirmation hearings about the possibility of nuclear war, Alexander Haig had replied that "there are things that we Americans must be willing to fight for . . . Clearly, in the nuclear age the responsibilities in this area become all the more awesome. But the point I wanted to make is there are things worth fighting for . . . We must structure our policy under that credible and justified premise."[19]

Undersecretary for Defense, James Wade, had made the same point even less equivocally. "We don't want to fight a nuclear war" he told a House subcommittee, " . . . but we must be prepared to do so if such a battle is to be deterred" and went on to add the injunction that "we must not fear war."[20] Similarly, that the Administration had turned its mind to the possibility of post-deterrence nuclear hostilities is clearly implied in the statement by National Security adviser William P. Clark in which he insisted that "we must be prepared to deter attack and *to defeat such attack should deterrence fail.*"[21]

2. *Limited nuclear war in Europe*

No single issue has served more to confirm the impression that the United States adheres to a notion of limited nuclear war than the successive statements made on the subject of a limited war within Europe or on a war limited to Europe. Given European sensitivities on this issue, these statements have been seized by the critics and given wide publicity.

At base, the contention is that the United States wishes to deter

---

[18] *The Weekend Australian* (June 5–6, 1982).
[19] Quoted by Tad Szulc, 16 *The Washingtonian* (1981).
[20] *Christian Science Monitor* (February 1, 1982).
[21] Address at Georgetown University, May 21, 1982, in *Official Text* (USICA, Canberra, May 25, 1982). (Emphasis added.)

the Soviet Union from any aggression against Western Europe but to do so while decoupling its deterrent from a threat that would entail destruction of continental United States. According to this account, limited nuclear war is the device whereby the United States maintains its extended deterrent while reducing the dangers to itself in the event that deterrence should fail. The decisions to produce the neutron bomb and to proceed with modernisation of the Long-Range Tactical Nuclear Force (LRTNF) in Europe (deployment of cruise missiles and Pershing II) is portrayed in this light: a Eurostrategic balance might, as it were, let the United States off the assured destruction hook.

Insofar as this image has been cultivated, US Government spokesmen have only themselves to blame. Tactless observations have fueled the fires of suspicion. For instance, in October 1981, President Reagan speculated on a nuclear war confined to Europe and said he "could see where you could have the exchange of tactical weapons against troops in the field without it bringing either one of the major powers to pushing the button."[22] The following month, the Administration's policy on nuclear weapon employment in Europe was thrown into further disarray by the open clash between Weinberger and Haig on the place of "demonstration" nuclear shots in NATO strategy, Haig claiming that such contingency plans existed and Weinberger insisting that this was simply a "suggestion" of the 1960s.[23]

The official rationale of US policy is, of course, the very reverse of that depicted by the critics. So far is the United States from seeking to decouple US security from that of Western Europe that the revamping of NATO's nuclear forces was requested by European Governments, and agreed to by the United States, precisely on the grounds that it would more effectively link the strategic nuclear deterrent to the tactical and conventional theatre balance. Richard Burt, Director of the State Department's Bureau of Politico-Military Affairs explained the cruise and Pershing deployments in these terms: "The United States took this step in the full knowledge that the Soviet Union would most likely respond to an attack on its homeland by US systems in Europe with an attack on the United States. Thus the emplacement of long-range US cruise and ballistic missiles in Europe makes escalation of any nuclear war in Europe to involve an intercontinental exchange more likely, not less."[24]

---

[22] *Christian Science Monitor* (October 21, 1981); *Washington Post* (October 21, 1981).

[23] See *International Herald Tribune* (November 6, 1981); *Washington Post* (November 6, 1981).

[24] Address to the Arms Control Association September 23, 1981 in 81 *Department of State Bulletin* (1981), pp. 56–57.

3. *The Neutron Bomb*

The neutron bomb has served as a microcosm of all the opposed arguments on the subject of limited nuclear war. Its proponents have proclaimed its deterrence, war-fighting, collateral damage-limitation and just-war virtues. Its critics have focused on its blurring of the nuclear threshold, on the dangers of its usability, on its deficiencies as a combat weapon and upon the scale of damage for the European battlefield that even its limited usage would entail. As already indicated, the enhanced radiation weapon was also a contributing factor to European unease about the battlefield burdens Europe would bear in the war-fighting scenarios emanating from Washington. The Administration announced its decision to proceed with production, but not deployment, of the neutron bomb in August 1981 (reportedly because, in August, Europe is on vacation and the protests would be muted).

More so than with any other weapon system, the case for the neutron bomb depends upon the validity of the deterrence paradox that it is the greater usability of the weapon that holds out the greater prospect of its non-use. It was on the grounds of its more effective deterrent power that the Reagan Administration was to sell the neutron bomb. It would be effective against a Soviet tank blitzkrieg, it would save lives and it would be safer for the European civilian population: for all these reasons, the Soviet Union would be deterred by the credibility of a NATO threat to employ them. In short, the case for the neutron bomb rests on the paradox that, because of the military rationality of the weapon and the greater propensity to resort to it, the effect is that of "actually reducing the likelihood that nuclear weapons would ever be used in Europe."[25] Thus Herbert Scoville explained the neutron bomb's attractiveness to Western political leaders on the grounds that "it might be easier to decide to use neutron weapons" and hence the bomb would "make it a little more credible that Western leaders would initiate the use of nuclear weapons."[26] It was precisely such reasoning that Scoville feared: we cannot enjoy the greater deterrent effect without also being aware of the reality of heightened threat on which it is predicated. The neutron bomb, therefore, encapsulates the atavism that is resurgent in nuclear war thinking: if the rhetoric still chooses to focus on the processes of deterrence, there yet remains the technological reality of new generations of nuclear weapons, the utility of which lies precisely in their military usability.

---

[25] *Op. cit.* (in note 7, above), p.1.
[26] *New York Times* (August 26, 1981).

4. *The MX missile*

While the public debate on MX in the United States has concentrated exclusively on its basing mode, the more important questions concern the strategic rationale for the missile itself. Those who would see the United States as seeking to acquire a genuine war-fighting nuclear capacity, those who would see the United States as moving increasingly towards a counterforce targeting doctrine and those who would see the United States as seeking an effective pre-emptive capability—all of those have looked very closely at the MX missile.

The MX will, by all accounts, be the most accurate missile in the United States nuclear arsenal. According to some reports, the Defence Department claims that, against a Soviet silo, it will have single shot kill probability of 92 per cent.[27] Even the White House has not been coy in admitting that it is the counter-silo features of MX in which the Administration is interested. In a background statement issued by the White House in support of MX it was candidly admitted that "early deployment of MX will break the Soviet monopoly on prompt counter-ICBM capabilities."[28] Likewise, Colin Gray saw the virtue of MX lying in its capacity to "threaten close to 75 per cent. of the total nuclear payload available to the Soviet strategic forces."[29]

The suspicion persists that such a countermilitary potential can be exploited only by way of a first strike and that it is the pre-emptive characteristics of the missile that are destabilising. Clearly, on this score, it is difficult to look beyond capabilities to the intentions which underly them. Many would maintain that a first strike makes no more sense for the United States than it does for the Soviet Union as there would still remain a survivable force capable of inflicting massive damage on the United States. Others have suggested that the United States lead in Anti-Submarine Warfare (ASW) makes the option marginally more attractive in Washington. In any case, those who suspect that there may be people in high places who are prepared to give the advocates of active damage-limitation (by way of pre-emption) at least a fair hearing, can draw no comfort from the expression of such views in US military journals: for instance, two authors have indicated that "selective counterforce strikes by MX could also serve the vital defensive purpose

---

[27] See, *e.g.* A. and A. Cockburn, "The Myth of Missile Accuracy" XI *Parameters* (1981), p.85.

[28] *New York Times* (October 3, 1981).

[29] "The MX ICBM and Nuclear Strategy," 14 *International Defense Review* (1981), p.861.

of reducing the Soviet ability to attack US targets by destroying their ICBMs prior to launch."[30]

5. *Trident II*

Traditionally, the submarine-launched ballistic missile (SLBM) has been regarded as a primarily countervalue weapon, lacking the accuracy of land-based missiles. The new generation Trident equipped with D-5 missiles is, however, presented as a weapon system with considerable countermilitary potential and is so described in the official statements in support of the system. Once again, even if the focus of the Reagan Administration has been on nuclear deterrence, it is *via* weapon systems that have specific countermilitary characteristics and that are designed to be used for specific military missions. The White House described the D-5 missile as having such accuracy that "they will allow us to use sea-launched missiles to attack any target in the Soviet Union, including their missile silos."[31] Comments made by Undersecretary of Defence for Research and Engineering, Richard DeLauer, would not have been such as to assuage Soviet fears of the underlying intentions of the US strategic modernisation programme: "The improved accuracy expected with development of the Trident 2 or Lockheed D-5 submarine-launched ballistic missile," DeLauer said, "will provide a counterforce capability enabling destruction of hardened Soviet targets and could even provide the capability for pre-emptive strike."[32]

6. *BMD and civil defence*

As part of its inherited countervailing strategy and its concern with developing a credible nuclear fighting force, the United States has been re-examining the question of ballistic missile defence (BMD) and, coupled with 1982 being the due date for the five-year review of the SALT I anti-ballistic missile (ABM) Treaty, this has led to a partial reopening of the ABM debate of the late 1960s.[33]

The terms of the debate appear, however, to be significantly different. In the 1960s, the ABM systems were frequently discussed as a defence for populations and it was their potentially destabilising consequences for mutual deterrence that led to the treaty prohibiting them in 1972. At the present time, BMD is discussed principally as a means of protecting land-based missile systems. Specifically,

---

[30] K.B. Payne and N. Pickett, "Vulnerability is Not an Adequate Strategy," *Military Review* (1981), p.71.

[31] *New York Times* (October 3, 1981).

[32] *Aviation Week and Space Technology* (October 26, 1981), p.49.

[33] See *e.g.* C. Gray, "A New Debate on Ballistic Missile Defence" XXIII *Survival* (1981), pp.60–71.

BMD is one of the remaining options being considered for the "survivable" basing of the MX.

To that extent, the parameters of the debate would seem to be less apocalyptic than in the 1960s: the discussion does not centre on the heavens-will-fall implications of population defence but rather on the stability-inducing contribution that BMD can make to the defence of vulnerable missiles, thereby reducing the incentives to launch first or on warning.

However, superficial appearances can be deceptive. The present context of BMD discussion is considered to have equally sinister and destabilising implications by those critics who view BMD as being associated with limited first-strike and escalation dominance concepts. In the credo of nuclear deterrence, survivable ICBMs aimed at populations are good; the protection of missiles, possibly for sequential counterforce missions in a protracted war scenario, is execrable.

In any case, the present Administration has given every indication that it wishes to consider seriously the BMD option. Weinberger gave an early intimation of this in April 1981,[34] and more recently Richard Perle, Assistant Secretary of Defense for International Security, answered a House Armed Services Committee question on the prospects of the ABM Treaty being cancelled by saying that "if . . . the only way we can defend our strategic forces is by the deployment of an ABM system that exceeds the terms of the treaty, I think you could find sufficient support for that. . . ."[35]

Closely associated with BMD in the public mind is the question of civil defence although, as indicated above, the association is not direct as defence of missile silos may have implications for the strategic balance that are quite different from those produced by protective measures for civil populations. Here again, however, there is ambiguity in what a programme of civil defence tells us about the wider strategic philosophy of the government which pursues it. At the one end of the spectrum, a concern with civil defence preparedness can be depicted as no more than a prudent intention to alleviate, even if only at the margins, the horrendous impact of nuclear war; at the other end, civil defence programmes, especially if found in the Soviet Union, are regarded as *prima facie* evidence of an intent to initiate and win nuclear wars. If the critics take the heightened profile of civil defence issues in the United States in recent years—regardless of whether there is greater substance under the publicity—as signifying gradual Administration acceptance of the

[34] *US News and World Report* (April 13, 1981), p.45.
[35] *Army Times* (March 8, 1982).

idea of nuclear war then the blame lies at least in part with various United States Government agencies which have fostered this association of ideas in their repeated attacks on Soviet civil-defence efforts. This said, civil defence officials have aggravated the situation by their frequently callous and flippant remarks on the impact of nuclear war. The philosophy of Undersecretary of Defense, T.K. Jones, that "everybody's going to make it if there are enough shovels to go around" and that the United States, with civil defence, would recover from a nuclear war in two to four years,[36] may not be representative of official thinking generally but it certainly caused even well-disposed observers of the United States strategic scene to think twice about the desirability of present trends.

6. *Command, Control, Communication and Intelligence (C^3I)*

When, in early October 1981, President Reagan announced his strategic programme, he was careful to emphasise the centrality of C^3I to what his Administration was trying to achieve: "I consider this decision to improve our communications and control systems as important as any of the other decisions announced today."[37] This position was an outcome of one of the first reviews that Reagan had requested, a review of "strategic connectivity"[38] which had revealed deficiencies in the C^3I area.

That the priority being assigned to C^3I should not be seen as reflecting adherence to concepts of limited nuclear war, spokesmen have been at some pains to point out. Fred Iklé, Undersecretary of Defense for Policy, informed an interviewer that more would have to be invested in C^3I but insisted that "this does not mean . . . an increase in the emphasis on nuclear war, and particularly not limited nuclear war."[39] But if it does not mean this, what does it mean?

Various authorities have pointed to the vulnerabilities inherent in C^3I systems. A General Accounting Office report of August 1981 delivered this message.[40] A Carter official who had worked on PD59 admitted that "there are limits, especially those arising from C^3I capabilities" constraining full implementation of the countervailing strategy.[41] Des Ball was graphically to illustrate the myriad of technical problems that could erode the capacity to control a nuclear war[42] and John Steinbruner has argued that even a relatively small

---

[36] See, *e.g. Los Angeles Times*, January 15, 1982; *New York Times*, March 17, 1982; *Washington Post*, April 1, 1982.
[37] *New York Times*, October 3, 1981.
[38] *Government Executive* (January 1982).
[39] *New York Times*, March 14, 1982.
[40] *New York Times*, August 6, 1981.
[41] W. Slocombe, "The Countervailing Strategy" 5 *International Security* (1981), p.27.
[42] *Can Nuclear War be Controlled?*, *op. cit.* in note 8, above.

number of nuclear weapons "are probably sufficient to eliminate the ability to direct US-strategic forces to coherent purposes."[43]

But what might these "coherent purposes" be if not to engage militarily, and with political objectives, in a limited nuclear war? In what other circumstances could survivable C^3I systems be a major priority? Despite Iklé's protestations, other official statements have emphasised the necessity of C^3I for the conduct of an ongoing and possibly protracted nuclear war which is, almost by definition, a limited one. The White House has conceded that C^3I systems are not as survivable as required and "could not operate reliably over an extended period after a Soviet attack, if that proved necessary."[44] Accordingly, in explaining the US programme, Secretary Weinberger told the Senate Armed Services Committee that "we will be initiating a vigorous R & D program leading to a command and control system which will endure for an extended period beyond any initial nuclear attack."[45]

CONCLUSIONS

Arguments as to whether the ultimate strategic intentions of either of the super-Powers are benign or malign tend to become theological. In the circumstances, it is probably wise to refrain from making pronouncements on these ultimate intentions.

A lesser conclusion can nonetheless be drawn. Even if we accept at face value the various statements that governments today are no more disposed to the idea of nuclear war than they were 30 years ago and that their principal interest resides in maintaining a deterrent-based peace, it is yet possible to distinguish between that end and the means of achieving it. In many subtle and pervasive ways, limited nuclear war ideas have suffused the intellectual framework of deterrence theory. The end, it is claimed, is to secure more effectively the nuclear peace. In the process, however, there is room for legitimate questioning as to whether this end may not be undermined by the means themselves. The more we plan for the execution of nuclear wars and the more that the operational details of nuclear war become a part of the normal, albeit rarified, discourse, the greater is the danger that we lose touch with reality. In seeking to convince the enemy of the sincerity of our nuclear preparations, we may commit the ultimate folly of convincing ourselves. And then the atavism of nuclear war, limited or not, would reign supreme.

---

[43] "Nuclear Decapitation" 45 *Foreign Policy* (1981–2), p.18.
[44] *New York Times*, October 3, 1981.
[45] Testimony of October 5, 1981, reproduced in XXIV *Survival* (1982), p.30.

THE REAGAN ADMINISTRATION
AND SUPER-POWER NUCLEAR RELATIONS

By

PAUL BUTEUX

THE interaction of the respective strategic doctrines of the two
super-Powers, as perceived by each of them, has been an important factor affecting their nuclear relationship in recent years. In
the case of the Reagan Administration, its strategic policy has
been very much affected by particular interpretations of Soviet
strategic doctrine. However, perceptions of Soviet doctrine and of
how that doctrine affects American strategic choices and objectives have been a significant element in the American debate over
strategic policy at least since the SALT I agreements of 1972. As
the meaning and implications of those agreements were examined
and analysed, and as what were seen as adverse shifts in the strategic balance occurred, which the continuing SALT process
seemed unable to curb, so questions as to the purposes and
assumptions underlying the Soviet Union's military efforts became
of increasing concern to American policy-makers. How these
questions have been answered has helped determine positions
taken with respect to strategic choices. So, in addition to the usual
debate over what kinds of forces were needed to serve what kinds
of political and strategic objectives, there has been added a vigorous discussion as to the meaning of the Soviet strategic doctrine
for the strategic posture of the Soviet Union, for Soviet views on
deterrence and, ultimately, for Soviet intentions. In the determination of current United States strategic policy, the pevailing
interpretations of Soviet strategic doctrine seem to have been a
factor as relevant as perceived trends in the strategic balance
itself.

I—THE IMPLICATIONS OF PARITY

American strategic thinking in the last decade has reflected considerable concern with the implications of parity and its status in the
Soviet-American relationship. Although many of the issues raised
are not in themselves new, but have recurred in one form or another
ever since the 1950s, the notion of parity has provided a new focus
and significance for them. Two general questions have been raised
as a result: the first concerns the meaning that is to be given to

strategic parity and to its interpretation in operational terms; the second, its value as an object of policy.

To say the least, the concept of parity has an elusive quality, and successive American Secretaries of Defense have sought different ways of giving substance to it in terms of weapons acquisition, strategic posture and strategic doctrine. None has seen the simple notion of numerical equality as a sufficient definition; not only because numerical indicators are inadequate measures of military capability, and not only because in terms of static indicators equality between the United States and Soviet Union has never existed, but also because a definition of parity in terms of numerical equality does not necessarily create a strategic balance seen as satisfactory by both sides. To achieve such a balance other factors have to be taken into account which enable the United States and the Soviet Union to meet their political and strategic objectives. Even though for arms control purposes both the United States and Soviet Union have been willing to accept equality in certain components of the strategic balance, each side has sought agreements in line with its different strategic and political objectives. Thus although the SALT agreements were meant to enshrine parity and by so doing provide an operational definition of it, and although the START proposals are designed purportedly to achieve the same end, strategic arms control has not achieved a military balance which is symmetrical in form or which, currently, both sides would accept as providing equal security. In the end, mutual acceptance of parity and the acceptability of any arms control agreement which defines it rest on a political bargain, and like any bargain its value to the participants will change with changing circumstances. The current American Administration has clearly taken the view that, as presently defined in existing arms control agreements, parity is no longer adequate for the achievement of United States strategic objectives and that a major effort must be made to bring about a change in the strategic balance. In future, strategic arms control must rest on a balance more satisfactory to the United States and, presumably, on a definition of parity which reflects this.

Secretary of Defense Casper Weinberger has defined United States strategic objectives in the following way: first, to deter military attack by the Soviet Union and its allies and friends. Secondly, in the event of attack, to deny the enemy victory and bring about a rapid end to the conflict on terms favourable to the interests of the United States and compatible with the political and territorial integrity of the United States and its allies. Thirdly, to promote arms control and, fourthly, to inhibit the further expansion of Soviet control and military presence in the world and induce the Soviet Union to withdraw from such countries as Afghanistan where it maintains its presence by force of arms. As well, the United States seeks to inhibit the Soviet Union's overall capacity to improve its military forces by preventing, in concert with allies, the flow of militarily significant technologies and material to the Sovet Union and by refraining from actions that serve to subsidise the Soviet economy. In sum, the aim is to deter, and if necessary defend against, the coercive use by the Soviet Union of its military power. By making a sustained commitment to redress any significant imbalance, the Secretary of Defense has argued that not only will American deterrent capabilities be strengthened, but the prospects for arms control and arms reductions will be improved.[1]

This is an interesting elaboration and expansion of a set of objectives which successive American Administrations have endorsed in one way or another since the beginning of the 1970s. The Nixon Administration was the first to redefine the strategic objectives of the United States in the light of the Soviet achievement of parity. As formulated by that Administration, these resulted in a requirement for a large and varied strategic arsenal sufficient to accomplish American strategic goals. "Sufficiency" was defined in such a way as to require a capacity for assured destruction which at the same time would provide no incentive for the Soviet Union to strike first in a crisis. In addition, it was important that American forces be perceived at least as equal (which meant that they not be perceived as inferior in *any* significant dimension) to those of the Soviet Union. At the same time, an emphasis was placed on both numerical equality and on the capacity to prevent the Soviet Union from acquiring the ability to cause greater damage to the United States than would be inflicted on the Soviet Union by the Americans in a nuclear war. Finally, though it was James Schlesinger who later as Secretary of Defense made flexible and limited options a central focus of American declaratory strategy, from the beginning of the Nixon Administration it was clear that the search for more flexible options was to be an important element in its strategic policy.[2]

All American Administrations from that of Richard Nixon onwards, including the present one, have sought to maintain these goals within the context of a changing strategic balance. However, the present balance is seen by many as threatening the ability of the

---

[1] Report of Secretary of Defence Casper Weinberger to the Congress on the FY 1984 Budget and FY 1984–88 Defense Programs (February 1, 1983.) p.16.

[2] The strategic policy of the Nixon Administration was elaborated in a number of early statements. A concise version can be found in the Statement of Secretary of Defence Melvin R. Laird before the House Armed Services Committee on the FY 1972–76 Defence Programme and the 1972 Defence Budget (March 2, 1971), p.62.

United States to meet the long-established criteria of sufficiency adequately. When numbers of Soviet launchers are combined with factors such as throw-weight, increased accuracy and an expanding inventory of warheads, then it is possible to argue, as the critics of SALT have done, that on the basis of indicators that successive Administrations have regarded as significant, the United States no longer has strategic equality with the Soviet Union. Concern about this state of affairs has been an important factor behind the revisions that have occurred in American strategic doctrine in recent years. The Carter Administration's formulation of the "countervailing strategy" and the accompanying revisions in targeting policy initiated in 1980 by Presidential Directive 59 (PD. 59) can be seen as an attempt to adjust American strategy to a changed strategic environment.

Where the Reagan Administration appears to have departed significantly from its predecessors with respect to strategic policy is in the ambitious way in which United States strategic objectives have been described. Not only has the Administration endorsed established criteria for sufficiency, but has gone beyond them and formulated requirements for the strategic arsenal that suggest an unwillingness to accept the constraints on American policy that are imposed by a strategic balance defined in terms of "sufficiency" alone. It is this which has raised the question of whether the Reagan Administration considers parity to be a desirable objective of policy at all. Certainly, there has been enough ambiguity in the Administration's position to suggest that parity is not acceptable if it does no more than deny the Soviet Union strategic superiority. Rather, the United States seeks a military balance that is compatible with the full range of American foreign-policy objectives and which holds out the prospect of securing them in competition with the Soviet Union. Not surprisingly, the Soviet Union has responded by arguing that the United States is engaging in a futile attempt to restore its past strategic superiority.

II—COUNTERFORCE AND THE CONTINUITY OF UNITED STATES POLICY

Despite the Reagan Administration's emphasis on the restoration of American military power, the main lines of the strategic build-up have followed a course laid down by earlier Administrations. As a result, the articulation of American policy has followed trends already established. Perhaps the most significant of these trends, because others can be understood as aspects of it, has been the shift in American declaratory strategy away from deterrence by threat of retaliatory punishment towards a strategy of denial, and away from assured destruction to strategies of nuclear utilisation.[3] It is this, rather than any dramatic shift of interest towards counterforce targeting, that is characteristic of recent United States declaratory strategic doctrine.

As more has been revealed about the contents of American targeting policy since the first Single Integrated Operational Plan (SIOP) was formulated in 1960, it is clear that the capacity to undertake counterforce strikes against the nuclear retaliatory capability of the Soviet Union, along with other military targets, has been a major and consistent objective of American strategy. But whereas the first SIOP was essentially a capabilities plan designed to maximise the utilisation of American strategic forces, since then revisions in the SIOP have sought to facilitate a wider range of employment options that would meet American objectives better if war were to occur, and which at the declaratory level at least, would conform better to American deterrence needs.[4]

Secretary of Defense Schlesinger's "limited nuclear options" strategy of 1974 represented the first major effort to reformulate nuclear weapons employment policy in the age of parity. Since then, there has been a persistent effort to expand the strategic options available and to acquire the capabilities appropriate to the options sought. In defining these options, the ability to discriminate between a wide range of military targets and urban and industrial "assured destruction" targets has been a crucially important objective. More flexible options have required greater accuracy, more refined warheads in terms of yield and nuclear effects, and much greater demands on command, control and communications. Recent and on-going United States nuclear weapons programmes have been directed to the improvement of strategic forces in all these respects.

Despite the seeming contradiction, the move towards deterrence by denial can be understood as a response to the loss of American strategic superiority. The commitment to policies that require what can be described broadly as "extended deterrence" has always demanded of the United States a strategic posture that offers more

---

[3] M. Keeny Jr. and W. Panofsky, "MAD versus NUTS: The Mutual Hostage Relationship of the Superpowers" 60 *Foreign Affairs*, Nr. 2, (Winter 1981/82), p.289.

[4] On the first SIOP see D.A. Rosenberg, "The Origins of Overkill: Nuclear Weapons and the American Strategy, 1945–69," 7 *International Security*, Nr. 4, (Spring 1983), pp.3–71. Informative discussions of more recent versions of the SIOP can be found in A.H. Cordesman, "Deterrence in the 1980s: Part I. American Strategic Forces and Extended Deterrence," *Adelphi Papers*, Nr. 175, I.I.S.S., London (Summer 1982); D. Ball, "U.S. Strategic Forces: How Would They Be Used?" 7 *International Security*, Nr. 3 (Winter 1982–1983), pp.31–60.

than the ability to retaliate in the event of a nuclear attack on the United States or its close allies. What the United States has sought has been the ability to deter a wide range of threats at thresholds below those that greatly risk a central nuclear exchange. In the jargon of strategic analysis, not only has the United States sought a strategic posture that enhances "crisis-stability," but has sought general "deterrence-stability" as well. This has been essential if only to make an extended deterrent commitment credible to the United States itself; but, in addition, such a capability enables the Americans to exploit the political advantages that flow from its possession. In other words, the United States seeks a strategic balance which gives bargaining leverage in any political confrontation with the Sovient Union; the simple deterrence of an unambiguous nuclear threat is not enough. The present Administration, like all others, has given priority in defining the objectives of its strategic policy to the prevention of nuclear war; however, again like all previous Administrations, it has also reaffirmed that the United States must possess the capability to respond to any Soviet threat in ways that make sense in terms of the national interest.[5] This in turn requires that the United States possess a credible means of responding appropriately to any Soviet action that is seen as threatening American interests.

As far as the strategic dimension is conerned, in the past the strategic balance was such that the United States could be satisfied with employment plans that provided for relatively massive strikes once a decision to employ nuclear weapons had been made. Despite Robert McNamara's emphasis in the early 1960s on the importance of strategic flexibility (which in its NATO dimension was endorsed as the strategy of flexible response), in fact until the mid 1970s little attempt was made, either in force or target planning, to develop means of implementing a genuine flexible options strategy.[6] Consequently, the countervailing strategy and the force requirements generated by it can be seen as representing a major effort to bring declared strategy and force planning into line. In effect, what the countervailing strategy has attempted to do is extend the principles of flexible response more fully into American strategic targeting options.

The strategic build-up which enabled the Soviet Union to claim

---

[5] See testimony of F.C. Iklé (Undersecretary of Defence for Policy) in *Strategic Force Modernization Programs*, Hearings before the Subcommittee on Strategic and Theatre Nuclear Forces of the Committee on Armed Services, U.S. Senate, (October 27, 1981), p.30.

[6] On this point see H.S. Rowen, "The Evolution of Strategic Nuclear Dotrine" in L. Martin (Ed.) *Strategic Thought in the Nuclear Age* (1979) pp.131–156.

parity with the United States has been the prime catalyst for these developments. No longer does the United States have the margin of superiority which would enable it to achieve its strategic objectives on the basis of a force posture offering United States decision-makers only the possibility of large, relatively undifferentiated use of nuclear weapons. The United States now faces an adversary which is seen as itself possessing options which threaten to nullify American declaratory strategy and to which the United States must respond in turn. In this respect, American interpretations of Soviet strategic doctrine have become crucial variables in the determination of American policy. Out of this has come the formulation of a number of controversial requirements for American nuclear forces. Among these are a capacity for nuclear war-fighting (or, at any rate, a capacity to deal with the supposedly war-fighting posture of the Soviet Union); a capability for endurance and the ability to conduct nuclear operations in a protracted war, and a revival of interest in the possibility of ballistic-missile defence.

One aspect of Soviet strategic doctrine that has had considerable effect on American strategic policy in recent years is the belief that the Soviet Union possesses a theory of victory in nuclear war. The targeting revisions initiated by P.D. 59 were designed, in large part, to covince the Soviet Union that it would not be able to "prevail" against the United States and its allies whatever the level of conflict, conventional or nuclear, and hence the designation of the policy as the "countervailing" strategy. A succinct and well-publicised argument that the Soviet Union's strategy is designed to fight and win a nuclear war has been made by Richard Pipes.[7] He, among many others, has argued that the Soviet Union has never accepted the principles of nuclear deterrence as understood in the United States; instead of understanding deterrence as the product of a capacity for mutual destruction, and designing their strategic posture accordingly, the Russians see nuclear forces, like armed forces generally, as serving fundamental political purposes. Pre-eminent among these purposes is the security of the Soviet Union, which is something best secured not be acceptance of a hostage relationship with the United States, but by a manifest ability to prevail in war. This requires a large and varied range of military capabilities which, when combined with an appropriate military doctrine for their use, will ensure that no adversary is in a position to coerce the Soviet Union by threat of force. In this view, the object of Soviet strategy is to prevent war by effectively constraining an opponent from initiat-

---

[7] R. Pipes, "Why the Soviet Union thinks it could fight and win a nuclear war, "64 *Commentary*, Nr. 1, pp.21–34.

ing it; a policy of deterrence by denial rather than by threat of punishment. The imperative towards a defensive strategy (in the sense of an ability to conduct a nuclear war in some kind of militarily significant way) does not mean however that the Soviet Union regards nuclear war as something which would be anything other than an unmitigated disaster. Nonetheless, the ability to fight such a war is the best means of insuring against it.[8] Although the interpretation of Soviet strategy is a matter of considerable debate, that the Soviet Union possesses a comprehensive and varied nuclear arsenal and well-developed military doctrines governing its operation seems incontrovertible. What is less clear is whether the Soviet Union sees its nuclear forces as a means of "compellence"; as a means of securing political advantages from the exploitation of perceived superiorities in the strategic balance, including what may be perceived as superior strategic doctrine.[9]

The prominence given by the Reagan Administration to Soviet war-fighting capabilities, and of the need of the United States to respond to them, has led to the Administration's own strategic policy being interpreted as moving towards nuclear war-fighting. The emphasis on flexible counterforce capabilities, with the concomitant capability of employing limited strategic options, lends itself to the charge that the United States seeks a limited nuclear war-fighting posture. Weight is added to this charge when the planned improvements and modernisation of American strategic forces are added to the NATO plan to deploy new intermediate-range missiles in Europe. The fear that the United States is planning for the possibility of limited nuclear war has become a politically potent force on both sides of the Atlantic, and has become a significant constraint on the ability of the United States to give credence to its declaratory strategy. No doubt in response to this, but nonetheless consistent with stated American policy of longstanding, the Reagan Administration has stressed that rather than fighting a limited nuclear war, the object of American policy is to strengthen deterrence by possessing the ability to threaten responses that are credible to the potential adversary. This requires the capacity to do more than respond to a nuclear attack. There is a need "to cope with threats across the entire spectrum of conflict" which would yield in turn

---

[8] On this point see J. Erickson, "The Soviet View of Deterrence: A General Survey," XXIV *Survival* Nr. 6 (November/December 1982), p.245.

[9] Hannes Adomeit has argued that the pattern of Soviet risk-taking has demonstrated ambiguity about the value of military forces for the "compellence" of a nuclear adversary, but has strongly recognised their value in *deterring* an adversary from taking military counteraction to Soviet initiatives. See "Soviet Risk Taking and Crisis Behaviour" in J. Baylis and G. Segal (Eds.) *Soviet Strategy* (1981) p.191.

"unquestionable" dividends in the event that deterrence failed.[10] In the view of at least one Administration spokesman, to designate this strategy as one of "nuclear war-fighting" rather than one of deterrence is simply facile.[11]

In substance, if not in rhetoric, there has been little in the Reagan Administration's strategic *doctrine* that departs from that of its predecessor. Thus, for example, there has been the same emphasis on the ability to target Soviet political and military leadership and other organs of control in the (rather truistic) belief that these are highly valued in the Soviet Union. There has been also the same emphasis on the importance to the United States of escalation control if, in the event of conflict, an enemy is to be convinced that there is nothing to be gained and much to be lost by further escalation. It is argued that control of escalation holds out the prospect of limiting the scope, duration and intensity of any conflict and of maintaining the credibility of the American extended deterrent. Understood in these terms, escalation control requires a strategic balance in which, even after a Soviet counterforce first-strike against United States nuclear forces, the "exchange ratio" would not favour the Soviet Union. What this means in other words, is that the Soviet Union should not be able by such an attack to bring about a strategically significant shift in the post-attack strategic balance.[12]

Similarly, the view that the United States needs to respond to a perceived Soviet capability, and military doctrine for the conduct of protracted war is not unique to the Reagan Administration. It flows from long-standing criticisms that American policy has neglected the implications of this and other aspects of Soviet strategic thinking. Again, the measures proposed and undertaken by the United States to strengthen the endurance of its strategic forces in order to nullify any protracted war advantage that the Soviet Union might have, can also be interpreted in turn as a search by the United States for the means to implement a war-fighting doctrine of its own. Some of those who suggest this seem to be motivated by a wilful unwillingness to come to grips with the complexities of contemporary strategy, and interpret any measure designed to increase the possibility of choice and control with respect to nuclear weapons as

---

[10] Weinberger, *op. cit.* in note 1 above, p.34.

[11] Iklé *loc. cit.* in Note 5 above.

[12] On the countervailing strategy see Report of the Secretary of Defense Harold Brown to the Congress on the FY 1982 Budget (January 17, 1981), pp.37–45. For the continuity of U.S. policy under the Reagan Administration see Weinberger, *op.cit.*, in note 1 above, pp.51–55. For the connection between escalation control and extended deterrence see the testimony of R. Perle (Assistant Secretary of Defence for International Security Policy), Hearings before the Committee on Armed Services, U.S. Senate, *Part 7: Strategic and Theatre Nuclear Forces*, (March 1, 1982), p.4370.

implying a propensity to use them. On the other hand, the very measures taken to counter the expanding range of Soviet options nonetheless generate a force posture that could serve war-fighting objectives. Whether or not war-fighting is seen as a desirable and possible objective or strategy will in the end by determined by the doctrines underlying it. On this point, there are undoubted ambiguities in the American position; but they are ambiguiuties that arise as much from Administration rhetoric as from the substance of declaratory strategic doctrine.

The argument for the necessity of building endurance into the American strategic posture was expressed by President Carter's Secretary of Defense, Harold Brown, in the following way: "Survivability and endurance are essential prerequisites to an ability to adapt the employment of nuclear forces to that entire range of potentially rapidly changing and perhaps unanticipated situations and to tailor them for the appropriate responses in those situations. And, without adequate survivability and endurance, it would be impossible for us to keep substantial forces in reserve."[13]

The current Administration has in no way departed from this view of the utility of endurance and of the necessity for strategic reserves to make it possible. And, like previous Administrations, it has given considerable attention to improving American Command, Control and Communication (C^3) capabilities with the object of enabling them to fulfil their management functions "throughout a sustained sequence of Soviet attacks."[14] Regardless of whether a capability of this kind is technically feasible, the strategic doctrine that requires it undoubtedly is one that envisages the conduct of military operations under strategic nuclear attack: in other words the conduct of nuclear war; even though it is assumed that such a war would be intiated by others.

Along with measures designed to increase endurance, and its prerequisite—survivability, other steps have been taken to modernise the strategic triad in order that long-standing strategic objectives can be maintained. However, a controversial concomitant of this endeavour is the enhancement of United States prompt, first-strike counterforce potential. It is not that even the most ambitious strategic procurement programmes of the Reagan Administration would deny the Soviet Union a capacity for assured destruction, but that current American strategic programmes will, in the absence of Soviet countermeasures, significatnly increase American hard-tar-

---

[13] Brown, *op. cit.* in note 12 above, p.41.
[14] Weinberger, *op. cit.* in note 1 above, p.54; Iklé, *op. cit.* p.34.

get capability against the Soviet ICBM force.[15] Quite apart from the contribution that this will make to the United States position in the strategic balance, some Administration spokesmen have suggested that if the Soviet Union should attempt to counter these American moves, then it will have the benefit to the United States and its allies of "stressing" the ability of the Soviet economy and govenment to maintain the necessary effort.[16] The notion that "arms-race attrition" is a suitable strategy for the United States is one of the few entirely novel contributions made by the Reagan Administration to the debate on American strategy.

There is an additional area in which American procurement and deployment plans can be interpreted as strengthening prompt counterforce potential. The planned deployment of *Pershing II* missiles in Germany can also be interpreted in this light because of their possible threat to Soviet C^3 in the Western military districts of the Soviet Union. (It should be pointed out, though, that the strategic rationale for the deployment of the *Pershing II* force does not rest on its prompt *strategic* counterforce capability). Nonetheless, the Soviet Union has chosen to interpret the *Pershing II* as a first strike threat, and the fact that the Soviet Union has done so is not only politically significant, but can also be seen as evidence that the Soviet Union views INF deployment as threatening some of the achievements of its own military build-up in Europe. Though the decision to deploy modernised theatre nuclear forces was taken by the United States in a different political and institutional context from that in which decisions affecting the strategic arsenal have been taken, the deployment of modernised INF is completely compatible with the limited-and flexible-options strategy of the United States.

III—SOVIET DOCTRINE

Just as American strategic doctrine has been marked by continuity so has that of the Soviet Union. However, in the Soviet case, the relevant doctrine is different in kind from that of the United States. If strategy is broken down into components according to various policy areas, then it is possible, for example, to speak of "declaratory," "operational," "arms control," and "force employment" policies. It is also possible to speak of each as having an appropriate

---

[15] An excellent analysis of this point can be found in J.S. Finan, "Arms Control and Central Strategic Balance: Some Technological Issues." XXXVI *International Journal*, Nr. 3 (Summr 1981).

[16] See *e.g.* R. Perle, *op. cit.* in note 12 above, p.4374.

doctrine associated with it. Generally speaking, the effective political debate about American strategy (when it has not been confused with political rhetoric) has been concerned with its declaratory aspects: those aspects that provide a rationale for budgetary decisions and in terms of which much public discussion of strategic policy takes place.[17] In contrast, open sources in the Soviet Union give much greater emphasis to the operatinal aspects of policy and to the force employment doctrine that underlies how in the event of war nuclear weapons might be used. And it is largely the force employment aspects of Soviet strategic doctrine that have had direct impact on American strategic policy in recent years. The Soviet Union makes use of declaratory strategy, but this tends, much more than is the case in the United States, to be placed at the service of specific foreign-policy objectives. For the Soviet Union, again much more so than for the United States, declaratory strategy functions as an agent of political warfare.

As has been suggested already, while accepting that the possibility of mutual destruction is an objective condition of contemporary international politics, the Soviet Union rejects the theory of deterrence as a basis for the design of its strategic posture and the determination of its operational doctrine. For the Soviet Union, deterrence is seen as part of a larger political objective having to do with war prevention, and the function of Soviet military strategy is to contribute to this objective by its manifest ability to defeat an opponent's designs.[18] In line with this view, it is no part of Soviet strategy to absorb an initial strike before retaliating with its remaining reserve of assured destruction forces. Nevertheless, for much of the post-Second World War period, regardless of its preferred strategy, the Soviet Union had little choice but to adopt such a posture. Given the size and technical character of its strategic forces, the Soviet Union was in no position to adopt the kind of "city avoidance" strategies proposed by Robert McNamara in the 1960s. All that the Soviet Union could fall back on was a declaratory threat to pre-empt in the event of a nuclear attack being threatened. Now, however, with the greatly increased number of warheads available

---

[17] Ball, *op. cit.* in note 4 above, pp.32–33.

[18] In addition to Pipes, *op. cit.* in note 7 above, pp.30–32 and Erickson, op. cit. in note 8 above p.243, see C. D. Blacker, "The Soviet Union after Brezhnev: Military Power and Prospects; 6, *The Washington Quarterly*, Nr. 2, (Spring 1983), p.58. That the Soviet Union accepts the reality of assured destruction is well argued by R.L. Garthoff in "Mutual Deterrence and Strategic Arms Limitation in Soviet Policy, "3 *International Security*, Nr. 1 (Summer 1978), pp.112–147. For a discussion of the ambiguities of the word "deterrence" in Russian and for the differences between Western and Soviet use of the concept; see, D. Holloway, *The Soviet Union and the Arms Race* (1983), pp.53–54.

to the Soviet Union at both the theatre and strategic levels, and with their greatly increased accuracies, the ability of the Soviet Union to plan for the minimising of enemy options through its own capacity for counterforce attacks is increased. When coupled with such complementary measures as civil defence and a continuing interest in ballistic missile defence, the Soviet Union has all the elements of a "damage limiting" strategy in place.

Although it is doubtful if the Soviet leadership could be convinced that it had the ability through pre-emption to deny the United States the possibility of a massively destructive response with its remaining reserve forces, the Soviet leaders may have considerable confidence in their abilit6 to deny the United States the option of limited and flexible use of nuclear weapons in the way predicated by the NATO strategic concept of flexible response. One fundamental difficulty with the idea of the countervailing strategy is that while it makes sense on the assumption of limited options being exercised initially by the Soviet Union; in the light of Soviet doctrine and strategic capabilities, it is difficult to see how the United Sates could initiate a strategic exchange to its own advantage. Indeed, a major consequence of the Soviet Strategic build-up has been not simply to deny the United States any basis for a functional notion of strategic superiority, but to call further into question American options which are crucial to their own strategy—including that of nuclear first use. In contrast, neither Soviet strategic doctrine nor its strategic posture require a specific first-use threat. The Soviet Union in the event of war might well attempt to strike first as part of its general tactics of surprise and seizing the military initiative, but Soviet notions of deterrence do not require a first-strike capability. Rather, the Soviet Union is more concerned with denying the United States that capability.

Crucial to an understanding of Soviet policy is recognition of Soviet Union's desire to ensure that the United States is constrained as much as possible from using its military power for political advantage. As the Soviet Union has increasingly asserted its status as a global power so has it deployed its forces accordingly. Along with this has occurred a renewed interest in the possibility of protracted war involving the use of nuclear and conventional forces on a World-wide basis, and one manifestation of this has been the development of a "combined arms" concept for all of its military forces. This should not be interpreted as a simple return to the Stalinst dogma of "permanently operating factors" in which the decisive impact of nuclear weapons on military operations was downplayed. Instead, the possibility of protracted global conflict can be seen as reflecting the expansion of Soviet military power and the desire to insure against as many contigencies as possible. It is typical of Soviet doctrine that (at least until recently), it has given far greater attention than has that of the United States to what might happen after war broke out and how a war might be fought after an initial nuclear exchange had taken place.[19]

The Soviet emphasis on war-fighting, rather than deterrence, flows from the distinction in Soviet strategic thought between the nature of war as a *political* phenomenon and the *military* doctrines underlying the actual conduct of operations. The notion of strategy as independent of political conditions makes no sense to the Soviet Union, and a lot of what would be considered as within the domain of strategy in the West is regarded in the Soviet Union as military doctrine, the development of which is the task of professional military staffs. It is, to say the least, methodologically dubious to draw too many conclusions about the political purposes of Soviet armed forces from the military doctrines applied to them. A lot of the debate over the meaning and content of Soviet strategy has been marked by confusion over the distinct difference in Soviet thinking between military doctrines and strategy properly so-called.[20]

Nonetheless, the forces actually acquired, and the operational doctrines applied to them, undoubtedly have strategic implications for the West in general and the United States in particular. The elimination of United States "compellence" advantage has already been noted, and the Soviet interest in seizing the initiative and in the use of surprise inevitably raises concern about the possibility of a Soviet first-strike regardless of the content of Sovient strategic thinking. Since the Soviet Union manifests little or no acceptance of American notions of deterrence and crisis stability, the mechanistic assumptions of much American strategic thinking inevitably fuels United States fears when the Soviet Union adopts forces and a military posture that does not conform with these assumptions. Thus the growth in capability of Soviet nuclear forces of all kinds, which the Soviet Union justifies on the basis of preventing the forces of imperialism from threatening or initiating the use of force, appear to the United States and others as far beyond the legitimate requirements of defence.

What is often lacking in American strategic theory (as opposed to

---

[19] W.R. Schilling, "U.S. Strategic Nuclear Concepts in the 1970s: The Search for Sufficiently Equivalent Countervailing Parity," 6, *International Security*, Nr. 2, (Fall, 1981), p.76. That the U.S. is currently giving greater attention to these matters reflects, perhaps, the presence in the Reagan Administration of F.C. Iklé who has written with considerable insight on this subject. See *Every War Must End* (1971), and "Can Nuclear Deterrence Last Out the Century?", 51 *Foreign Affairs*, Nr. 2 (January 1973).

[20] Erickson, *op. cit.* (in note 8 above), pp.243–244.

United States political rhetoric) is the recognition, explicit in Soviet strategic thinking, that the relationship between the two global super-Powers is essentially one of political conflict and inevitably adversarial in nature. From the Soviet point of view, the armed forces of both contenders must reflect this fact. Hence the rejection of many American ideas abut nuclear strategy and the determination not to allow the United States to establish the "rules of nuclear engagement" by its own strategic doctrine.

This helps explain the apparent contradiction between the Soviet Union's rejection of the idea of limited nuclear war while at the same time building and deploying forces that would enable the Soviet Union to conduct one. Again the explanation lies in the Soviet understanding of strategic thinking and operational doctrine. For the Soviet Union, it is not the nature of weapons that determines the scope of war, but the political objectives that the participants seek. The Soviet approach to limited war falls into the *ius ad bellum* tradition in which limits in war follow from the political and precedural context within which war takes place. This is in contrast to American limited war thinking which conforms more closely to the *ius in bello* school and focuses more on the substantive limitations on conduct that might be practised in war.[21] If the Soviet Union interprets Amercian objectives as the regaining of military superiority and the ability to exercise escalation control, then from the Soviet point of view any conflict with the United States could not be limited whatever the technical possibilities of the forces involved.[22] The Soviet Union requires forces able to conduct military operations whatever the political context and whatever the military environment, but in the event of war with the United States the stakes would be so great that escalation to all-out war would be the most likely result.

Soviet nuclear forces have been designed to cover a complete range of theatre and strategic targets while retaining a substantial survivable reserve. At the same time, evidence of a reload capacity for both intermediate and strategic nuclear forces conforms to the possibility of protracted war being included in Soviet military planning. Ultimately, Soviet military requirements are determined by how the Soviet Union interprets the political framework within which the Soviet-American strategic relationship operates. During the late 1960s and the 1970s, the political framework was one of détente, and the Soviet Union saw détente as the result of a fundamental restructuring of international relations brought about by a

---

[21] I. Clark, *Limited Nuclear War* (1982) pp.16–25.
[22] Erickson, *op. cit.* (in note 8 above), p.246.

shift in the "correlation of forces."[23] The growth of Soviet military power and the reaching of parity with the United States has made a major contribution to this result. Now, the evident determination of the current Administration of the United States to challenge Soviet military achievements and assert its own definition of détente must be seen as profoundly disturbing to the Soviet Union.

CONCLUSIONS

The Soviet Union's interpretation of such United States initiatives as PD.59 and the proposed deployment of new intermediate nuclear forces in Europe as being first-strike in their implications, part of an American drive for strategic superiority, should be seen as something more than simply political propaganda, but as representing a genuine Soviet strategic assessment. If this is the case, then the prospects for stability in the Soviet-American strategic relationship are not good for, after all, this Soviet assessment is but the obverse side of the American reaction to the strategic policies of the Soviet Union. A neglected area of the study of arms races is relevant here: that is how the interaction of strategic doctrines affects the military planning and acquisition policies of adversaries.

In this respect, it has been suggested recently that in the United States changes in strategic thinking have led to a trend towards a "reverse convergence" of American and Soviet strategic doctrines.[24] Rather than the Soviet Union increasingly emulating United States ideas about deterrence and strategic stability, which many American strategists once confidently expected would happen, the United States is more and more attracted by Soviet strategic doctrine. This is particularly noticeable in the case of those American strategists who have advocated much greater attention to such areas as nuclear war-fighting and strategic defence as a means of overcoming perceived strategic weaknesses; areas that have long been stressed in Soviet strategic doctrine. However, in my view, to suggest that either in strategic posture or in actual declaratory doctrine reverse convergence is occurring is to misread the case. What has happened rather is that as the United States has sought the means to maintain strategic objectives under a strategic balance which no longer confirms major areas of American superiority, a degree of what might be termed "strategic parallelism" has occurred. Because recent American Administrations have shown

[23] R. J. Mitchell, "A New Brezhnev Doctrine: The Restructuring of International Relations, "XXX *World Politics*, Nr. 3 (April 1978), pp.366–390.

[24] D. W. Hanson, "Is Soviet Strategic Doctrine Superior?" 7 *International Security*, Nr. 3 (Winter 1982/1983) pp.61/63.

greater interest in nuclear war-fighting than in the past, and because capabilities compatible with a war-fighting posture have been acquired, a convergence of Soviet and American doctrines should not be inferred. After all, the strategic interests of the two super-Powers remain very different, as do the political and cultural bases which generate these interests. As long as this is the case, then the strategic doctrines of the two super-Powers will remain very different too.

Although there have been strong elements of continuity in American strategy over the past decade, and which are clearly present in the strategic policy of the Reagan Administration, it is in the scale and kind of forces that the strategy is seen as requiring, and in the range of political objectives that the American strategy is to serve, that the Reagan Administration has departed from recent trends. This has been reflected more in the political rhetoric of the Administration than in its strategic doctrine, but many observers, including perhaps the Soviet leadership, have noted the radicalism of the rhetoric rather than the continuity of doctrine. Nevertheless, the perception that the Soviet Union had achieved a measure of military superiority and that is military build-up effectively had been unrestrained by arms control, motivates the Reagan Administration to seek the restoration of American military power. When coupled with global political objectives that appear little different from those associated with the heyday of containment, it is difficult to avoid the conclusion that the Reagan Administration has sought to restore a margin of superiority characteristic of a military balance that is satisfactory to a status quo Power whose global position is under challenge.

NUCLEAR-WEAPON DEVELOPMENTS AND THE GENEVA TALKS

By

FRANK BARNABY

and

STAN WINDASS

I—THE NUCLEAR ARSENALS

Nuclear warheads are of two types—strategic and tactical. Range is the main distinguishing factor between them, the former having very long intercontinental ranges, defined in the SALT II Treaty as greater than 5,500 kilometres.

Strategic nuclear weapons are deployed on intercontinental ballistic missiles (ICBMs), submarine-launched ballistic missiles (SLBMs), and strategic bombers. Soviet and American ICBMs have ranges of up to about 15,000 km, modern SLBMs have ranges of up to about 8,000 km, and strategic bombers have unrefuelled operational ranges of up to about 6,000 km. Some strategic ballistic missiles carry many warheads—up to 14 modern multiple warheads are independently targetable on targets which are hundreds of kilometres apart. (They are called multiple independently targetable re-entry vehicles, or MIRVs.) Strategic bombers carry free-fall nuclear bombs and air-to-ground missiles armed with nuclear warheads.

The United States had, at the mid-point of 1983, 1,613 strategic ballistic missiles,[1] 1,045 ICBMs and 568 SLBMs. Of these, 1,118 (568 SLBMs and 550 ICBMs) are fitted with MIRVs. Two hundred and seventy-two B-52s are operational as strategic bombers, carrying 1088 nuclear free-fall bombs; 1,114 short-range attack missiles with nuclear warheads; and about 200 air-launched Cruise missiles (ALCMs). These United States strategic nuclear forces carry about 9,700 nuclear warheads—2,100 on ICBMs, 5,200 on SLBMs and 2,400 on bombers. These warheads can deliver a total explosive power of about 3,100 megatons (Mt)[2]; 1,400 by ICBMs, 300 by SLBMs and 1,400 by bombers.

---

[1] Data on nuclear arsenals are given in *World Armaments and Disarmament*, SIPRI Yearbook 1983, London (1983), and *The Military Balance 1983–1984*, International Institute for Strategic Studies, London (1983).

[2] Megaton (Mt) is equivalent to the explosive power of 1 million tons of TNT.

The Soviet Union had, at the mid-point of 1983, 2,378 strategic ballistic missiles—1,398 ICBMs and 980 SLBMs. Of these, up to 1,032 (244 SLBMs and 788 ICBMs) are thought to be fitted with MIRVs. Some 143 Soviet long-range bombers may be assigned an intercontinental strategic role. These Soviet strategic nuclear forces carry about 8,000 warheads on ballistic missiles—about 6,000 on ICBMs and 2,000 on SLBMs. These warheads can deliver about 6,000 Mt, about 5,000 Mt by ICBM and 1,000 Mt by SLBM. The bombers may carry about 300 nuclear weapons—about 150 as free-fall bombs and the rest as short-range attack missiles. The explosive power of these aircraft-delivered warheads totals about 300 Mt.

Tactical nuclear weapons are deployed in a wide variety of systems including howitzer and artillery shells, ground-to-ground ballistic missiles, free-fall bombs, air-to-ground missiles, anti-aircraft missiles, atomic demolition munitions (land-mines), ground, air, and submarine-launched Cruise missiles, torpedoes, naval mines, depth charges, and anti-submarine rockets. Land-based tactical systems have ranges varying from about 20 km or less (artillery shells) to a few thousand kilometres (intermediate range ballistic missiles). The explosive power of tactical nuclear warheads varies from about 10 tons to about one megaton.

The United States deploys tactical nuclear weapons in Western Europe, South Korea and the United States, and with the Atlantic and Pacific fleets. The Soviet Union deploys its tactical nuclear weapons in Eastern Europe, in its own Western territories, and east of the Urals, as well as with its fleets.

According to Arkin, Cochran, and Hoenig,[3] the United States nuclear arsenal contains over 26,000 nuclear weapons (strategic and tactical), down from the peak of some 32,000 reached in 1967. Today's weapons are spread over 25 types ranging from portable land-mines, weighing a mere 70 kilogrammes to strategic bombs, weighing about 3.6 tons. The explosive power of the weapons varies considerably from the equivalent of about 10 tons of TNT for the W54 atomic land-mine to that of 9 million tons of TNT for the B53 strategic bomb. Twelve types of United States nuclear weapons are currently deployed in European NATO countries; 6,000 nuclear warheads are deployed throughout all NATO countries.

Projected nuclear-warhead production in the United States from now until about the mid-1990s, may involve the production of some 30,000 new warheads, of which about 14,000 are for weapons in current research and development programmes. The likelihood is that

---

[3] W. M. Arkin, T. B. Cochran and M. M. Hoenig, *Nuclear Weapons Data Book Vol. 1* (1983).

the United States will deploy 23,000 new nuclear warheads by the end of the 1980s. Making allowance for the fact that about 17,000 warheads will be withdrawn from the stockpile, or replaced, during this time the number of nuclear warheads will grow to 32,000 by 1990.

The Soviet nuclear arsenal is somewhat smaller than the American. Together the super-Powers have deployed about 45,000 nuclear weapons. For comparison, the nuclear arsenals of the other established nuclear-weapons Powers (the U.K., France, and China) contain a total of about 2,500 nuclear warheads. The total explosive power of the American and Soviet nuclear arsenals is roughly 15,000 megatons—equivalent to over one million Hiroshima bombs, or to 750 times all the high explosive used in all the wars in history. The super-Power nuclear arsenals are now, and have for many years been, much larger than needed for any conceivable military, political or strategic reason.

II—MODERNISATION
OF STRATEGIC NUCLEAR WEAPONS

The accuracy of a nuclear weapon is normally measured by its circular error probability (CEP), the radius of the circle centred on the target, within which half of a large number of warheads fired at the target will fall.[4] In both the United States and the Soviet Union the CEPs of ballistic missiles, ICBMs and SLBMs, and of tactical nuclear weapons are continually being improved. In the United States, for example, improvements have been made in the guidance system of the Minuteman-III ICBM involving better mathematical descriptions of the performance of the inertial platform and accelerometers during flight, and better pre-launch calibration of the gyroscopes and accelerometers. With these improvements, the CEP of the Minuteman-III is about 200 m, compared with 400 m for the Minuteman-II. At the same time the design of the Minuteman warhead has been improved so that for the same weight, size, radar cross-section and aerodynamic characteristics, the explosive power of the warhead has been increased from 170,000 tons (170 kt) of TNT equivalent to 330 kt. The new Minuteman-III warheads delivered with greater accuracy than their forerunners could destroy Soviet ICBMs in their silos (hardened to withstand over-pressures

---

[4] CEP figures must be treated with caution. Figures quoted are those measured over test ranges; it is not certain, to say the least, that these CEPs would be achieved under operational conditions. (See M. Bunn and K. Tsipis, The Uncertainties of a Pre-emptive Nuclear Attack, 249 *Scientific American*, Nr.5, November 1983, pp.32–41.

of 1,500 pounds per square inch) with a probability of success of about 57 per cent. for one shot and about 95 per cent. for two shots.

The improved land-based ICBM force significantly increases United States nuclear-war fighting capabilities. There will be further increases by the MX missile system now under development. The guidance for the MX will be based on the advanced inertial reference sphere (AIRS), an all-altitude system which can correct for movements of the missile along the ground before it is fired. A CEP of about 100 m should be achieved with this system. If the MX warhead is provided with terminal guidance,[5] CEPs of a few tens of metres are feasible.

The most formidable Soviet ICBM is the SS-18. This is thought to have a CEP of about 450m with the accuracy soon being improved to about 250m. Typically, each SS-18 warhead would appear to have an explosive power of either about 500 kt or 800 kt. With the higher accuracy, the lethality of a SS-18 warhead will be comparable with that of a United States Minuteman-III warhead. The Soviet Union also has the SS-19 ICBM, which is thought to be similar to that of the SS-18 and equipped with a similar warhead. Some of both the SS-18s and SS-19s are MIRVed, the missiles carrying 6, 8, or 10 warheads. In one of the single-warhead versions, the SS-18 is thought to carry a 20 Mt warhead, probably the world's biggest. (Incidentally, the total amount of high explosives used by man in *all the wars in history* has been calculated as about 20 million tons, the same amount as the explosive power of just one of these Soviet warheads.) The other Soviet MIRVed ICBM, the SS-17 carries 4 warheads each with an explosive power of 750 kt; the CEP is about 450m. So far, up to 788 of the Soviet ICBMs have been MIRVed, compared with 550 in the United States. The Soviet MIRVed ICBM force carries a total of up to about 5,000 warheads. The United States MIRVed ICBM force carries 1,650 warheads.

The Soviet strategic ICBM force is an increasing threat to the 1,000-strong United States Minuteman ICBM force, as the accuracy and reliability of the Soviet warheads are improved. On both sides, the land-based ballistic missile forces provide a nuclear-war fighting element in the nuclear policies, in that the land-based missiles are increasingly targeted on small hardened military targets. The submarine-based strategic forces, however, still provide an element of nuclear deterrence by mutual assured destruction: their missiles are inaccurate enough to be targeted on the enemy's cities and industry.

---

[5] Using a laser or radar system to scan the ground around the target, this locks on to a distinctive feature in the area, and guides the warhead with great accuracy onto the target.

III—STRATEGIC NUCLEAR SUBMARINES

The super-Power navies operate a total of 96 modern strategic nuclear submarines (34 American and 62 Soviet), equipped with SLBMs. A single United States strategic nuclear submarine, for example, carries about 200 warheads, enough to destroy every Soviet city with a population of more than 150,000 people. American cities are hostages to Soviet strategic nuclear submarines to the same extent as Soviet cities are to American strategic submarines. In fact, just four strategic submarines on appropriate stations in the oceans could destroy most of the major cities in the Northern Hemisphere.

The most common operational class of Soviet ballistic missile submarine is the Delta-class, carrying 12 or 16 SLBMs, the missiles having ranges of over 8,000 km. The SS-N-18, the missile carried by Delta-class submarines, is the first Soviet SLBM to be MIRVed. These missiles could hit most targets in the United States from Soviet home waters.

By the mid-part of 1983 the Soviets had deployed 224 SS-N-18s, each equipped with up to 7 MIRVs, each MIRV having a yield of about 200 kt. The SS-N-18s are carried on 14 Delta-class submarines. The other main operational Soviet SLBM is the SS-N-8, with a range of about 8,000 km and a single 800 kt warhead. Two hundred and ninety two SS-N-8s are deployed, mainly on 22 Delta-class submarines. The Soviet Union also operates 24 Yankee-class strategic nuclear submarines, each carrying 16 SS-N-6 SLBMs, a 3,000 km range missile carrying either a 1-Mt warhead or two 200-kt warheads. The two warheads cannot, however, be independently targeted and can only hit targets not very far apart.

In 1980, the Soviet Union launched a very large strategic nuclear submarine, the Typhoon. This 160 m long boat displaces, when submerged, 25,000 tons and carries 20 MIRVed SLBMs. One has recently become operational, equipped with a new, more accurate ballistic missile, the SS-N-20. This SLBM carries about nine warheads, each with a yield of 200 kt, over a range of about 8,000 km. At mid-1983, the Soviet Union had deployed up to 980 SLBMs, up to 244 of them MIRVed, in its 62 modern strategic nuclear submarines. These SLBMs are capable of delivering about 2,000 nuclear warheads, about 30 per cent. of the total number of warheads in the Soviet strategic nuclear arsenal.

The United States now operates two types of SLBM—the Poseidon and the Trident-I. Each Poseidon carries on average 9 MIRVs, each with a yield of 40 kt; each Trident-I carries on average 8 MIRVs, each with a yield of 100 kt. Trident-I SLBMs are deployed on Trident submarines and on Poseidon submarines. The Tridents are new boats of which three were in operation by mid-1983. They are approximately twice as large as the Poseidon missile submarines which they are replacing. Each Trident carries 24 Trident SLBMs, with ranges of about 7,300 km. Seven more Trident submarines are being built. They should become operational at the rate of about one a year. Trident-I SLBMs are being retro-fitted into Poseidon strategic nuclear submarines. So far, 12 Poseidons have been fitted with the new ballistic missiles. Nineteen other Poseidon boats are operational; each carries 16 Poseidon missiles, with ranges of about 4,500 km.

The extra range of the Trident SLBMs allows the submarines carrying them to operate in very much larger areas of the oceans and still be within range of targets in the Soviet Union. The submarines do not then have to expose themselves to the same extent to Soviet anti-submarine warfare systems.

The Americans plan to increase the accuracy of their SLBMs so that they will become as accurate as land-based ballistic missiles. The CEPs of the Poseidon and Trident SLBMs are about 450m. The accuracy of SLBMs will be further improved by the use of mid-course guidance techniques together with more accurate navigation of the ballistic missile submarines. The deployment of terminal guidance on the warheads will give CEPs of a few tens of metres. SLBMs will then be so accurate as to cease to be only deterrence weapons aimed at enemy cities and become nuclear-war fighting weapons able to destroy enemy strategic nuclear forces.

Soviet SLBMs are significantly less accurate than their American counterparts. Operational Soviet SLBMs are thought to have CEPs typically exceeding 1,000 m. But the accuracy of the missiles will steadily improve and eventually become as accurate as American ones. The SS-N-18, for example, may have a CEP of 600 m.

IV—STRATEGIC BOMBERS

The United States is continually modernising its strategic bomber fleet. Currently B-52s are being provided with air-launched Cruise missiles (ALCMs)—25 per bomber. The Reagan Administration also plans to build 100 B-1B bombers to replace some of the ageing B-52s. The first B-1Bs should be operational in 1986 and they will also carry ALCMs. The United States is also doing intensive research into the Advanced Technology Bomber, or "Stealth" aircraft. This programme involves the development of radar-absorbing materials and aircraft shapes to give a very small radar cross-section,

Table 1

United States Strategic Nuclear Forces (mid-1983)

UNITED STATES	Delivery vehicle	No. deployed	No. of warheads per delivery vehicle	Total no. of warheads	Total delivery capability (Mt)
Land-based (ICBMs)	Minuteman II	450	1	450	540
	Minuteman III	250	3	750	128
	Minuteman III (Mark 12A)	300	3	900	302
	Titan II	45	1	45	405
Sub-total		1,045		2,145	1,375
Sea-based (SLBMs)	Poseidon C-3	304	10	3,040	122
	Trident I (C-4)	264	8	2,112	210
Sub-total		568		5,152	332
Strategic bombers	B-52	272			
	bombs		4	1,088	1,088
	SRAMs			1,114	220
	ALCMs			200	40
Sub-total		272		2,402	1,348
TOTAL		1,885		9,699	3,055

Source: *World Armaments and Disarmament, 1983,* SIPRI Yearbook (1983).

as well as terrain-following and other systems to avoid detection by Soviet air-defence systems.

The ALCM is a sub-sonic, nuclear-armed, winged vehicle, about six m long, weighing less than 1,360 kg, with a range of about 2,500km, a CEP of 100 m, and a nuclear warhead of about 200 kt. The ALCMs could be launched outside Soviet territory against air defence systems, to destroy their radars and anti-air-craft missiles. Following B-52s would then be able to penetrate into Soviet territory to attack targets with their nuclear bombs and ALCMs. The missiles are accurate enough to be used against small hardened military targets and, because they have relatively small radar cross-sections, are difficult to detect by radars on the ground.

Unlike the United States, the Soviet Union maintains an extensive air defence system based on a family of surface-to-air missiles and a large number of interceptor aircraft. The Soviets will probably extend their air-defence system to be able to cope with the Cruise

Table 2

Soviet Strategic Nuclear Forces

SOVIET UNION	Delivery vehicle	No. deployed	No. of warheads per delivery vehicle	Total no. of warheads (independently targetable)	Total delivery capability (Mt)
Land-based (ICBMs)	SS-11	260	1	260	260
	SS-11	290	3 MRV	290	290
	SS-13	60	1	60	45
	SS-17	120	4	480	360
	SS-17	30	1	30	180
	SS-18	150	8	1,200	1,080
	SS-18	58	1	58	1,160
	SS-18	100	10	1,000	500
	SS-19	30	1	30	150
	SS-19	300	6	1,800	990
Sub-total		1,398		5,208	5,015
Sea-based (SLBMs)	SS-N-5	9	1	9	9
	SS-N-6	96	1	96	96
	SS-N-6	288	2 MRV	288	115
	SS-N-8	292	1	292	240
	SS-N-17	12	1	12	12
	SS-N-18	224	1, 3, or 7	1,000	220
	SS-N-20	20	up to 9	150	36
Sub-total		941		1,847	728
Strategic bombers	Bison	43	2	86	86
	Bear	100	2	200	200
Sub-total		143		286	286
TOTAL		2,482		7,341	6,029

Source: *The Military Balance 1983–1984*, International Institute for
Strategic Studies, London, 1983.

missiles now being deployed by the United States. This will probably involve deploying Airborne Warning and Control System
(AWACS) aircraft to constantly patrol the Soviet borders to detect
incoming air or ground-launched Cruise missiles, and alert and control fighter aircraft and surface-to-air missiles to shoot enemy missiles down. There are those who believe that the main reason for the
deployment by the United States of Cruise missiles is to provoke the
Soviet Union into spending very large sums on counter-measures,
like AWACS.

Table 3

The SS20 compared with its precedessors, and with some of the NATO missiles assigned to Europe

Missile	SS4	SS5	SS20	Pershing 1A	Pershing II	GLCM	Poseidon
Year First Deployed	1959	1961	1977	1969–71	1983(?)	1983(?)	1971
Range (*miles*)	1200	2500	3100	450	1000–1200	1500	2900
Mobility	fixed	fixed	mobile, but must be launched from pre-prepared launch sites	mobile, but must be launched from pre-surveyed sites	mobile; can be launched from any location	mobile; can be launched from any location	submarine-launched
Reaction Time (*time between initial order and launch*)	8 hours	a few hours	up to 1 hour	about 1 hour	several minutes	several minutes	about 15 mins.
No. of warheads per missile	1	1	3	1	1	1	10
Warhead Yields (*kilotons*)	1000	1000	150	60–400	5–50	200	50
Accuracy (*CEP measured in yards*)	2500	1200	800 if deployed as planned 450 if launched from fixed silos	450	40	50	500
Probability of a single warhead destroying hardened (1000psi) target	.2%	9%	6%	8–24%	99.99%	100%	7%

Source: O. Greene, *Europe's Folly: the facts and arguments about cruise* (1983).

V—MODERNISATION OF TACTICAL NUCLEAR WEAPONS

Both the United States and the Soviet Union are modernising their tactical nuclear arsenals. Tactical nuclear weapons have a shelf-life of 20 or so years after which they must be withdrawn from the arsenal or replaced. This is because the fissile and fusion material in the weapons, particularly tritium, decays and other materials deteriorate. NATO announced in November 1983, for example, that it would withdraw 1400 obsolete tactical nuclear weapons from Europe, over a five-year period (reducing the number deployed from 6,000 to 4,000). Modernisation is inevitable if nuclear weapons are continually deployed.

Among the new types of nuclear weapons planned for NATO are Pershing II missiles and ground-launched Cruise missiles. These weapons are so accurate as to be perceived as nuclear-war fighting weapons; both have a CEP of about 50 m. Although less accurate than the American missiles, the Soviet SS-20, an intermediate range ballistic missile, may soon become accurate enough to be a nuclear-war fighting weapon, given the relatively large explosive power of its warhead.

The Soviet SS-20, first deployed in 1976, is a two-stage mobile missile, with a range of about 5,000 km. About 360 of the missiles were deployed by mid-1983; about 240 are targeted on Western Europe (from sites West of the Urals) and the rest on China and possibly other Asian targets (from sites East of the Urals). Each SS-20 normally carries three MIRVed warheads with a yield said to be about 150 kt. The CEP of the SS-20 as deployed is thought to be about 800 m. This would give it about a 7 per cent. probability of destroying a military target hardened to about 300 psi; comparable with that of a United States Poseidon SLBM. The SS-20 is replacing, on a one-to-one basis, the old, inaccurate SS-4 and -5s, intermediate-range ballistic missiles deployed in the 1960s.

The Pershing II, to replace the Pershing I missiles deployed in West Germany, will be provided with a sophisticated new guidance system called RADAG. When the warhead approaches its target a video radar scans the target area and the image is compared with a reference image stored in the warhead's computer before the missile is launched. The computer controls aerodynamic vanes which guide the warhead onto its target with an accuracy unprecedented in a missile with a range of 1,800 km. The missile is the only ballistic missile able to penetrate a significant distance into the Soviet Union; it could, for example, reach Moscow from its sites in West Germany. The plan is to deploy 108 Pershing IIs with warheads having yields in the kilotonnage range.

NATO also plans to deploy 464 ground-launched cruise missiles between 1983 and 1988, in West Germany, Italy, the United Kingdom, Belgium, and the Netherlands. The missiles will have ranges of about 2,500 km and carry warheads with yields of 200 kt.

VI—CONFLICTING PERCEPTIONS

The decision to deploy Pershing II and ground-launched Cruise missiles was taken by NATO as part of a "twin-track" decision. The other track was arms control negotiations between the United States and the Soviet Union. Behind this straightforward decision however lay a great deal of confusion, due to conflicting perceptions about the nature and purpose of the nuclear system. It is these conflicting perceptions which undermined the negotiations and created stresses in the Alliance—stresses which can only be resolved when a new concept of defence is developed.

The Germans on the whole stressed the symbolic and political nature of the proposed deployment of Cruise and Pershing II. This symbolism had two aspects to it. One was the concept of *coupling* European nuclear systems to the United States; and the other was the idea that Pershing and Cruise were a *balance response* to the SS-20. It followed from this that if the Russian SS-20s disappeared, there would be no need for the Allies to deploy intermediate range nuclear missiles. The threatened deployment was seen very largely in bargaining-counter terms, and had little relationship to military strategy or doctrine.

The British officials, on the other hand, emphasised the need for modernisation as a function of the deficiencies of flexible response. NATO doctrine in the British view required the capability to strike the Soviet Union with systems based in Europe. Existing capabilities, all based in the United Kingdom, were ageing and in need of replacement. Modernisation was required irrespective of developments in Soviet capabilities. The SS-20 was not essential to this argument though its deployment made the case stronger.

The Americans, however, tended to maintain that NATO should have nuclear capabilities for a "wider range of contingencies than that of a selective response." In their opinion, Intermediate-Range Nuclear Forces are military assets which must have a demonstrative military use to be credible. They believe that theatre nuclear forces constitute war-fighting capabilities rather than political signalling assets.[6] It is significant that these graduated views of the West Germans, the British and the Americans reflect their geographical situation in relation to a possible "theatre" nuclear war.

VII—THE COURSE
OF THE GENEVA NEGOTIATIONS

The "twin-track" decision to prepare, to deploy and simultaneously to negotiate was announced by NATO on December 19, 1979. The date for the first deployment of the new weapons, should the negotiations fail, was fixed for December 1983, just four years later. Negotiations, however, did not actually commence in Geneva until November 20, 1981—23 months later—and half-way to deployment.

The talks had no official name because the two sides could not

---

[6] The source of this information on West German, British and U.S. perceptions is the Interim Report of the Special Committee of the North Atlantic Assembly on Nuclear Weapons in Europe (September, 1981), pp.6–7.

agree on the basic agenda. However, for convenience we shall use the common NATO name Intermediate-Range Nuclear Force (INF) negotiations.

The opening position of the United States was declared in a draft treaty on February 2 which proposed, following Reagan's speech of November 18, 1981, to cancel deployment of Pershing II and ground-launched Cruise missiles if the Soviet Union would "dismantle" all their SS-20, SS-4 and SS-5 missiles world-wide. An associated NATO declaration of December 11, 1981, stated that "Reductions in other US and Soviet nuclear systems could be sought in subsequent phases."

The opening position of the Soviet Union was laid out in a proposal of February 12, 1982. This proposal was that any agreement must take into account *all* intermediate-range nuclear armaments (range 1000 km+) installed in Europe and intended for use in Europe (*i.e.* air and sea as well as land-based British and French as well as United States); reduction of the present number (almost 1000 on each side) to 300 units on each side by 1990, with an intermediate threshold of 600 units up to 1985; the parties to refrain from deploying new nuclear weapons in Europe during the negotiations and present weapons to be frozen at their current qualitative and quantitive level. The ultimate goal was "A Europe free from all types of medium range nuclear weapons." Subsequent clarification revealed that the zone under consideration in the Soviet proposal was the whole of Europe "from the mid-Atlantic to the Urals, and from the Arctic to Africa."[7]

The United States zero option was generally perceived on both sides to be non-negotiable. Zero is any case a difficult bargaining position to start from, since any change from zero is a change of principle as well as of degree. However, it is clear from the preliminary discussions that NATO officials knew that the Soviet Union could not accept the zero option, for the obvious reason that it would have meant "unilaterally" abandoning, under threat, a major weapon system which had been in existence (albeit in a less developed form) for 25 years, and which formed an integral part of Russian military strategy.

It is not quite clear that the Russian "zero option" was seen from the beginning by the Russians as totally non-negotiable. However, the Soviet proposal turned out in fact to be as un-negotiable for the Americans as the American one was for the Soviets. This was

---

[7] Brezhnev Speech, Bonn, November 25, 1981. This became known as the Soviet "zero option."

because of fundamental differences of perception which were expressed in total disagreement over the agenda. Agenda disagreements were first of all over which area of the world should be included. The United States position was that the agreement should be "world-wide". The Soviet position was that any agreement should relate strictly to Europe. Secondly, there was the problem of British and French nuclear-weapons systems. The Russians wanted these counted in the negotiations, since the negotiations were about all "forward-based" long-range NATO systems—including those of France and the United Kingdom, while the United States insisted that French and British systems were irrelevant. Thirdly, there was a disagreement about the categories of weapon to be counted. The Soviet Union maintained that *all* long-range nuclear systems in the defined area should be counted—land, sea and air-based. The United States maintained that only *land-based* missiles should be counted—specifically the SS-20s, SS-4s and SS-5s, and the threatened (but not yet deployed) ground-launched Cruise missiles and Pershing IIs; only, in fact, the weapons which the Soviet Union had, and the United States did not have.

In the light of these underlying agenda difficulties, it is very hard to maintain that the two sides were initially involved in the same negotiations. Basically the Russians rejected the whole concept of the "twin-track," which related existing SS-20s to the threatened deployment of Cruise missiles and Pershing IIs. They were not participating in that particular discussion, but were proposing an alternative one.

The final phase of the negotiations began with the United States shift from the "zero option" on March 30, 1983—nine months before deployment, and 13 months after the United States zero option had first been proposed. The new US offer was for "substantial reduction in planned deployment of Pershing IIs and ground-launched Cruise missiles" if the Soviet Union agreed to reduce medium-ranged missiles "to an equal number on a global basis."

Following this United States shift there were a series of last minute shifts on both sides in the final run-up to deployment. The United States suggested various levels of "balance" between Cruise and Pershing II missiles on the United States side and SS-20s on the Soviet side; and the Russians proposed various reductions in SS-20s related to British and French nuclear forces. The United States, however, remained quite firmly committed to some deployment of the new systems, and the USSR equally firmly committed against; and this led to the final breakdown of the talks.

VIII—THE NITZE–KVITSINSKY COMPROMISE

During the course of the negotiations two tentative agreements were discussed by the chief United States and Soviet negotiators, Nitze and Kvitsinsky, but never ratified by either government. The content of these proposals suggests that the proposed Pershing II deployment was in fact the key problem.

The first tentative proposal was drafted on July 16, 1982, following an informal discussion between Nitze and Kvitsinsky during a "walk in the woods" in the Jura Mountains near Geneva. On the Soviet side what was striking about this draft was that it proposed some very radical shifts towards the United States "agenda." It accepted comparability between existing Soviet and threatened United States systems (75 Cruise missiles versus 75 SS-20s), limitations on Soviet deployment outside Europe, and the formal exclusion of British and French systems. The only major (and highly significant) gain in return for these major Soviet concessions was to be the non-deployment of Pershing II missiles.

On the United States side, the gains were as great as the price the Soviet Union was to pay; and the only major price for these gains (apart from a limitation on aircraft numbers) was the non-deployment of Pershing IIs. Subsequently, a number of senior officials on both sides came round to the view that the Nitze-Kvitsinsky compromise should have been accepted. On November 13, 1983, just before the final breakdown of the talks, Nitze and Kvitsinsky had a second walk, this time in a Geneva park, and it appears that a proposal was unofficially discussed which was not dissimilar from the previous compromise. It may well have involved a Russian concession over the "counting" of French and British nuclear-weapon systems. It certainly involved the non-deployment of Pershing IIs. Whatever it was, this compromise was also rejected by the United States. To make their point finally clear the Russians waited for the deployment of Pershing II before walking out of the talks on November 23, 1983.

The core of the difficulty was therefore the United States determination to retain the right to deploy the new missiles for perceived military reasons, and the Soviet refusal to ratify such deployment. Since Pershing II is militarily a highly significant weapon, and the ground-launched Cruise missile militarily much less significant, it is just conceivable that a deal involving a small Cruise-missile deployment could have slipped through; but over Pershing II there was a total and irrevocable contradiction from the beginning to the end.

It is impossible to see how this could have been otherwise. In order to reach an agreement for the deployment of Pershing II missiles, the Soviet Union would have to ratify, in treaty form, the deployment of a weapon of a kind appropriate for a first-strike nuclear capability against the Soviet Union. Whereas such weapons might have been accepted *de facto* the idea that they could be accepted *in treaty form* is absurd. Underlying the agenda difficulties therefore were radical problems relating to the nature of nuclear doctrine and the super-Power confrontation.

IX—UNDERLYING PROBLEMS

(i) *Asymmetry*. The first of these underlying problems is the contrasting geophysical situation of the two super-Powers.

The Soviet Union occupies only one third of the Euro-Asian land mass, and has an extensive land frontier with the allies of the United States in central and southern Europe and in Turkey. It also has a massive land frontier with the unpredictable Middle East, and with China in the Far East with a potential threat off-shore from Japan. The United States on the other hand, together with its ally Canada, occupies the whole of the North American land mass, and has traditionally claimed and exercised dominance over the South American land mass.

If the world is seen in terms of a super-Power balance therefore and it is this presupposition we eventually have to question), the Soviet Union cannot but perceive itself as encompassed by forward bases of the opposing super-Powers, while the United States enjoys the relative security of a vast ocean frontier. Since the basic geophysical situation is thus perceived as profoundly asymmetrical, there can be no agreement on *localised* weapon systems between the super-Powers on a basis of equality simply in weapon systems. What matters more is where they are.

Local or theatre weapon systems in Western Europe are inevitably seen by Russia in the super-Power balance context as the front line of a "forward" system of the United States. The systems of the Soviet Union targeted on Europe are seen as totally dissimilar, since they are not "forward" systems of the Soviet Union aimed at the United States. The problem would of course be duplicated in the Far East were Japanese systems to be deployed.

A common view of Western negotiations, however, is that the Russian insistence on "counting" the French and British nuclear-weapon systems in the negotiations was basically a bargaining policy; and if we move from the context of threat perceptions to the context of the arms control "game," there is some justification for this view. At the outset of the negotiations there had to be some statement on the Russian side as to what should be counted, and clearly some kind of "balance" would have to be shown. Since there are no United States European-based systems—comparable with the SS-20s, and since Russia was unwilling to sanction new NATO deployments, it did make "bargaining sense" from the outset to count the British and French systems in balance against the SS-20s—especially as any agreement reached along those lines would give the Soviet Union treaty control over the British and French nuclear-weapon deployments.

In terms of military thinking however, (as opposed to negotiation-game thinking) there is very little sense in balancing SS-20s against British and French nuclear weapons. The Soviet SS-20s, as we have seen, are essentially a modernisation of the SS-4s and SS-5s deployed in Europe since the 1960s. These weapons are related to Soviet war-fighting capabilities which in military thinking must relate to the possibility of fighting a war in Europe.

The evidence of the INF negotiations suggests that the Russians may well have been prepared to reduce the number of SS-20 war-heads targeted in Europe to about 300, but that the military would refuse to go below this, for military war-fighting reasons—and this is assuming *no* additional United States deployments. Any deployment of Cruise and Pershing II missiles would necessitate additional warheads because they would introduce additional prime targets. On the United States side a similar difficulty stood in the way of any agreement *not* to deploy Pershing II missiles. This new category of missiles was clearly seen by the nuclear-war-fighting elements in the Pentagon to make a substantial increase in the war-fighting capability of the United States in Europe.

(ii) *Nuclear-War Fighting*. The second underlying problem was the drift towards nuclear-war fighting doctrine, as distinct from nuclear deterrence achieved by some kind of mutual-assured-destruction (MAD) balance. The drift towards nuclear-war fighting doctrine should not, however, be attributed to any particular administration. It is inherent in the logic of post-MAD deployment of "less than MAD" nuclear weapons.

Clearly, some kind of possible use of "less than MAD" weapons must be envisaged, and this must be a pre-MAD use (rather than a MAD or post-MAD use). The question arises, would the use of less-than-MAD weapons escalate to MAD, or would it not? If the use of the lesser weapons would escalate to MAD, then they are seen to be superfluous. They are simply part of the mutual suicide system, and the threat to use them loses all credibility. They become part of what Kissinger called the "creeping paralysis" of nuclear weapons.

The only way of avoiding this is to argue that escalation would not *necessarily* occur, and that a tactical nuclear war *could* be controlled and limited. But if you say a nuclear war could be controlled and limited, that means you must elaborate a controlled and limited nuclear-war fighting option—and you must make it credible. This means that you must have the ability to prevail or "win." Clearly, it is no use planning for an exchange in which you "lose." This is only a straightforward application of a very simple principle: there's no point in threatening a war unless you can fight it, and there's no point in fighting a war unless you can in some sense "win" it. The *purpose* of acquiring this capability may well be "deterrence"; but it is quite different from deterrence by MAD. Meanwhile, technology by its own momentum continues to develop "better" weapons, *i.e.* more accurate, more flexible weapons better adapted to the purpose of fighting a "limited" nuclear war. An effective tactical deterrent therefore moves logically and technologically towards an effective tactical nuclear-war winning capability. In calculating the force level required for such a capability, balance has little relevance. The number of weapons you need depends entirely on your nuclear-targeting policy, and on the need to prevail.

Balance, however, is more commonly perceived as producing some kind of security, through "balance of power," or as providing a basis for negotiated agreements about force levels. How true is this?

The idea that such a balance of nuclear-war fighting capability could provide any kind of security is illusory. Unlike traditional "balances of power," which depend on the idea of long drawn-out military contests, the balance of first-strike and nuclear-war prevailing capability means that victory is assured to the side which is quickest on the draw. The temptation to "draw" in a time of crisis would be overwhelming, if only to prevent the other side doing so. The situation (though entirely "balanced"), would be the end of all deterrence, because provided you strike first there is nothing left to deter you. The idea that such a capability on either side could be ratified by treaty is bizarre in the extreme.

Unfortunately, it is not possible to take refuge in the illusion that the prospect of nuclear war is so terrible that no-one will initiate it. Theories of "decapitating" first-strike are now being developed, and the exceedingly complicated decisions involved are being increasingly computerised. The danger is not so much in the reality as in the perception of a nuclear-war winning and first-strike capability; and this perception is increasing.

In essence, this means that it is no longer possible, with the development of "extended deterrence" and nuclear-war fighting doctrine, to depend on the idea of balanced threat and counter-threat at every level as a possible basis either for security, or for arms control negotiations in the traditional mode, dominated by the mythology of balance and leading to treaty formulations. On the contrary, "balance" at every level is an endlessly permissive recipe for a steady advance towards nuclear war.

BEIRUT 1982

AN INTERDISCIPLINARY TEST CASE

By

GEORG SCHWARZENBERGER

"Yet do ye who pass me by bewail my fate and shed a tear in honour of Berytus
that is no more"

BARBUCALLUS (after Beirut's destruction by earthquakes and fire—sixth century
A.D.)

PICTURES of Beirut, flashed across the world's television screens, have become part of a collective memory: Israel's massive invasion of the Lebanon in 1982; the helplessness of a symbolic United Nations Force; discreet absence of Lebanese forces, except "Free-Lebanese" contingents under Israels "guidance" in Southern Lebanon; the prolonged bombardment of West Beirut by Israeli land, sea and air forces; the walkabouts by Yasser Arafat and his staff amid the ruins of Beirut; the remains of bestial massacres in the refugee camps near Beirut Airport; PLO bunkers and tunnels, filled with weapons and ammunition, below the rubble of the camps and residential areas, and one solitary witness to human concern: the visit to the Beirut refugee camps by the Chancellor of London University as President of the "Save the Children" Fund.

PART ONE

FOCUS ON BEIRUT

What appears to matter more than the particular aspects of these and other relevant pictures—especially those of the 1958 United States intervention in the Lebanon[1] and the Lebanese Civil War 1975–76—for the understanding of International Relations as an interdisciplinary and synoptic field of studies, are the typical and universally significant facets of these happenings.

Varied experiences and experiments over half a century with

---

[1] See Y.B.W.A., Vol. 13 (1959), pp.236 *et seq.*

world affairs in general and the particular area[2] that, before being misnamed the Middle East, was more poignantly described as the Levant—and, perhaps more logically, as the Near East—suggest examination of Beirut 1982 on three, and increasingly exacting, levels: power, law and ethics.

Power

On an empirical basis, successive international societies suggest three basic working hypotheses:

First, while the application of force in inter-group relations may be triggered off accidentally, at some point further escalation depends on conscious—if possibly ill-informed—decisions.

Secondly, even leaders who draw their inspirations from metarational sources are severely limited in their choice of few available strategies, tactics and instruments of international relations.

Thirdly, while highly integrated groups (communities) may draw on more sublimated motivations, action in relations between groups in states of lesser cohesion (societies) tends to be based, at best, on awareness of reciprocal interests. Yet, frequently it is little more than an assertion of superior power (understood as a mean between force and influence) and, in the last resort, the application of force.

In a Hellenistic legend, Beirut, or Berytos (Phoen.: the town of wells or springs) as it was then called, was founded by one of the many gods in Phoenician cosmology. Since the days of the Canaanite city-States, a lengthy list of warrior-leaders from Rameses II and Nebuchadnezzar onwards have perpetuated their presence on the cliffs of the Dog River (*Lycus*—Nahrel-Kalb outside Beirut).

Probably, none of these war-lords would have found anything unusual in the 1982 Israeli advance into the Lebanon. Yet, some might have reflected on the deeper reasons why this invasion should have come to a halt in West Beirut. They might have thought of a number of plausible explanations: shortage of expendable manpower for any serious street-fighting in Beirut or in more intensive mountain warfare; pressures from third Powers or inside Israel, or a desire to offer some manoeuvring-space to a "co-operative" Lebanese government in Beirut.

The scale of destruction wrought by Israel on enemies and by-

---

[2] See below under Law, p. 298; "In Praise of Folly" (London Quarterly of World Affairs 1946, pp.194 *et seq*.) and "Priorities for Solving the Arab-Israeli Conflict" (Letter to the Editor of *The Times*, London, June 2, 1967).

Part One of this paper is based on the *Montague Burton Lecture 1983*, delivered on February 7, 1983 in the University of Leeds under the title of *Focus on Beirut* (also separately available in the *Montague Burton Lectures* series, published by Leeds University).

standers alike in Beirut might well have appeared congenial to most of these conquerors, and they might have dismissed lightly the human and other costs of this display of overwhelming force. Yet, the more sophisticated among them might have wondered about long-range policies behind the bombardment and the subsequent massacres of Palestinians by units in Phalangist uniforms and in liaison with Israeli command-posts. They might have considered these policies to be fully in line with rational objects of their own terrorist policies: creation of panic and a mass exodus of survivors of the bombardment and massacres. Recalling some of their own exercises in policies of *divide et impera*, more than one of the empire-builders might also have credited the brains behind the events of Beirut with a desire to "involve" the Maronite faction on the Israeli side in the war and awareness of the possibility of the auxiliaries getting out of hand.

The visions of the earlier conquering heroes were echoed in style by one of the last in the Dog-River galaxy: General Gouraud, the first French High Commissioner under the League of Nations Mandate for Syria and Lebanon. In 1920, he greeted his charges "on the shore of this sea of many legends that has seen the triremes of Phoenicia, Greece and Rome and now, by a happy fate, brings you . . . the blessing of French peace."

Law

During the millenium when Beirut formed part of the Roman Empire, it became a major port, centre of learning and meeting ground of a multitude of races, religions and civilisations.

To survivors of the waves of invasion and counter-attack by Muslims, Crusaders, Mongols, Mamluks and other armed hosts, Beirut's imperial past may well have appeared as a golden era of law and order. The tribulations of the population in these dark ages are recorded in a harrowing report by ibn-Battutah, a fourteenth-century Muslim traveller from North Africa, on his northward journey on *Via Maritima* from Egypt to Beirut.

The report was brought to the attention of the Chairman of the Legal Section of a select institution (the Academy of the Nether World or, for short, ANW). On his initiative, it was decided that the Section should discuss the Report.

Participants in the discussion included custodians of treaties of Egyptian and Hittite rulers of the Lebanon; Papinian and Ulpian of the Beirut Law School; law-clerks of the Crusaders' Principalities and an eminent adviser to Salah-al-Din, also known as Saladin.

With collective experiences extending over three millenia, the meeting reached consensus on two points:

First, the most rational and effective protection against anarchy was the availability and firm use of irresistible force at an early stage of any serious threat to law and order. This implied strong government and a corps of well-co-ordinated or, preferably, self-co-ordinating lawyers in legal teaching and practice.

Secondly, the object of world peace could best be attained through world law in a world State. Until this state of perfection was reached, the inevitable struggle for the mastery of the world could perhaps be shortened by the most cost-effective use of any means that were likely to ensure this end in the shortest possible time, at minimal cost and with maximum effect. If an example had to be made, a fellow academician from the Messianic Section had found the answer: "Now go and smite Amalek, and utterly destroy all they have, and spare them not; but slay both man and woman, infant and suckling, ox and sheep, camel and ass."[3]

It was through the kindness of a trusted friend—an *alter ego* since the days when I first became immersed in a related Near-Eastern issue: the League of Nations Mandate for Palestine (*Tübinger Abhandlungen* (1929))—that I was able to study the Minutes outlined above. This life-long counsel also left me a note on relevant legal developments since the 15th century of our time. I am only allowed to make my acknowledgments to him in his professional capacity as D.A., which an astute reader may take to stand for Devil's Advocate (*advocatus diaboli*).

The gist of D.A.'s analysis can be condensed into seven rules:

(1) Every sovereign State must ensure that its territory is not being used as a base for hostile operations against another sovereign State with which it is at peace or linked by relevant consensual engagements.

(2) Under pre-1914 international customary law, armed reprisals and resort to war on any ground is legal. Subsequent limitations of *jus ad bellum* rest on a consensual basis. They suffer from serious shortcomings regarding any independent and impartial verification of contested assertions. In particular, this applies to explanations offered by veto-Powers and governments under their protection that a particular action is justified by Article 51 of the United Nations Charter.

(3) Under the customary law of international responsibility, a State may protect its own nationals abroad but not interfere with the treatment by another State of its own subjects or any stateless inha-

---

[3] Samuel, Bk. I, Ch. 15, v. 3.

bitants of its own territory. Apparent exceptions of "humanitarian" intervention in the 19th century rested on the consent of the Ottoman Porte. In particular, this applies to the mandate granted by the Concert of Europe to France after the 1860 massacre of Christians by Druzes in Beirut under the eyes of strong Ottoman forces, and with surreptitious assistance from local authorities.

(4) Jurisdiction regarding breaches of the traditional laws and customs of war is limited to the State responsible for the forces concerned. Similarly, during a state of war, any enemy State into whose hands alleged war criminals have fallen may exercise over them an extraordinary wartime jurisdiction. This responsibility is limited to wars between subjects of international law but extends in favour of irregular forces allied with, or controlled by, belligerents. Such irregular forces must comply with four requirements: They must be commanded by a person responsible for his subordinates, wear a fixed distinctive emblem recognisable at a distance, carry arms openly and conduct their operations in accordance with the laws and customs of war (1907 Hague Regulations).

(5) The extension in 1945 and after of war crimes *jure belli* to crimes against humanity and crimes against peace can be justified by the *co-imperium* of the victors then exercised in Germany, consent by Japan and estoppels created by the unanimous adoption in 1948 of a supposedly declaratory Resolution on the subject by the United Nations General Assembly and the subsequent admission of new members on the assumption of their concurrence with the 1948 Resolution.

(6) The 1948 Genocide Convention, to which Israel, Lebanon and Syria are parties, covers only acts committed with *intent* to destroy, in whole or part, a national, ethnical, racial or religious group *as such*. Jurisdiction regarding the trial of alleged offenders is entrusted to the competent courts of the State in the territory of which the act has been committed.

(7) Other relevant conventions such as the Geneva Conventions of 1929 and 1949 and the Additional 1977 Protocols to the 1949 Conventions, in which the laws and customs of war have been developed, apply only between the Parties to these instruments. Similarly, pertinent resolutions of the United Nations General Assembly are purely recommendatory.

Implications and conclusions

From this analysis, six implications and conclusions appear to follow regarding the Israeli invasion of Lebanon and the Beirut massacres of 1982:

(1) Assuming that armed attacks on Israeli territory had been launched from Lebanese territory and terrorist bases there established, the Israeli invasion of the Lebanon, the destruction of these bases and the continuing presence in Lebanon until these threats are removed can be justified on the ground of self-defence under Article 51 of the United Nations Charter. This conclusion is independent of the continued applicability of the General Armistice Agreement of 1949 between Israel and Lebanon.

(2) It is hard to believe that competent tribunals of the State "in the territory of which the acts were committed"—that is, Lebanon—would be able or willing to try persons charged with genocide under the 1948 Convention.

(3) As a Party to the 1949 Geneva Conventions on the Protection of War Victims, Israel is bound—as are Lebanon and Syria—to apply these Conventions in favour of war victims of other Parties and irregular forces allied to, or under the control of, another Party, provided that such forces fulfil the four conditions taken over from the 1907 Hague Regulations. Both Lebanon and Syria being Parties to the 1949 Conventions, the P.L.O. armed forces may be considered to be allied with Syria, and some of its units to be under Syrian control. As none of the three States mentioned is a Party to the additional 1977 Protocols, these developments of the 1949 Conventions may be ignored.

(4) In the 1949 Geneva Conventions, the following grave breaches have been singled out from other war crimes under the laws and customs of war and are treated as especially reprehensible: "wilful killing, torture and inhuman treatment, including biological experiments, wilfully causing great suffering or serious injury to body or health, and extensive destruction and appropriation of property, not justified by military necessity and carried out unlawfully and wantonly." The Israeli bombardment of Beirut and the September 1982 massacres call for examination also from this angle.

(5) In accordance with general international law, any Party to the 1949 Geneva Conventions may make representations to other Parties regarding the non-observance of their duties under these multilateral treaties and insist on full compliance with the Conventions. The exercise of these rights does not depend on involvement of any Party in a particular armed conflict. As Parties to the 1949 Geneva Conventions, each of the permanent members of the Security Council of the United Nations is able to invoke the Conventions in relation to any other Party it may consider to be guilty of breaches of the Conventions.

(6) The Parties to the 1949 Conventions have undertaken "to enact any legislation necessary to provide effective penal sanctions

for persons committing, or ordering to be committed, any of the grave breaches" of the war crimes enumerated under (4) above.

Moreover, each Party is "under the obligation to search for persons alleged to have committed, or to have ordered to be committed, such grave breaches, and shall bring such persons, regardless of their nationality, before its own courts."

The Israeli Commission of Inquiry and the Lebanese Administrative Commission on the 1982 Beirut massacres hardly measure up to the minimum requirements of military courts for the trial of alleged war criminals under the laws and customs of war, nor can they be regarded as tribunals or courts in the meaning of the 1948 Genocide Convention or the 1949 Conventions on Victims of War.[4]

The two sets of legal rules considered differ in formulation and sophistication. Yet, they lead to remarkably similar results: *de facto* immunity from effective legal control of the mighty and less mighty under their protection.

The reason is not far to seek. The sectoral international societies of earlier ages have coalesced into a global activity area. Yet, they all are international systems of power politics, overtly or in disguise as are those of the two post-World War periods. Thus, it would have been expecting too much from the victors in the last world war to do more than administer to the vanquished the law laid down retrospectively on war crimes in the wider meaning. For all practical purposes, those sufficiently powerful remain above the law because they are stronger than the law. More than 300 years ago, Pascal (*Pénsees*—1670) described succinctly what, in all ages, the servants of the mighty are tempted to do: "Being unable to make what is just strong, we have made what is strong just."

Ethics

International ethics, like international law, is primarily conditioned by international society, rather than the reverse.

Across the ages, leading nations have asserted their own superiority as standard-bearers of civilisation over savages and barbarians alike.

As an essentially ethical test, civilisation has its uses. Yet, to be acceptable as generally relevant, it has to be *universalised* so as to cover the chief civilisations that, through the ages, have emerged from pristine savagery. It has to be *relativised* so as to make manifest the savage and barbarian elements in all civilised groups, and it has to be "*dynamised*" so as to emphasise the room there always is for

---

[4] See, further, below, p. 305 *et seq.*

further improvement and the constant danger of descent to post-civilised barbarism.

To remind ourselves of the gulf between aspiration and achievement in contemporary world civilisation, it suffices to recall that, since the area bombings in the Second World War and the man-produced mushroom-clouds over Hiroshima and Nagasaki, over one hundred and forty wars have taken place, a cosmic armament race towards further overkill-capacity that makes reciprocity meaningless is rapidly accelerating, and scenarios for a "winnable" Third World War are proliferating.

It appears appropriate to preface consideration in ethical perspective of the issues before us by three cautions: the need for stringent self-criticism, rather than censoriousness about others; the limiting effect of a highly stratified world on freedom of choice, especially on the lower levels of the world pyramid, and the primary responsibilities of any driver for his own vehicle and his charges in the carousel of what, to all appearances, is an increasingly irrational world.

Against this less than promising background, three issues, which are directly relevant in the context of Beirut 1982 and after, may be singled out: the ethical autonomy of the standard of civilisation; the relevance of the Lebanese and Israeli inquiries into the massacres; and finally, relevant ripostes from, or on behalf of, suspects-in-chief.

Ethical autonomy of the standard of civilisation. In the fields of auxiliary law-creating processes (general principles of law recognised by civilised nations), recognition of States and governments, international responsibility, the law of armed conflict and on a consensual level as, for instance, regarding the protection of human rights, the civilisation-test has been incorporated in international law. Yet, this formative influence on international law has not affected the distinct and autonomous character of the civilisation-standard as an ethical test of international conduct. It hardly needs elaborating that, on this level, the Israeli bombardment of West Beirut and, *a fortiori*, the 1982 massacres fall far below any but a mock-standard of civilisation.

Relevance of the Lebanese and Israeli inquiries. The Lebanese Government limited its inquiry into the Beirut massacres of 1982 to the establishment of an *ad hoc* administrative commission, operating secretly and charged with the task of reporting to the Lebanese Government.

The Israeli Commission of Inquiry was established under a

general statute: the Commission of Inquiry Law.[5] The Commission had on its Bench two members of the Israeli Supreme Court and a retired general. While it was entitled to decide itself on the public or secret character of its meetings, it was severely limited in the personal, functional and geographical scope of its investigations. It too, was restricted to the submission of a secret report, to be published at the Government's discretion.[6]

The institution of the two Commissions had the probably not unintended effect of almost instant sedatives on internal and world public opinion. In Lebanon, the Beirut massacres were swiftly overshadowed by subsequent fighting between Maronite Christians and Druzes as well as between pro- and anti-Syrian Muslim factions. In Israel, quarters near to the Prime Minister let it be known that he saw compensations in an adverse report by the Commission: It would enable the Government to appeal to the electorate as the final judge.

Incidentally, such a move might also be thought to transfer individual guilt to an ever welcome scapegoat. Yet, let the ultimate fate of the "sin-offering" be recalled: The terrorised beast was not just driven into the wilderness and there let loose, but right to the precipice and, it may be presumed, driven right over it.[7]

The codes of criminal procedure of most civilised legal systems contain provisions on the presumption of innocence and benefit of doubt in favour of the accused. Yet, all these presumptions are rebuttable on the balance of available evidence. On the ethical level, the balance of credible evidence is all that matters.

Ripostes for consideration. While I was struggling with the appropriate evaluation of Beirut 1982, D.A. happened to drop in again. With deserved asides on my almost automatic—and negative—reactions to zealotism, messianic outpourings and hypocrisy of any kind, D.A. left some notes to use as I saw fit. They are a first draft of his forthcoming pleadings as *advocatus diaboli* at a session of the World Tribunal of Public Opinion (WTPO) on Beirut 1982:

(1) Nothing could be less convincing and counter-productive than any selective application of ethical standards. In a highly stratified world society, the tone was set by the small international oligarchy within the international aristocracy of sovereign States and, foremost, by the two super-Powers of the Eighties. It had to be recalled

---

[5] No. 5729—in 1968, as amended in 1972 and 1979.
[6] See, further, below, p. 305 *et seq.*
[7] Lev. Ch. 16. 10 (*New English Bible* version).

that, in their preparations for doomsday-warfare, these and other Powers showed a remarkable willingness—in conditions they presumed to determine for themselves—to expose their supposed charges to a Massada on a world scale. It should also be remembered that meanwhile, they acted in areas under their hegemonial control with even less concern for the tenets of world civilisation than other predecessors in empire-building. Thus, the Tribunal should apply in favour of any accused all that remained of any standard of world civilisation: the standard of the least-disfavoured barbarian.

(2) If the Tribunal considered the acts and omissions under consideration to fall below even the lax standards of contemporary world society, the personal responsibility of any suspect should be established by the preponderance of probabilities and the credibility of defences advanced. In judging pleas of ignorance and excuses put forward, it would be absurd to ignore proved association in the past of any of the accused with terrorist activities and outrages.

(3) If the Tribunal decided to discharge any of the accused, it was advisable to mention expressly that such an act of clemency merely meant parity with other, and possibly, worse offenders who were not before the Tribunal.

In reflecting on the wider significance of the three injunctions, I was reminded of a passage in Spinoza's *Tractatus Politicus* (1675–77): "When I have applied my mind to politics so that I might examine what belongs to politics with the same freedom of mind as we use for mathematics, I have taken my best pains not to laugh at the actions of mankind, not to groan over them, not to be angry with them, but to understand them."

Finally, it appears advisable to check critically the significance of the three levels of analysis chosen in this paper:

Power-tests can do little more than assist in a pragmatic assessment of happenings in terms of cost-effectiveness: by reference to objectives aimed at and the costs—political, economic, military, legal and ethical—incurred in attempts at their realisation.

Legal tests provide normative standards which, in view of the adjustment of international law to the needs of open power politics and power politics in disguise, are highly relative.

Ethical tests, if not similarly watered down but applied against the background of the challenges held out by what is best in world civilisation, can perhaps serve the most salutary purposes. They can furnish the world with a mirror-image of itself, and the world may not like what it sees.

PART TWO

THE KAHAN AND MACBRIDE REPORTS

One of the shock-waves from the September 1982 massacres resulted in the near-unanimous Resolution of the General Assembly of the United Nations, condemning the outrages and calling for an international inquiry into the happenings.[8]

---

[8] Adopted at the Seventh Emergency Special Session of the General Assembly (September 24, 1982—A/RES/ES—7/9 without reference to a Main Committee) by 147 votes to 2 (Israel and the U.S.A.) with no abstentions:

"*The General Assembly*,

Having considered the question of Palestine at its resumed seventh emergency special session,

Having heard the statement of the Palestine Liberation Organisation, the representative of the Palestinian people,

Recalling and reaffirming, in particular, its resolution 194 (III) of December 11, 1948,

Appalled at the massacre of Palestinian civilians in Beirut,

Recalling Security Council resolutions 508 (1982) of June 5, 1982, 509 (1982) of June 6, 1982, 513 (1982) of July 4, 1982, 520 (1982) of September 17, 1982 and 521 (1982) of September 19, 1982,

Taking note of the reports of the Secretary-General relevant to the situation, particularly his report of September 18, 1982,

Noting with regret that the Security Council has so far not taken effective and practical measures, in accordance with the Charter of the United Nations, to ensure implementation of its resolutions 508 (1982) and 509 (1982),

Referring to the humanitarian principles of the Geneva Convention relative to the Protection of Civilian Persons in Time of War, of August 12, 1949, and to the obligations arising from the regulations annexed to the Hague Conventions of 1907,

Deeply concerned at the sufferings of the Palestinian and Lebanese civilian populations,

Noting the homelessness of the Palestinian people,

Reaffirming the imperative need to permit the Palestinian people to exercise their legitimate rights,

1. *Condemns* the criminal massacre of Palestinian and other civilians in Beirut of September 17, 1982;

2. *Urges* the Security Council to investigate, through the means available to it, the circumstances and extent of the massacre of Palestinian and other civilians in Beirut on September 17, 1982, and to make public the report on its findings as soon as possible;

3. *Decides* to support fully the provisions of Security Council resolutions 508 (1982) and 509 (1982), in which the Council, *inter alia*, demanded that:

(a) Israel withdraw all its military forces forthwith and unconditionally to the internationally recognised boundaries of Lebanon;

(b) All parties to the conflict cease immediately and simultaneously all military activities within Lebanon and across and Lebanese-Israeli border;

4. *Demands* that all Member States and other parties observe strict respect for the sovereignty, territorial integrity, unity and political independence of Lebanon within its internationally recognised boundaries;

5. *Reaffirms* the fundamental principle of the inadmissibility of the acquisition of territory by force;

6. *Resolves* that, in conformity with its resolution 194 (III) and subsequent relevant resolutions, the Palestinian refugees should be enabled to return to their homes and property from which they have been uprooted and displaced, and demands that Israel comply unconditionally and immediately with the present resolution;

7. *Urges* the Security Council, in the event of continued failure by Israel to comply with the demands contained in resolutions 508 (1982) and 509 (1982) and the present resolution, to

The indignation of the 147 governments voting for the Resolution exhausted itself in this gesture. Yet, under the pressure of public opinion at home and abroad, the Israeli Government considered it advisable to establish a commission of inquiry on the massacres. The Commission's Final Report was published during the middle of February 1983 (*Events at the Refugee Camps in Beirut—Kahan Report.*)[9]

At about the same time, a private group published a report by what was termed "the International Commission to inquire into reported violations of International Law by Israel during its invasion of the Lebanon" (*Israel in Lebanon—MacBride Report*).[10]

In response to a request by D.A.,[11] I prepared some comparative notes on the two Reports which, with his concurrence form Part Two of this paper.

The two Reports will be considered under seven heads: establishment and composition of the two Commissions; objects and scope of the inquiries; organisation; procedure; evidence, normative standards, and recommendations by the Commissions.

1—Establishment and Composition of the Commissions

1. *Kahan Commission*

The Kahan Commission was established under an Israeli Statute, the Commission of Inquiry Law.[12]

The Israeli Government would have preferred an *informal*

---

meet in order to consider practical ways and means in accordance with the Charter of the United Nations;

8. *Calls upon* all States and international agencies and organisations to continue to provide the most extensive humanitarian aid possible to the victims of the Israeli invasion of Lebanon;

9. *Requests* the Secretary-General to prepare a photographic exhibit of the massacre of September 17, 1982 and to display it in the United Nations visitors' hall;

10. *Decides* to adjourn the seventh emergency special session temporarily and to authorise the President of the latest regular session of the General Assembly to resume its meetings upon request from Member States."

See also the Leading Article in *The Times* (London, September 20, 1982): *After the Massacre*, and the Report by C. Smith from Beirut in *The Observer* (London, September 19, 1982), and the evidence regarding the massacres in *The Times* (London, September 24, 1982).

[9] Authorised translation into English—Jerusalem (1983).

On the "political somersault prompted by a loss of internal and external credibility" of the Israeli Government and leading to the establishment of the Kahan Commission, see Ch. Walker's report in *The Times* (September 29, 1982), and the reaction by Ch. Herzog, a former chief of Military Intelligence and, subsequently, President of Israel in *The Sunday Times* (September 26, 1982).

[10] Ithaca Press, London (1983).

[11] See above, p. 297.

[12] No. 5729 of 1968, as amended in 1972 and 1979. Published January 8, 1969 (Vol. 23, 1968–69, *Laws of the State of Israel*, pp.32 *et seq.*) See also the *Kahan Report*, App. A, p.1; *Laws of the State of Israel*, Vol. 26 (1971–72), Nr. 14, and *ibid.* Vol. 33 (1978–79), Nr. 37, and P. Elman, "The Commissions of Inquiry Law, 1968" (6 *Israel Law Review* (1971), pp.398 *et seq.*).

inquiry by Chief Justice Kahan, President of the Israeli Supreme Court, on the Beirut massacres. Yet, in view of two pending petitions to the Supreme Court for an inquiry under the 1968 Statute, the President thought that it would be improper to accept the invitation.[13] The Government then proceeded on the basis of the 1968 Statute.

Under the 1968 Statute, the President of the Supreme Court appoints the Chairman and, as a rule, two other members of a commission of inquiry.[14]

The President decided to act himself as Chairman of a statutory commission of inquiry into the Beirut massacres. In addition, he appointed Justice Barak of the Israeli Supreme Court[15] and Major-General Efrat (Reserve Israeli Defence Forces).[16]

2. *MacBride Commission*

The Commission had been called into existence on the initiative of "a small group of concerned and influential persons in the United Kingdom" which "appealed for sponsors and for funds to defray the cost involved" in establishing and operating the *ad hoc* Commission.[17]

Its composition was as follows: *Chairman*: S. MacBride, S.C. (former Irish Minister for External Affairs and Assistant Secretary-General, United Nations); *Vice-Chairman*: Professor R. Falk (International Law—Princeton University); K. Asmal (Senior Lecturer in Law—Trinity College, Dublin); Dr. B. Bercusson (Lecturer in Law—Queen Mary College, University of London); Professor G. de La Pradelle (Private Law—University of Paris X) and Professor S. Wild (Semitic Languages and Islamic Studies—University of Bonn).[18]

2.—*Objects and Scope of the Inquiries*

1. *Kahan Commission*

Under the 1968 Israeli Statute, it is the purpose of commissions of inquiry to examine matters which, in the Government's view are "at

---

[13] *The Times* (London, Spetember 25, 1982) (L. Plommer—Jerusalem).

[14] s.4, "Commissions of Inquiry Law, 1968" (*loc. cit.* in n. 12 above, p.32).

[15] *Kahan Report*, p.1. See also the laudatory assessment of Mr. Justice Barak in the Special Issue of *Time* (New York): "Verdict on the Massacre" (February 21, 1983), p.10.

[16] *Kahan Report*, p.1. For a similarly positive evaluation of Major-General Efrat, see *Time*, *loc. cit.* (in n. 15, above), p.10.

[17] *MacBride Report*, p. VII. See also *ibid.* p.281, and below, n. 39.

[18] *MacBride Report* p. IV. See also *ibid.* p.VII.

the time of vital public importance" and require "clarification" by investigation and report to the Government.[19] The terms of reference of commissions of inquiry are settled by the Government.[20]

The Israeli Government defined the terms of reference of the Kahan Commission as including "*all* the facts and factors connected with the atrocity [*sic*] carried out *by a unit of the Lebanese Forces* against the civilian population in the Chatilla and Sabra camps.[21]

The identification by the Israeli government of the supposed perpetrators of the atrocities was an almost contemptuous attempt to exclude from the Commission's jurisdiction an essential fact of the subject-matter yet to be investigated by the Commission. The Government received the rebuke it deserved from the Commission. The insouciance was also duly remembered in the Commission's self-description: Commission of Inquiry into the *events* at the Refugee Camps in Beirut.[22]

The Commission recorded a visit to Beirut but without indication of the date or the parts of Beirut included in this *descente sur les lieux*.[23] Yet, it "was no allowed to enter the area of the events.[24] The Commission remained silent on the identity of the powers so concerned about, presumably, its safety.[25]

The Commission also reported that it had "made an effort" to collect evidence from "outside the juridical boundaries of the State of Israel" and had taken "all necessary steps" to bring witnesses from outside Israel before the Commission.[26]

---

[19] s.1, Commissions of Inquiry Law 1968 (*loc. cit.* in n. 12, above, p.32).
[20] *Ibid.* section 2(a), *loc. cit.* in n. 12, above, as amended in 1979 (p.100).
[21] *Kahan Report*, p.1 (emphasis added).
[22] Emphasis in title added. The Commission put on record that, in this area, it "found it necessary to deviate somewhat from the stipulations of the Cabinet's resolution, which represents the Commission's terms of reference. . . . It is our opinion that we would not be properly fulfilling our task if we did not look into the question of whether th atrocities spoken of in the Cabinet's resolution were indeed perpetrated by the Phalangists" (*ibid.* p.3). See also below, n. 65.
Yet according to a letter from the Kahan Commission to Major Haddad, who appeared before the Commission, the Commission accepted that the "Lebanese forces mentioned in the Cabinet mandate to the Commission did not include his forces, which were shown as "the army of free Lebanon in Southern Lebanon." (M. Brilliant's report in *The Times*, December 6, 1982). See also the *Kahan Report*, pp.48 and 60, and below, text to nn. 26 and 68.
[23] *Ibid.* p.1.
[24] *Ibid.*
[25] Instead, the Commission "viewed television footage filmed near the time of the events at the camps and their surroundings" (without indication of the sources of these films, *ibid.* p.1). See also the report on the Commission's visit in *The Times* (London, October 20, 1982).
[26] *Ibid.* p.1.

2. *MacBride Commission*

The MacBride Commission limited its inquiries to the responsibilities incurred by *Israel* from her invasion of Lebanon until the termination of the massacres on September 18, 1982.[27]

More particularly, the Commission's terms of reference covered the possibility that, in invading Lebanon, Israel might have committed "breaches of international law." It also decided to examine whether, and if so how far, "were the Israeli authorities involved, directly or indirectly, in the massacres or other killings that were reported to have been carried out be Lebanese militia men" in the two camps between 16 and 18 September, 1982.[28]

The Commission or sub-commissions visited a number of countries, including (in alphabetical order) Israel, Jordan, Lebanon and Syria, for purposes of discussion, information and collection of evidence.[29] The Israeli Government permitted the members of the Commission to enter Israel but refused to co-operate with the Commission because it "regarded the terms of reference of the Commission as being too limited and one-sided.[30]

3—*Organisation*

Some worthwhile insights can be gained from the internal organisation and operation of the two Commissions.

1. *Kahan Commission*

The number of sessions (60) held by the Commission and the size of the evidence before it[31] permit inferences on the workload of the Commission's infra-structure, including its three staff investigators, and the Commission's judicial co-ordinator, Judge Bartov.[32] Yet, to judge by the evidence considered in the *published* section of the Commission's Report, the mountains of paper before the Commission yielded little new. It had all been revealed months before in the reports of investigative journalists, especially those based on Beirut.[33]

The reliability of this evidence creates a presumption in favour of the reports from the same sources on matters in Appendix B to the

---

[27] *MacBride Report*, p. V.
[28] *Ibid.*
[29] *Ibid.* pp. VIII–IX.
[30] *Ibid.* pp. VII and IX.
[31] *Kahan Report*, p.1.
[32] *Ibid.* p.5.
[33] See the reports cited below, especially those by R. Fisk, L. Jenkins and Ch. Walker. See also below, text to n. 62.

Commission's Report: the sections of the Report withheld from publication because the Commission considered this "essential in the interest of protecting the nation's security or foreign relations."[34] These impressive journalistic efforts also assist in checking the evidence used and evaluated in the MacBride Report.[35]

2. *MacBride Commission*

Five facets of the Commission's work assist in assessing the Commission's Report:

(1) The plenary sessions of the Commission for consideration of evidence and findings extended over eleven days.

(2) The Commission's hearings in the countries listed above were chaired by the Commission's Vice-Chairman.[36]

(3) An undisclosed portion of the evidence before the Commission was selected and analysed by a team of nine research workers who also, during their employment for three months, "undertook research in different fields of the Commission's mandate."[37]

(4) The co-ordination and editing of the "various portions" of the Commission's Report was undertaken by one of the members of the Commission.[38]

(6) In the Report, the "generous financial support from many sources" is acknowledged and, "in an even more comprehensive sense," the Commission's indebtedness to the members of, and the adviser to, the Convening Committee.[39]

4—*Procedure*

1. *Kahan Commission*

In the absence of express provisions in the 1968 Statute or regulations thereunder, the Commission had a free hand in determining its own procedure.[40] In particular, it was "not bound to follow the rules of procedure of a court."[41]

The Commission emphasised that its procedures were "not those of a criminal court." Thus, the rule that, "in order to convict

---

[34] *Kahan Report*, p.2.
[35] See below, p.315, and *MacBride Report*, pp.199 *et seq.* (list of witnesses and organisations who gave evidence to the Commission).
[36] See above, text to n. 18, and *MacBride Report*, p. VII.
[37] *Ibid.* p. IX. See also *ibid.* pp.217 and 281.
[38] Mr. Kader Asmal (see above, p.307; *MacBride Report*, p. IX).
[39] *Ibid.* pp. VII and 281 (names of the members of the Convening Committee). See also above, n. 17.
[40] s.7, Commission of Inquiry Law 1968 *loc. cit.* (above, p.306, in n. 12) p.32.
[41] *Ibid.* s.8(*a*) (*ibid.* p.33).

someone, his guilt must be proven beyond reasonable doubt," did not apply in its proceedings.[42] Yet, the Commission was aware of the likely consequences of its findings and conclusions "from a social and ethical standpoint.[43] Thus, in accordance with the 1968 Statute, the Commission sent notices to nine persons "likely to be harmed by the inquiry or by its results" so as to enable them to protect themselves by attendance before the Commission, examination of witnesses and presentation of their own evidence.[44]

While some of the hearings of the Commission were held in public, others were held in camera.[45]

2. *MacBride Commission*

The Report contains little concrete information on the procedural aspect of the Commission's work. Ultimately, as the Chairman wisely observed, views on this aspect of the Commission's work, as on others,[46] are questions of confidence in the "objectivity, independence, qualification and standing of the members of the Commission."[47] On each of these points, all its members are entitled to generous presumptions in their favour.

Attention should also be drawn to the Chairman's efforts to secure official Israeli co-operation with the Commission's work.[48]

5—*Evidence*

1. *Kahan Commission*

Unless otherwise provided in the 1968 Statute, commissions of inquiry are "not bound by the rules of evidence."[49] The "may admit any evidence in any manner deemed to be expedient."[50] The Chairmen and, ultimately, the commissions have, however, wide powers to summon witnesses, require the production of documents or other exhibits and order the taking of evidence abroad.[51]

Three possible limitations of the Kahan Commission's freedom of action should be borne in mind:

---

[42] *Kahan Report*, p.4.
[43] *Ibid*. p.4.
[44] s.15, Commissions of Inquiry Law 1968, *loc. cit.* (in n. 12 above), pp.34–35 and *Kahan Report*, p.4). See also App. A (Resolution of the Commission of November 24, 1982).
[45] *Ibid*. p.108.
[46] See below under 6 (b) and 7 (b).
[47] *MacBride Report*, p. VIII.
[48] *Ibid*. p. VII. See also above, text to n. 30.
[49] s.8(b), Commissions of Inquiry Law 1968, *loc. cit.* (in n. 12 above), p.33.
[50] *Ibid*. s.8(a) (*ibid*. p.33).
[51] ss.9 *et seq*. (*ibid*. pp.33 *et seq*.).

(1) *Terms of reference.* As with any combination of words, the Commission's terms of reference are open to wide and narrow constructions. While, in a narrow interpretation, the emphasis would be on the three-day period of the September 1982 massacres, a wide interpretation would probably tend to fasten on "all the facts an factors connected" with the massacres.[52]

In deciding to exclude matters of an "indirect or remote" connection,[53] the Commission attempted to steer a middle course and keep its options open right to the end of its deliberations.

(2) *Public and secret elements.* It is for the commissions under the 1968 Statute to decide on their withdrawal into secret sessions, the exclusion and evaluation of evidence, the non-publication of specific reasoning and recommendations and even the secrecy of the whole of their reports.[54]

If, as with the Report of the Kahan Commission, portions of the Report remain secret "since, in our opinion, non-publication of this material is essential in the interest of protecting the nation's security or foreign relations",[55] this decision inevitably affects the credibility of any of the published sections of the Report; for, if the Commission qualified any of its assertions, evaluations and recommendations in the published sections by reference to others in the secret portions of the Report, it might offer clues to the contents of what was to be hidden from public gaze.

(3) *Unstated assumptions.* In the prototypes of commissions of inquiry or governmental initiative,[56] it was probably taken for granted that a government with powers to appoint the chairmen or all the members of such commission, and to decide on their terms of

---

[52] See above, text to n. 21.

[53] *Kahan Report*, pp.2–3.

[54] ss.18(a) and 20(a), Commissions of Inquiry Law 1968, *loc. cit.* (in n. 12 above), pp.35–36, as amended in 1979 by the addition of "foreign relations of the State or classified procedures of the Israeli Police" as grounds for sitting in camera and non-publication of the whole or parts of reports (*ibid.* 1978–79, p.101). See also below, p.322, n. 28.

[55] *Kahan Report*, p.2. See also *ibid.* pp.12 and 108, and the page, following Appendix A: "Appendix B (SECRET)."

[56] An essential difference between the British Tribunals of Inquiry (Evidence) Act 1921 (11 Geo. 5, Ch. 7) and the Israeli Commissions of Inquiry Law 1968 should be born in mind: the establishment of commissions under the 1921 Act depends on Resolutions of both Houses of Parliament (s.1(1)).

On the history of tribunals of inquiry in England since the 17th century, see G.W. Keeton, *Trial by Tribunal* (1960), pp.21 *et seq.*; on the connections between the British model and the Commissions of Inquiry Ordinance, issued by the British Mandate Administration for Palestine in 1921, and the Israeli legislation of 1968, see Elman, *loc. cit.* (in n. 12 above), and Sir Cyril Salmon, "Tribunals of Inquiry," 2 *Israeli Law Review* (1967), pp.313 *et seq.*

For a critical examination of the Franks Report on *The Falklands War*, see, for instance, Ch. Wain, *The Listener* (London) (January 27, 1983).

reference, would not be the prime suspect in investigations to be held.

Regarding the subject-matter of the inquiry by the Kahan Commission, the opposite assumption was widely considered to be more appropriate.[57] The attempt made by the Israeli Government to prejudge one of the facts yet to be established could but deepen doubts previously held.[58]

Implications. The three factors considered may explain some of the least persuasive passages in the Commission's Report. More particularly, five facets of the Commission's findings and recommendations call for close examination:

(1) exclusion of any matter on the ground of its indirect or remote connection with the massacres[59];

(2) harsh treatment of evidence from sections of the Israeli military establishment which had been opposed to close contacts with the Phalange and its active involvement in any fighting[60];

---

[57] On Deputy Prime Minister Levy's statement at the meeting of the Israeli Cabinet on September 16, 1982, see the *Kahan Report*, p.50.

Although, apparently, treated as an "outsider" in his adopted country, the reaction of a reporter and editor of world reputation and the highest integrity to the news of the Beirut massacre was unqualified: "All of us realised it had been organised by our army" (J. Timerman, *The Longest War* (1982), p.157). The renowned author of *Prisoner Without a Name, Without a Number* was similarly explicit in his forecast on the *Kahan Report* (*The Longest War*, p.159).

See also below, p.314 *et seq.*

[58] See above, text to n. 22.

[59] See above, text to n. 53. In the *Kahan Report*, the rational element in Phalangist policies of terror is adequately emphasised: In order to improve, *inter alia*, the "demographic balance between the Christians and Muslims in Lebanon, . . . the Phalangist leaders proposed removing a large portion of the Palestinian refugees from Lebanese soil, whether by methods of persuasion or other means of pressure" (p.8). See also *ibid.* p.11, and above, p. 312.

The Commission must have been aware of comparable rationalisations offered by, and on behalf of, the Israeli Prime Minster and Minister of Defence in connection with the massacres at *Deir Yassim* (1948) and *Quibia* (1953), the former carried out by Irgun and the latter by an army unit under Major Sharon's command. See, for instance, M. Begin, *The Revolt* (1959—translated from the Hebrew by S. Katz), pp.162 *et seq.*; E. Silver in *The Guardian* (London, February 9 and April 9, 1983) and further, the leading article "Dare Call it Terrorism" in *The Times* (London, August 7, 1982); Mohammad Tarbush in *The Observer* London, (September 29, 1982); R. Fisk in *The Times* (London, September 29, 1982); Ch. Walker (*ibid.*), and M. Horsnell and E. Mortimer (*ibid.* March 7, 1983).

The pleas of ignorance offered on both occasions by the leaders of these units were hardly more credible than the long-standing policies of the Phalangist leaders considered in the Report. See also below, n. 62.

[60] According to the testimony by the Israeli Director of Military Intelligence, he had not even been informed "that it had been decided to send the Phalangists into the camps, and that they were operating there" (*Kahan Report*, pp.30 and 84–85). See also *ibid.* p.77: the Commission's refusal to concern itself with what it termed a "logical contradiction" and its evaluation of other relevant evidence, (*ibid.* pp.81 *et seq.*); the report by L. Jenkins in *The Guardian* (London, October 1, 1982), and below, p.320, nn. 12 and 13.

(3) severe recommendations regarding officers who, well in time, had warned their superiors of less than civilised characteristics of the Phalangist militia[61];

(4) acceptance at face value of denials and excuses made by the suspects-in-chief[62];

(5) exculpations of higher echelons on the ground of imperfections in the "functioning of establishments."[63]

On any of these areas, it is advisable to check findings of the Kahan Commission by reference to reports from international relief organisations and investigative journalists of proved independence, competence and integrity[64] and the evidence in the MacBride Report.[65]

2. MacBride Commission

In accordance with its more extensive time-scale than that prescribed to the Kahan Commission, the MacBride Commission considered that it had convincing evidence on three central issues relating to the Beirut massacres:

(1) "complicity by Israeli military and civilian officialdom in the massacres carried out by the Lebanese militias (Phalange, Haddad)" in the massacres.[66]

(2) contact between the Israeli Minister of Defence and the Prime Minister "minutes" after hearing of the explosion of a large bomb in the Phalangist headquarters in Beirut and death of Bashir Gemayel, the President-Elect of Lebanon, and the decision of the two Israeli key-figures on the immediate occupation of West Beirut.[67]

(3) identification of the Phalange and Major Haddad's militia as the "main and probably, exclusive, perpetrators of the massacres.[68] The Commission did not find "authoritative" evidence on active

---

[61] See below, p.320. In the *Kahan Report* the pointlessness of repeated advice contrary to the "sympathetic approach" of Mossad in favour of active cooperation with the Phalange and the support for this policy in the highest political and military echelons of the Israeli establishment is acknowledged but not accepted in mitigation of the Military Intelligence officers concerned. See also *ibid*. pp.83–84, on the "subjebective" element in the pro-Phalangist attitude of Mossad to the Phalange, the testimony by the Head of Mossad, *ibid*. p.9, and on the "advantages" to be derived from this "emotional" involvement, *ibid*. p.68.

[62] See, further, the *Kahan Report*, pp.5, 27, 44–45, 51–52, 59, 65 and 82–83; the *MacBride Report*, p.168; above, n. 59, and below, pp.320–321.

[63] *Kahan Report*, pp.85 and 100 *et seq*. See also below, p.320.

[64] See also the *Kahan Report*, pp.42–43, and above, note 33.

[65] See also above, text to n. 35, and below under (2). The supply by Israel to the forces of Major Haddad and the Phalangists of uniforms "similar to those" worn by the Israeli Defence Forces (*Kahan Report*, pp.7–8) may explain some of the contradictions on the identity of the actual participants in the massacres.

[66] *MacBride Report*, p. XIV. See also *ibid*. pp.165–166.

[67] *Ibid*. pp.165 and 183, n. 5. See also p.166.

[68] *Ibid*. pp.176–177.

participation of Israeli or other armed forces on the spot.[69] Yet, it considered as established the "reckless disregard" by Israel of probable consequences of the entry of the Lebanese militia into the camp,[70] assistance by Israel to the militia from outside[71] and lack of adequate control over the militia whose members obeyed Israeli officers whenever such control was exercised.[72]

In view of the contacts established by the MacBride Commission in Beirut[73], its view on the value of the likely evidence in the Lebanese Government Report deserves to be noted. As this investigation was "exceedingly constrained by Phalange influence"[74], the Mac-Bride Commission reached the common-sense conclusion that little new—and, it may be added, trustworthy—evidence was likely to emerge from this source.[75]

6—Normative Standards

It is probably a sound proposition that, in any objective sense, there are no facts but only value-judgments in varying degrees. Yet, pragmatically, the lawyer's distinction between facts and normative standards has its uses. It emphasises the purely negative character of "facts" which include anything of a non-normative character.

---

[69] *Ibid.* p.177. See also Major Haddad's interview with R. Fisk in *The Times* (London, September 23, 1982) that *"officially"* he "did not have any men in Beirut," and that his forces did "nothing" without co-ordination with the Israeli Army, and the reports by E. Silver in *The Guardian* (London, September 25, 1982) on "New claims that Israeli army helped plan the attack" and *ibid.* (November 2, 1982) on evidence implicating "Haddad's men," by L. Plommer in *The Times* (London, September 25, 1982) and by Ch. Walker (*ibid.* November 2, 1982).

In the *Kahan Report*, any suggestions of a "conspiracy or plot" by the "Israeli political echelon or from the military echelon in the Israeli Defence Forces" are treated as "unfounded" accusations (pp.51–52). Yet, the reference to I.D.F. does not cover Mossad, and there are several gradations which fall short of the extremes of conspiracy and non-involvement. On Israel's "indirect" responsibility, see *ibid.* pp.54 *et seq.* and below, p.316.

[70] *MacBride Report*, p.179.

[71] *Ibid.* p.180.

[72] *Ibid.* p.180.

[73] See above, p.309 and below, n. 75.

[74] *MacBride Report*, p.164.

[75] *Ibid.* See also L. Jenkin's Report from Beirut in *The Guardian* (London, December 30, 1982), and the interview by Claude Khouri with Asaad Germanos, the Lebanese Prosecutor General in charge of the Lebanese Government inquiry into the September 1982 massacres, in *Monday Morning* (Beirut, February 21, 1983), pp.40–41. According to the summaries published in Beirut in *Le Reveil* and *L'Orient: Le Jour* (June 21, 1983), the Prosecutor General attributed full legal responsibility to the Israeli Armed Forces under the 1949 Geneva Convention IV but exculpated them from active participation in the events inside the camps. In his view, neither the Lebanese Armed Forces nor the Christian militias had any advance knowledge of the massacres which were perpetrated by unknown persons who had suffered in previous years from Palestinian abuse.

1. *Kahan Commission*

Subject to the Israeli Statute of 1968 on Commissions of Inquiry[76] and the terms of reference settled by the Israeli Government,[77] the Kahan Commission was free to limit itself to a purely factual inquiry or apply any normative standards of its choosing. Yet, whatever choice it would make and preference it would voice might well be indicative of undisclosed reasons behind such decisions.

Responsibility. Once the Commission had decided that "all the facts and factors" connected with the Beirut massacres[78] included the issue of *responsibility* for the massacres, the Commission had to determine the normative system by reference to which this responsibility arose.

A variety of choices existed: The Commission could base its findings on international or (Israeli and/or Lebanese) municipal law. It could also rely on moral standards, be they those of a society or community in the sociological meanings of these terms.[79]

The Commission adopted an eclectic approach. It considered the responsibilities for the massacres primarily in legal terms but held that it was not its "function as a commission of inquiry to lay a precise legal foundation for such legal responsibility."[80]

It does not appear to be self-evident why the Commission should have generalised as it did on the duties of commissions of inquiry, nor why a commission with a majority of senior judges should have preferred to leave anything imprecise that could be made more precise.

Legal Status of Israeli Forces in Lebanon. Similarly, the Commission declined to determine the legal position of Israel and the Israeli Forces in Lebanon and West Beirut. It merely held contingently that, *if*, at the time of the massacres, Beirut was to be regarded as occupied territory—"and we do not determine that such indeed is the case from a legal perspective"—it is "the duty of the

---

[76] See above, text to n. 12.

[77] See above, text to n. 21.

[78] Terms of reference (see above, text to n. 21). The Kahan Commission considered that its investigations also obtained a wider "importance from the perspective of Israel's moral fortitude and its functioning as a democratic State that scrupulously maintains the fundamental principles of the civilised world" (*Kahan Report,* p.107). See also below, p.322, and, for a more realistic view of some of the weak spots in Israel's democratic structure, the penetrating analysis by Y. Peri, "Between Battles and Ballots, *Israeli Military in Politics*" (1983), p.175 *et seq.*

[79] See, further, the writer's *Power Politics. A Study of International Society* (1941—3rd ed. 1964, pp.12 and 213 *et seq.*).

[80] *Kahan Report*, p.54.

occupier, according to the rules of usual and customary international law, to do all it can to ensure the public's well-being and security."[81] In this context, *"public"* is hardly an appropriate description. Yet, its use suggests some inhibition about employing more relevant technical terms such as *non-combatants* or *civilian population.*[82]

Instead of coming to grips with whichever relevant legal system applied, the Commission engaged in moralising exercises on a level of high abstraction and at a respectful distance from the international law of belligerent occupation.[83] It decided to operate in the sphere of obligations "applying to every civilised nation and the ethical rules accepted by civilised peoples."[84]

In consonance with the normative standards selected, the Commission offered apposite authority: a passage in the Book of Deuteronomy on what the Commission called the "beheaded heifer." Perhaps what impressed itself subconsciously on the Commission was the plea of the elders: "Our hands have not shed this blood neither have our eyes seen it."[85] It may have reminded the Commission of similar pleas of the suspects-in-chief before it.[86] Yet, once the Commission introduced bibical authority and comments on it in the Talmud, it might have reflected on a feature that might be more relevant for its own inquiry than symbolic protestations of innocence by the elders of the city: the difference between a *no man's land* and an area under *effective control* of occupation forces.

Similarly, the Commission might have explained the rules of the international law applicable in battle zones, suitably supported (if not on the secret list) by citations from relevant Israeli military manuals. Instead, it reflected on the need to combine toughness with minimum standards of "combat morality" and, in this respect, the deplorably low standards of the various Lebanese groups and the (higher) "norm" applied by the Israeli Defence Force.[87]

A hypothetical line of thought may provide a clue to the Commission's extraordinary reasoning: If the Commission had concentrated on a legal analysis, could it have avoided considering the adequacy of the transformation into Israeli law of the 1948 Geno-

---

[81] *Ibid.*
[82] See, further, the writer's *International Law*, Vol. II (1968), p.109 *et seq.*
[83] *Kahan Report*, pp.54 *et seq.*
[84] *Ibid.*
[85] *Book of Deuteronomy* (Ch. 21: v. 6–7).
[86] *Kahan Report*, pp.58 *et seq.* pp.64 *et seq.* and pp.100–108. See also above, p.314.
[87] *Kahan Report*, p.58.

cide Convention[88] and the 1949 Geneva Conventions on the Protection of War Victims,[89] not to speak of Israel's attitude to the relevant 1899 and 1907 Hague Conventions[90] and the treatment under Israeli law of traditional war crimes, committed by persons under Israeli jurisdiction?[91] Moreover, the Commission might have been expected to recommend improvements in Israeli law under any of these heads as well as examine relevant acts and omissions—and those responsible for them—by Israeli State organs with powers more adequate than those of the Commission.

In addition, on the level of jurisdiction on war crimes and issues of a similar character, the inadequacy of the Commission's identification of *acts* with *direct* responsibility and of *omissions* with *indirect* responsibility would have been revealed.[92] The *corpus* of judgments on war crimes offers authority on the criminal responsibility of those who, in hierarchical relations, have duties to act but fail to perform them, and these duties can hardly be determined by oversimplifications such as contrasts between complicity equalling direct responsibility and anything else constituting "merely" indirect responsibility on the vaguest of normative levels.[93] Yet, would it have been compatible with the "security of the State"[94] and Israel's "foreign relations"[95] to open this Pandora's box?

---

[88] Crime of Genocide (Prevention and Punishment) Law (1950) *Laws of the State of Israel*, Vol. 4 (1949–50), Nr. 31, pp.101 *et seq.*

See especially, s.5: "A person who has committed, outside Israel, an act which is an offence under the Law, may be prosecuted and punished in Israel as if he had committed the act in Israel" (p.101). Under s.9, the Minister of Justice is charged with the implementation of this Law (*ibid.* p.102).

See also the *MacBride Report*, pp.193 and 194 *et seq.* (Majority Note on Genocide and Ethnocide—the two dissenters (*ibid.* p.197) are not named).

[89] Subject to reservations regarding the use of the Red Shield of David as the emblem and distinctive sign provided in the Conventions, Israel became a party to all four 1949 Geneva Conventions on July 6, 1951. The Conventions were included in Vol. I of the *Israel Treaty Series* but, apparently, not formally transformed into Israeli law. See also R. Lapadoth, *La Conclusion des Traités Internationaux en Israël* (1962), pp.31 *et seq.*

[90] One June 17, 1962, Israel became a party to Hague Convention I of 1907 on the Pacific Settlement of International Disputes. See also *loc. cit.* in n. 82 above, pp.9 *et seq.*

[91] On the law applied by Israeli Courts in the *Eichmann* Trial, see below, n. 92, and the writer's *International Law and Order* (1971), pp.237 *et seq.*

[92] See, further, J. Hall, *General Principles of Criminal Law* (1947), pp.215 and 247 *et seq.*, and G. Williams, *Criminal Law* (1978), pp.34, 42, 68 *et seq.*, and pp.233 *et seq.* See also the *Legal Material* submitted by the Israeli Attorney General to the District Court of Jerusalem in the *Eichmann* case (Part Three: *Involvement in Crime*, August 8, 1961), the Judgment of the District Court in the *Eichmann* case (Criminal Case 40/61), ss.189 *et seq.*, and the Judgment of the Supreme Court sitting as a Court of Criminal Appeal (Criminal Appeal 336/61), rejecting the appeal, and *loc. cit.* (in n. 82, above), Vol. II, pp.443 *et seq.*

[93] See, further, Vol. II, *ibid.* and pp.826 *et seq.* (bibliography).

[94] *Kahan Report*, p.108. See also *ibid.* p.2, and above, p.312.

[95] *Ibid.*

2. *MacBride Commission*

Under its terms of reference,[96] the MacBride Commission was encouraged to apply international law to the acts and omissions of Israeli organs from the Israeli invasion of Lebanon until the termination of the massacres.[97]

The Commission's legal findings can be summarised under six heads:

(1) *Self-defence* under Article 51 of the United Nations Charter, narrowly construed[98]:

(2) war of aggression as a crime under international law[99];

(3) legitimation of wars of national liberation by "law-making" United Nations resolutions[1];

(4) declaratory character of humanitarian conventions on the law of armed conflict, including the two 1977 Geneva Protocols to the 1949 Conventions and the 1981 United Nations "Convention" on Specific Conventional Weapons[2];

(5) a controversial use of the de Martens-Clause in the Preamble of Hague Convention II of 1899[3];

(6) Reference to four legal principles, formulated so that "the more specific and applied content of the law of war can be deduced[4];

Each of the Commission's propositions and its application to the factual situations (which themselves need careful checking) calls for further examination by reference to the tests provided in Article 38 of the Statute of the International Court of Justice.[5] By virtue of their incorporation as an integral part in the United Nations Charter and, thus, near-universal acceptance, these criteria constitute the most reliable safeguards against excursions into the wonderland of *lex ferenda.*[6]

---

[96] See above, p.308.

[97] *MacBride Report*, pp.1 *et seq.*

[98] *Ibid.* pp.14 *et seq.* See above, p.297 *et seq.*, and, further, *loc. cit.* (in n. 82, above), pp.28 *et seq.*

[99] *MacBride Report*, pp.20, 187 and 190–191. See also above under I (2) and *loc. cit* (in n. 82, above), pp.478 *et seq.*

[1] *MacBride Report*, pp. XIV–XV and 20–26. See also G.I.A.D. Draper, *Wars of National Liberation and War Criminality* in M. Howard (Ed.), *Restraints on War* (1979), pp.157 *et seq.*, and, further, the writer's *The Dynamics of International Law* (1976), pp.5 and 77 *et seq.*

[2] *MacBride Report*, pp. XIV–XV and 27 *et seq.* See, further, *loc. cit.* (in n. 1 above) (1976).

[3] *MacBride Report*, pp. XIX and 49. See also *ibid.* pp. XV and 27 *et seq.* See also above, n. 82, pp.21–22.

[4] *MacBride Report*. p. XIX. Anything *can* be done. The legal issue appears to be whether it *may* be done.

[5] See, further, *loc. cit.* (in n. 82, above), Vol. I (1957), pp.25 *et seq.*

[6] See, further, *ibid.* pp.6 and 25 *et seq.* and n. 1 above (1976), pp.8 *et seq.* See also *I.C.J. Reports 1969*, pp.43–44, and *1974*, pp.23–24.

7—Recommendations

1. Kahan Commission

What the Commission had done was to reduce legal responsibility to a political responsibility, but with high moral overtones: "The end never justifies the means, and basic ethical and human values must be maintained in the use of arms."[7]

The Commission's recommendations indicate the limited significance of applying these standards to the acts and omissions of the persons investigated.

Category one (highest political and military echelons):

(1) *Prime Minister, Foreign Minister and Head of Mossad*: polite rebukes—no concrete recommendations.[8]

(2) *Minister of Defence*: in view of established defects in the discharge of his duties, recommended that *if* the Prime Minister thought it necessary, it would be for him to consider the removal of the Minister of Defence from his office.[9]

(3) *Chief of Staff*: "grave conclusions" but, in view of his impending retirement, no further action recommended.[10]

(4) *G.O.C. Northern Command*: no concrete recommendation.[11]

Category Two (military echelons on middle levels):

(1) *Director of Military Intelligence*: "extremely serious omissions" in discharging the duties of his office. Recommended that he should not continue in his office.[12]

(2) *Division Commander Brigadier General*: Recommended that, for three years, he should not serve as field commander.[13]

---

[7] *Kahan Report*, p.107. See also above, p.316.

[8] *Kahan Report*, p.105. See also *ibid.* pp.64, 72 and 85 *et seq.* On the background of the chief suspects, see also the assessments by Peri, *loc. cit.* above, n. 78 (*Index of Names*, pp.334 *et seq.*). Until September 12, 1982, Major-General Hofi (named in *The Times*, London, October 20, 1982)—on his previous record, see Peri, *loc. cit.* (in n. 78, above), pp.90, 244 and 258)—was the head of Mossad and, then, his Deputy took over (*Kahan Report*, p.87).

[9] *Kahan Report*, pp.105–106. See also *ibid.* pp.67 *et seq.*

[10] *Ibid.* p.106. See also *ibid.* pp.74 *et seq.*, and, on the reduction by the Chief of Staff of the sentence passed on Lieutenant *Pinter* "for the murder of three prisoners of war in South Lebanon in 1977," and personal connections, Peri, *loc. cit.* (in n. 78, above), pp.272–273 and 321, n. 21 (in conjunction with p.269).

[11] *Ibid.* p.105. See also *ibid.* pp.43 and 89 *et seq.* and the report by Ch. Walker, *The Times* (London, November 1, 1982).

[12] *Kahan Report*, p.106. See also *ibid.* pp.81 *et seq.*; Ch. Walker's Reports in *The Times* (London, February 10 and 12, 1983), and above, n. 60.

[13] *Kahan Report*, p.106. See also *ibid.* p.93 *et seq.* and Brigadier General Yaron's impressive admission of individual and collective guilt: "The mistake, as I see it, the mistake is everyone's. The entire system showed insensitivity . . . I did badly, I admit it" (*ibid.* p.47). See also D.J. Goldberg, *The Times* (London, February 26, 1983), and above, n. 60.

Category Three (improvements in the functioning of the establishments concerned): The Commission recommended measures to prevent the repetition of occurrences such as:

(1) the Prime Minister learning "about the events in the camps from a BBC broadcast on Saturday (September 18, 1982) afternoon."[14]

(2) the head of Mossad also learning only at the Cabinet session on Thursday (September 16, 1982), when the Phalangists were already in the camps, about the decision taken the day before that the Phalangist militia should enter the camps.[15]

(3) sins against military red tape: reports "not always handled according to the standing procedures," and worse to follow: some reports "not recorded in the designated log books"[16];

(4) an epidemic of "faulty" memories.[17]

The Commission summed up the purpose of its inquiry as bringing "to light all the important facts relating to the perpetration of the atrocities; it therefore has *importance* from the perspective of Israel's moral fortitude and its functioning as a democratic State that scrupulously maintains the fundamental principles of the civilised world."[18] So it has and even more so has the manner in which the Israeli Government has chosen to "implement" the Commission's recommendations.[19]

2. MacBride Commission

Three of the recommendations of the MacBride Commission reflect the Commission's thinking:

(1) Probably the least controversial of the Commission's recommendations is the suggestion to pay greater attention to the implementation of the 1949 Geneva Conventions.[20] Yet, some Parties to these Conventions may be hesitant to apprehend Israeli and Lebanese leaders—and even more so those responsible for massacres elsewhere—and "use their national courts to carry out this responsibility."[21]

(2) The Commission recommended that Israel should make reparation for all damages done in Lebanon by violation of international

---

[14] *Kahan Report*, p.100.
[15] *Ibid.*
[16] *Ibid.* p.103.
[17] See, for instance, *ibid.* pp.36, 38, 45, 104 and 106. See also above, nn. 62 and 63.
[18] *Kahan Report*, p.107.
[19] See, for instance, the leading article in *The Times* (London, February 9, 1983) and the reports by Ch. Walker in *The Times* (London, February 12 and March 22, 1983).
[20] *MacBride Report*, p.192.
[21] *Ibid.*

law to the Government of Lebanon, reimbursement to voluntary
bodies for the cost of supplies and services provided by them and
arising from the Israeli invasion and occupation of Lebanon.[22] Alas,
this recommendation is based on an interpretation of international
law that, in generalised terms, would probably fall short of general
acceptance even by *ad hoc* supporters of this recommendation.[23]

(3) The Commission recommended that the United Nations
should set up a special international tribunal to "investigate and
prosecute individuals charged with crimes of State, especially in
connection with the Chatilla and Sabra massacres."[24]

Unless acclaimed as sticks with which to beat a particular
offender, Recommendations (2) and (3) are likely to remain Pla-
tonic. Yet, if these Recommendations are examined in the light of
the reasons why they hardly correspond to international law as it
stands[25] nor would be appreciated in a generalised form, they can
claim at least some educational value.

For Further Consideration

It would be instructive to know what the members of the two—or
three[26]— Commissions thought of the Reports of their counterparts.

While I was reflecting on this possibility, D.A. dropped in again[27]
and suggested three points for further consideration:

(1) in relation to the *Kahan Report*: the almost tragic impact, on
men of high calibre, of the mentality pervading a particular type of
garrison State.[28]

(2) in relation to the *MacBride Report*: the effect of the "committed" international law prevailing in the Commission on the credibility of international law.[29]

(3) in relation to *both Reports*: the dilemmas created for "persons

---

[22] *Ibid.* pp.192–193.
[23] See above, p.319, n. 6.
[24] *MacBride Report*, p.193.
[25] See above, p.319, n. 6.
[26] See above, pp.302 and 315, nn. 73 and 74.
[27] See above, p.298.
[28] See H.D. Lasswell, "The Garrison State," 46 *American Journal of Sociology*, pp.455 *et seq.* (1941); Peri, *loc. cit.* (in n. 78 above), and Mr. Eban's observation that "at no stage, was McCarthism more intense or more rampant in the United States than it is in Israel today" in *The Times* (London, December 18, 1982). See also above, n. 54, and below, n. 30. For some purposes, awareness of the "schizophrenic" element in Israeli society (as in most other social groups), which D. Horowitz (see, further, Peri, *loc. cit.* (in n. 78 above), pp.8 and 331–332) emphasises, may also be helpful.
[29] See, further, *loc. cit.* above, p.319, n. 1. (1976), pp.5 and 77 *et seq.* and Y.B.W.A., Vol. 37 (1983), pp.292 *et seq.*

of good will"[30] by insufficient consideration in time of the fundamental incompatibilities between their judicial and academic functions and the *ad hoc* tasks they undertook at their peril.[31]

PART THREE

INTERDISCIPLINARY READING

1—*Power*

Barbucallus, (*Anthologia Graeca Palatina*, Book IX).

Battutah, ibn, *Tukfat al-Nuzzar* (translated by C. Defrémery and B.R. Sanguinetti), Vol. I (1893).

Churchill, Charles H., *Mount Lebanon* (3 vols., 2nd. ed., 1853).

——, *The Druses and the Maronites* (1862).

Cramer, R.B., and Steele-Perkins, "Beirut", *Observer Magazine*, December 5, 1982.

Gibbons, E., *The History of the Decline and Fall of the Roman Empire* (1788).

Gilmour, D. *Lebanon: The Fractured Country* (1983).

Gurney, O.R., *The Hittites* (1952).

Heller, M. *A Palestinian State. The Implication for Israel* (1983).

Heren, L., Ghandi: The horror the film omits" *The Times* (London, December 4, 1982).

Herzog, C. *The Arab-Israeli Wars* (1982).

Higgins, R., *United Nations Peacekeeping 1946–1967, Documents and Commentary*, Vol. I: *The Middle East* 1969.

Hitti, P.K., *Lebanon in History* (1967).

---

[30] *Kahan Report*, p.108. As with the professed illusions of the Kahan Commission on Israeli democracy (see above, n. 78), which may reflect national "discipline," rather than a lack of understanding of interdisciplinary issues, the proposition advanced in the Report on "*the* correct approach, from a legal and public standpoint, to the problem of the personal responsibility of the political echelon" (p.61) indicates a remarkable unwillingness to face the factors in their own national environment which appear to have conditioned the Commission's own approach to the wider issues of their inquiry.

The Commission's appeal to "all persons of good will" (*ibid.* p.108) to accept its assurance that "the inquiry was conducted without any bias" (*ibid.*) can be accepted without reservation. Yet, what this amounts to can be judged only if and when the secret parts of the Report become publicly available.

The *Kahan Report* provides evidence of a marked preference for Mossad, as compared with Military Intelligence. Correspondigly, the warnings issued by the latter appear to be unduly undervalued (see above, p.297, n. 6 and p.303, n. 12).

On the role of Mossad in relation to the Phalange, see also the *Kahan Report*, pp.7 *et seq.*, and, more generally, on the various Israeli secret services, Peri, *loc. cit.* (in n. 78, above) (Index under *Intelligence* and *Secret Services*).

See also above p.305, text to n. 28.

[31] On other facets of the problem of judicial incompatibilities, see Y.B.W.A., Vol. 27 (1973), pp.434 *et seq.*

Hourani, H.H., *Syria and Lebanon* (1946).
——, *Arabic Thought in the Liberal Age, 1789–1939* (1962).
Howard M., "Pacification and its Victims," *Times Literary Supplement*, (London), April 15, 1983.
Hurewitz, J.C., *Diplomacy in the Near and Middle East, A Documentary Record* (2 vols., 1956).
Issawi; C.K., *Economic History of the Middle East and North Africa* (1982).
Jansen, M., *The Battle of Beirut* (1982).
Kissinger, H., *The White House Years* (1979).
——, *Years of Upheaval* (1981).
Lasswell, H.D., "The Garrison State," 46 *American Journal of Sociology* (1941).
Machiavelli, N., *Discorsi*. Book Two: *Methods of Expansion; Diplomacy and War*, and *Administration of Conquered Territory*; Book Three: *Salus Populi Suprema Lex* (1531).
Monroe, E., *Britain's Moment in the Middle East 1914–1971* (1981).
Moore, J.N., (ed.) *The Arab-Israeli Conflict* (3 vols., 1975).
Morgenthau, H., *Politics in the 20th Century* (1962), Vol. II, Chap. 30: "The Lebanese Disaster."
Mortimer, E., *Faith and Power, The Politics of Islam* (1982).
Mouterde, R., *Le Nahr el-Kalb* (1932), Plate VI.
Parkinson, F., *The Philosophy of International Relations* (1977).
Polk, W.R., *The Arab World*, (1980).
Porter, H., *History of Beirut* (1912).
Reid, R.R., "Syria 1859–1863," *Cambridge History of British Foreign Policy*, Vol. II (1923).
Rondot, P., *Les Chrétiens d'Orient* (1955).
Rosenthal, E., "The Role of Islam in the Modern National State," 16 *Year Book of World Affairs* (1962).
Runciman, S.A., *History of the Crusades* (3 vols. 1951–55).
Salibi, K.S., *Crossroads to Civil War: 1958–1976* (1976).
Schwarzenberger, G., *Power Politics: A Study of World Society* (1941—3rd ed. 1964).
Sella, A., *Soviet Political and Military Conduct in the Middle East* (1981).
Smith, A., "From International Relations to World Politics," Leeds University, *Montague Burton Lecture* (1982).
Toynbee, A.J., *A Study of History*, Vol. XII, Chap. 13: "The Configuration of Syriac History" (1961).
Winstone, H.V.F., *The Illicit Adventure: The Story of Political and Military Intelligence in the Middle East from 1898–1926* (1982).
Woolfson, M., *Prophets in Babylon: Jews in the Arab World* (1980).

Wright Q., *A Study of War*. Vol. I, Chap. 7: "Historic Warfare" (1942)

Yadin, Y., *The Art of Welfare in Biblical Lands* (1963).

Yirmish, D., *War Journal* (1983).

2—*Law*

Atiyah, P.S., *Law and Modern Society* (1983).

Bar-Yaacov, N., *The Israeli-Syrian Armistice* (1967).

——, "Keeping the Peace between Egypt and Israel 1973–1980," 15 *Israel Law Review*(1980).

Blum, Y.Z., "The Beirut Raid and the International Double Standard," 64 *American Journal of International Law* (1970).

Bowett, D.W. *Self-Defence in International Law* (1958).

Boyle, F.A. "Upholding International Law in the Middle East," 4 *Arab Studies Quarterly* (1983).

Brownlie, I., *International Law and the Use of Force by States* (1963).

Butler, W.E., (ed.) *International Law in Comparative Perspective* (1980).

Cardahi, C., "Le mandat de la France sur la Syrie and le Liban," 43 *Recueil*, Hague Academy of International Law (1933).

Cheng. B., (ed.) *International Law: Teaching and Practice* (1982).

Collinet, P. "Histoire de l'école de droit de Beyrouth," *Etudes historiques sur le droit de Justinian*, Vol. II (1925).

Davis, H.M., *Constitutions, Electoral Laws, Treaties of States in the Near and Middle East* (1947).

Dinstein, Y., "The New Geneva Protocols," 33 *Year Book of World Affairs* (1979).

——, "Legal Aspects of the Israeli Incursion into Lebanon and the Middle East Conflict," *Research Report*, Institute of Jewish Affairs, London (1983).

Draper, G.I.A., *The Red Cross Conventions* (1958).

Falk, R.A., "The Beirut Raid and the International Law of Retaliation," 63 *American Journal of International Law* (1969).

——, *The Status of Law in International Society*, Chap. 22: "The Quest for World Order and the Vietnam War" (1970).

Fawcett, J., *Law and Power in International Relations* (1982).

Feinberg, N., *The Legality of a "State of War" after the Cessation of Hostilities* (1961).

Friedmann, W., "United States Policy and the Crisis of International Law," 59 *American Journal of International Law* (1965).

Green, L.C., "Superior Orders and the Reasonable Man," 8 *Canadian Yearbook of International Law* (1970).

Green, L.C., "International Law and the Control of Terrorism," 17 *Dalhousie Law Journal* (1983).

Higgins, R., "The June War: The United Nations and Legal Background," 3 *Journal of Contemporary History* (1968).

Kassem case: (1969) See *Israeli Military Prosecutor* v. *Omar Mahud Kassem and Others*, 4 *Revue des Droits de l'Homme*, p. 536 *et seq.* (1971).

Keeton, G.W. *Trial by Tribunal* (1960).

Khadduri, M., "The Franco-Lebanese Dispute and the Crisis of November 1943," 38 *American Journal of International Law* (1944).

——, *War and Peace in the Law of Islam* (1955).

——, and Liebesny, H.J., *Law in the Middle East* (2 vols., 1955).

Lauterpacht, E., *Jerusalem and the Holy Places* (Anglo-Israeli Association, 1968).

Lauterpacht, H., *International Law and Human Rights* (1950).

MacBride, S., and Others, *Israel in Lebanon*: Report of the International Commission to enquire into reported violations of International Law by Israel during its invasion of the Lebanon (1983).

Macdonald, R.St.J., and Johnston, D.M. (eds.), *The Structure and Process of International Law* (1983).

Maine, Sir Henry Sumner, *Ancient Law* (1861).

Peri, Y., *Between Battles and Ballots*: Israeli Military in Politics (1983).

Rougier, A., "La théorie de l'intervention d'humanité," 17 *Revue génerale du droit international public* (1910).

Rosenne, S., *Israel's Armistice Agreements with the Arab States* (1951).

Schwarzenberger, G., *International Law*, Vol. II: "The Law of Armed Conflict," Part Six: "Enforcement of the Rules of Warfare" (1968).

Schwebel, S.M., "What Weight to Conquest?" 64 *American Journal of International Law* (1970).

Smith H.A., *The Crisis in the Law of Nations* (1947).

Stone J., *Aggression and World Order* (1958).

Stowell, E.C., *Intervention in International Law* (1921).

Tunkin, G.I., "The New System of International Law," in G.M. Wilner (ed.), *Jus et Societas* (1979).

United Nations, International Law Commission. "Draft Code of Offences against the Peace and Security of Mankind," *Compendium of Relevant International Instruments*. A/CN. 4/368 (1983).

Wright, Q., "Bombardment of Damascus." 20 *American Journal of International Law* (1926).

——, "United States Invervention in the Lebanon," 53 *ibid.* (1959).

3—*Ethics*

Alexander, Y., and Kittrie, N.N., *Crescent and Star. Arab and Israeli Perspectives on the Middle East Conflict* (1973).

Arendt, H., *Men in Dark Times* (1970).

Burton, Sir Montague, *The Middle Path* (1943).

Calder, R., *The Inheritors*. Part Four: "The Streams of Civilisation." (1961).

Cheng, B. (Ed.), *International Law: Teaching and Practice* Chap. 5: "International Law and the Problem of Political World Order" (1982).

Collingwood, R.G., *The New Leviathan* (1942).

Davies, Lord, *Nearing the Abyss* (1936).

Elman, P., "The Commission of Inquiry Law, 1968", 6 *Israel Law Review* (1971).

Erasmus, D., *Stultitiae Laus* (1514).

Esposito, J.L. *Islam and Development: Religion and Sociopolitical Change* (1980).

Goren, A.A. (Ed.), "Dissenter in Zion," Collected Writings of J.L. Magnes (1982).

Hackett, Sir John, *The Third World War: The Untold Story* (1982).

Hawkes, J., *Man on Earth*. Chap. VI: "Civilisation." (1954).

Howard, M. (ed.), *Restraints on War* (1979).

Institut International de Recherches et de Formations en vue du développement, "Étude préliminaire sur les besoins et les possibilités de développment au Liban" (1959–60).

Jaeckh, E., *Weltsaat* (1960).

James, A., *The Politics of Peace-Keeping* (1969).

Jaspers, K., *Die geistige Situation der Zeit* (1931).

Keeton, G.W., *National Sovereignty and International Order* (1939).

Laqueur, W., *The Terrible Secret: The Suppression of Information about Hitler's 'Final Solution'* (1980).

Laski, M., *The Offshore Island* (1959).

Lasswell, H.D., *World Politics and Personal Insecurity* (1935).

Mason, H.L., "Imponderables of the Holocaust," 34 *World Politics* (1981).

McDougal, M.S., and Feliciano, F.P., *Law and Minimum World Order* (1961).

Morris, W., *The Clowns of God* (1981).

O'Brian, C.C., *The United Nations, Sacred Drama* (1968).
Pearce, J., *Under the Eagle: U.S. Intervention in Central America and the Caribbean* (1981).
Orwell, G., *1984* (1949).
Owen, R.B., "Memorandum on the Soviet Intervention in Afghanistan," U.S.A. Dept. of State, 74 *American Journal of International Law* (1980) pp. 418 *et seq.*
Schwarzenberger, G., *International Law and Order* (1971), Chap. 11: "The Legality of Nuclear Weapons," and Chap. 13: "The Eichmann Trial."
——, *The Dynamics of International Law* (1976) Chap. 5: "The Law of Armed Conflict: A Civilised Interlude?" 1976.
Schweisfurth, T. *Sozialistisches Völkerrecht?* (1979).
Sternberg, F., *The Coming Crisis* (1947).
Timerman, J., *The Longest War* (1982).
Vincent, R.J., *Non-Intervention and International Order* (1974).

CUMULATIVE INDEX
VOLUMES 26–38
(1972–1984)

(Roman numerals refer to the volume, Arabic to the pages)

Crises, the anatomy of—*cont.*
   patterns, 18–19
   typology, 19–22
      non-nuclear, 19
      nuclear, 18, 19
   See also under Crises and Survival.
Culture, xxxii,
   African, 258
   analysis of, 251–267
      concepts, 253, 263–264
      disciplines, 252, 255–256
      levels, 252, 256, 264
   See also under International Relations, place in; *and* Culture, factor of, in Global International Order.
Culture, factor of, in Global International Order, xxxiv, 252–264
Culture in world affairs,
   importance of, 254–260
   study of, 260–263
Curle, A., xxx, 5–13

DETENTE.
   East-West, xxxii, 3–4, 8–22, 50, 64–75
   economic co-operation, 64–75
   France, and, 13–14
   Helsinki conference (CSCE), after, 8–22
      "allied" States on both sides, and, 12–14
      attitudes towards, 15–18
      code of conduct?, 18–22
      non-aligned European States, and, 14–15
      Soviet view of, 9–11
      United States view of, 11–12
   irreversible, 13
   Southern Africa, in, 117–118
   West German concept of, 14
   See also below.
Détente,
   East-West, xxxv, 63, 166, 266–278
      function and limits of, 276–278
      Helsinki Final Act, 62–78, 275, 277. *See also under* Human Rights.
      international law, and, 266–278
      Southern Africa, in, 155
      See also above.
Deterrence, ageing of, xxxvi, 10–24
   convergence of circumstances, 18–21
   economies of defence, new, 13–15
   ends and means, 11–13
   flexible response, 11
   grand strategy, case for, 21–24
   military consequences, 15–18
   research and development, (R.&D.), 13, 19, 22
Developing States,
   more equal than others, xxxii, 286–302
      demands, 288–293
      international law, 287–288, 293–298
      lesson, the, 301–302
      result, the, 299–301
   See also under Third World.
Dickstein, H.L., xxvi, 245–265

U Thant—*cont.*
  acting Secretary-General of UN, 43
  Burma's permanent representative at UN, 43
  Cambodia and Thailand,
    de Ribbing mission, 54
    Gussing mission, 54
  Congo, operation in,
    Rwanda and Burundi, Dorsinville mission, 54
  criticisms, general, 45–57
    opportunities and limits, Secretary-General's, 63–64
    personality, 46–52
    record, 52–60
    1967, 47–49, 60–63
  critics of, 43–64
  Cuba, withdrawal of Soviet missiles from, 45, 53
  Cyprus, 58
  Equatorial Guinea, 54, 55
  good offices, 55, 56
  Indo-Pakistan conflict, 46
  Middle East, 46
    UNEF, removal of, 47–51
  personality, 46–52
  Secretary-General of UN, 44–64
  Soviet Union, and, 45, 53
  Vietnam War, and the, 44–46, 53
  West New Guinea (West Irian), 54, 57
    Bunker mission, 54
  Yemen observer mission, 57–58
  See also under United Nations, Departments, Secretariat.

VAIZEY, J., xxx, 243–257
Vazquez, M.S., xxvii, 301–315
Vickers, Dame Joan, xxviii, 219–231
Vietnam War, xxviii, 33, 72, 74, 92, 108, 294, 305
  after-effects of, 63
  Gulf of Tonkin incident, 47, 305
  Okinawa, and, 93
  North Vietnam,
    Japan and, 111
    UN, membership of, 236, 249
  South Vietnam,
    UN, membership of, 236, 249
    United States, 63, 72, 86–87
Vincent, R.J., xxvii, 332–344; xxix, 34–55; xxxi, 8–26; xxxiv, 252–264; xxxvii, 25–38, 42

WALDHEIM, K., xxxvii, 81–96
  Austrian Ambassador to the UN, 82
  Director-General,
    Political Affairs Department Austrian Foreign Ministry, 82
  Secretary-General, UN,
    arrival, 82–83
    attitudes, 83–84
    contacts, 84–86
    dénouement, 95–96
    good offices, 86–87
    peace-keeping, 87–92
    response, 92–95
War, concept of, xxx, 133–149